"A unique, extraordinary, and profoundly challenging book. . . . (*The Way*,) in working out the presuppositions and implications of ecological theory, from epistemology to economics, may be seen both as an attempt to exhibit the ecological worldview itself, and to put it to work in current dilemmas of policy. . . . Goldsmith's urgent and prophetic book [is] destined to disturb the dogmatic slumbers of all the conventional philosophies."

— TIMES LITERARY SUPPLEMENT

"*The Way* is a masterpiece, by one of the best-informed persons on the planet. In my opinion, this book is the most profound, most penetrating, most hard-hitting analysis available of why modern society is not sustainable on planet Earth and what will have to change in order to make it so."

— WILLIS HARMAN, President of the Institute of Noetic Sciences
and author of *Global Mind Change*

"Edward Goldsmith's *The Way* is a compendium of fresh insight and incisive criticism of reductionistic mainstream science, organized into sixty-six cellular chapters that add up to a whole that is greater than the sum of its parts."

— HERMAN E. DALY, co-author of *For the Common Good*

"*The Way* is an original, brilliant critique of the modernist world view and its supporting structure, the mechanistic paradigm in science and marketplace economics. Goldsmith ranges, with awesome knowledge, through ecology and other natural sciences, anthropology, history and philosophy. Sure to be furiously debated, his new book should be read by ecologists, environmentalists, and virtually everyone who has an interest in the earth and its future."

— DONALD WORSTER, author of *Nature's Economy*

"Goldsmith has not only the courage to challenge modern science, but the vision to define the ecological alternatives."

— HELENA NORBERG-HODGE, author of *Ancient Futures*

"Goldsmith has written a masterpiece. It is ecological philosophy not in the usual sense of environmental ethics, but an all-embracing system in which the traditional concerns of Western philosophy and science are given an entirely new context." — J. DONALD HUGHES, author of *Ecology in Ancient Civilizations*

"*The Way* is an important work, and in several ways rather original. The author is well known all over the world. Tens of thousands are grateful for what he has done through a long life of devoted work. They will cherish this magnum opus." — ARNE NAESS, author of *Ecology, Community, and Lifestyle*

# THE WAY

## An Ecological World-view

Edward Goldsmith

SHAMBHALA
Boston
1993

Shambhala Publications, Inc.
Horticultural Hall
300 Massachusetts Avenue
Boston, Massachusetts 02115

9  8  7  6  5  4  3  2  1

First Shambhala Edition
Printed in the United States of America on acid-free paper  ∞
Distributed in the United States by Random House, Inc.

Library of Congress Cataloging-in-Publication Data

Goldsmith, Edward, 1928–
The way: an ecological world-view/Edward Goldsmith.
p.  cm.
Originally published: London: Rider, 1992.
Includes bibliographical references (p.    ).
ISBN 0-87773-882-3
1. Human ecology—Philosophy.   2. Environmental protection.
3. Conservation of natural resources.   4. Gaia hypothesis.
I. Title.
GF21.G63   1993          92-50460
304.2—dc20               CIP

# Contents

# Introduction

Modern humanity is rapidly destroying the natural world on which it depends for its survival. Everywhere on our planet, the picture is the same. Forests are being cut down, wetlands drained, coral reefs grubbed up, agricultural lands eroded, salinized, desertified, or simply paved over. Pollution is now generalized – our groundwater, streams, rivers, estuaries, seas and oceans, the air we breathe, the food we eat, are all affected. Just about every living creature on earth now contains in its body traces of agricultural and industrial chemicals – many of which are known or suspected carcinogens or mutagens.

As a result of our activities, it is probable that thousands of species are being made extinct every day. Only a fraction of these are known to science. The earth's magnetic field is being changed, with no one knows what possible consequences. The ozone layer that protects humans and other living things from ultra-violet radiation is being rapidly depleted; and our very climate is being so transformed and destabilized that within the next forty years we will experience climatic conditions in which no human has ever lived before.

By destroying the natural world in this way we are making our planet progressively less habitable. If current trends persist, in no more than a few decades it will cease to be capable of supporting complex forms of life. This may sound far-fetched; unfortunately, it is only too realistic. My colleagues and I have documented the trends and the likely outcome, *ad nauseam*, in *The Ecologist* over the last 21 years.

Why, we might ask, are we doing this? The answer is that our society is committed to economic development – a process which by its very nature must increase systematically the impact of our economic activities on an environment ever less capable of sustaining them, and ever more deeply degraded by them. An idea of the gross mismatch between the impact of human activities and the environment's capacity to sustain them is provided by the fact that we now co-opt, for our own use and for our various economic activities, fully 40 per cent of the Biosphere's terrestrial Net Primary Production (NPP). What is more, if economic activities continue to expand at the present rate, within no more than a few decades we will co-opt 100 per cent of NPP – which, of course, is not remotely conceivable.

All this is of little, if any, concern to our political leaders. They continue to go about their normal business as if the problem did not exist. Thus, though 170 scientists sitting on the Inter-Governmental Panel on Climate Change (IPCC), set up by the United Nations, have warned them that carbon dioxide emissions must be reduced by 60–80 per cent immediately if we wish to avert a climatic catastrophe, the British government has just undertaken the largest road-building programme in the country's history and talks happily of doubling the number of cars on the roads by the end of the century. The American administration openly admits that, whatever the climatic consequences, it plans to go on increasing carbon dioxide emissions into the foreseeable future. Industrialists are, if anything, even less concerned. The oil industry has been very active in lobbying governments to prevent them from taking any measures that, in the interests of reducing $CO_2$ emissions, might lead to a reduction in oil consumption and a consequent dip in sales. In general, a major constraint on government action to tackle the serious environmental problems that face us is imposed by the lobbying efforts of powerful industrial groups intent on defending their petty short-term interests, come what may.

More surprising, however, has been the almost total indifference with which the academic world has viewed this critical problem. Its acknowledged role is to provide governments and society at large with knowledge that serves the public interest and maximizes the general welfare. But how can it achieve this task if it systematically ignores the fatal process that is rendering our planet ever less habitable and, unchecked, must inevitably lead to the extinction of our species along with countless others? Our academics bring to mind those Australian Aborigines, who, when they first sighted Captain Cook's impressive ship sailing up the Australian coast north of Botany Bay, took no interest in it but maintained their normal activities as if this strange monster was simply not there. Perhaps they hoped – consciously or unconsciously – that by ignoring it to the point of not recognizing its existence they might induce this aberration to go away and leave them alone.

The parallel is more than superficial. In both cases a life-altering challenge is systematically ignored because a prevailing world-view declares it to be inconceivable – indeed, is proved wrong if the challenge is shown to exist. The American anthropologist A. F. C. Wallace shows convincingly that tribal peoples will go to any lengths to preserve their 'cognitive structure or mazeway' (see Chapters 18 and 66) as he refers to it. A scientist will go to equal lengths to do so – as Thomas Kuhn, Michael Polanyi, Gunther Stent and other enlightened philosophers of science have shown.

The world-view which today's academics share with everybody else in our society I refer to in this book as modernism. It is faithfully reflected in the specific paradigms of the academic world – the paradigm of economics or the paradigm of science, for example. One of the two most fundamental tenets of the world-view of modernism and its academic paradigms is that all benefits, and therefore our welfare and our real wealth, are derived from the man-made world; this means, in effect, that they are the product of science, technology and industry, and of the economic development that these make possible. The inestimable benefits provided by the normal functioning of the Biosphere – such as a favourable and stable climate, fertile soil and fresh water, without which life on this planet is not possible – are totally ignored and assigned no value of any kind.

The second fundamental tenet of the world view of modernism follows quite logically from the first: it is that to maximize all benefits, and hence our welfare and our wealth, we must maximize and venerate economic development. To question the efficacy of this fatal process, or to suggest that it might not be entirely beneficial, is to blaspheme against the holy writ of modernism. For mainstream scientists it is blasphemous to show that the modernization of agriculture in the Third World is the main cause of malnutrition and famine in those countries; or that modern medicine has failed to prevent an increase in the global incidence of just about every disease with the exception of smallpox. Nor will any believer accept that the terrible social and environmental destruction we are witnessing today has been wrought by this sacred process. Instead, it will be imputed to deficiencies or difficulties in its implementation – government interference, corruption among local officials, freak economic or climatic conditions that are unlikely to occur again, or good old human fallibility.

In this way the world-view of modernism prevents us from understanding our relationship with the world we live in and adapting to it so as to maximize our welfare and our real wealth. Instead modernism, and the paradigms of science and economics in particular, serve to rationalize economic development or 'progress' – the very behaviour that is leading to the destruction of the natural world with consequences for all to see: poverty, malnutrition and general human misery.

How, one might ask, is it possible for our 'objective' scientists to behave in so unobjective a manner? The answer is that science is *not* objective – a fact that has been well established by Michael Polanyi, Thomas Kuhn and other philosophers of science. One reason why scientists accept the paradigm of science and hence the world-view of modernism is that it rationalizes the policies that produced the world in which they, and indeed all of us, have been brought up. It is very difficult for people to avoid regarding the world they live in – the only one they have ever known – as the normal condition of human life on this planet. Just as an abandoned child who sleeps in the sewers of Rio de Janeiro and lives off petty crime and prostitution regards his or her lot as totally normal, so scientists, observing the world as a whole, do not easily detect abnormality in the fact that our rivers have been transformed into sewers; that our drinking water is contaminated with human excrement, pesticide residues, nitrates, radionuclides and heavy metals; that our agricultural land is eroding faster than soil can possibly form by natural processes; that our natural forests are being systematically replaced with ecologically vulnerable and soil-destroying monocultures of fast-growing exotics, that our cities are increasingly ugly, chaotic and polluted – or that our children spend most of their spare time watching violent and sadistic films on television. All this, and much else that is totally aberrant and destructive, most mainstream scientists will take to be normal.

This general human tendency to regard the only world we know as normal is reflected in the disciplines that are taught in our schools and universities. Thus the modern discipline of economics is based on the assumption that the destructive economic system that is operative today is normal; the discipline of sociology on the assumption that our modern atomized and crime-ridden society is normal; our political science on the assumption that the elected dictatorships that govern modern nation states are normal; and our agricultural science on the assumption that large-scale, mechanized, chemical-based agriculture (which rapidly transforms arable land into desert) is normal. It simply does not occur to many academics that what they take to be normal is very atypical in the light of humanity's total experience on this planet – necessarily short-lived, and totally aberrant. They are like biologists who have only seen cancerous tissue and understandably mistake it for a healthy organism, failing to distinguish between pathology and physiology.

Another reason why our scientific community still accepts the paradigm of science is that, though it paints the most misleading picture of reality, it is nevertheless a totally coherent and self-consistent whole. This must be so, for scientific theories are not adopted by mainstream science because they have been proved to be true by experimentation in controlled laboratory conditions, or even as a result of simulation on a mathematical model, but because, first and last, they happen to fit in particularly well with the paradigm of science. The disciplines which these theories constitute are only judged to be scientific, and hence worthy of being taught in our schools and universities, if they conform to the reductionistic and mechanistic paradigm inspired by Newtonian physics – and this in spite of the fact that Newtonian physics is supposed to have been disposed of by quantum theory.

The Behaviourists made psychology conform to this model. The neo-Darwinists and, even more so, the sociobiologists did the same for biology. Modern sociology is no stranger to mechanism and reductionism, and the development of the new ecology in the 1940s and 1950s has created a Newtonian ecology. In this way all academic knowledge from the most trivial to the most important is forced into science's Procrustean paradigm, stretching or shrinking to fit an atomized and mechanistic world in which people are no more than machines, their needs purely material and technological – precisely those that the state and the industrial system are capable of satisfying. At the same time, because within this paradigm any social and ecological problem that might arise must necessarily be of a mechanistic nature, an appropriate technological solution can be prescribed. It is all very neat and very logical, this pure and perfect figment of the scientist's imagination.

The paradigm of science is also a totally homeostatic system. (see Chapter 24) It is capable of perpetuating itself, however wide the gap may be between the world it depicts and the world as it really is. For if knowledge is only accepted to the extent that it fits the paradigm, any knowledge that does not fit, however true and important it might be, is by the same token ruthlessly rejected. This disposes of all theories based on the assumption that the world is orderly and purposive rather than random; organized rather than atomized; cooperative rather than purely competitive; dynamic, creative and intelligent rather than passive and robot-like; self-regulating rather than managed by some external agent; tending to maintain its stability or homeostasis rather than to change perpetually in an undefined direction: in other words, all theories based on the assumption that the world is alive rather than dead and machine-like.

It would seem that none of the basic principles that must underlie a Gaian ecology will fit the paradigm of science; nor will the world-view of modernism accommodate the policies needed to bring to an end the destruction of the planet and to develop a sustainable and fulfilling way of life. We thus require a new world-view, with which ecological principles are reconcilable, and which recognizes the urgency of remedial policies. Not surprisingly, many people are working towards the development of such a world view. Among them are Arne Naess, George Sessions, Warwick Fox and others in the Deep Ecology movement; Murray Bookchin and his Social Ecology group; Henrik Skolimowski and Ecophilosophy; Ashis Nandy and his colleagues, who have developed a telling critique of Western science; and Fritjof Capra's Elmwood Foundation.

I have tried in this book to state clearly the basic principles underlying an ecological world-view. These principles are all closely interrelated, forming an all-embracing and self-consistent model of our relationship with the world in which we live. I have worked at the book, on and off, for several decades, but in recent years it has undergone a considerable change. It was always clear to me that the inspiration must come from the world-view of vernacular societies, in particular from the chthonic world-view of the earliest period when people everywhere really knew how to live in harmony with the natural world. I have often been criticized on this score. However, it has always seemed to me presumptuous to postulate a world-view of an ideal society for which there is no precedent in the human experience on this planet and whose biological, social and ecological viability has never been demonstrated. If Karl Marx made that mistake, so too do today's adepts of economic development or progress, who seek to create a man-made technological world without asking themselves whether we are capable of adapting to it, or whether the Biosphere is capable of sustaining it for more than a few decades.

What has struck me more recently is that the main features of the world-view of early vernacular societies were everywhere basically the same. They emphasized two fundamental principles that necessarily underlie any ecological world-view. The first is that the living world or Biosphere is the basic source of all benefits and hence of all wealth, but will only dispense these benefits to us if we preserve its critical order. From this fundamental first principle follows the second, which is that the overriding goal of the behaviour pattern of an ecological society must be to preserve the critical order of the natural world or of the cosmos (a term which I shall use in a rather general way to denote the universe as it is seen through the eyes of vernacular, and hence of ecological peoples).

A cursory study of the world-view of vernacular and, in particular, chthonic humanity shows that many societies actually had a word for such a behaviour pattern: the R'ta of the Indians in Vedic times; the Asha of the Avestas; the Maat of the ancient Egyptians; the Dharma, another Hindu concept later taken up by the Buddhists; and the Chinese Tao. These terms can often refer to the critical order of the cosmos, but they are generally used to denote that path or Way that must be taken in order to preserve its critical order. If many other societies do not have a specific term for it, the concept of the Way is nevertheless built into their world view. Explicit or implicit adherence to the Way is critical. It is only by following it that a society can subordinate all political and economical considerations to the overriding imperative of maintaining the critical order of the cosmos. Hence the title of this book.

The task of trying to build a coherent and self-consistent world-view has been more difficult than I originally thought, because it has meant describing each of its constituent principles or propositions in terms of all the others, and hence in terms of the whole. Its structure is thus circular. To assist the diligent reader I have placed, after each principle or proposition mentioned in a given chapter, a bracketed chapter reference which can be consulted when a fuller explanation is sought.

Like all syntheses of this sort, the book cannot be regarded as the work of a single person. I owe much to many people, both dead and alive. There is no space to mention many of the former, but who they are will soon become clear to the reader. I started the work that led to its writing in the 1950s. For a long time I worked in isolation. One of the first people I discussed it with was Ion Gresser of the Institut du Cancer at Villejuif near Paris, who taught me to look at analogies between natural systems and vernacular societies. Another was Joel de Rosnay who, in the early 1960s, introduced me to the General Systems Theory of Ludwig von Bertalanffy, which has coloured all my thinking ever since. I am very grateful, too, to Armand Petitjean. I spent much time over the years in the remarkable library of his beautiful house at S. Hippolyte du Fort in the Cevennes. I have benefited enormously from his wisdom and erudition on just about all the subjects I deal with in this book. I have learned a lot, too, from Jacques Grinewald whose encylopaedic knowledge of the history of science and scientific thought has been of great value to me. I am also particularly indebted to that remarkable man, James Lovelock, who was my neighbour in Cornwall for many years, and whose Gaia thesis I (and a lot of other people) regard as absolutely vital to the development of an ecological world-view. My colleague Peter Bunyard and I organized, with his full cooperation, a number of symposia at Camelford in Cornwall to examine some of the more important implications of his thesis. These symposia, among other things, enabled me to establish contact with important thinkers on the subjects dealt with in this book, such as Lynn Margulis, Brian Goodwin, David Lambert, Mae Wan Ho and Peter Saunders, who are carrying to its logical conclusion the work of J. H. Woodger, C. H. Waddington, Paul Weiss and the other great organismic biologists – in an era when sociobiology and the 'selfish gene' have become the orthodoxy.

I am indebted too, to Eugene Odum, one of the few remaining academic ecologists whose work has not been perverted to fit the paradigm of mechanistic science. His writings have been an important part of my education. The history of ecological thought I learned primarily from Donald Worster, during the conversations we had together and from his seminal book *Nature's Economy*. I would like to mention my friend, Helena Norberg-Hodge, who 'knows it all' and whose long discussions with me inform this work. I am indebted, too, to Robert Mann, Grover Foley and Andrew McFarlane for the many evenings we have spent together discussing these issues in Auckland, New Zealand; to Rajni Kothari, Ashis Nandy, Vandana Shiva and their colleagues at the Centre for the Study of Developing Societies in New Delhi; to Paul Blau and my other friends of Ecoropa, with whom I have had many enlightening discussions, and to that scientific arch-heretic, Rupert Sheldrake. I am also indebted to Satish Kumar, who introduced a new dimension into my life in 1974 by arranging for me to spend four months with the Gandhi Peace Foundation in New Delhi. It was as a result of my stay there that I realized the incalculable relevance of the thought of Mahatma Gandhi to the development of an ecological world view. It was also then that I met most of my Indian friends, from whom I have learned so much. I must thank too Sunderlal Bahuguna and Mohammed Idris who, along with Richard St Barbe-Baker 'the Man of the Trees', are among the most inspiring people I have ever met.

I am particularly indebted to Krishna Chaitanya, possibly the greatest polymath of all time, who is not only one of India's leading art critics, but has written an eight-volume history of Mayalayam literature (the literature of the state of Kerala where he was born) and a ten-volume history of world literature; he has nevertheless found time to write a remarkable five-volume synthesis of the physical and social sciences (physics, chemistry, biology, psychology, sociology and ecology) of which I have made shameless use, and from which I have quoted many passages. Krishna Chaitanya is also the author of many erudite studies of India's cultural heritage: it is from him that I learned of the Vedic principle of the R'ta (the Way), the behaviour pattern adhered to by early Indian society to maintain the critical order of the cosmos. I must acknowledge, too, the encouragement I have received from my very close colleagues, Peter Bunyard and Nicholas Hildyard, with whom I have worked for many years. Nicholas, by taking over the task of running *The Ecologist* with its associated activities, which he does incomparably better than I ever did, has provided me with the leisure to write this book. I must also thank Arne Naess who, after reading a summary of this book in *The Ecologist*, urged me to complete it and get it published. I thank my very close friend John Aspinall for having so enriched my life during all the years I have been writing this work, my brother Jimmy for his great support and my wife Katherine for hers (also for putting up, over the years, with the anti-social way of life that is the lot of a writer committed to a long-term project).

I must also thank Brian Goodwin, Jacques Grinevald, Nicholas Hildyard, Donald Hughes, James Lovelock, Arne Naess, Jerry Ravetz, Wolfgang Sachs, Guiseppi Sermonti, Denys Trussell, and Donald Worster, who have so kindly consented to read the original manuscript of this book and have pointed out errors and made other valuable comments.

Finally, I must thank Tessa Strickland, my editor, for her enthusiasm. Without her, this book would never have been published – also Denys Trussell who has helped me finish it, Mike Kirkwood my very patient copy editor, Annie Ouvry who has typed it over and over again, Hilary Datchens, Lynda Wright and Simone Hawkins who over the years have typed a mountain of notes and various drafts.

### References
References for all quotations and for many of the works referred to in the text are provided in the Bibliography which doubles as an author index.

# Chinook Blessing Litany

●

We call upon the earth, our planet home, with its beautiful depths and soaring
   heights, its vitality and abundance of life, and together we ask that it

*Teach us, and show us the Way.*

We call upon the mountains, the Cascades and the Olympics, the high green
   valleys and meadows filled with wild flowers, the snows that never melt, the
   summits of intense silence, and we ask that they

*Teach us, and show us the Way.*

We call upon the waters that rim the earth, horizon to horizon, that flow in our
   rivers and streams, that fall upon our gardens and fields and we ask that
   they

*Teach us, and show us the Way.*

We call upon the land which grows our food, the nurturing soil, the fertile fields,
   the abundant gardens and orchards, and we ask that they

*Teach us, and show us the Way.*

We call upon the forests, the great trees reaching strongly to the sky with earth in
   their roots and the heavens in their branches, the fir and the pine and the
   cedar, and we ask them to

*Teach us, and show us the Way.*

We call upon the creatures of the fields and forests and the seas, our brothers and
   sisters the wolves and deer, the eagle and dove, the great whales and the
   dolphin, the beautiful Orca and salmon who share our Northwest home,
   and we ask them to

*Teach us, and show us the Way.*

We call upon all those who have lived on this earth, our ancestors and our friends, who dreamed the best for future generations, and upon whose lives our lives are built, and with thanksgiving, we call upon them to

*Teach us, and show us the Way.*

And lastly, we call upon all that we hold most sacred, the presence and power of the Great Spirit of love and truth which flows through all the Universe . . . to be with us to

*Teach us, and show us the Way.*

———

# ONE

# Ecology is a unified

# organization of knowledge

●

*What we find among the Zuni of New Mexico is a veritable arrangement of the universe. All beings and facts in nature, the sun, moon and stars, the sky, earth and sea, in all their phenomena and elements; and all inanimate objects as well as plants, animals and men, are classified, labelled and assigned to fixed places in a unique and integrated system in which all the parts are coordinated and subordinated one to another by 'degrees of resemblance'.*
ÉMILE DURKHEIM AND MARCEL MAUSS

*Each profession makes progress, but it is progress in its own groove. Now to be mentally in a groove is to live in contemplating a given set of abstractions. The groove prevents straying across country, and the abstraction abstracts from something to which no further attention is paid, but there is no groove of abstractions which is adequate for the comprehension of human life. Thus in the modern world, the celibacy of the mediaeval learned class has been replaced by a celibacy of the intellect which is divorced from the concrete contemplation of the complete facts.*
A. N. WHITEHEAD

———

1

Ecology emerged as an academic discipline towards the end of the last century, largely in response to the realization that biological organisms and populations were not arranged randomly but, on the contrary, were organized to form 'communities' or 'associations' whose structure and function could not be understood by examining their parts in isolation. Both Frederick Clements and Victor Shelford, two of the most distinguished pioneers of the discipline in the USA, defined ecology as the 'science of communities'. 'A study,' they wrote, 'of the relations of a single species to the environment conceived without reference to communities and, in the end, unrelated to the natural phenomena of its habitat and community . . . is not properly included in the field of study.'

In the 1930s, the Oxford ecologist Arthur Tansley coined the term 'ecosystem' which he defined as a community taken together with its abiotic environment, much as James Lovelock's 'Gaia' sees the Biosphere and its abiotic context. It is probable that Clements or Shelford, living today, would see ecology as the 'science of ecosystems'. Eugene Odum, possibly the most distinguished of modern ecologists (and one of the few remaining 'holists'), defines ecology as the science of 'the structure and function of nature' or 'the structure and function of Gaia' (the natural world or the biosphere taken together with its atmospheric environment). For Odum, ecology is thereby a superscience or unified science as it was for Barrington Moore, the first President of the American Ecological Society. For him, ecology was not just another scientific discipline, but a science 'superimposed on the other sciences', the science of synthesis essential to our understanding of the structure and function of the Biosphere. 'Will we be content', he asked the St Louis branch of the society in 1919,

> to remain zoologists, botanists, and foresters, with little understanding of one another's problems, or will we endeavour to become ecologists in the broad sense of the term? The part we play in science depends upon our reply. Gentlemen, the future is in our hands.

His words would sound singularly out of place at a meeting of the American Ecological Society today, still more so at a meeting of its British equivalent.

J. H. Woodger, the British theoretical biologist, also considered that

> there ought to be a most general science, not immersed in particular subject matter, but dealing with the relationship between various special sciences, and trying to synthesize their most general results.

Neither the Biosphere nor any of its constituent processes can be explained fully in terms of the separate impermeable disciplines into which modern knowledge has been divided. As Russell Ackoff, the founder of Operations Research, notes,

> some of the questions that we ask of Nature – in contrast to the problems it presents to us – can be classified as physical, chemical, biological and so on, but not the phenomena themselves . . . . Automobile accidents can be viewed at least as physical, biological, psychological, sociological, and economic phenomena. To study them in any one of these ways is to exclude variables which are relevant from other points of view.

Kenneth Craik makes the same point: 'Getting used to the dark,' he asks, 'is it physics, chemistry or physiology?' Ragnar Granit, the Nobel laureate and neurophysiologist, answers that it is quantum physics, photochemistry, chemistry, physiology and psychology. Even what appears to be a purely physical phenomenon, like the movement of planets, cannot be understood purely in physical terms. As Ackoff writes,

> experience of planetary motion is as much a biological, psychological, sociological and economic phenomenon as it is physical.

The Biosphere does not conform to the arbitrary divisions into which knowledge has been divided. Even the best-established barriers turn out to be of relative value only. Thus when Friedrich Wöhler synthesized urea, the barrier between the *organic* and the *inorganic* suddenly shattered, as did that between the *animate* and the *inanimate,* once the virus was found to manifest certain conditions associated with life on being confronted with a

---

3

source of protein, and at other periods to display the normal behaviour pattern of a crystal. A. N. Whitehead even refused to accept that there was any fundamental barrier separating physics from biology. 'Physics', he wrote, 'is the study of small organisms, biology of big organisms.' Ludwig von Bertalanffy showed that, at a certain level of generality, the behaviour of all living entities, or natural systems, is governed by the same laws. This basic principle underlies his General Systems Theory.

The compartmentalization of knowledge into different disciplines makes it possible to view life processes in isolation, apparently subject to laws of their own. In this way totally aberrant theories have been constructed and, in some cases, have remained to this day the official doctrine of science – though their absurdity would be apparent to all were we to accept the fundamental unity of life processes. An example is the mechanomorphic theory of life.

René Descartes divided the things of this world into two categories – the *res extensa* and the *res cogitans*. The former, he maintained, was the domain of science, the latter the domain of theology. The object of this totally artificial division was to carve out a sphere of influence for science, freeing it from the shackles of theological control; at the same time, the Church was reassured that science was not threatening to take over its territory. Only by studying the *res extensa* separately from the *res cogitans* was it possible for Descartes to see the world as a vast machine, the mechanomorphic thesis that still underlies modern science and helps to rationalize economic development and the modern industrial enterprise.

The compartmentalization of knowledge has also led to the perception of economic activity – the distribution of resources within a society – as separate from the society itself and from the rest of the Gaian hierarchy. Modern economics abstracts the phenomena it studies from the natural world. As Nicholas Georgescu-Roegen points out, the economic process is depicted as a 'circular diagram, a pendulum movement between production and consumption within a completely closed system'. It is thus seen as governed exclusively by its own laws rather than by those that govern all the other processes occurring within the natural world. As a result, the fact that there is a continuous mutual influence between the economic process and our physical environment carries no weight with the standard economists. And the same is true of Marxist economists who swear by the Marxist dogma that everything nature supplies man is a spontaneous gift. . . . [I]n Marx's famous diagram of production, too, the economic process is presented as a completely circular and self-sustaining affair.

Once it is admitted that the economic process influences and, in turn, is influenced by biological, social and ecological factors, generally known as 'externalities', then an effort is made to 'internalize' them by quantifying these mutual influences in the language of economics. This may be a reasonable procedure, as Hermann Daly and John Cobb concede, when the externalities involved are of a minor nature; but once it is the very capacity of the earth to support life that has to be internalized, then 'it is time to restructure basic concepts and start with a different set of abstractions that can embrace what was previously external.' In effect, this means rewriting economics in the light of a unified theory of the Biosphere. (see Chapter 19)

Further barriers separate the disciplines in which we study behaviour, ontogeny and evolution, with equally obscurantist consequences. To say that a population has evolved is to say that neither its ontogeny nor its behaviour are the same today as they were at some moment in the past. To understand evolution we therefore need to understand ontogeny and behaviour – the processes that have actually undergone change – not separately but as part of the whole evolutionary pattern.

Ontogenic development is clearly goal-directed, since it leads to the development of a standard phenotype. It is also dynamic and highly coordinated, since all its different stages are closely interwoven into a single strategy. It can also monitor its responses and correct diversions from the course it must take to achieve its goal. That the day-to-day behaviour of non-human animals also displays these same features nobody will deny, yet they are denied by neo-Darwinists, indeed by all mainstream scientists, to the evolutionary process itself. The geneticist Theodosius Dobzhansky, for instance, while accepting the purposiveness of ontogeny, since organs grow to fulfil future functions, still dogmatically insists that this is not true of phylogeny.

Furthermore, with the hardening of Darwinist theory under the auspices of August Weissmann and William Bateson, any feedback between behaviour and ontogeny on the one hand and evolution on the other, as implied by Lamarck, is fervently denied. This means that the instructions that determine the evolutionary process are seen as issued blindly, uninfluenced by their effects on the processes to which they give rise – a phenomenon unknown in the living world and cybernetically impossible in an adaptive life process. However, once ontogeny, behaviour and evolution are seen together as part of a single process, the operation of feedback processes of some sort becomes incontestable. (see Chapter 19)

The compartmentalization of knowledge also makes possible the totally artificial distinction between behaviour occurring *within* the highly ordered and cooperative internal environment of an organism and that occurring *outside* it. It is only by insisting on that arbitrary dichotomy that the idea of natural selection, closely associated as it is with the 'survival of the fittest' (Charles Darwin suggested the two might be different terms for the same thing) can possibly be postulated as the basic mechanism of evolution. Indeed, the notion put forward by the nineteenth-century German biologist Wilhelm Roux that selection occurs at different levels of organization within the internal environment of an organism – for instance at the level of the cell and the tissue – did not gain full acceptance because natural selection and the struggle for survival were difficult to envisage within an internal environment where cooperation and homeostasis were so marked. In general, only by studying evolution in a restricted context has it been possible to perpetuate the neo-Darwinist myth that the process is individualistic, competitive, random and hence non-directive – one that is not subject to biospheric control and hence cannot be distinguished from the anti-evolutionary enterprise to which our industrial society is committed (see Chapter 64).

If ecology is to become Barrington Moore's superscience, the key to our relationship with the Biosphere, then it must provide a framework which articulates all other disciplines to provide a coherent picture of that relationship.

———

# TWO

# Ecology seeks to establish the laws of

# nature

●

*For Gods and men alike, (in the eyes of Homer) there are certain destined bounds which normally and systematically circumscribe their power. It is just possible to exceed them: but only at the cost of provoking an instant Nemesis.*

F. M. CORNFORD

*Almost everywhere in the world, man has been disregarding the Divine Law and the Laws of Nature, to his own undoing. In his pride, he has rampaged over the stage of the earth, forgetting that he is only one of the players put there to play his part in harmony and oneness with all living things.*

RICHARD ST BARBE-BAKER

———

To study the structure and function of the Biosphere and its constituent natural systems is to seek out their pattern. The general features of this pattern are non-plastic, which is another way of saying that they are subject to constraints – in this case, the particular set of constraints ensuring behaviour that will maintain the stability of the Biosphere. It is these constraints that we must refer to as the laws of nature or Gaian laws.

They are not absolute laws, as were those that Laplace and Descartes saw as applying to the mechanistic world they depicted. Gaian laws can be violated, but only at a cost – that of reducing stability, both directly at a specific level of organization and indirectly at other levels in the Gaian hierarchy including that of the Biosphere itself.

Adherence to a specific set of laws is required to maintain the order and hence the stability of a natural system; if these laws are disregarded the degradation and eventual demise of the system will follow. As we move from one level of organization to the next up the hierarchy of the Biosphere, so new sets of laws – usually referred to as 'emergent laws' – become operative. These laws do not supersede those operative at the lower levels but complement them.

Thus, if a man is to remain healthy, his behaviour must accord with a set of physical, chemical, biological, psychological, social and ecological constraints. Among other things, he must breathe fresh air, drink clean water, feed himself properly and live in an environment that has not diverged too drastically from that to which he has been adapted by his evolution and upbringing. As a member of a larger natural system, the family, he must behave in a husbandly way towards his wife and in a fatherly way towards his children, or his family will simply disintegrate. The family in turn is part of a community, and the community is part of a wider society contained within one of the ecosystems which constitute our Biosphere. If the Gaian hierarchy is to maintain its stability, all the individual living things that compose it must obey a veritable hierarchy of laws, which together constitute the laws of nature. It is the failure of modern man to observe the constraints necessary for maintaining the integrity and stability of the various social and ecological systems of which he is part that is giving rise to their disintegration and destabilization, of which the increased incidence of wars, massacres, droughts, floods, famines, epidemics and climatic changes are but the symptoms.

The very principle of a Gaian law is incompatible with the reductionist thesis that is essential to modern science, according to which natural systems are no more than the sum of their constituent parts and thus have no identity, no integrity and no stability. It is incompatible with the notion of randomness, also critical to modern science, in terms of which life processes are no more than accidental, chance happenings. It is incompatible with the notion of causality. Thus Robert Boyle objected to the notion of laws because for him, as for all other reductionist scientists, events cannot be 'caused' by laws, only by antecedent events. When an arrow is shot from a bow, he insisted, 'none will say that it moves by a law, but by an external impulse'. And Gaian law is also incompatible with the empiricist thesis that only observable events are real, all theoretical explanations of life processes being ignored.

Since laws cannot be totally denied, scientists have now demoted them to the status of 'statistical regularities'. This means that there is no reason why laws should apply to the world we live in other than that they have, on the whole, been observed to do so. The statistical view of the world provides a means of reconciling the embarrassing evidence for an orderly world, and hence one governed by laws, with the paradigm of science.

However, even this concession to reality is regarded as unacceptable by Ilya Prigogine, the Belgian chemist and Nobel laureate who has become an intellectual cult figure in France, Belgium and elsewhere. Prigogine considers that the only universal laws are those of classical thermodynamics (see Appendix 1). However, they only apply to those things that are near 'thermodynamic equilibrium' and are thereby in a 'state of homogeneity' – to a world in which all energy is in its final degraded or homogeneous state, and all matter, by inference, in a state of disorder or randomness: the primeval soup, in other words. Since living things do not fall within this category, the laws of classical thermodynamics cannot apply to them, and since there are no other laws, it must follow that the behaviour of living things is not subjected to any laws at all.

This sounds very much like the worst sort of mediaeval casuistry, yet Prigogine assures us that it is the only view that a scientist can possibly adopt – for it is the only one that is reconcilable with statistical theory.

When the Newtonian paradigm was in fashion, he admits, there were indeed laws. However, it was by specifically rejecting the notion that nature is governed by laws that it became possible to free science from the 'Newtonian myth' (see Appendix 1).

The French philosopher and social theorist Edgar Morin seems to have accepted the Prigogine mythology in its entirety. It is only in 'popular epistemology', he tells us, that one finds reference today to the laws of nature. In other words, only the stupid and the uneducated still believe that nature is governed by laws. Modern science has abolished them all and has thereby liberated man so that he is free to create his own laws and to determine the course of his own evolution, and hence of his own destiny. This is exactly the message required to rationalize our modern individualistic and competitive society – the global free-for-all that is leading to the rapid destruction of our planet in order to satisfy short-term economic and political interests.

The world-view of ecology asserts that the opposite is true. The critical feature of the Biosphere is an order which can only be maintained if all life processes within the Biosphere are subjected to laws or constraints – whether self-imposed or imposed by the larger systems of which they are part and that make up the Gaian hierarchy (see Chapter 61). These constraints are precisely those that will lead living things to behave homeotelically (see Chapter 53) towards the Biosphere. Significantly, chthonic man has always recognized a hierarchical set of laws governing at once his own behaviour, his society, the natural world and the cosmos, laws which it was his moral duty to observe as vigorously as possible.

---

# THREE

# Ecology studies natural systems in their Gaian context

●

*If perception is ordinarily highly dependent on context, then stripping away context may be a strategy of doubtful value.*
KARL POPPER

*Whereas the laboratory method's power lies precisely in its isolation of the phenomenon to be studied, ecological science is, on principle, anti-isolationist. It is the science of totalities. As such it is anti-scientific, as science at present is usually conceived and practised.*
LYNN WHITE

Scientific method involves studying the behaviour of living things in 'controlled laboratory conditions' – which means isolating them from the larger systems of which they are part. The information thus gained would be less questionable if these larger systems were no more than random arrangements, but they are not. Living things are the differentiated parts of the hierarchy of natural systems that make up the Biosphere, and the Biosphere has a critical structure which enables it to maintain its homeostasis in the face of environmental challenges (see Chapter 36) and to provide each of its subsystems with an optimum environment (see Chapter 24).

This principle has obvious implications. A natural system behaves very differently within its natural environment from the way it behaves once subjected to an artificial environment which bears little relationship to that in which it evolved, and hence from the natural system of which it is a differentiated part. This is true at all levels of organization within the Gaian hierarchy.

Thus, at a molecular level, a haemoglobin molecule in solution has a different affinity for oxygen than when it is inside a red blood cell. A cell that has been removed from an egg at an early stage in its development, as the famous German embryologist Hans Driesch showed, can develop into a whole organism, instead of developing into a differentiated part of an organism. Michael Polanyi, the Cambridge-based philosopher of science, notes that the reason for this is that 'the behaviour of a cell depends on its position in a total pattern' which means that 'cell interaction is . . . of crucial importance', an embarrassing fact that cannot be explained in terms of reductionist science. This is true not just of isolated cells, but also of tissues – that is why grafting and budding and in general modern tissue culture are, in general, practicable.

Paul Weiss, though he himself was a laboratory biologist, notes that biochemists tend to

> study organic chemical interactions (e.g. enzyme reactions) in physically orderless or deliberately disordered states (test tube solutions or tissue pulp). This is a technical necessity and a lot can be learned through these methods. But they fall far short of reproducing the way things happen in the living system. They

can show, at best, what might happen, but not what actually does happen in the organized state; for in an organism, chemical reactions occur, in the first place, 'not ubiquitously and indiscriminately, as in a mixture, but rather in critical patterns of localization and segregation,' and, secondly, without the pampering and nursing care of a learned experimenter.

The same is true of the behaviour of organisms. As Eugene Odum notes, 'many insects are destructive pests in an agricultural habitat but not in their natural habitat where parasites, competitors, predators or chemical inhibitors keep them under control.'

The more the environment of living things differs from that in which they evolved, the more their behaviour is likely to be maladjusted, un-adaptive or heterotelic. Thus the responses of a laboratory animal, con-fined in a box or cage, to the sight of a piece of cheese, are likely to provide very little valid information as to the normal behaviour of the members of its species towards the food on which they normally feed, because such animals have not been adapted by their evolution or upbringing to living in boxes or cages, or to dealing with isolated pieces of cheese. They will thus be biologically, socially and cognitively maladjusted to dealing with such an artificial situation (see Chapter 47). In the first place, living things do not react blindly to stimuli. They seek to make sense of them, and as the Ges-talt psychologist Keith Oatley notes, 'that sense will include the whole context in which the material is presented.' But how can they make sense of something when its context has been systematically removed – when a 'context-free situation' has been created to satisfy the exigencies of scien-tific method?

Experiments carried out in the impoverished environment of a labora-tory, as Krishna Chaitanya notes, are biased 'against cognition and in-telligence. They have been set up in such a way as to lend credence to the myth that living things simply react blindly and robot-like to specific stimuli.' This impression can be communicated still more vividly if the animals have been *brought up* in the aberrant conditions of a laboratory, where their cognitive faculties have been stunted. Until recently, it was generally assumed that baboons were individualistic, competitive and aggressive creatures – a notion based on a study conducted by Lord Zuckerman, at one time chief scientist to the British government, of baboons in the London Zoo. When they were actually studied in the wild, however, he found them to be orderly, cooperative, and peaceful, though their social groupings were highly hierarchical. It then became clear that Zuckerman's baboons were unsocialized and delinquent, their behaviour somewhat resembling that of equally unsocialized urban slum-dwellers.

The behaviour of children, brought up in extreme isolation from their natural social and biological environment, is even more aberrant. They seem incapable of any but the most rudimentary understanding, like Peter of Hanover, a child brought up in isolation and later exhibited as a sort of curiosity in eighteenth-century London. Eventually people got bored with him and he was made to work as an agricultural labourer. It was found that he could work perfectly well, but simply could not understand the meaning or purpose of what he was doing. When asked to load a wheelbarrow with manure, he would do so very efficiently but, not knowing what the manure was for, would proceed to empty the wheelbarrow and fill it up again repeatedly until made to stop.

The fact is that living things, studied in isolation from the natural systems within which they developed phylogenetically and ontogenetically, are little more than freaks; their behaviour cannot be regarded as providing valid information on normal homeotelic behaviour within the Biosphere.

# FOUR

# Ecology is holistic

●

*Our final aim is to bring human behaviour within the framework of the physical sciences.*

LORD ADRIAN

*If the organism is a hierarchical system with an organization above the chemical level, then it is clear that it requires investigation at all levels, and the investigation of one level (e.g., the chemical) cannot replace that of higher levels.*

J. H. WOODGER

*We have to start with a concept of the whole organism as the fundamental entity in biology and then understand how this generates parts that conform to its intrinsic order – resulting in a harmoniously integrated, though complex, organism.*

BRIAN GOODWIN

The early academic ecologists were so impressed by the way living things are organized to form a community, and hence the extent to which they are interrelated, that they compared the community to a biological organism. C. C. Adams, in the first American book on animal ecology, published in 1913, insisted that

> the interactions among the members of an association are to be compared to the similar relations existing between the different cells, organs, or activities of a single individual . . . The physiological needs and states of an association have as real an existence in individual animals as similar needs in the cell or cells which compose the animal's body.

This view of the ecological community became so well established that for Daniel Simberloff it is a superorganism, 'ecology's first paradigm'. F. S. Bodenheimer wrote in 1953 that the concept of the community as an organism is stressed in nearly every textbook of ecology and, 'backed by established authority, is generally regarded if not as a fact, then at least as a scientific hypothesis not less firmly founded than the theory of transformation' (or evolution). It is this concept above all, he wrote, 'that distinguishes ecology from biology proper.'

The holism of the early ecologists is irreconcilable with the paradigm of science in terms of which the world is seen as random, atomized, and mechanistic. Unfortunately, it is the latter view of the world that is alone capable of generating the science-based manufactured goods required to satisfy commercial ends (pesticides, antibiotics and genetically engineered micro-organisms, for instance). The holistic approach, on the other hand, does not yield the sort of practical information required for this purpose. As the ecologist N. W. Pirie notes,

> those who are obsessed by the interactions of everything with everything else . . . are of necessity diffuse. Practical conclusions are not drawn from the holistic contemplation of totality.

For that reason alone, ecology had to be transformed, but there were other reasons. Ecology had to become respectable if it was to be taught in universities and this meant conforming to the paradigm of reductionist science. The process started in the 1940s.

The Cambridge zoologist and ethologist W. H. Thorpe defines reductionism as 'the attribution of reality exclusively to the smallest constituents of the world and the tendency to interpret higher levels of organization in terms of lower levels.' The justification for this is that only discrete particle-like entities are real. For only they are measurable; only they can be studied with precision, in controlled laboratory conditions. It is these assumptions that still underlie the 'analytical' or 'reductionist' nature of modern science.

Because it is physics that deals with the smallest constituents of the world (those at the lowest level of organization) it is considered the only real science – 'Aristoscience', as the Australian philosopher of science John Passmore calls it. And the New Zealander Lord Rutherford, one of the fathers of nuclear physics, went so far as to say that 'science is either physics, or stamp-collecting.' The gratuitous assumption that all knowledge about the world we live in can be reduced to the language of physics is unquestioned, and scientific progress consists largely in the achievement of this task. The Nobel laureate Francis Crick, co-discoverer of the genetic code, states the reductionist credo very explicitly. 'Eventually', he writes, 'one may hope to have the whole of biology "explained" in terms of the level below it, and so on right down to the atomic level.' It is becoming clearer that the enterprise Crick proposes will never be realized, nor can it be. Nevertheless, the basic philosophy of reductionism has survived unscathed and has led to the most obscurantist trends in the disciplines dealing with life processes at the higher levels of organization.

As Alexander Koyre, perhaps the foremost Newtonian scholar, notes:

> the unholy alliance of Newton and Locke produced an atomic psychology, which explained (or explained away) mind as a mosaic of 'sensations' and 'ideas' linked together by laws of association (attraction); we have had, too, atomic sociology, which reduced society to a cluster of human atoms, complete and self-contained each in itself and only mutually attracting and repelling each other.

17

Koyre disowns these products of 'physics envy' in the name of Newton himself, assuring us that he 'is by no means responsible for these, and other monstra, engendered by the over-extension – or aping – of his method.'

The reductionist and mechanistic ecology which came into being in the 1940s is another such monster. One of its main architects was the Oxford ecologist Arthur Tansley. He denied the basic holistic principle that the whole is more than the sum of its parts and hence not amenable to study by reductionist method. 'These "wholes",' he wrote, 'are in analysis nothing but the synthesized actions of the components in associations.' A mature science, in his view,

> must isolate the basic units of nature [and must] 'split up the story' into its individual parts. It must approach nature as a composite of strictly physical entities organized into a mechanical system. The scientist who knows all the properties of all the parts studied separately can accurately predict their combined results.

The reductionist approach to ecology is usually traced to the earlier writings of the botanist Herbert Gleason, whose article 'The individualistic concept of the plant association' was first published in 1926 and presented and discussed at the International Botanical Congress that year. Initially, it was very badly received. In the words of Robert McIntosh, Gleason was 'anathema to ecologists.' Gleason himself admitted that, for ten years after the publication of his article, he was 'an ecological outlaw'. His thesis simply did not fit in with the ecological paradigm of the times. However, as the latter was transformed to conform with the paradigm of science and hence with the world view of modernism, so Gleason's ideas became increasingly acceptable until eventually they became part of accepted biological wisdom. McIntosh, the best known historian of ecological thought, refers to them as 'a viable and expanding tenet of current ecological thought', while P. A. Colinvaux, in a well-known textbook, goes so far as to describe the holistic view of the community as a 'heresy'. Other modern ecologists go further and claim that their work has provided incontestable proof of the validity of Gleason's philosophy. J. T. Curtis, for instance, tells us that 'the entire evidence of the plant ecology study in Wisconsin' – in which he was involved – 'can be taken as conclusive proof of Gleason's individualistic hypothesis of community organisation'. The American ecologist R. H. Whittaker regards his 'gradient analysis' as providing similar evidence.

How, one might ask, can they possibly make such claims? The answer is that science provides a means of collating data but not of interpreting them; inevitably they are interpreted in terms of a scientist's particular paradigm. Thus, if Curtis and Whittaker believe that the Biosphere is 'atomized' and 'random', they will probably interpret the results of their experiments in such a way as to rationalize their reductionist faith.

Gleason's main argument is that only the individual is 'real'. Larger associations, such as ecological communities or human communities, are abstract entities that only exist in the eyes of the beholder. 'An association has no real identity of its own', he writes, from which it must follow that 'its behaviour is only understandable in terms of that of its components.' It merely represents 'the coincidence of certain plant individuals and not an organic entity itself'. Whittaker bases his case for the reductionistic approach on the same argument: 'an association is not a concrete natural community', he assures us. 'It is an abstraction from the unlimited complexity and intergradation of communities, a class produced by an ecologist's choice of a class concept or definition.'

Natural systems, however, especially those at the higher levels of organization such as societies and ecosystems (and, of course, the biosphere itself) are incomparably more complicated than billiard balls, atoms and the other relatively simple entities that physicists study. As Wolfgang Kohler notes,

> if organisms were more similar to the systems which physics investigates, a great many methods of the physicist could be introduced in our science without much change. But in actual fact, the similarity is not very great. One of the advantages which makes the physicist's work so much easier, is the simplicity of his systems . . . . An amoeba is a more complicated system than all systems of the inanimate world.

Living systems display all sorts of qualities that inanimate things display only in an embryonic or latent way if at all – qualities which become very much more developed as we move up from simple forms of life to more complex ones, such as humans. The important point is that these qualities are not apparent from a study of the system's constituent parts, but only once we see the system as a whole. Thus, the coordination of the behaviour of the parts by the whole is only apparent once one has identified the whole. That living systems cooperate not just with each other but with the whole – that they are homeotelic, seeking thereby to maintain the critical order or stability of the whole, is also only evident from a holistic perspective.

As the great Indian polymath Krishna Chaitanya notes, 'seen from below, a mechanism may look self-sufficient; but from above, it can be seen as being utilized for a purpose which transcends the apparent self-sufficiency of its operations'. On the other hand, as Ludwig von Bertalanffy writes, the essential difference between events, ordered 'so as to maintain the system' and 'those running wild to destroy it' is clearly obscured by considering biology and indeed sociology in physical terms. 'What does "health" or "norm" mean in contrast to "disease" and "pathology"?' he asks. 'Nothing, so far as the laws of physics and chemistry are concerned. . . . But without these and similar notions, there would be no science of medicine and indeed biology.' Nor, one may add, would it be possible to note the essential distinction between heterotelic and homeotelic processes or between evolution and anti-evolution.

Reductionist science clearly cannot help us understand the problems caused by the disintegration of a larger system, such as an ecosystem or Gaia herself, whose principle features it continues to deny, and whose very existence, except in a metaphorical sense, it continues to question. Passmore feels that it is precisely because of this insistence on understanding the world in terms of physics that scientists have been so unsuccessful in understanding the real problems that face us today.

> If we are still ignorant about most of the phenomena we encounter in our daily life – whether it be human nutrition or the life history of animals – this ignorance can in part be set down to the aristoscientific emphasis on a very different kind of knowledge.

Eugene Odum, though he admits the successes of the reductionistic approach, considers that

> cell-level science will contribute very little to the well-being or survival of human civilization if we understand the higher levels of organization so inadequately that we can find no solutions to population overgrowth, social disorder, pollution and other forms of societal and environmental cancer.

It is probably by seeking to understand the simple in terms of the complex, rather than the complex in terms of the simple, that one can best understand the true nature of our relationship with the world of living things. A. N. Whitehead intimated this when he suggested that the concept of the organism should be extended downward to include the particle. W. H. Thorpe was more explicit: 'We have to work back into the physical sciences, equipped with the concept of organism derived from the biological sciences.'

---

# FIVE

# Ecology is teleological

●

*The attitude of biologists to teleology is like that of the pious towards a source of temptation which they are unsure of their ability to resist.*

SIR PETER MEDAWAR

*The Gaia hypothesis . . . is an alternative to that pessimistic view which sees nature as a primitive force to be subdued and conquered, and that equally depressing picture of our planet as a demented spaceship, forever travelling, driverless and purposeless, around an inner circle of the Sun.*

JAMES LOVELOCK

The teleological explanation of the life process centres on its goal – Aristotle's 'final cause' – rather than on its antecedent cause, which alone is accepted by the scientific community. Teleology, the neurophysiologist and Nobel laureate Ragnar Granit tells us, is required to answer the question of *why* things happen, without knowing which it is very difficult to answer the question of *how* things happen.

This must be true of any entity or process. Thus Robert Fuller and Peter Putnam tell us that

> a skilled electronics engineer is often unable to derive the function of a rather simple electronic circuit, despite a complete knowledge of the network and the properties of its elementary units. On the other hand, if one has a guiding idea as to the overall function of the circuit, then it is possible to examine the component parts and see just what role they play in this function.

In this case, the elementary units only acquire meaning once their function within the electronic circuit is established. Granit's example is the discovery of how the eye adapts to light and darkness.

> When rods and cones were discovered in the vertebrate retina, had it not become evident that rods dominated in retinas of the night animals and cones in those of daylight animals this discovery would have remained an observation of but limited consequence. Instead, understanding of its meaning (why) made it a cornerstone in a large body of biological research dealing with the adaptation of the eye to light and darkness, rod vision and cone vision, and the rod-free central fovea of the human retina.

Rods and cones, however brilliantly they are described, only acquire meaning once one knows what they are for. In the same way, it is only once one has established the goal of any organism or natural system that one is in a position to ask how it achieves this goal. This is often referred to as the cybernetic method.

It is exactly how James Lovelock developed his famous Gaia thesis.

> To examine the earth cybernetically is to ask the question 'What is the func-

tion of each gas in the air or of each component of the sea?' Outside the context of Gaia, such a question would be taken as circular and illogical, but from within it is no more illogical than asking: 'What is the function of the haemoglobin or of the insulin in the blood?' We have postulated a cybernetic system; therefore, it is reasonable to question the function of the component parts.

Thus, Lovelock starts off by pointing to the extraordinary constancy of the chemical composition of the Biosphere – the oxygen and carbon dioxide content of the atmosphere, for instance, and the salt content of the sea. He then searches for mechanisms that could assure this constancy. Ralph Gerard notes how the physiologist proceeds in precisely the same way.

> The physiologist's whole life is concerned with problems of organic purpose, though he rarely likes to say it, particularly in public. We see purposeful behaviour all through the body; it is the only way it makes sense to us. And then we look for the mechanisms to account for it.

In terms of the paradigm of science, this teleological method of building up knowledge is totally illegitimate. To accuse a scientist of using a teleological argument is to accuse him of being unscientific, indeed, of being a veritable charlatan. Very few scientists would be willing to take that risk. Even James Lovelock does not admit that his argument is teleological. The Daisy World model developed by Andrew Watson of the Marine Biological Association at Plymouth, to which Lovelock attaches so much importance, is primarily designed to show that cybernetic processes need not be teleological. However, to model a rudimentary and hypothetical cybernetic process is one thing; but it would prove quite another to build a realistic model capable of demonstrating that the very much more sophisticated cybernetic behaviour of complex forms of life in the real world is non-teleological.

Scientists will go to the most extraordinary lengths to make it appear that the statements they make are non-teleological. One ruse is to deny the purposiveness of life processes altogether and to argue that nature only *appears* purposeful. Julian Huxley tells us that 'at first sight the biological sector seems full of purpose. Organisms are built *as if* in purposeful pursuit of a conscious aim.' But the truth lies in those two words *as if*. As the genius Charles Darwin showed, the purpose is *only an apparent one*. He adds that,

> No conscious seizing of opportunities is here meant [by the use of the word purpose], nor even an unconscious sensing of an outcome. The word is only a convenient label for these tendencies in evolution; that what can happen usually does happen; changes occur as they may and not as would be hypothetically best; and the course of evolution follows opportunity rather than plan.

The opposite is true. 'Opportunism' is itself a teleological concept. An adaptive individual does not seize any opportunity to bring about a random change, but clearly one that suits its purposes – one that it judges to be 'hypothetically best' – for itself and for the hierarchy of natural systems of which it is part.

More devious expedients are resorted to in order to make it appear that scientists can avoid arguing teleologically. One device – a purely linguistic one – is to formulate an obviously teleological statement in such a way that it no longer appears teleological. David Merrell notes how throughout modern biological literature we find

> a great array of teleological jargon bearing witness, as it were, to the homeorhetic tendency of living systems. Biologists are always talking of one thing occurring, 'for the purpose of something' or, 'in order that something might happen' or, 'serving the function of something' and so on.

However, philosophers still go to great lengths to show that these statements can be translated into a non-teleological form. This often leads them 'into a morass of circumlocutions'. Thus biologists, as Granit notes, have been 'prepared to say a turtle came ashore *and* laid its eggs,' but not that 'it came ashore *to* lay its eggs.'

The cybernetician Peter Calow also shows how it is possible to translate teleological propositions into non-teleological language. Thus the teleological statement 'the function of the vertebrate heart is to pump blood' can be translated into non-teleological language simply by saying that 'the heart is a necessary condition for the circulation of blood in vertebrates'.

Another device resorted to by mainstream scientists is to provide a purely mechanistic explanation of purpose. The inspiration came from the favourite toy of cyberneticians: the machine with feedback. These machines are programmed in such a way that they seek to achieve a goal. They avoid teleology in the sense that they are not seen as tending towards a final cause, hence their behaviour does not require some sort of super-natural explanation. The principle involved is reconcilable with that of causality, reductionism, statistical method and, of course, mechano-morphism. Indeed, as Henri Atlan puts it, 'this new type of goal directed-ness is acceptable in that it is not derived from theological idealism, but from neo-mechanism' – in other words, science had found its own 'acceptable' metaphysics. It came to be known as 'teleonomy', a term first used by Colin Pittendrigh and later taken up by Julian Huxley, Ernst Mayr, Jacques Monod, C. H. Waddington and other leading biologists.

The acceptance of teleonomy only enables us to ask the question 'why' rather than 'how' within a limited sphere, that of the functioning of a machine. However it tells us nothing of why the machine has been made to function in this way, nor why it has been set its goal. Yet the de-velopment of molecular biology, culminating in the decoding of the genetic code by Francis Crick and his colleague James Watson, has further increased the credibility of the notion of teleonomy. Living things, molec-ular biologists maintain, give the impression of tending towards a goal or final cause, but this is only because they have been programmed like machines to move in this direction. Instead of a computer programme, the *deus ex machina* is now the genetic programme.

However, no life process can be understood in terms of the informa-tion with which it has been programmed, because the larger systems of which it is part constitute an environment with which it is constantly interacting and from which it derives much of the information required for its development. Thus a developing embryo acquires information during the entire embryological process, first from the cytoplasm, then from the womb; later, when the child is born, it acquires further information from its family and, as it grows up, from the community and ecosystem of which it is part.

One of the main attractions of Darwinism for scientists is that its basic concepts appear to be non-teleological, but that is an illusion. Competition, for example, implies competition for something. Since competition, for Darwinists, is intimately linked with the notion of the 'survival of the fittest', it means competition to survive. But why should living things want to survive? We assume that they do, but this is a gratuitous assumption. Stones do not want to survive, particularly.

Another key neo-Darwinist concept, natural selection, is equally teleological, a point hammered home relentlessly by P.-P. Grassé. 'There cannot be selection without purpose [intention]', he writes, and 'by explaining the evolution of the fittest in terms of selection, they [the neo-Darwinists] are endowing all living things with an inherent goal.' In reality, the concept of selection is of use to neo-Darwinists because it provides a means of delegating to a vague and undefined environment the teleological functions that alone can explain the development and proper functioning of the natural world. It is, of course, a desperately feeble subterfuge, but mainstream scientists appear to be easily taken in.

Ecology has to be teleological, for purposiveness is possibly the most essential feature of the behaviour of living things. Only a methodology that accepts this can enable us to understand the roles that living things play within the Gaian hierarchy of which they are the differentiated parts.

---

# SIX

# Ecology explains events in terms of their role within the spatio-temporal Gaian hierarchy

●

*At the present day, the whole subject of causation is in a chaotic state. Men of science, on the one hand, who use the notion, appear to be too busy amassing facts to trouble themselves much about what they mean by it, and philosophers, on the other hand, seem, for the most part, from the time of Hume onward, to entertain beliefs on this subject which are very difficult to harmonize with the use of the notion in biological science.*

J . H . WOODGER

*The meaning of any natural thing or event cannot be fully grasped or explained scientifically until we discover its relations to the components of the orderly flow of process we call our cosmos.*

C . JUDSON HERRICK

Mainstream science sees an event in the real world as the result of a 'cause'. A cause is a discrete event that has been observed empirically by the process of induction to precede the effect in time, on the basis of which it is assumed that it will always have the same effect.

This principle of explanation fits in perfectly with the paradigm of science. It is reductionistic, the cause being a discrete event; mechanistic, since the cause is a switch which triggers off a specific effect; predictable, since switches are not creative or intelligent; compatible with the notion of randomness, since the causal process occurs in isolation from all other processes; and non-teleological, since the cause must necessarily precede the effect.

However, it provides a very misleading picture of events in the real world, for a life process – contrary to the impression conveyed by neo-Darwinism – does not occur in a void but as an integral part of a much wider process: the evolution of the Biosphere itself. A life process also evolves for a purpose, that of fulfilling a specific function within the hierarchy of the biosphere, so as to contribute to the maintenance of its critical order and hence its stability. For this reason it can only be explained in terms of its role or purpose within the spatio-temporal Gaian hierarchy. It is this explanation that must be taken to be its cause – that is, if the term 'cause' is to be of any use in the understanding of life processes.

What is more, the same cause will not always trigger off the same effect, for if a living thing cannot achieve its goal in the normal way, it will seek to do so in a different way, displaying the principle of 'equifinality'. Clearly, one cannot explain a life process in terms of a single event if it can achieve its goal even when the event does not occur. (see Chapter 25)

If a normal homeotelic process cannot be explained in terms of isolated discrete causes, nor can a heterotelic process (see Chapter 41) that disrupts the functioning of natural systems and prevents them from achieving the goal they were designed to achieve. The reason is that such a heterotelic event can trigger off a veritable chain reaction of ever more heterotelic events. That event which is taken to constitute a cause may thus be but one of a very long series of events, each one of which can be regarded as constituting a cause. Consider the following passage from the writings of George Perkins Marsh, a nineteenth-century American diplomat and one of the most important precursors of today's ecology movement.

> The aquatic larvae of some insects constitute, at certain seasons, a large part of the food of fresh water fish, while other larvae, in their turn, prey upon the spawn and even the young of their persecutors. The larvae of the mosquito and the gnat are the favourite food of the trout in the wooded regions where those insects abound. Earlier in the year, the trout feeds on the larvae of the Mayfly, which is itself very destructive to the spawn of the salmon, and hence by a sort of house-that-Jack-built, the destruction of the mosquito that feeds the trout, that preys on the Mayfly, that destroys the eggs, that hatch the salmon, that pampers the epicure, may occasion a scarcity of this latter fish in waters where he would otherwise be abundant. Thus all nature is linked together by invisible bonds, and every organic creature however low, however feeble, however dependent, is necessary to the well-being of some other among the myriad forms of life with which the Creator has peopled the earth.

What then is the cause of the epicure's frustration? Why has he been deprived of his smoked salmon? The obvious answer is that the mayfly has eaten the salmon's eggs. But is that a sufficient cause? Obviously not, since mayflies would not have been a problem if there had been enough trout around to eat them. The absence of the appropriate number of trout is thus another cause of this sad event. But it is not a sufficient cause either, since if there had been enough mosquito larvae around for the trout to eat, they would not have left the area; hence the absence of mosquitoes can also be regarded as a cause, though still not a sufficient cause, for if people had not killed the mosquitoes, there would still have been plenty of larvae. Clearly we must consider the problem in greater depth. To begin with, it would appear that the people in the area once used to put up with the mosquitoes; why then, we might ask, do they not now? Perhaps people had recently moved into the area who were particularly sensitive to mosquito bites. Perhaps, too, they had been persuaded by a chemical company to get rid of the mosquitoes, which they would otherwise have tolerated, by spraying them with an insecticide that the company happened to manufacture. But why should people be stupid enough to poison their environment with carcinogenic pesticides? Why, too, should chemical companies be allowed to manufacture them? To answer these questions would mean describing the nature of our industrial society and how it actually came into being.

Of course, in such a society, it is politically and commercially convenient to take the most immediate cause as determinant and ignore all others. This appears to justify the most superficial treatment possible, accommodating rather than changing the social and economic structures on which we have become dependent for the satisfaction of our short-term interests. Such technical fixes are the stock in trade of the corporations into which our society is organized. If the cause of crop damage is seen to be a specific pest, this justifies waging chemical warfare against it (which suits the pesticide manufacturers); if the cause of an infectious disease is taken to be a specific microbe, this justifies the use of antibiotics to eliminate it (which suits the pharmaceutical industries). The adoption of these solutions, moreover, stimulates other commercial activities such as transport, banking and retailing, all of which provide jobs, contribute to the tax revenue of the state and, temporarily at least, improve our material welfare.

Unfortunately, technological expedients only solve technological problems. They cannot reverse the disruption of natural systems. Alleviating the symptoms, they render the problems more tolerable and thus perpetuate them. René Dubos, the Franco-American microbiologist and father of what might be referred to as the ecology of health, pointed out over 40 years ago that microbes are not the cause of infectious disease. Man will always be inhabited by vast populations of microbes; indeed, according to the American microbiologist Lynn Margulis, known for her work on microbial ecology and the Gaia thesis, we harbour in our bodies as many microbial cells (*prokaryotes*) as animal cells (*eukaryotes*), most of them playing an essential role in our metabolism. Dubos traced the source of diseases to a breakdown in the critical balance between man and his microbial populations precipitated by a range of possible factors: old age, malnutrition, exposure to low-level radiation, to chemical pollutants, or to a virus that disrupts the immune system.

Louis Pasteur, who first incriminated the micro-organism, eventually saw the error of his ways. 'The microbe is nothing', he admitted on his deathbed. 'The terrain is everything.' W. R. Day, an authority on plant diseases, also sees very clearly that blaming the parasite leads to the neglect of fundamental causes. An infectious disease may be caused by a subtle combination of factors which reduces the resistance of an organism, making it vulnerable to an attack which under normal conditions it would repel with ease. The recent deaths of dolphins in the North Sea, for example, point to its contamination by low levels of all sorts of heavy metals, chemicals and radionuclides, which combine to reduce the effectiveness of the immune systems of sea mammals against the viruses that have been officially implicated. The truth is that the North Sea has simply ceased to provide a viable habitat for dolphins and many other forms of life.

The same is probably true of the degradation of forests in Europe and on the east coast of North America where trees have died in increasing numbers. The designated killer is 'acid rain' containing high levels of sulphuric acid created when sulphur dioxide emissions from factories combine with the moisture in the atmosphere. But trees are ill and dying in areas where there is little or no sulphur dioxide pollution. It is more likely that a subtle combination of pollutants of all sorts – in the air, in the rainfall and in the soil itself – is responsible, leaving us to face the depressing fact that late industrial society is giving rise to conditions which cannot sustain complex forms of life like large trees. Such conditions are the opposite to those that obtain in a climax ecosystem, in which everything conspires to prevent epidemics of this sort.

It is impossible to understand the daunting problems that confront us today in terms of the narrow scientific concept of causality. Instead, they must be examined within their total Biospheric context. When we do this, it becomes clear that our problems must be solved not by technological means (which only mask the symptoms) but by addressing the underlying social and ecological maladjustments. As clearly, this will mean bringing about fundamental changes to our society and our economy, and to their relationship with our increasingly degraded Biosphere, so that the preservation of its critical order becomes our overriding goal.

---

# SEVEN

# Fundamental knowledge is inherited

●

*Deductivism, in mathematical literature, and inductivism in scientific papers are simply the postures we choose to be seen in when the curtain goes up and the public sees us.*

SIR PETER MEDAWAR

It is fundamental to modern science that all knowledge is obtained by empirical observation. This implies, among other things, that a child is born with a virgin mind – the *tabula rasa* of the empiricist philosophers – on which, during its upbringing, empirical knowledge is systematically registered. This thesis is consistent with the view that a living thing is a temporal isolate, but it is incompatible with our knowledge of the continuity and stability of natural systems.

The ethologist Robert Fantz noted that new-born chicks, from the moment they were born, pecked 100 times more often at spherical than at pyramidal objects. The Nobel laureate Niko Tinbergen found that newly hatched herring gull chicks preferred pecking at objects which resembled the bill of the parents, from which they were fed. Marked preferences for certain specific objects were also established among baby chimps. Fantz also showed that children displayed a greater interest in flat objects that were painted to look like human faces than in flat objects on which the features of a human face were painted in a scrambled pattern, while they largely ignored similar objects on which no human features were painted.

Fantz regards his experiments as demonstrating that living things are born with 'innate knowledge of the environment' – a knowledge which 'provides a foundation for the vast accumulation of knowledge built up through experience'. This must be so: each generation of living things inherits genetic information which reflects the experience of its ancestors, going back into the mists of time. Only in this way can a species (and the Gaian hierarchy of which it is part) display continuity or stability. Morphogenesis – including the morphogenesis of the individual's brain, and hence of its capacity to build up knowledge – must display continuity or stability. But what is true of morphogenesis is also true of behaviour. These processes are simply different stages in the same Gaian process. It follows that the behaviour of successive generations also displays continuity – which, in any case, we know empirically to be true and this requires that an individual inherits a rudimentary model of its relationship with its environment, reflecting the behavioural experience of its cultural group, its race and its species.

We know that the evolutionary development of all life processes proceeds from the general to the particular. This is true of the development of the hierarchical organization of knowledge (the cybernism) on the basis of which behaviour is mediated. The generalities of a cybernism, what is more, being non-plastic, must colour the rest of the information that is 'built up through experience'. It is thus the most general and hence the most fundamental knowledge that must be inherited, while that which is 'built up through experience' is derived from it, during the interplay between behaviour and its field – the ordered environment within which behaviour occurs.

---

# EIGHT

# Fundamental knowledge is ineffable and we mainly have access to it by intuition

●

*What we cannot speak of, we must be silent about.*
LUDWIG WITTGENSTEIN

*The Tao that can be told is not the eternal Tao.*
LAO-TZU

For empiricist philosophers, and hence for our mainstream scientists, knowledge must be entertained consciously and must be expressible in language, for only such knowledge is observable. However, there is every reason to suppose that knowledge that is entertained subconsciously, and thereby cannot be articulated, plays an essential part in determining our behaviour patterns.

Michael Polanyi refers to such knowledge as 'ineffable' and notes how 'all professionals possess a mass of professional knowledge of this sort . . . they know many more things than they can tell, knowing them only in practice, as instrumental particulars, and not explicitly as objects'. All the knowledge that they cannot tell, he takes to be 'ineffable', and its use to guide our behaviour 'an ineffable process of thought'.

Arthur Koestler notes that our instincts are 'notoriously inarticulate'. 'We can describe intellectual processes in the most intricate detail, but have only the crudest vocabulary even for the vital sensations of bodily pain – as both physician and patient know to their sorrow.' Neurophysiologically, the seat of our instincts and emotions, and of our values too, lies in our primitive brains, the first to develop during the course of our cerebral evolution. It is the knowledge organized in these brains of which we are unconscious and cannot articulate. The seat of our readily articulated conscious knowledge, on the other hand, seems to be the neo-cortex, the newest of our brains. Significantly, attempts to mediate at the 'high' conscious level functions designed to be mediated at the 'lower' one lead to maladjustments and failures. The psychologist Victor Frankl notes how many psychological problems involving failure on the part of patients to fulfil basic behavioural functions are attributable to this cause.

> In clinical practice, often we are confronted with patients who are, so to speak, over conscious of what they are doing, and this interferes with performance, be it the performance of the sexual act (sexual neurosis) or the performance of any artistic work (vocational neurosis).

In Frankl's terms this is the phenomenon of *hyper-reflection,* to be countered by *de-reflection,* which means turning a patient's attention away from himself and his own activity.

Michael Polanyi describes the same phenomenon in slightly different terms.

> If a pianist shifts his attention from the piece he is playing to the observation of what he is doing with his fingers while playing it, he gets confused and may have to stop. This happens generally if we switch our focal attention to *particulars* of which we had previously been aware only in their subsidiary role.

This is usually referred to as self-consciousness. In the example of 'stage fright' it consists in 'the anxious riveting' of the would-be actor's attention on 'the next word or note or gesture' to be remembered. This accent on the details 'destroys one's sense of the context which alone can smoothly evoke the proper sequence of words, notes or gestures'. The cure is to allow one's mind to 'operate with a clear view to the comprehensive activity in which we are primarily interested'.

This suggests that different types of behaviour – if they are to be adaptive – must be mediated at the appropriate cerebral level. An essential part of the skills displayed by Polanyi's professionals, pianist and actor, and by Frankl's lover and artist, is closely bound up with their instincts, emotions and values, and must be mediated at the level of the primitive brains. This is even more obviously true of our basic physiological functions, such as the digestion of our food and the circulation of our blood. If they were to depend for their proper functioning on the conscious knowledge organized into our neo-cortex, we would probably not survive for a single day.

It is possible that our most fundamental knowledge of our relationship with the world around us falls into this category. Indeed, if our society and the Gaian hierarchy of which it is part are to maintain their stability or continuity, then this fundamental knowledge must be passed on from generation to generation largely intact. It is only the particularities of such knowledge that can be modified with impunity by articulate consciousness.

The process whereby we apprehend our ineffable knowledge is usually referred to as 'intuition'. It is itself mysterious and ineffable. One such fundamental intuition is the unity or 'one-ness' of the living world. For the Bantu, as Placide Tempels writes, this is the supreme wisdom which cannot be acquired in schools or universities. For Alexander von Humboldt, 'the harmonious unity of nature' lies 'beyond the realms of positive knowledge' and is 'accessible only to the vivid and deep emotions'. The Haiku scholar R. H. Blyth suggests that only our intuition can enable us to understand the whole, while the intellect can understand something 'as a part but not as a whole'. For deep ecologists this one-ness of the natural world is 'the central intuition of deep ecology'.

———

# NINE

# Ecological knowledge is built up by organizing knowledge in the mind

●

*Overt intelligent performances are not clues of the working of the mind,* they are those workings.
GILBERT RYLE

*How can one explain scientific discovery and artistic originality without reference to mind and imagination?*
ARTHUR KOESTLER

If the concepts of 'ineffable knowledge' and 'intuition' are foreign to the paradigm of science, so is that of the mind itself, for its workings are not observable in the sense in which material objects are observable. Thus to David Hume only impressions (sensations) and ideas were real, the mind being regarded as no more than the sum total of our impressions and ideas. Gilbert Ryle insisted that there could be no mind as distinct from its workings and that any statement about the mind was meaningless. This, in broad terms, has been the position of empiricist philosophers ever since.

When John B. Watson and the American behaviourist school sought to eliminate from their field of study all the metaphysical speculation of their predecessors and turn their subject into a 'hard science', they denied the existence of the mind in the same way as did Hume and Ryle. Any introspective concept that could not be observed and quantified was taken as non-scientific and had to be eliminated. Consciousness, for instance, which empiricists since Descartes had always taken to be the seat of knowledge, Watson regarded as 'neither a definable or usable concept' and as 'merely another word for the concept of the soul . . . of more ancient times'. As he pointed out, 'no one has ever touched a soul or seen one in a test tube'. This was E. C. Tolman's position, too. 'All that can ever be observed in human beings', he insists, 'is behaviour' – and this is all one can talk about scientifically. Since all behaviour is random, there is no need for the mind as an instrument of coordination.

According to Watson, when a dressmaker designs a new gown, he does not have any picture in his mind of what the gown will look like when it is finished. This would be teleological behaviour, which is quite unacceptable to science. Besides, how can one quantify a picture and explain it in the scientifically respectable terms of physics and mechanics?

> All the dressmaker does is call in his model and she picks up a new piece of silk, and throws it around her; he pulls it in here, he pulls it out there. . . . He manipulates the material until it takes on the semblance of a dress.

A painter, too, plies his trade in this way. 'Nor can the poet boast of any other method.' Indeed, we get new 'verbal creations such as a poem or a brilliant essay', he insists, 'by manipulating words, shifting them about until a new pattern is hit upon.' The same attitude is displayed by the members of the behaviourist school of sociology. George A. Lundberg considers the search for human motives to be unscientific on the grounds that it is 'an animistic pursuit'. It is under the influence of such ideas that sociology has degenerated into the study of the observable atoms of social behaviour.

Evolution is seen by neo-Darwinists and socio-biologists in the same way.

> The organic raw material is manipulated in a random manner – a tail is added here, a pair of wings there, and eventually, the appropriate pattern is hit upon and preserved because it happens to be the fittest.

The only scientifically acceptable method of acquiring primary knowledge is by induction, which involves the acquisition of data by cumulative individual observations and correlation. The more often a correlation can be made, the more are we justified in believing that the events will continue to occur together and, indeed, that they constitute a 'cause and effect' relationship.

This method of acquiring knowledge fits in perfectly with the paradigm of science. It is a reductionist concept, since each observation can be regarded as an 'atom' of cognition, just as each 'bit' is an atom of information, each 'reflex' an atom of behaviour, each sense datum an atom of perception, and each 'meme' (to use Richard Dawkins's term,) an atom of culture. It can be quantified, since observations can be counted. It also fits in with the view of behaviour as random rather than orderly or teleological, passive and robot-like rather than dynamic and creative. But it has very serious failings. Hume was the first to point to the limitations of induction. There was no logical reason, he argued, for supposing 'that those instances of which we had no experience resemble those of which we have had experience', which means that 'even after the observation of the frequent or constant conjunction of objects, we have no reason to draw any inference concerning any object beyond those of which we have had experience.' However, Hume considered that induction, in spite of this failing, still provides the only valid way of building up knowledge. Indeed, he is usually regarded as its original proponent.

Other epistemologists, including Immanuel Kant and later Karl Popper, have taken the logical objection more seriously. However, this issue does not seem to be the critical one, for no method of acquiring 'synthetic' knowledge can provide us with logically indubitable knowledge. What we require is a means of acquiring knowledge that has the greatest likelihood of being true – different degrees of likelihood being required for different purposes. The critical question is whether induction is the means of satisfying even this more modest criterion, and it can be shown that it is not.

One reason is that one can push Hume's argument against the validity of induction a stage further. Because of the nature of life processes (which logicians do not appear to be concerned with) the fact that events have been observed to occur together does not mean that they will continue to do so indefinitely. 'Our expectation of life', Michael Polanyi notes,

> does not increase with the number of days we have survived. On the contrary, the experience of living through the next 24 hours is much less likely to recur after it has happened 30,000 consecutive times than after only 1000 times. Attempts to train a horse to do without food will fall down precisely after the longest series of successes; and the certainty of amusing an audience by one's favourite joke does not increase indefinitely with the number of its successful repetitions.

The truth is that the building up of knowledge requires more than the accumulation of individual observations. These must be interpreted in the light of a model of our relationship with our environment. *Thought* is required – a non-quantifiable, non-reductionistic, non-mechanistic activity, whose very existence is not consistent with the paradigm of science. Without it, 'without theoretical interpretation,' in Popper's formulation, 'observation remains blind – uninformative.'

Cause and effect relationships, established on the basis of indiscriminate empirical observations, must indeed provide very questionable conclusions. After the racial riots in Britain in 1981, a public enquiry was set up under the chairmanship of Lord Scarman to determine its causes and propose measures to prevent their recurrence. The Brixton residents group 'Concern' argued that simply to engage more policemen would not solve the problem. To confirm this thesis, they published a study establishing that between 1977 and 1980, the period during which crime really began to escalate in Brixton, 'the number of policemen exceeded the established level for the area by 113 per cent'. From this they drew the conclusion that 'more police increased the crime rate'. They may, of course, have been right, but it is more realistic to see the growing crime rate in Brixton and elsewhere as a symptom of social and cultural deprivation against which the police, however numerous, can do very little.

It is only among the simplest forms of life, for whom mental activity is still relatively rudimentary, that knowledge is acquired by something approaching the inductive method. To train an earthworm to find its way through a maze requires considerable patience. The correlation between taking the wrong path and receiving an electric shock is made only after repeated lessons. On the other hand, as we move to less simple forms of life there is a corresponding increase in mental complexity (see Chapter 51) and hence in the ability to think and to interpret experiences. The number of empirical observations required before learning occurs is proportionately reduced. In fact, one could formulate a law to the effect that the role of induction is inversely proportionate to the degree of organization in an animal's mental model of its relationship with its environment. The more one knows about the behaviour of a natural system, the smaller the number of observations required to understand it and predict how it is likely to change. If this were not so, what would be the point of acquiring knowledge? In what way would an authority on a subject be more capable of solving a problem in his field than a layman?

As we shall see, perception involves detecting rather than merely receiving signals – a living thing detects only signals that appear to be relevant to the achievement of its behavioural goal. (see Chapter 14) Such signals are said to attract its 'attention'. Polanyi notes that the role of attention is ignored by psychologists and other inductive scientists, while Popper tells of an experiment that he carried out with his students, in which he simply asked them to observe. The students looked a little flummoxed. He then said:

I hope you are all cooperating and observing. However, I fear that at least some of you, instead of observing, will feel a strong urge to ask what do you want me to 'observe'?

If this were so, he told them, then his experiment had been successful for its object was to show that 'in order to observe, we must have in mind a definite question which we might be able to decide by observation.'

Interestingly enough, Charles Darwin, in his autobiographical sketch, insisted that he 'worked on Baconian principles, and, without any theory, collected facts on a wholesale scale.' But, later in the same book, he admits that he could not resist forming a hypothesis on every subject. In his correspondence, he is even more explicit on this subject. Thus, in a letter to Henry Fawcett, he writes, 'how odd it is that anyone should not see that all observation must be for or against some view.' And in a letter to H. W. Bates, 'I have an old belief that a good observer really means a good theorist.' Medawar considers that these comments reflected 'his true opinions as opposed to the opinions which he felt became him.' Polanyi also denies that a scientist's discoveries are the product of the inductive method. De Broglie's wave theory, the Copernican system and the theory of relativity 'were all found by pure speculation guided by criteria of internal rationality.'

W. H. Thorpe sees scientific progress as being largely achieved by

great leaps of imaginative insight; leaps which, at the time they were made, may have had very little experimental or observational basis .... In some respects ... many of the most important theories in the history of science are arrived at as much by the modes of thought of the artist and of the pure mathematician as by those popularly considered to be characteristic of scientists

— by a mysterious process, he might have added, that could well be referred to as intuition.

---

# TEN

# The mind contains a hierarchical organization of instructions and an associated model or dynamic map

●

*For living processes to occur a ready made model of the final product, i.e. of the goal, is required, or at any rate a template with the same degree of specificity to guide a proper order of assemblage.*

PAUL WEISS

To do its work, the mind (like any other cybernism) must be endowed with a set of instructions capable of triggering off a coordinated sequence of actions such as those involved in the development of an embryo or an ecosystem. But that is not enough. For a coordinated sequence of actions – or a strategy – to maintain itself along the path or chreod that will achieve its goal, a *model* is required of the end-product or goal, of the path that it must follow to achieve it, and of all possible sources of disturbance that could have to be counteracted if the goal is to be achieved. The gene provides such a model.

Norman Horowitz notes:

> It seems evident that the synthesis of an enzyme – a giant protein molecule consisting of hundreds of amino acids arranged end to end in a specific and unique order – requires a *model* or *set of instructions* of some kind. These instructions must be characteristic of the species; they must be automatically transmitted from generation to generation, and they must be constant yet capable of evolutionary change. The only known entity that could perform such a function is the gene. There are many reasons for believing that it transmits information by acting as a model or *template*.

The relationship between the genome and the protein that it synthesizes must be functionally the same as that existing between *any* cybernism and the life process that it helps to mediate. In each case, information organized in a cybernismic medium is translated into a behavioural mode: instructions are translated into action. The model must thus be highly purposive – not objective or, in Keith Oatley's words, 'neutral in the sense in which an encyclopaedia typically is'. On the contrary, the model is best seen as formulated in the language of the system's pattern of instructions. For instance, it is because a traditional society's fundamental instructions are of a moral nature that its cultural model is formulated in the language of morality.

Instructions and potential instructions are organized in accordance with the stage in the process at which they will be required; in accordance, too, with the probability of their being required by the occurrence of conditions to which the behaviour they mediate is adaptive. The model thereby provides a picture of those aspects of the system's relationship with its field or environment relevant to the implementation of the instructions enabling the system to achieve its goal.

In a military campaign the commander issues his orders, organized hierarchically as all orders must be. The most general order will be to defeat the enemy; the less general orders specify how, in the changing conditions of the battlefield, this ultimate goal is best to be achieved. They will be revised constantly in the light of the data gathered by intelligence officers on the deployment of friendly and enemy troops. The data will not just be piled up somewhere, for adaptive behaviour cannot be mediated on the basis of data, or even a data bank. For behavioural purposes, the data must be organized to constitute a model, thus becoming information. (see Appendix 2)

Specialized staff officers do this, methodically moving little symbols representing friendly and enemy formations across a map that usually covers one wall of the room, tent or caravan that serves as the commander's headquarters. It is only by consulting this 'dynamic map' that the commander knows what instructions, at any given point in the campaign, will make victory more probable. Any other approach would simply be 'muddling through', much as our politicians do today. But theirs is not the way of nature. The behaviour of the Biosphere and its component subsystems, we know to be coordinated and committed to a long-term strategy of survival. We can thus postulate that all behaviour, including the evolutionary process itself, must be controlled by a dynamic model analogous to the set of instructions associated with a general's map.

It is a comparatively recent idea that humans and other animals possess in their minds a dynamic model of their relationship with their environment. H. Head, the neurologist, was possibly the first to suggest that information was organized in the brain to form representations or 'schemata'. This idea was taken up by Karl Lashley, who found it useful as a means of understanding the behaviour he observed in his own animal experiments. In 1932, F. C. Bartlett published his classic, *Remembering*. He showed that remembering can only be understood if it is realized that 'the past operates as an organized mass rather than as a group of elements each of which retains its specific character' and that 'remembering is not the re-excitation of unnumerable fixed, lifeless traces, it is an imaginative reconstruction'.

Thus, if a group of people are told a story and are, at a later date, asked to repeat it, each will do so very differently, for each will reconstruct it in the light of his personal mental model or world-view. What remains of the original story is a person's general attitude to it, which reflects all the attitudes and prejudices, if we like to call them that, that underlie his own particular world-view. His principal preoccupation is not to recall the events with the greatest possible precision, but to reconstruct the story in accordance with his world-view.

At about this time, C. Judson Herrick also noted that in order to explain the subtleties of behaviour one must postulate the existence of stable arrangements of information in the brain which he referred to as 'neurograms'. The first really explicit statement of the thesis, however, was Kenneth Craik's. He contended that the brain, in order to fulfil its function, *must provide a model of the physical world*. Only an organism equipped 'with a small scale model of externality and of its own possible actions within its head' can try out various alternatives, determine which is the most adaptive, and react to future situations before they occur – thus making use of the knowledge of past events to deal with the present and future and to adapt successfully to its environment.

Michael Polanyi also found it necessary to explain learning in this way.

> A rat which has learned to run a maze will show a high degree of ingenuity in choosing the shortest alternative path when one of the paths has been closed to it. This behaviour of the rat is such as would be accounted for by it *having acquired a mental map of the maze*, which it can use for its guidance when faced with different situations within the maze.

In this way, a rat does not have to rely on induction and hence on random trial and error to find its way out of the maze, any more than does a man.

The rat can best be regarded as being endowed with a mind. This mind, the seat of the instincts, emotions, values and sociability which provide the rat with the appropriate guidelines of an adaptive homeotelic behaviour pattern. It also provides the rat with a closely associated cybernismic model of its relationship with its environment.

# ELEVEN

# Ecology is qualitative

●

*I often say that when you can measure something you are talking about and express it in numbers, you know something about it, but if you cannot express it in numbers your knowledge is of a meagre and non-satisfactory kind.*
LORD KELVIN

*The further away economics strays from reality, the better it can be sold as 'scientifically precise'.*
JUDE WANNISKI

*As long as we have lips and voices*
*which are to kiss and sing with*
*who cares if some one-eyed son of a bitch*
*invents an instrument to measure Spring with*

e. e. CUMMINGS

The basic knowledge of vernacular man was contained in his myths and formulated in the language of abstract concepts such as 'fate', 'justice' and 'law', and in the language of gods and spirits – concepts that had a clear meaning to him in terms of his world-view, and could be taught to children in songs, play and theatrical performances. It was a language of the people, not of their experts: a human language. Plato also sought to understand the world in terms of abstract ideas or 'universals', while abstract concepts such as 'origins', 'essences', 'qualities' and 'goals' continued to be in vogue during the medieval period.

Quantification came with the search for objective and precise knowledge. Galileo laid down that only the quantifiable was real, which meant that the non-quantifiable was outside the field of science. The new philosophy of nature developed by Descartes and Galileo anticipated the Newtonian idea that nature could be understood in terms of physical atoms moving through space and time. To isolate the characteristics of matter in motion, that could be measured and related by mathematical laws, was to understand the workings of nature. As Descartes himself said, 'give me extension and motion and I will construct the universe.'

Quantifiable concepts such as space, time, weight, velocity, acceleration, inertia, force and momentum were the subject matter of Galileo's new science, replacing the more subjective knowledge that could not so easily be quantified. The seventeenth century saw the development of further quantifiable abstractions such as 'the force of gravity', 'space pervading ether', 'mass' and also 'power' and 'energy'. Two great eighteenth century works on mechanics, Lagrange's *Traité de mécanique analytique* and Laplace's *Mécanique céleste*, purported to prove that nature is governed by precise and all-embracing mathematical laws and served to enshrine the quantitative method.

Since then science has not looked back. As Morris Kline writes, 'the history of modern science is the history of the gradual elimination of gods and demons and the reduction of vague notions about light, sound, force, chemical processes and other concepts to number and quantitative relationships.' This process has been a great success in the field of physics, where the concepts used have been relatively simple and hence easy to quantify, especially when employed in isolation from the more complex systems studied by biologists and sociologists. C. P. A. Pantin notes that physics has been able 'to become exact and mature just because so much of the whole of natural phenomena is excluded from this study.' But, as Paul Weiss argues, 'there is no reason for us to downgrade nature,' to meet the physicist's inadequacy.

That is precisely what mainstream science has done. One of the problems has been to define the concepts in terms of which complex systems are described with any sort of accuracy. Unfortunately, this has rarely been done. As J. H. Woodger notes,

> Nothing in biology is more striking than the contrast between the brilliant skill, ingenuity and care bestowed upon observation and experiment, and the almost complete neglect or caution in regard to the definition and use of the concepts in terms of which its results are expressed.

This is also a problem in psychiatry. The Nobel prize winning novelist Isaac Singer notes how accurately the textbooks have 'defined' the idiot, the cretin, the imbecile, the epileptic, the hysteric, the hypochondriac and the neuresthenic.

> But what do the impressive Latin words actually refer to? A vague set of symptoms at best. As the cynic puts it 'the psychotic builds a castle in the air; the neurotic lives in it, and the psychiatrist collects the rent.'

Similarly, most basic terms used by ecologists have never been properly defined. Thus G. H. Orians distinguishes between nine types of *stability* and David Merrell notes twenty-one different ways in which scientists use the term *competition*. In the philosophy of science, the terms used are equally vague. Margaret Masterman once accused Thomas Kuhn of using the term *paradigm* in twenty-two different ways. Predictably, difficulties arise when these vague or ambiguous concepts are quantified. Thus the term *diversity* is used at once to denote the number of species in an ecosystem and, at the same time, their 'equitability' or relative sizes. These are basically two different concepts that could only be represented by a single quantity if they were known to be precise functions of each other, so that a change in the value of one would automatically lead to a predictable change in the value of the other, which is not so: in fact, the relationship between the two concepts has yet to be determined with any sort of accuracy. Other terms used in ecology are also very difficult to quantify. Biomass is an example. Ramon Margalef points out that a tree 'includes much dead tissue' to which the term biomass cannot strictly apply.

The preoccupation with quantification has led scientists to develop concepts and indeed whole theories partly at least because they could be expressed in quantifiable terms, regardless of whether anything in the real world corresponds to them. Many of the concepts of neo-Darwinism fall into this category, natural selection being a case in point. It should realistically be seen as acting on the phenotype – the living animal. As C. H. Waddington notes, if a horse is to survive in the natural world, it must run fast enough to escape from predators and 'it is irrelevant, whether it can run fast because it has been trained by a good horse trainer or because it has a nice lot of genes.' However, natural selection acting on the phenotype is extremely difficult to quantify, for which reason neo-Darwinists prefer to see it as acting on the genotype, a process very much easier to model.

Modern ecologists are preoccupied with energy because this concept is particularly easy to quantify. S. D. Putman and R. J. Wratten, who see ecology as 'a quantitative exact science' like physics, assure us that it is via the concept of energy that such an ecological science can be developed. As for the ecosystem, R. V. O'Neill states explicitly that it is 'fundamentally an energy processing system', while Putman and Wratten see 'any biological system – individual, population or community – as a system for the transfer, storage and dissipation of energy', a thesis with which Robert McIntosh seems to concur. Yet Putman and Wratten themselves would concede with Margalef that the central concept of energy flow is vitiated because 'it is impossible to estimate the total amount of degraded energy involved in ecosystem dynamics'.

Quantifiable or not, the idea that the basic role of living things is to process energy is simplistic and naive. It is, of course, reconcilable with the paradigm of science, which sees living things as no more than machines, but it bears no possible relationship to reality.

Michael Polanyi has shown how mental concepts undergo simplification as they enter language. In effect, we *leave out* all the information that cannot be expressed in language, much of it because we are not aware of knowing it. Polanyi, as we have seen, refers to such knowledge as ineffable. The language of mathematics imposes still further simplification which means that still more information must be left out.

Scientists are unlikely to entertain the possibility that a proposition about the behaviour of complex systems couched in the language of mathematics can provide *less* rather than *more* accurate information. To demonstrate that this can be so, one might draw on the critical distinction made by Robert Mann, editor of *New Zealand Environment*, between precision and accuracy. By formulating a proposition quantitatively, one undoubtedly makes it more precise – but only at the cost of reducing its ability to represent the real world. Precision, in fact, is only achieved at the cost of accuracy.

# TWELVE

# Only qualitative vernacular models can provide the informational basis for adaptive behaviour

●

*It is only in quantitative ecosystem ecology that the rich details of natural history become reduced to 'brute' transfers of conservative substances, because the real details have so far proved too diverse, complex and generally difficult to represent and quantify. Every ecologist who has ever made an energy or material flow model of an ecosystem, is painfully aware of its deficiencies in terms of relevant information omitted . . . . A model reduces the intricate beauty and awesome complexity of a piece of living nature to what is by comparison a flat, pallid image of the reality . . . . An ecosystem model, no matter how sophisticated or difficult to produce, is but a shadow of its prototype.*
B. C. PATTEN AND EUGENE ODUM

Knowledge is seen by mainstream science as organized into man-made structures, such as logic or mathematics, from which propositions can then be deduced. The philosopher of science W. M. Elsasser considers that if science were sufficiently advanced all its propositions could be deduced in this way. However, mainstream science is increasingly disposed to understand the structure and function of a complex system (such as a society or an ecosystem) by modelling it mathematically. This involves determining first the relevant variables (systems analysis) and then their interrelationships (modelling). A change occurring in the real world can then be simulated by modifying the value of the appropriate variables and interrelationship – the effect that this will have on all the other variables and interrelationships providing an indication of how the change is likely to affect the real world. Simulation can be seen as a very much more sophisticated form of deduction. It is particularly attractive because living things seem to proceed in a very similar way when they seek to understand events in the real world. Unfortunately, however, this methodology is fraught with problems.

To begin with, there is no established methodology for choosing the variables and interrelationships. They are chosen first of all because they are modellable, which means above all that they can be quantified. Unfortunately, many of the most relevant variables and interrelationships in a complex system are non-quantifiable. Neither is there a valid methodology for choosing which of the quantifiable variables and interrelationships will be taken into account. This is left to the initiative of the modellers and, inevitably, the choice will reflect the world view with which they have been imbued. In view of the very high cost of building mathematical models of complex systems – which can often run into hundreds of thousands if not millions of dollars – the chances are that the modernist world view of governments, multinational corporations and international agencies will be reflected in the model.

The same problem occurs in the choice of the basic assumptions underlying a mathematical model, which the modellers are expected to state explicitly. Such assumptions are not those that must underlie the model if it is to represent the real world with the greatest accuracy, but those that are required for purely technical model-building reasons. Thus, among the assumptions underlying a model built by A. J. Nicholson to mimic the stable relationship between predators and their prey, are firstly that the predator and the prey have synchronized generations, which means that they are of the same length and start at the same time. Needless to say, this simply does not occur in the real world.

Further assumptions in Nicholson's model are equally unrealistic. The generations are assumed to be discrete with no overlap between them. The predator searches randomly, contrary to the known behaviour of predators which is dynamic, intelligent and consistent with a specific interpretation of the situation in which they find themselves. The predator never becomes satiated and goes on eating members of the prey species indefinitely, which we know not to be the case. Finally, the robot-like predator has a 'constant searching efficiency' which means that it is unaffected by the food it eats, the mood it is in, or the time is has spent seeking out its prey.

In short to build a mathematical model at all, its architect must simplify his creation until it bears very little relationship to the real world it is supposed to be modelling. This does not seem to concern our modellers unduly, their principal preoccupation being to ensure that their model is a self-contained and logically consistent construct. At this they are very skilful.

Consider the mathematical model provided by S. D. Putman and R. J. Wratten of the process of ecological succession towards a climax. (see Chapter 50) Since the traditional explanation is incompatible with the idea of progress and thereby unacceptable to modern ecologists, an alternative explanation is provided. Putman and Wratten and others tell us that succession is simply an example of a 'regular Markov chain', in which 'characteristic probabilities depend only on a current state and not any previous state.' As the chain develops it eventually settles into a pattern 'in which various states occur more or less with characteristic frequency that are independent of initial states.'

It is argued that this final 'stationary distribution' of states is the analogue of the climax community and that climaxes must occur by the statistical certainty that the Markov process always settles into a stable pattern. What is more, if a community is temporarily disturbed, something like the original community returns. This too is a function of Markovian processes. Finally, Markovian development, like succession, is characterized by rapid changes followed by undetectably slow changes. This means that stability, in the naive sense of 'absence of change', increases 'tautologically' as succession proceeds. 'None of these characteristics', Putman and Wratten significantly insist, is 'necessarily of biological origin.' The biological systems are not in themselves the explanation for the process. Researchers have shown the 'close fit' between Markovian processes and succession. The most 'sophisticated' of such researchers, we are told, is F. S. Horn, who insists that 'general properties of succession are direct statistical consequences of a species-by-species replacement process, and have no uniquely biological basis.'

The whole argument is an example of a fallacy we can best refer to as 'mathematical realism'. Children often think that because a word exists there must be something in the real world that corresponds to it, a notion known as 'nominal realism'. Jean Piaget cites, among many examples, a child who says that 'pigs are rightly named because they are so dirty', and 'the sun is rightly named because it is so hot.'

Oxford linguistic philosophers are similarly guilty of what might be called 'linguistic realism' when they assume that there must be some intrinsic and universal wisdom in the structure of the English language which casts light on the workings, say, of the Biosphere – when, in reality, what is offered is a very crude representation, suitable only for conversational purposes.

Putman and Wratten, like Horn and other modern ecologists, are committing the same error. They suppose that because someone has developed a mathematical model which simulates, in a rudimentary manner, some aspects of the real world, then it must be capable of simulating, in a scientific manner, all aspects of the real world. It is of course, astonishing that a mathematical model of a Markov chain can imitate, however crudely, any aspect at all of such real-world processes as succession to a climax. That one must therefore be able to derive other, scientifically acceptable information about succession from the behaviour of a Markov chain is absurd – just as absurd as to suppose that because a puppet can be made to resemble a policeman, an examination of the cotton wool with which it is stuffed will enable you to understand a policeman's digestive system or the circulation of his blood. What they are proposing is, in fact, little more than a modern form of divination – but because the diviners are scientists, performing their rituals on scientifically consecrated premises, they enjoy credibility among the naive and the gullible. (see Chapter 51 and Appendices 2 and 3)

Simulation on a mathematical model is no substitute for the interpretation of real-world situations in the light of the world-view of vernacular man, or through a 'cognized model' of his relationship with his environment. It can of course, be argued that such models are not 'scientific' in that they do not conform to 'objective' reality. However, the role of knowledge is not to depict reality in the manner of an encyclopaedia, but in order to mediate adaptive homeotelic behaviour. Roy Rappaport sees cognized models as offering vernacular populations a distinctive means of maintaining themselves in their environment. They should not be judged in accordance with the

> extent to which they are identical with what the analyst takes to be reality, but the extent to which they direct behaviour in ways that are appropriate to the biological well-being of the actors and of the ecosystems in which they participate. The criterion of adequacy for the cognized model is not its accuracy but its adaptive effectiveness.

The Colombian anthropologist Gerardo Reichel-Dolmatoff sees the mythology of a vernacular society as providing its members with a model of their relationship to the society and to its natural environment, in the light of which they seek to interpret environmental changes and to monitor their behaviour pattern so as to reduce changes to a minimum and maintain the society's stability. The vernacular model is naturally formulated in the language of the society's mythology, and the interrelationships that are seen to exist between the gods and spirits who control society and the natural world are carefully established and explained in mythological terms. (see Chapter 22) Thus among the Canelos Quichua Indians of Ecuador, as N. E. Whitten tells us, playing flutes, singing songs and telling myths punctuates discussion of Amasanga (who controls the weather, the thunder and lightning) Nungui (who controls the soil-base for the roots of garden-life and pottery clay) and Sanghui (who controls water). These activities are, among other things, mechanisms for associational or analogic linking of cosmological and ecosystem knowledge to social rules and breaches, and social dynamic to cosmological premises.

Problems such as a shortage of game, soil erosion, a shortage of clay for making pots, or bad weather can all be interpreted in terms of the model and attributed to some maladjustment in the relationship between the various gods that control these resources, which in turn can be related to some failure on the part of society to fulfil its obligations towards them. The model is holistic rather than reductionistic: the spirits are not the atomized components of the Biosphere but, on the contrary, reflect its truly hierarchical nature.

The vernacular model is formulated in a language which all can understand and which thereby empowers all to act in a coordinated manner if necessary. This is in stark contrast with a mathematical model, formulated in an esoteric tongue which only a handful of specialists can really understand and act upon.

For all these reasons a cognized or vernacular model satisfies the basic requirements of a cybernetic system in a way that the scientific mathematical model cannot. The vernacular model, in fact, is alone capable of providing the informational basis for homeotelic and hence homeostatic behaviour at the social level.

# THIRTEEN

# Ecology is subjective

●

Te matauranga o te Pakeha
The knowledge of the white man
He mea whakato hei tinanatanga
is propagated
Mo wai ra?
For whose benefit?
Mo Hatana?
For Satan's?
Kia tupato i nga whakawai
Be wary of its temptations
Kia Kaha ra, kia kaha ra
Be strong and firm.
Te matanranga o te Pakeha
The knowledge of the white man
Patipati, a Ka mura whenau
Engulfs you, then confiscates land.
Kia kaha ra, e hoa ma
Be strong, friends.

Ka mutu ano
Land is all we have.
Te tanga manawa
To rest a beating heart
Oranga, a oranga
And for our livelihood
Te matanranga o te Pakeha
The knowledge of the white man
Ka tuari i te penihana oranga
Gives out social security benefits.
Hei aha ra?
Why?
Hei patu tikanga
To kill customs
Patu mahara
To kill memory
Mauri e
To kill our sacred powers.

TUINI NGAWAI OF NGATI POROU

Scientific knowledge purports to be objective; that is seen to be its main virtue, decisively separating it from the sort of knowledge entertained by ordinary people. Objective knowledge is knowledge that is free of the personal beliefs, values and metaphysical ideas of its entertainer; hence it is knowledge that is neutral with regard to the achievement of any specific goal.

Actually, scientific knowledge is epistemologically no different from other forms of human knowledge. We like to think that human knowledge is something very special. But it is simply a particular kind of information and there is every reason to suppose that it must be organized and made use of in the same way as other forms of information. It is thus significant that objective information plays no part in the strategy of the Biosphere. The information used by natural systems at all levels of organization is not objective but subjective.

The information contained in a fertilized egg is not objective; it consists of that which is required to permit the development of the embryo into a child. The information contained in the cultural 'cognized' model of a vernacular society is not objective. As Roy Rappaport makes clear, its role is to ensure the adaptation of a particular society to the specific environment in which it lives; it is thus only in terms of its ability to achieve this goal that it can be judged.

Though scientists will deny it, this is also how scientific models are judged. Francis Bacon, 'the father of modern science', was the first to insist that science be ruthlessly separated from values ('the idols of the understanding') – but he did nothing of the sort. His scientific knowledge, far from being 'value free' set out explicitly and purposefully to give man power over nature. 'Truth and utility are perfectly identical', he writes in the *Novum Organum*, and 'that which is most useful in practice is most correct in theory.'

Instead of putting aside the old values of good and evil to create a value-free factual knowledge, Bacon simply replaced them with the values of 'useful' and 'useless'. It was a critical time in the history of human affairs. The New World had just been discovered and the financial opportunities provided by plunder and the slave trade seemed limitless. It is not surprising, as Benjamin Farrington notes, that the Christian values of mercy and love should, in such circumstances, have been so easily forgotten, nor that the cynical values of Baconian science should have been so readily accepted. After all, they were precisely those that best served to rationalize our efforts to exploit these new opportunities. 'In Baconian ideology,' Donald Worster writes, 'the Good Shepherd of the Christian tradition had become a scientist and technocrat. Science offered the means for building a better sheepfold and creating greener pastures.'

All the models developed by human societies, including the world-view of modernism and the closely associated paradigm of science, are necessarily 'cognized' and hence subjective. One reason is that man, like all other living things, is a *participant* in the life of the biosphere, whereas in the Western philosophical tradition he has always been regarded as a *spectator* and hence as an entertainer of 'objective' knowledge. This principle has now been accepted, in theory at least, in modern physics. Werner Heisenberg showed that it is impossible to eliminate the influence of the observer and this led him to formulate his 'principle of uncertainty'. Unfortunately, uncertainty has yet to affect the way most physicists look at the world, let alone the practitioners of such disciplines as chemistry, biology, anthropology, sociology and ecology.

For vernacular man, on the other hand, there was what Ashis Nandy calls 'a continuity between the observer and the observed'. For Toshihiko Izutsu,

> the highest degree of knowledge is always achieved when the knower, the human subject, becomes completely unified and identified with the object so much so that there remains no differentiation between the two. For differentiation or distinction means distance, and distance in cognitive relationships means ignorance.

That knowledge, whether scientific or not, must be subjective also follows from the fact that the procedures with which our evolution has equipped us for perceiving our relationship with our specific environment are purely subjective. Contrary to the assumptions of our empiricist philosophers, they are simply not designed to provide us with an objective representation of the world. This principle is worth looking at in some detail.

Observation or perception, which is supposed to be the source of all our knowledge, begins with the detection of data. It is active rather than passive, detecting rather than merely receiving, and it is also highly selective. Instead of accumulating available data in a random fashion, as empiricists assume we do, we isolate those which appear relevant to our behaviour pattern (a minute percentage of the total) from those which do not. As C. Judson Herrick notes:

> The skin is sensitive to mechanical vibrations up to 1,552 per second, but beyond that point feels only a steady push. The ear is aware of sound travelling by wave lengths of 13 mm up to 12,280 mm, but does not hear sounds below or above these limits. The skin is aware of heat-waves only from .0008 mm to .1 mm long. The eye takes cognizance of light waves from .0008 mm to .0004 mm, but misses electric waves, ultra-violet waves, X-rays, gamma rays and cosmic rays, running from wavelengths of .0004 mm to .000,000,000,008 mm.

Sense data outside this range are simply ignored, since during the course of our evolution they have not proved of any relevance to the achievement of our behavioural goal.

This genetically determined selection is complemented by a culturally determined one. At any given moment, we detect only a minute percentage of the data we are genetically equipped to detect – those that our upbringing and experience within a particular culture have taught us to regard as relevant to our behaviour. Detection can only occur on the basis of a pre-existing mental model whose generalities reflect the experience of the species and whose particularities are largely those of the individual within his cultural group. It is in the light of this model that the relevance of different data to his behaviour pattern is determined.

What is more, what we detect with our sensing apparatus is not what we *see*. We do not detect the actual constituents of our environment, such as dogs, trees and rocks, but only patterns of light and shade. These are then interpreted by us in the light of our mental model. A perception is thus a hypothesis based on a particular paradigm. Only in this way can we explain how we can differentiate between movements in our environment and shifts of the image on the retina due to the movement of our own eyes, how we are capable of perceiving 'phantom colours' such as white and purple, which constitute gaps in the spectrum in terms of our detecting procedures, or how we can distinguish between extreme cold and extreme heat, both of which transmit identical messages to the brain. Only in this way can we understand why babies see everything the right way up, for if they were to depend on their detecting mechanisms, they would see everything upside down.

Only in this way can we understand our extraordinary ability to handle fragmentary data. When we read a page of print we may not even notice printing mistakes such as missing letters or even missing words. We subconsciously fill in the gaps. This is possible, Keith Oatley points out, 'because we have a prior knowledge of what we are looking at'. More precisely, we interpret the signals we detect in terms of the mental model we have built up of the subject.

Many experiments, including those carried out by Solomon Asch at Harvard, reveal that people can be induced by suggestion and the force of public opinion to see things very differently from the way they previously saw them. Suggestion and the force of public opinion can change the mental models in terms of which people apprehend the world about them. Thomas Kuhn wrote that this is precisely what occurs in the scientific world after a 'paradigm shift'. Thus, Lavoisier, who discovered oxygen, 'saw oxygen where Priestley had seen dephlogisticated air and where others had seen nothing at all.' In learning to see oxygen, however, Lavoisier also had to change his view of many other more familiar substances. He had, for example, to see a compound ore where Priestley and his contemporaries had seen elementary earth, and there were other such changes besides. At the very least, as a result of discovering oxygen Lavoisier saw nature differently. One might even say that he 'worked in a different world'.

If observation is a purely subjective process, then so are the other means whereby we acquire knowledge, such as intuition and thought itself. We judge the validity of a proposition or hypothesis by determining to what extent it fits in with a subjective model of our relationship with our environment. The truth is that man is simply not designed by his evolution to entertain objective knowledge. As Karl Popper put it, 'knowledge in the objective sense is knowledge without a knower.' This empiricist philosophers have totally failed to realize. Thus Popper discards the epistemology of Locke, Berkeley, Hume and even Russell, for they all assume the possibility of objective knowledge in the conventional sense of the term. He thus dismisses the entire school of empiricist philosophy, which they created, and which provides the basic epistemological foundations of modern science.

Michael Polanyi goes further than Popper. If knowledge is objective, he considers, then 'we must accept the virgin mind, bearing the imprint of no authority, as the model of intellectual integrity.' Only a new-born child possesses such a virgin mind and is thereby able to pass judgements on all questions 'without any preconceived opinions'. But such judgements would necessarily be of a rudimentary nature, as a child would not yet be intelligent enough to understand fully the issues it was called upon to judge. To do so, it would have to grow up, but for its mind to remain virgin and hence objective it 'would have to be kept unshaped until then by any kind of education. It must be taught no language, for speech can be acquired only a-critically, and the practice of speech in one particular language carries with it the acceptance of the particular theory of the universe postulated by that language. An entirely untutored maturing of the mind, would however, result in a *state of imbecility*. For these reasons, Polanyi considers that objective knowledge is an illusion and that we should accept that knowledge, whether scientific or not, is necessarily subjective. Popper, on the other hand, still thinks that objective knowledge is possible – even though it may be, strictly speaking, 'knowledge without a knower'. Such scientific knowledge he sees as made up of logical constructs of different sorts: 'conjectural theories', 'arguments' and, presumably, mathematical models. It is precisely the role of science to build up such constructs. Popper postulates 'three worlds'. The first world is the real world; the second that of subjective knowledge of the real world; and the third that of objective knowledge of the real world, which he sees as the product of humans, just as 'honey is a product of bees or spider's webs of spiders'.

It is true that such constructs have a measure of autonomy in that changes occurring in the real world can be translated into or 'simulated' by changes in the structure of the construct, in accordance with clear rules. If the construct is a particular language, for instance, simulation is achieved in accordance with the grammatical rules of the language in question. If it is symbolic logic, it is done in accordance with the rules of symbolic logic; if a mathematical model, in accordance with the rules of mathematics. Changes occurring within these constructs, it can be argued, are insulated from human subjectivity by virtue of the fact that they occur in accordance with the laws that govern them.

That is undoubtedly the case once the constructs have been brought into being, but we must not forget that the constructs are man-made in the first place and for that reason reflect human cultural patterns which are clearly highly subjective. Indeed, Benjamin Lee Whorf maintained that each language faithfully reflects the metaphysical system of the society that developed it, a thesis much discussed and generally confirmed by semanticists and anthropologists over the last decades. That a mathematical model reflects the metaphysical system of the society that developed it, is perhaps even more evident. It is generally accepted that a mathematical model is no better than its basic assumptions. If these are wrong, then the answers the model provides will also be wrong. As the critics of model building put it: 'garbage in, garbage out'.

The subjectivity of all the various disciplines into which we have divided modern knowledge is equally clear. Their function is above all to help rationalize, and hence legitimize, different aspects of the enterprise of economic development, or progress, to which our society is so resolutely committed. Thus Adam Smith's *Wealth of Nations* showed that by behaving in the most egoistic way possible we maximize not only our own material interests but also those of society at large – a cheerful philosophy which rationalized the individualism and egoism that marked the breakdown of society during the industrial revolution. Darwinism was rightly described by Oswald Spengler as 'the application of economics to biology', Darwin's 'natural selection' being but a biological version of Smith's 'invisible hand' and serving, above all, to legitimize the Promethean enterprise of our modern society by making it appear to be a natural process.

Scientific knowledge, as is pointed out throughout this book, serves to rationalize the paradigm of science and hence the world view of modernism on the basis of which economic development, or progress, alone makes sense. A similar comment can be made about knowledge organized by today's ecological movement. There is no reason to suppose that the ecological world view – in its different variants – is any more objective, less value-laden or less purposeful. Just as modern scientific knowledge is designed to rationalize the paradigm of science, so ecological knowledge is designed to rationalize the world view of ecology.

---

# FOURTEEN

# Man is cognitively adjusted to the environment in which he evolved

●

*What a curious idea it is, this fear that has haunted us since the age of Bacon, that knower and known cannot be trusted along in one another's company but must be chaperoned by a sober and censorious methodology . . . lest they should have illegitimate intercourse and produce bastards of fantasy.*

THEODORE ROSZAK

The perfection of man's cognitive endowment for the purpose of assuring his adaptation to his biological and social environment is an essential principle of the ecological world-view. This principle was always clear to vernacular man and has been expressed in a wide variety of ways. Philosophers since the days of Parmenides have insisted that the mind can understand reality only because they both have the same structure or logos. It was also the first article of faith of Goethe's philosophy of nature that there is 'a perfect correspondence between the inner nature of man and the structure of external reality, between the soul and the world' (see Bortoft, 1986). Henry David Thoreau referred to it as 'Nature looking into Nature'. Paul Tillich refers to what he regards as the rational structure of the mind as 'subjective reason' and to the rational structure of reality as 'objective reason'.

This principle is incompatible with the scientific assumption that subjective knowledge is necessarily imperfect and that only objective scientific knowledge displays sufficient accuracy to provide the basis of rational and hence adaptive behaviour. Charles Darwin would have agreed with this, on interesting grounds. Intuitively, he felt that the natural world could not really have been brought into being by random changes. However, he did not feel that he could trust 'the convictions of man's mind' for it 'has been developed from the mind of lower animals'. And he asks, 'would any one trust in the convictions of a monkey's mind, if there are any convictions in such a mind?' This is also the view of the neo-Darwinists and sociobiologists. Thus, R. L Trivers, a noted sociobiologist, regards as 'very naive' the view that 'natural selection favours nervous systems which produce ever more accurate images of the world'. On the contrary, he tells us, it is very much more probable that 'our genes are deceiving us and filling us full of the glow of having achieved absolute truth.' Edward O. Wilson sees things in much the same way. His attack on intuitionism is based on the notion that we cannot depend on our judgements precisely because they are the product of evolution and thereby totally undependable.

It is also true that in terms of the neo-Darwinian theory of evolution, an individual need not be capable of correctly apprehending his environment in order to survive, for behaviour is not seen to be part of the evolutionary process. What is more, living things are not seen as correctly apprehending or understanding their relationship with their environment but as reacting to it blindly, like Pavlov's dogs. Behaviour, like evolution, is thus seen as a passive process stage-managed by an anonymous environment.

It is encouraging, however, that a number of our more thoughtful scientists have, by implication at least, rejected such assumptions, realizing that the living brain, after a billion years or so of being shaped by the environment, is suited to it with an accuracy that is both remarkable and profound. C. H. Waddington points to a 'congruity between our apparatus for acquiring knowledge and the nature of the things known' and suggests that the human mind 'has been shaped precisely to fit the character of those things with which it has to make contact.' Konrad Lorenz goes still further. He notes that the way we experience the outside world, and indeed the 'a priori' forms of intuition, are 'organic functions based on physical and even mechanical structures of our senses and of the nervous system' and these 'have been adapted by millions of years of evolution.' Jean Piaget goes so far as to say that our cognitive functions are an extension of organic regulations and must be seen as differentiated organs for regulating our relationship with the external world, which must therefore clearly serve the ends of human life.

# FIFTEEN

# Ecology is emotional

●

*Reason flows from the blending of rational thought and feeling. If the two functions are torn apart, thinking deteriorates into schizoid intellectual activity and feeling deteriorates into neurotic life-damaging passions.*

ERICH FROMM

*People need more than to understand their obligation to one another and to earth; they also need the* feeling *of such obligation.*

WENDELL BERRY

Nineteenth-century naturalists were unashamedly emotional in their descriptions of nature. This is particularly true of the great German geologist and naturalist, Alexander von Humboldt, who described the tropical forests of Brazil with emotion and with awe. Charles Darwin, who particularly admired Humboldt, wrote of the Brazilian forests in the same vein, in a letter to Professor Henslow:

> Here I first saw a tropical forest in all its sublime grandeur . . . . Nothing but the reality can give any idea how wonderful, how magnificent it is. . . . I formerly admired Humboldt, I now almost adore him; he alone gives any notion of the feelings . . . on first entering the tropics.

This is a long way from the detached, impersonal, 'objective' approach of today's scientists, for whom, as Donald Worster notes, a tropical forest is but

> a resource to be mapped and dissected, and whose constituents are classified and catalogued increasingly for the benefits of some organization that is only interested in their utilitarian potential.

Modern science has banned the emotions. This is the inevitable consequence of decreeing that scientific knowledge must be objective – a vain decree since man, by his very nature, is incapable of entertaining objective knowledge, just as he is incapable of effectively suppressing his emotions. Michael Polanyi speaks of 'the overwhelming elation felt by scientists' at the moment of making a scientific discovery, 'an elation of a kind which only a scientist can feel and which science alone can evoke in him.' He cites as an example Kepler's elation at discovering his Third Law: 'nothing holds me', he wrote, 'I will indulge my sacred fury.'

The same degree of passion is displayed by scientists in their diatribes against those who attack their beliefs, and threaten their 'cognitive structure' (see Chapter 18). Against these critics veritable witch-hunts have been mounted, comparable to those the medieval church aimed at the proponents of new heresies. Take the witch-hunt against Rachel Carson, who dared suggest that synthetic organic pesticides, whose development in the 1940s was seen as one of the great scientific achievements of that period, actually did more harm than good and should be phased out. Rachel Carson's message was undoubtedly a very subversive one and clearly more than mainstream scientists could take: the reaction was quick and venomous. William B. Bean wrote in *Archives of Internal Medicine* that *Silent Spring*, from the scientific point of view, is 'so much hogwash'. *The Limits to Growth* (the first report to the Club of Rome, written by Donella and Dennis Meadows and others) also drew fierce fire. It was lambasted by the editors of both *Nature* and *Science*, the two principle scientific journals in the English-speaking world, and by Lord Zuckerman, then chief scientist to the British Government, as 'arbitrary speculation' and 'unscientific nonsense'.

The reaction of the scientific world to Immanuel Velikowsky's heretical book *Ages in Chaos* was even more hysterical, as is well documented by Harold Brown. Among other things, there was a concerted effort to force the publisher to take the book out of print. Scientists wrote numerous infuriated letters to the publishers, and actually boycotted their salesmen and text books. The attack was so powerful, that the publishers simply had to give in, even though it was one of their most profitable books. This does not seem to be the way that truly objective scientists would react to the publication of a dissenting book. It was the reaction of highly emotional, indeed almost hysterical people who felt that the dissenter threatened to undermine scientific doctrines to which they were professionally and psychologically committed.

The truth is that man is simply not designed to behave in a non-emotional way, which is one of the reasons why he is incapable of entertaining objective knowledge and behaving 'rationally'. Those imbued with the paradigm of science see this insuppressible human emotionality as a terrible human failing. Some go so far as to attribute it to a defect in our neuro-psychological evolution which has prevented our neo-cortex – the seat of our intelligence – from dominating our primitive reptilian brain, the seat of our emotions.

Arthur Koestler considers that this terrible evolutionary blunder can only be remedied by systematically subjecting man to some form of chemotherapy. But the suppression of man's emotions would mean the eclipse of his closely associated values, his religiosity, his spirituality, his ability to sing and dance, laugh and weep, love and hate, of everything, in fact, that makes him human – all in the interests of making him more rational and machine-like, more adaptive to the aberrant and necessarily short-lived surrogate world that science has helped bring into being.

Up to a certain point, man can 'isolate' himself, to use Sigmund Freud's expression, from his emotions, splitting 'cognition from affect'. Freud saw this as an 'ego defence' or, in Ashis Nandy's words, 'a psychological mechanism to help the human mind cope with unacceptable or ego-alien inner impulses, and external threats.' It involves distancing himself emotionally from a situation or an act which to a normal emotional human would otherwise be intolerable, 'distancing', as Bruno Bettelheim notes, being a 'psychological device, which both the victim and his oppressor have to use'. It is precisely by reducing a victim to an object that one can face treating him in an inhuman way, which is why Aimé Césaire equates colonialism with 'thingification'.

Scientists involved in designing instruments of mass destruction, such as nuclear bombs, must also be capable of distancing themselves emotionally. Robert Jungk describes his encounter with a mathematician he met on his last visit to Los Alamos.

> His face was wreathed in a smile of almost angelic beauty. He looked as if his gaze was fixed upon the world of harmonies. But in fact, he told me later, he was thinking about a mathematical problem whose solution was essential to the construction of a new type of H-bomb.

Jungk adds that this scientist never bothered to watch the trial explosion of any of the bombs he had helped produce. To him, 'research for nuclear weapons was just pure mathematics untrammelled by blood, poison or destruction.'

But is Jungk's mathematician as unemotional as he seems? Undoubtedly not. The scientific education does not suppress the emotions; it merely displaces the object of the emotions. Instead of teaching people to feel emotional about their family, their community, their traditional culture, their religion and the beauty of their natural environment, they are taught instead to feel emotional about the scientific enterprise and the surrogate world it brings into being. Nor is the emotional attachment of the scientist to his work irrelevant to its achievement. Polanyi notes that 'scientific passions are no mere psychological by-product'; instead they have a logical function which contributes an indispensable element to science: 'passions charge objects with emotions, making them repulsive or attractive; positive passions affirm something as precious.' It follows that 'The excitement of the scientists making the discovery is an intellectual passion, telling that something is intellectually precious, and more particularly, that it is precious to science.' In the same way, it can be argued that the witch-hunts mounted by the scientific community against those who threaten the credibility of the scientific enterprise are also 'precious to science'.

The ecology we need is not the ecology that involves viewing the biosphere on which we depend for our survival at a distance and with scientific detachment. We will not save our planet through a conscious, rational and unemotional decision, signing an ecological contract with it on the basis of a cost–benefit analysis. A moral and emotional commitment is required. Indeed, one of the key tasks of ecology must be to redirect our emotions so that they may fulfil the role they were designed to play in helping us preserve the critical order of the Biosphere.

---

# SIXTEEN

# Ecology is a faith

●

*Unless ye believe ye shall not understand.*
ST AUGUSTINE

*Science has remained predominantly an anti-rationalistic movement, based upon a naive faith.*
A. N. WHITEHEAD

Vernacular man believed unquestioningly in the sacred principles under-lying the cultural pattern with which he was imbued. Since they had been formulated by his ancestors who lived at the beginning of time they had to be true. Who was he to doubt the ancestral wisdom which these principles so clearly embodied?

For St Augustine, knowledge was a gift of grace for which we must strive under the guide of antecedent belief. He ruled Christian minds for nearly a thousand years, until the end of the seventeenth century. Then came the development of 'objective science' which was and still is seen as free of all contamination from subjective and irrational human elements such as our emotions, our values, our beliefs.

John Locke, in particular, distinguished between faith and knowledge, persuasion and certainty. It was particularly important to root out faith or belief, for it was associated with religion and superstition. Michael Polanyi tells us that 'all belief was reduced to the status of subjectivity: to that of an imperfection by which knowledge fell short of universality.' Without belief, however, there can be no knowledge. 'For all truth', as Polanyi notes, 'is but the external pole of belief, and to destroy all belief would be to deny all truth.'

This is the main theme of his seminal book *Personal Knowledge*. Into every act of knowing 'there enters a tacit and passionate contribution of the person knowing what is being known' and this, rather than being a flaw, is 'a necessary component of all knowledge'. The idea that reason and intelligence alone are the source of our understanding is sheer illusion.

> Tacit assent and intellectual passions, the sharing of an idiom and of a cultural heritage, affiliation to the like-minded community; such are the impulses which shape our vision of the nature of things on which we rely for our mastery of things. No intelligence, however critical or original, can operate outside such a fiduciary framework.

That this must be so follows from the fact that the human neo-cortex, which is possibly the seat of our intellectual activities, has not been de-signed by its evolution to function by itself as an autonomous instrument of control, any more than has the gene. The lower parts of the brain, which may be regarded as the seat of our values and emotions, have an equal and possibly a greater role to play in determining adaptive human behaviour.

Our leading philosophers of science and our more thoughtful scientists fully realize that science, too, is a faith, in that scientists accept uncritically the basic assumptions that underlie it. Karl Popper considers that 'scientific discovery is impossible without faith in ideas which are of a purely speculative kind,' and which is 'completely unwarranted from the point of view of science'. A. N. Whitehead points out that 'the faith in the order of nature which has made possible the growth of science is a particular example of a deeper faith' which 'cannot be justified by any inductive generalization.' Emile Meyerson notes that 'research is always dominated by preconceived ideas.' C. H. Waddington agrees that a scientist's work is influenced by his metaphysical beliefs, a point also made by Ludwig von Bertalanffy, Paul Feyerabend and others. To say this is no more than to say that the scientist's work reflects the paradigm in terms of which he approaches it, and indeed the wider paradigm of science which has shaped his whole professional life.

Science, in many respects, is just another religion. Thomas Kuhn accurately describes the scientific community as being a sort of priesthood. John Passmore compares 'aristoscientists' with medieval theologians. In many ways they are the priests of our industrial society. It is they who provide the information on the basis of which the industrial process is mediated and without which it could not occur. It is they, too, who have formulated the world view that provides its rationale. What is more, like other priesthoods, they have couched their holy texts in an esoteric language which no outsider can understand, and which confers on them an aura of mystery and sanctity. They have defined truth in such a way that they alone have access to it, for it must be established by a set of scientific rituals which only they can perform: only they possess the necessary scientific skills; only they are equipped with the requisite scientific technology; only they have access to the holy places where, in order to be valid, these rituals must be performed.

It is not surprising that their writings are imbued with an aura of sanctity previously reserved for the holy texts of the established religions. Indeed, if a proposition is classified as 'scientific', then it must be true, indeed incontestable; if, on the other hand, it is branded as 'unscientific', then it must be the work of a charlatan. This has provided the scientific priesthood with the power to prevent any undesired deviation from scientific orthodoxy, just as the Catholic establishment of the Middle Ages could excommunicate any heretic whose teachings were a challenge to its authority. In this way, science has not banished faith. It has just substituted faith in modern science for faith in conventional religion.

Ecology, with which we must replace it, is also a faith. It is a faith in the wisdom of those forces that created the natural world and the cosmos of which it is part; it is a faith in its ability to provide us with extraordinary benefits – those required to satisfy our most fundamental needs. It is a faith in our capacity to develop cultural patterns that will enable us to maintain the integrity and stability of the natural world.

# Seventeen

# Ecology reflects the values of the

# Biosphere

●

*For primitive man, the universe as a whole is a moral or social order, governed
not by what we call natural law, but rather by what we might call moral or
ritual law.*

A. R. RADCLIFFE-BROWN

*Moral behaviour for the Bantu is behaviour that serves to maintain the order of
the Cosmos and hence that maximizes human welfare; immoral behaviour is that
which reduces its order, thereby threatening human welfare.*

PLACIDE TEMPELS

*A thing is right when it tends to preserve the integrity, stability and beauty of the
biotic community. It is wrong when it tends otherwise.*

ALDO LEOPOLD

For vernacular man, the laws of nature were essentially moral laws. In ancient Greece, the natural world was seen to be governed by abstract cosmic forces, in particular Moira (fate) and Dike (justice, law and morality). These concepts are not really distinguishable. As F. M. Cornford notes, 'the ordinance of fate is not a mere blind and senseless barrier of impossibility: it is a moral decree – a boundary of right and wrong.' The order of nature was a moral order: Cornford considers that for the ancient Greeks this was 'an obvious, unchallengable truth' and, indeed, 'the most important truth about the world.' This could probably be said for all vernacular people, even today. What is more, their idea of what constitutes morality is likely to be the same as that of the ancient Greeks.

If we turn to the moral philosophers of our own times to determine what is the moral system of industrial man, we learn that it is no longer connected in any way with our behaviour towards our society, or nature, or the cosmos. Instead it functions in a complete void. Thus Anthony Flew writes of G. E. Moore, probably the most influential moral philosopher of this century, that his 'argument proceeds as if it were in suspense outside space and time; and, incidentally, in complete isolation from the progress of the natural and human sciences.' He could have said much the same of the arguments of most moral philosophers of recent times. (see Appendix 3)

The importance of ethics today is also played down. Thus T. L. S. Sprigge tells us that 'our moral life is not the most important aspect of our life' and that 'we should conform to morality but seek our satisfaction elsewhere.' The so-called 'emotivist' school of moral philosophy goes further, regarding moral statements as 'non-factual': neither true nor false, they merely reflect someone's non-rational emotions. This is clearly the view that best fits the paradigm of science.

The ethical attitudes of modern scientific thinkers cast considerable light on the metaphysical assumptions and world-view underlying their scientific beliefs. The social Darwinists such as Herbert Spencer in the UK and William Graham Sumner in the USA saw nature as random, chaotic, atomized, competitive and aggressive: they felt that it was natural, desirable and indeed moral that man should behave in the same way. Another school of thought on morality is represented by T. H. Huxley, Gaylord

Simpson, Jacques Monod, Edward O. Wilson, Richard Dawkins and other contemporary sociobiologists. They agree that nature is 'red in tooth and claw' but they consider that it is man's duty, on the contrary, to declare war against nature. As Huxley puts it, 'the ethical progress of society depends not on imitating the cosmic process, still less in running away from it, but in combating it.'

The third school can be represented by C. H. Waddington and Julian Huxley. They too saw nature as 'red in tooth and claw'. However, they rejected T. H. Huxley's view that this meant that man's behaviour also had that tendency, as well as his view that we should wage war against nature. They felt that nature was evolving and as it did so, it would become more cooperative. It is thus by observing the laws of evolution that man can be moral.

If we look carefully through their writings on morality we find that, in spite of their obvious differences, the scientists of all three schools have much in common – above all, they faithfully reflect the fundamental principles underlying the paradigm of science. Thus, a cardinal tenet of modernist ethics is that morality begins with modern man and that one cannot talk of primitive man, or of other forms of life, as being 'moral'. This was the view of both T. H. Huxley and Julian Huxley after him. Waddington felt that 'it is only when we pass on from the sub-human world to deal with the evolution of man that ethics must, in its own right, enter the picture.' In a similar vein, Simpson tells us that 'there is no ethics but human ethics and a search that ignores the necessity that ethics be human, relative to man, is bound to fail.'

Morality is also associated by such scientists with the acquisition of knowledge and hence with the development of science. Monod and Simpson actually preached an 'ethic of knowledge'. The former sees this as being the only possible ethic for modern man; 'animistic' or primitive man, by contrast, believes in teleology, which is irreconcilable with objective or 'authentic' knowledge. Julian Huxley considers that since knowledge is good, its acquisition essential for assuring the march of progress, it must follow that 'social morality' includes 'the duty of providing an immense extension of research, and its integrated planning to provide the basis for desirable change.' Scientific knowledge even makes democracy possible. Joseph Needham considers that 'democracy might . . . be termed that practice of which science is the theory', while 'the subjective and the irrational are anti-democratic; they are the instruments of tyranny.'

Ethics is also seen as depending on consciousness, purpose, knowledge and all the other supposedly unique endowments of modern man, for it is only by means of these that there can be reason and choice, and thus morality. Monod tells us that the ethic of knowledge differs from all previous ethics in that it has been adopted by an act of conscious choice. Simpson tells us that choice is morally good. 'Blind faith', on the other hand, 'is morally wrong.' It must follow that as knowledge builds up, our rational choices will 'evolve'. This means that our ethics must be flexible rather than absolute or universal. Change, Simpson insists, is 'the essence' of evolution, and for that reason alone 'there can be no absolute standard of ethics.' Waddington also considers that an evolutionary ethic 'cannot be expected to be absolute but must be subject to evolution itself'; in particular it must 'be the result of responsible and rational choice in the full light of such knowledge of man and of life as we have.' This was also essentially the view of Julian Huxley.

The ethic of modernism is also an *individualistic* ethic. Simpson argues that even if we wished to derive an ethic from nature it would still be individualistic, for evolution tends towards individualization, as opposed to higher integration as ecologists once maintained. Man must be aware of 'the goodness of maintenance of this individualization' and promote 'the integrity and dignity of the individual.' For sociobiologists only an individualistic ethic is even conceivable. Man's overriding goal is the proliferation of his genes. The notion that in the natural world this goal may be subordinated to the needs of the community, the species or the natural world itself is considered 'unscientific' and those who suggest it, as does V. C. Wynne-Edwards, are mercilessly derided. The occasional occurrence of such 'altruistic behaviour' is acknowledged but is explained away as providing, in specific circumstances, the best means of satisfying the individual's overriding goal of maximum gene-proliferation.

There is a terrifying logic to this argument. For 'conscious' and 'rational' modern man – supposedly bereft of a subconscious, of emotions, of faith, allowed no attachments save of a rational and contractual nature, and without identity in an anonymous mega-society committed to perpetual growth – there *can* be no alternative to the individualistic ethic.

It is logically justified in another way. The ethic of modernism is the product of the conscious choice of the individual, who is seen as external to the Gaian hierarchy and free of the laws that govern its behaviour. Based on 'objective' and hence 'scientific' knowledge, this ethic can be sanctioned or authenticated by no authority but that of the individual himself, endowed as he supposedly is with unique intellectual and moral gifts, and armed with the unique potentialities offered by scientific knowledge. Not surprisingly, Simpson tells us that 'man can cherish values if he wishes to', but they are his own, self-imposed values. No absolute ethics can be found 'outside of man's own nature'. Monod is of the same mind. 'The ethic of knowledge', he writes, 'would not be imposed on man. It is he on the contrary who would impose it on himself.' For the evolutionists (among them Julian Huxley and C. H. Waddington) modern man also authenticates his own moral choices, although these are also 'natural' because they reflect the fundamental direction of the evolutionary process.

Above all, the ethic of modernism is the ethic of progress. As Julian Huxley writes, 'social organization should be planned not to prevent change, nor merely to permit it, but to encourage it.' This is also logical, for if all benefits are derived from the technosphere on which progress depends, then ethical behaviour must clearly be that which best serves to preserve the order of the technosphere and, indeed, improve and expand it.

Fortunately, other thinkers, mainly non-scientists, have in recent times returned to a more realistic view of morality. Among the first to react against the ethic of modernism were the precursors of today's ecology movement. Aldo Leopold, for instance, formulated his famous land ethic. 'Harmony with land', he wrote,

> is like harmony with a friend. You cannot cherish his right hand and chop off his left. That is to say, you cannot love game and have predators, you cannot build the forest and mine the farm. The land is one organism.

Human welfare depends on extending the circle of cooperative, communal relatedness to encompass all beings. Such an ecological ethic, as Donald Worster sees it, would change man's role from master of the earth to 'plain member and citizen of it.'

In the 1940s Ralph Gerard and the other members of the Chicago school of ecology saw nature as providing moral inspiration. The nature they saw was essentially cooperative, rather than 'red in tooth and claw'. 'If nature is found to be a world of interdependence', Gerard wrote, 'then man is obliged to consider that characteristic a moral dictum.' The evolutionary trend towards closer integration was, he argued, 'like a straight path through a dense wood, requiring of the pathfinder that he remain on the track and follow it through.' This path is the Way which endless generations of vernacular man have taken to be moral, serving to maintain the integrity and stability of the world of living things.

—————

# EIGHTEEN

# A proposition can only be verified in terms of the paradigm or model of which it is part

●

*Scientific knowledge in any era is what the scientist actively takes as such, and the scientific knowledge of one era may be rejected as error in the next.*
HAROLD BROWN

If mainstream scientists assure us that a thesis, however likely it may seem, has not been verified empirically, it will be branded as unscientific and unworthy of being taken seriously. The consecrated formula is that 'there is no evidence' that it is true, the evidence being exclusively provided by empirical verification in 'controlled laboratory conditions' isolated from the world of living things. If complementary evidence is admitted – epidemiological evidence in the field of health, for instance – this, too, must be empirical. Empirical verification can also be complemented by theoretical arguments, but these are considered of secondary importance.

Logical positivism is the epistemological doctrine that justifies this position. Its main tenet is that the criterion for the acceptability of a proposition – distinguishing a scientific from a metaphysical proposition, sense from nonsense – is empirical verification. Verification is based on induction, and is invalid on that count alone. The reason is that neither an observation, nor an experiment, nor even a series of observations and experiments, can establish a thesis or general principle. At best they can only show that the observation or experiment is compatible with that thesis. But of course, most propositions can be shown to be compatible with a large number of different theses, many of which are likely to be irreconcilable with each other. The philosopher of science Jerry Ravetz shows that one could 'verify' in this way 'the hypothesis that the moon is made of mouldy cheese. One need only deduce that it would then have spots, and then establish that the predicted spots do exist.'

The philosopher Harold Brown regards the fact that 'universal propositions cannot be conclusively verified by any finite set of observation statements' to be the 'central difficulty' of logical positivism. To be consistent, logical positivists would have to regard universal propositions as meaningless metaphysics, but this they clearly cannot do without losing all credibility. They get round the problem by insisting that they are not propositions at all, but merely 'rules which allow us to draw inferences from observation statements to other observation statements.' This is playing with words in the worst tradition of medieval casuistry.

On the other hand, more sensible logical positivists have given up the strict verificationist position. While they require that a meaningful proposition must at least be testable by observation and experiment, they accept that the results need not be conclusive. Rudolf Carnap, one of the fathers of logical positivism, proposed replacing the principle of verification with that of 'gradually increasing confirmation'. This marked the establishment of a new school of epistemology called 'logical empiricism'.

Another problem with empirical verification is that it is based on observation. As we have seen, to observe something means forming a hypothesis about it in the light of one's world-view, while the act of observation which serves to verify the hypothesis is itself the product of this paradigm or world-view, and hence no more objective than the proposition it serves to verify.

Thus Karl Popper noticed as far back as 1919 how currently accepted theories such as Marx's theory of history, Freud's psychoanalysis and Adler's individual psychology seemed to explain almost everything within the fields to which they applied, so much so, that those who subscribed to the theories underwent an 'intellectual conversion or revelation' and 'saw confirming instances everywhere: the world was full of verifications of the theory. Whatever happened always confirmed it.' Arthur Koestler, who in his youth in Hungary was a member of the Communist Party, later admitted that this is precisely what used to happen to him. 'My party education', he wrote, 'had equipped my mind with such elaborate shock-absorbing buffers and elastic defences that everything seen and heard became automatically transformed to fit a preconceived pattern.'

Popper regards such behaviour as 'uncritical'. Scientists do not behave that way. Science is distinguished from metaphysics by its application of the 'critical approach', which means that scientific theories must be formulated in such a way that they can be refuted by empirical means. Newton's theory, for example, predicted deviations from Kepler's laws (due to the interactions of the planets) which had not been observed at the time. It exposed itself thereby to attempted empirical refutations whose failure validated the success of the theory. Einstein's theory was tested in a similar way. 'Only if a theory successfully withstands the pressure of these attempted refutations', Popper asserts, 'can we claim that it is confirmed or corroborated by experience.' Scientists, in formulating a theory, are thereby 'taking a risk', which astrologers, Marxist historians, psychoanalysts and individual psychologists do not take. In other words, 'the criterion of the scientific status of a theory is its falsifiability or refutability, or testability.'

This thesis has in turn been much criticized on a number of obvious counts. To begin with, falsifiability still depends on observation, and is thereby still subject to all the limitations applying to the empirical method. As Sir Peter Medawar notes,

> We could be mistaken in thinking that our observations falsified a hypothesis; the observations themselves could have been faulty, or may have been made against a background of misconception; or our experiments may have been ill-designed. The act of falsification is not immune to human error.

Popper himself admits this. Falsifiability is also based on induction and, as we have seen, one cannot argue from observations or experiments to theories, nor can one disprove theories in this way.

C. H. Waddington considers that the falsifiability principle applies only to very simple events such as those studied by physicists. The reason is that all sorts of devices can be resorted to in order to maintain the validity of a hypothesis concerning the behaviour of complex natural systems. Imre Lakatos sought to replace the principle of 'naive falsification' by 'sophisticated falsification', which involved confronting the scientific theory with an alternative one. 'There is no falsification', he wrote, 'but the emergence of a better theory', though this is still not enough; what is required is a 'series of theories . . . usually connected by a remarkable continuity which welds them into a "research programme".' This, Lakatos admits, is roughly what Thomas Kuhn refers to as a paradigm. However, a programme takes a long time to develop, and it must not be killed off prematurely by pointing to a single inconsistency. For this reason, 'one must treat budding programmes leniently' for it is unfair to falsify theories until they are fully developed. Falsifiable theories must therefore be tolerated at least in their early stages.

For Kuhn, this is not sufficient. He rejects Popper's view that science is still concerned, as was Greek science, with fundamental issues. This is simply not true of modern science, in which the accent shifts from the discussion of fundamentals to what he calls 'problem solving'. Those involved in this latter activity share the same paradigm, whose validity is taken for granted and hence does not require testing. Kuhn actually goes so far as to say that 'it is precisely the abandonment of critical discourse that marks the transition to a science', after which 'the critical discourse recurs only at moments of crisis, when scientists must choose between competing theories', and it is only then that they behave like Greek scientists or philosophers.

In normal conditions, testing still occurs, of course, but it is not the fundamental issues (current theory) that are tested but only the details or technicalities of the theory, the experimenter's skill at 'problem solving', while the paradigm itself is never tested and can be guaranteed to emerge unscathed even if it were to be tested. As John Watkins notes,

> if the outcome of such a 'test' is negative, it does not fit the theory but backfires on the experimenter. His prestige may be lowered by the failure of his attempt to solve a puzzle; but the prestige of the paradigm within whose framework he makes the attempt is so high that it will scarcely be affected by such little local difficulties.

Not surprisingly, Kuhn considers that it is only very superficial propositions that are falsified, except when the paradigm of which it is part is in crisis and due to be replaced with a new paradigm.

The trouble is that when there is a confrontation between two paradigms, the victor is not necessarily that which would be chosen on the basis of any sort of empirical verification or falsification. For there is no rational discourse between the proponents of different paradigms. They speak different languages, see things in a fundamentally different way and therefore cannot really communicate. Moreover, as Michael Polanyi observes, scientific controversies 'never lie altogether within science.' This is perhaps an understatement. Indeed such controversies are likely to be highly emotive, quasi-religious affairs. In general, one can say that people, whether they be primitive tribesmen, businessmen, bureaucrats or professional scientists, will do everything they can to preserve their paradigm in the face of knowledge that appears to undermine it, a principle referred to by the anthropologist A. F. C. Wallace as 'the Principle of the Preservation of Cognitive Structure'.

Polanyi describes three strategies currently in use for preserving a cognitive structure when confronted with experiences which would appear to invalidate it. The first is to defend the principle that seems to be invalidated with reference to another principle; this is possible because of the circularity of world views or paradigms. Edward Evans-Pritchard notes how this is done by the Azande tribe of Uganda when faced with such experiences. For them 'the contradiction between experience and one's mystical notion is explained by references to other mystical notions.' Polanyi points out that belief in the usefulness of mathematics as a means of understanding the world is based on the same self-reinforcing circularity, since

> every assertion of a deductive system can be demonstrated by, or else shown to be, implied as axioms of the others. Therefore, if we doubt each assertion in its turn, each is found confirmed by circularity and the refutation of each consecutive doubt results in strengthening the belief in the system as a whole.

Another technique mentioned by Polanyi for maintaining the stability of beliefs in the face of conflicting evidence is to 'expand the circle in which an interpretive system operates.' In this way, 'elaboration of the system' can be readily supplied to cover 'almost any conceivable eventuality.' This device he calls 'the building up of ancillary hypotheses.' Scientific theories which 'possess this self-expanding capacity' are 'epicyclical', an allusion to the epicycles which were used in the Ptolemaic and Copernican theories to represent the uniform and circular movement of planets. According to Polanyi, 'all major interpretive frameworks have an epicyclical structure which supplies a reserve of subsidiary explanations for difficult situations.' Polanyi cites Evans-Pritchard's description of the epicyclical character of Azande beliefs. The Azande believe in the powers of the poison oracle. The oracle answers questions through the effects on a fowl of a poisonous substance called *benge*. The oracle poison is extracted from a creeper gathered in a traditional manner, which is supposed to become effective only after it has been addressed in the words of an appropriate ritual. Suppose that the oracle, in answer to the same question, says 'yes' and immediately afterwards, 'no'. For us, this would discredit the oracle, but Azande culture provides ready-made explanations for such contradictions. Evans-Pritchard lists no fewer than eight ready-made explanations which can account for the oracle's failure. They may insist that the wrong type of poison had been used, or a breach of taboo committed, or that the owners of the forest where the poisonous creeper grows had been insulted and avenged themselves by making the poison ineffectual.

Scientists, Polanyi points out, behave in just the same way. They are no more likely than an Azande medicine man to accept evidence that could invalidate any aspect of their belief. This could not be better illustrated than by Lakatos's story of the imaginary pre-Einsteinian physicist.

On the basis of Newtonian mechanics, of Newton's law of gravitation (N) and of the accepted initial conditions, (I), the physicist calculates the trajectory of a newly discovered small planet, (p). Unfortunately, however, the planet does not follow the expected trajectory. How does the physicist react to this? Does he accept that Newtonian mechanics are wrong? That the law of gravity (N) does not apply? Undoubtedly not. He suggests that there must be a hitherto unknown planet, p', which perturbs the path of p. He calculates the mass, orbit, etc., of this hypothetical planet and then asks an experimental astronomer to test his hypothesis. The planet p' is so small that even the biggest available telescopes cannot possibly observe it: the experimental astronomer applies for a research grant to build yet a bigger one. In three years' time, the new telescope is ready. Were the unknown planet p' to be discovered, it would be hailed as a new victory of Newtonian science. But it is not. Does our scientist abandon Newton's theory and his idea of the perturbing planet? No. He suggests that a cloud of cosmic dust hides the planet from us. He calculates the location and properties of this cloud and asks for a research grant to send up a satellite to test his calculations. Were the satellite's instruments (possibly new ones, based on a little-tested theory) to record the existence of the conjectural cloud, the result would be hailed as an outstanding victory for Newtonian science but the cloud is not found. Does our scientist abandon Newton's theory, together with the idea of the perturbing planet and the idea of a cloud which hides it? No. He suggests that there is some magnetic field in that region of the universe which disturbed the instruments of the satellite. A new satellite is sent up. Were the magnetic field to be found, Newtonians would celebrate a sensational victory. But it is not. Is this regarded as a refutation of Newtonian science? No. Either yet another ingenious auxiliary hypothesis is proposed or . . . the whole story is buried in the dusty volumes of periodicals and the story never mentioned again.

For Polanyi, to preserve the stability of one's world-view, paradigm or cognitive structure is entirely human. To suppose that such a demonstration of self-interest can be avoided by developing a more objective science is no more than a pious hope – a notion based on no knowledge of any kind. It is also an error to suppose that this is a human *failing*. It is not. It is, in fact, highly adaptive, indeed essential, in order to maintain the continuity or stability of a human social system. All organizations of information in the natural world are and must be capable of maintaining their stability in the face of environmental challenges.

The problem, of course, as Polanyi does not fail to point out, is that the devices used for stabilizing 'a true view of the universe, may "equally stabilize an erroneous [one]".' That, of course, is in the nature of things. The procedures that make possible homeotelic life processes (see Chapter 53) can be misdirected to promote heterotelic ones instead. (see Chapter 41) But the possibility of such errors is systematically reduced as we move from a 'disclimax' or neo-pioneer society (see end of Chapter 64), in which people's ideas will be largely random and individualistic, to a climax society in which people will be imbued with the world-view consistent with behaviour that best assures the preservation of the critical order of the cosmos.

---

# NINETEEN

# The Biosphere is one

●

*The most fundamental of my intellectual beliefs is that the idea that the world is a unity, is rubbish. I think the universe is all spots and jumps, without unity and without continuity, without coherence or orderliness or any of the other properties that governesses love.*
BERTRAND RUSSELL

*For primitive man, the supreme wisdom consists in recognizing the unity and order of the living world, a term we must take as including the world of the spirits.*
PLACIDE TEMPELS

*The entire range of living matter on earth, from whales to viruses, and from oaks to algae, could be regarded as constituting a single living entity, capable of manipulating the earth's atmosphere to suit its overall needs and endowed with faculties and powers far beyond those of its constituent parts.*
JAMES LOVELOCK

---

Traditional man knew that the world is one, that it is alive, orderly and hierarchically organized, and that all the diverse living things that inhabit it are closely interrelated and cooperate in maintaining its integrity and stability. In ancient Greece, the 'Pythagoreans', as Donald Hughes writes, 'held that the world is spherical, animate, ensouled and intelligent.' Plato saw it as a 'living creature, one and indivisible, containing within itself all living creatures which are by nature akin to itself.' What is more, this living creature was 'endowed with soul and reason'. The Stoics, Hughes tells us, also saw the cosmos as a sentient being 'which is rational, harmonious, and of which all living things are part. It is also self-sufficient, since it nourishes and is nourished from itself.'

This view of the world was also that of Linnaeus and his followers in the seventeenth century and of the Natural Theologists of the eighteenth and nineteenth centuries, among them John Ray, William Derham, William Paley and Thomas Morgan. The latter wrote of the 'perfect unity, order, wisdom and design' of the natural world, 'by which every individual is necessarily related to and made a dependent part of the whole.' For him, the biosphere could only be the work of a 'Universal designing mind' which 'contrived, adjusted and disposed the whole into such order, uniformity, concordant beauty and harmony and which continues to support, govern and direct the whole.'

Aldo Leopold, that great American precursor of the ecological movement, also saw the earth as one: 'we must realize the indivisibility of the earth – its soil, mountains, rivers, forests, climate, plants and animals, and respect it collectively; not as a useful servant but as a living being.' More recently, advances in cytology and molecular biology have led scientists, whose interest had previously been monopolized by the extraordinary diversity of living things, to realize that underlying it all is a basic unity that is very difficult to explain in terms of the paradigm of science, in terms of which knowledge is so strictly compartmentalized.

The geneticist Theodosius Dobzhansky notes that underlying the great diversity there are profound similarities. The genetic imprints in all living things can be read in the language of DNA and RNA, and the protein building blocks of all living things are made up of the same twenty aminoacids. Both Francois Jacob and Jacques Monod also note how similar all living things are at the microscopic level. And if the materials are the same throughout the living world, so is the pattern of construction. Thus the French biologist Armand de Ricqles is struck by the fact that all vertebrates, fish, amphibians, reptiles, birds and mammals are built according to the same organizational plan in spite of important anatomical differences. 'What', he asks, 'does this unity of design imply? This is a big question which comparative anatomy began to ask in the eighteenth-century and has not ceased to ask.'

It implies, of course, that as evolution proceeds superficial changes occur to adapt different forms of life to specialized environments, and yet the basic features of life remain the same – an evolutionary achievement that is difficult to reconcile with currently accepted evolutionary theory. It implies too that the overriding goal of living things is to preserve the critical order and hence the stability of the Gaian hierarchy of which they are part. It would also seem that Gaia is a single self-regulating natural system, at once a life-process and the unit of evolution (see Chapters 20, 21).

The Scottish geologist and natural philosopher James Hutton, writing in 1788, was possibly the first scientist in the modern world to recognize the unity of nature. The idea was put forward once again by the Austrian scientist Edouard Suess in 1875. He saw the earth as 'a Living World that is a system of living animals and plants' and coined the term 'Biosphere' to apply to to the living world together with its geological substrata. The modern idea of the Biosphere, however, is usually accredited to the Russian scientist, Vladimir Vernadsky. He saw it as a 'Living Organism', and quite rightly claimed that this had the widest possible implications for all the other disciplines in terms of which modern man seeks to understand the natural world and its functioning.

The notion that the world of living things, together with its atmospheric environment, also constitutes an entity can probably be traced to Larmarck. He saw the development of living organisms as an integral part of a wider subject (*The Physics of the Earth*) which included the study of the atmosphere (meteorology) and of the earth's crust (hydrogeology). None of these disciplines could be understood without reference to the others, pointing to the need for a truly holistic science of the natural world. Suess also saw the Biosphere in this way and described plants reaching deep into

the soil to feed and, at the same time, rising into the air above to breathe –
thus accentuating the close interaction between the lithosphere and the
atmosphere. Vernadsky's Biosphere included 'the whole atmospheric tro-
posphere, the oceans and a thin layer in the continental regions expanding
down about three kilometers or more.' His position contrasted with that
of Frederick Clements and Victor Shelford. Though they were among the
fathers of holistic ecology, they nevertheless insisted that the community
and its environment should not be regarded as forming part of the same
ecological entity.

Critical to the development of the modern theory of the Biosphere was
the realization that atmosphere was a creation of living things rather than
the product of purely physical and chemical forces. This was first suggested by Alfred Redfield and later, in 1841, by the French scientists, Jean
Baptiste Dumas and Jean Baptiste Boussingault. In the early 1970s the idea
was taken up by the atmospheric chemist James Lovelock who described
the process involved in great detail. 'The atmosphere of dead planets, like
Mars and Venus,' he notes, 'is in chemical equilibrium.' On the other
hand,

> the chemical composition of the atmosphere [of our planet] bears no relation
> to the expectations of steady-state chemical equilibrium. The presence of
> methane, nitrous oxide, and even nitrogen in our present oxidizing atmos-
> phere represents a violation of the rules of chemistry to be measured in tens of
> orders of magnitude.

What is still more extraordinary is that many of the gases that compose
the atmosphere are unstable in each other's presence. They should not
coexist, which suggests that they have to be continuously emitted on a
very large scale if they are to persist in the atmosphere. As Lovelock puts
it,

> we have an abundance of oxygen, 21 per cent of the atmosphere, and a trace of
> methane, at 1.5 parts per million. We know from chemistry that methane and
> oxygen will react when illuminated by sunlight, and we also know the rate of
> this reaction. From this, we can confidently conclude that the coexistence of

the two reactive gases methane and oxygen at a steady level requires a flux of methane of 1000 megatons a year. This is the amount needed to replace the losses by oxidation. Furthermore, there must also be a flux of oxygen of 4000 megatons a year, for this much is used up on oxidizing the methane. There are no reactions known to chemistry which could make these vast quantities of methane and oxygen starting from the available raw materials, water and carbon, and using solar energy.

For Lovelock, there is only one answer:

There must be some process at the Earth's surface which can assemble the sequence of unstable and reactive intermediaries in the programmed manner to achieve this end. Most probably this process is life.

What also requires explaining, as Lynn Margulis points out, is that if our planet were a dead one, like Venus or Mars, the atmosphere would be composed of more than 95 per cent carbon dioxide, yet it contains no more than 0.3 per cent – again, that which is required to support life. The explanation is photosynthesis – that essential activity of plant and algal life that is at the same time responsible for maintaining the requisite level of oxygen in the atmosphere. Thus living things, in taking up carbon dioxide and emitting oxygen, are creating precisely that combination of the two gases in the atmosphere that is required for maintaining life on our planet. They are also creating conditions most favourable to life when generating methane and other atmospheric gases or taking up or otherwise neutralizing gases in the atmosphere that are surplus to the requirements of life. This suggests 'that the atmosphere is not merely a biological product', Lovelock concludes, 'but more probably a biological construction; not living but like a cat's fur, a bird's feathers, or the paper of a wasp's nest, an extension of a living system designed to maintain a chosen environment.' He denies, however, that his thesis is teleological.

It is essential to Lovelock's thesis that living things could not create precisely the atmospheric environment they require if they were not organized to constitute a single cybernetic system – the biosphere. This global living entity, in conjunction with the atmospheric environment it has created, constitutes a bigger natural system that Lovelock refers to as Gaia, after the Greek goddess of the earth, and that I also refer to in this book as the Biosphere. He defines Gaia as

> a complex entity, involving the Earth's biosphere, atmosphere, oceans and soil; the total constituting a feedback or cybernetic system which seeks an optimal physical and chemical environment for life on this planet.

In particular, he stresses that Gaia is thereby capable of maintaining its stability or homeostasis in the face of change, for its climate has remained remarkably stable over the last few hundred million years in spite of the fact that the heat from the sun, during this period, has increased by about 30%.

No credible rebuttal of Lovelock's thesis has been published by the mainstream scientific community, nor is one likely to be. Many of its far-reaching implications are considered in this book.

---

# TWENTY

# Gaia is a spatio-temporal entity

●

*An object separated from its history is clearly not the kind of thing that could possibly exist.*

C. D. BROAD

*We are beginning to grasp that societies, like the individuals which compose them, and like life in general, have a time dimension. They are processes, and their direction in time is as important a part of their nature as their organization at any particular time.*

JULIAN HUXLEY

Gaia, and indeed all natural systems, exist in time as well as in space. There can be no atemporal system any more than there can be a non-spatial process. As J. H. Woodger puts it:

> A frog without a life history is as impossible as a life history without a frog. A frog in pickle is a cross-section of its history as a living organism, and anatomy is biology with the time dimension omitted. Anatomy studies the organism in 'timeless space'.

The languages of some vernacular societies, including a number of Indian tribes of the American North-West, accentuate the temporal aspect of the world around them, as Benjamin Lee Whorf showed so convincingly. Others, including those of European societies, tend to accentuate, on the contrary, their spatial aspect. The members of many North American Indian tribes, as Mirca Eliade tells us, saw the cosmos as 'a living being that is born, grows and dies on the last day of the year, to be reborn with the new year.' Thus, instead of saying 'a year has passed', the Yokuts say 'the world has passed'. If the sacred houses of the Algonquins and the Sioux are designed to provide a representation of the cosmos, they provide at the same time a representation of the year. What is more, if the cosmos was seen as dying at the end of each year, then it was man's duty to assure that it was annually reborn. Indeed, many of the ceremonies of vernacular people were re-enactments of the original act of creation ('cosmogenesis'), designed to assure the continuity of the cosmos. Vernacular man thus understood that the behaviour of successive generations of men and other living things is critical to cosmic continuity and the prevention of a reversion to the original chaos.

Mainstream science, on the contrary, sees no connection between the behaviour of living things, their development (morphogenesis), their physiology and the fate of the Biosphere – whose very existence as a self-regulating natural system most mainstream scientists still deny. They do not even see any connection between the behaviour of man and other living things and the evolutionary process, which is seen as occurring independently of adaptive changes undergone by them. All these processes are seen as distinct, largely unrelated and governed by a different set of laws.

Fortunately, a few more enlightened scientists see things differently. Thus Woodger sees all adaptive changes as 'different eras in the same process'. In his classical studies of infant behaviour, the psychologist Arnold Gesell notes that the early instinctive reactions of a child are no more than a continuation of the embryological activities that brought it into being. Henri Bergson, too, points to the continuity between embryogenesis and behaviour. 'How', he asks, 'can one draw the line between the constructive processes of the bird's embryonic development and the constructive process by which it builds its nest?' Charles Lumsden and Edward O. Wilson point to the same continuity, asserting that 'there is no fundamental break in the process between tissue formation and behaviour.'

If morphogenesis and behaviour are part of the same process, physiology and behaviour must be similarly linked. Edmund Sinnott notes that breathing, for instance, is a physiological process but also 'a part of the way an animal behaves' and that 'these two processes are part of a single strategy.' It follows that morphogenesis and physiology are also part of the same process. Indeed, 'in any living system', Sinnott writes, 'changes involved in growth are essentially the same as those concerned with the maintenance of vital activities and the repair of tissues.'

It is thus realistic to regard these processes, taken together, as corresponding to the wider process normally referred to as ontogeny. In turn, it is realistic to regard ontogenies as constituting the evolutionary process itself. That this must be so should be clear from the following consideration: when we say that evolutionary change has occurred, we mean that ontogenetic processes at a particular moment in time are no longer the same as they were in the past, which means that they have been subjected to morphogenetic, physiological and behavioural changes. This being so, it seems very unrealistic to study these changes outside their evolutionary context, just as it seems unrealistic to study evolutionary change, as does mainstream science, separately from the changes undergone by the constituent life processes in terms of which it manifests itself.

# TWENTY ONE

# Gaia, seen as a total spatio-temporal process, is the unit of evolution

●

*To Freud the unconscious is chiefly a receptacle for things repressed. He looks at it from the corner of the nursery. To me it is a vast historical storehouse.*
CARL JUNG

*A country which has lost the sense of its own past has no understanding of its present and no direction for its future.*
WINSTON CHURCHILL

A fundamental flaw in the neo-Darwinian thesis is that the individual organism is seen as the basic unit of evolution. But what is so special about the individual organism? Is there such a fundamental difference between its adaptive strategies and those of other natural systems that it can be viewed as totally distinct from them? The answer is, unquestionably, no.

Life processes at all levels of organization, including the evolutionary process itself, are designed according to the same plan, being purposeful, dynamic, creative and intelligent. What is more, their adaptive strategies are all geared to maintaining the stability or homeostasis of the entire Gaian hierarchy – *a sine qua non* for the maintenance of their own homeostasis (see Chapter 53). In addition, the larger systems, from Gaia downwards, control and coordinate the behaviour of their constituent parts. For these reasons, the individual cannot conceivably be regarded as the sole unit of evolution. It can only be Gaia herself, and we can best refer to evolution as the Gaian process.

A process, however, is an abstraction unless it has a spatial aspect, just as an entity is an abstraction if seen atemporally. The temporal and spatial abstractions in terms of which we are accustomed to think about Gaia are, in fact, only different aspects of the same reality, the spatio-temporal system that is Gaia. It follows that there must be a perfect correspondence between the temporal Gaian abstraction and the spatial Gaian abstraction, just as there must be a perfect correspondence between our digestive process and our digestive system, seen as a physical entity. The neo-Darwinian thesis involves, on the other hand, radically isolating the structure of the Biosphere, viewed spatially, from that of the Biosphere as a process – the former being seen in all its complexity and sophistication, the latter being reduced to the crude interplay between two machines – a generator of randomness and a sorting machine.

To determine the main features of the Gaian process, it must therefore suffice to establish what are the main features Gaia sees as a spatial or at least a contemporaneous abstraction which must be the main features of Gaia seen as a temporal abstraction, and of Gaia seen as a complete spatio-temporal System. Let us look at a few of its particularly significant features. The first is that Gaia, seen as a spatial abstraction, is hierarchical, being made up of larger systems that are divided into smaller and still smaller systems. The same must also be true of Gaia seen as a temporal abstraction or spatio-temporal process, which is a hierarchy made up of long-lived life processes that are divided up into ever shorter-lived life processes.

Thus there are tens of thousands of generations of cells within the lifespan of a single individual organism. Individuals have very much shorter lifespans than do the families of which they are the temporal as well as the spatial constituents. Beyond families stretch communities; beyond communities, societies or ethnic groups; beyond these, the human species, which in turn is unlikely to survive for longer than a fraction of the history of the biosphere itself.

Another essential feature of the Biosphere seen as a spatial abstraction, is that it displays order. As we shall see, (see Chapter 27) order in a spatial abstraction corresponds to purpose in a temporal abstraction. In a hierarchical spatio-temporal system this means that the parts must behave homeotelically to the Gaian hierarchy as a whole in order to maintain its stability, and thus their own. James Lovelock sees the development of Gaia and the maintenance of its stability over hundreds of millions of years as the result of the coordinated action of living things – in particular, bacteria.

Thus, the evolution of species, as opposed to the overall Gaian evolutionary process, can only manifest itself in terms of changes occurring to a succession of ontogenies. These ontogenies cannot be understood as separate and individual processes. They are the differentiated parts of phylogeny, which in turn is closely integrated with the myriad other phylogenies that make up the Gaian process. What, then, is the role of ontogenies and their constituent sub-processes – morphology, physiology and behaviour? The answer can only be: to provide the evolutionary process as a whole with the localized and short-term information required to ensure that it remains adaptive to the changing circumstances in which it occurs. In modern language, it provides the feedback without which no cybernetic process is possible. This was implicit at least to the evolutionary theory of Lamarck, but it is hotly denied by mainstream science, which sees evolutionary change as exclusively the result of changes affecting the genes of individual living things. As neither morphogenesis nor the development of a child into an adult, nor its physiological or behavioural experience are considered to affect the genetic material in any way, these processes are seen as totally isolated from the evolutionary process. (see Appendix 4)

Another relevant feature of the Gaian hierarchy, seen as a spatial or perhaps more realistically a contemporaneous entity, is that the smaller constituent entities are controlled and coordinated by the larger ones – Gaia herself controlling in this way the whole hierarchy that it constitutes. It can be shown that this must also be true of the Gaian process or evolution, which means that the past and the future must control the present.

In evolution, as in all natural processes, the whole precedes the part: in other words, the more general the features of a natural system, the earlier they must have been established. Thus the decision that a particular organism was to be a bird rather than a reptile or mammal was taken many millions of years ago. Those required to determine what family, genus, species or variety it would belong to were taken correspondingly later and in that order. The more trivial or specific the characteristics that distinguish an individual from the other members of its variety or species, the later its period of development. (see Chapter 54)

The nineteenth-century German philosopher and naturalist Ernest Haeckel very significantly showed that the embryos of different vertebrates such as chickens, tortoises and humans were, at particular stages in their respective developments, so similar that they could not be told apart. However, as they developed, so did they grow correspondingly different. This led him to formulate his biogenetic law, according to which, ontogeny recapitulates phylogeny, which, though it has been reconsidered and reformulated by Gavin de Beer, remains in its essence, fundamentally true.

The similarity in the form of these different embryos at the specific stages of their respective developments reflects their common early history. This early history is largely indelible. The reason is that the information which is transmitted from one generation to the next reflects the total experience of the species, not just its short-term experience. This is essential since the short-term experience could be non-representative, indeed aberrant: life processes based on it would then be heterotelic, serving to satisfy the short-term needs of individuals of a particular generation without, at the same time, serving those of the hierarchy of spatio-temporal systems of which they are part, and in such conditions the Gaian process would lose its continuity or stability.

If behaviour is to be based on information that reflects the total experience of a species, then this information must be non-plastic, which we know to be the case. It is only the shortest and most recent experience that is plastic and hence modifiable, and that can thereby change for the sake of preventing bigger, more destructive changes affecting the system's generalities. The information transmitted from one generation to the next must reflect the total experience of the species for another associated reason. It is that evolution is cumulative and incremental. During the evolutionary process, new information does not replace the old – it merely supplements it.

Significantly, the nervous system has also evolved by a process of successive accretions, the second and later the third nervous systems being added without displacing the older nervous systems. Paul McLean and Arthur Koestler lament the fact that the neo-cortex does not completely dominate the older brains – which would be necessary if man were, as both of them feel he should be, truly 'rational'. As McClean writes, 'the reptilian brain is filled with ancestral lore and ancestral memories and is faithful in doing what its ancestors say, but it is not a very good brain for facing up to new situations.' Neither of them realizes that rationality by itself (if there is such a thing) could only lead to chaos and that it is a prerequisite for the continuity of our species and hence for its survival that our 'rationality' be controlled precisely by the 'ancestral lore and ancestral memories' that reflect the total experience of our species.

Vernacular and, particularly, chthonic societies, lacking formal political institutions, are effectively governed by a Council of Elders. They are the living custodians of the society's cultural wisdom, which, in effect, reflects its total experience. For this reason, a chthonic society has often been referred to as a gerontocracy, or government by the old. However, the ultimate custodians of the traditional wisdom are the ancestral spirits who developed it. For this reason such a society is best seen as a necrocracy, or government by the dead. Ancestor worship is an essential feature of the religion of such societies; it is the influence of the values of which the ancestors are the custodians that holds sway. Lafcadio Hearn notes how this is true of traditional Japanese society. 'In all matters', he notes, 'the dead, rather than the living, have been the rulers of the nation and the shapers of its destiny' – as indeed they have ruled and shaped the destinies of all chthonic societies. No voices from the grave have spoken with greater authority than the mythical ancestors – the 'Dawn Beings', as A. R. Radcliffe-Brown refers to them, who lived in that sacred period known by certain Australian tribes as the 'World Dawn', Mirca Eliade's *in illo tempore*. In that sacred period they enacted the traditional law that was to govern for all time their society, the natural world and the cosmos itself. The traditional law was sacred on all these counts, and the non-plasticity of the traditional information that reflected the total experience of the society and that was passed down from one generation to the next was thus assured. Adaptation to new environmental changes, in such conditions, in-volved only the imperceptible changes which the shaman and the Council of Elders could reconcile with the society's mythology and the traditional law that it served to rationalize. Such a society would thus be seen as governed by the total spatio-temporal hierarchical entity going back to the 'Dawn Period' when it first arose. In this way, the principles governing the transmission of cultural information are precisely those governing the transmission of genetic information which ensures the stability of natural systems at a biological level of organization.

But it is not just the past, but also the future that controls the present; for the shorter processes serve the purpose of the larger processes that en-compass and outlive them. Indeed, within the Gaian process, individual life processes are designed in such a way as to maintain the critical order of the Gaian process indefinitely – that is, until such time as massive geo-physical change gives rise to conditions that lie outside its 'tolerance range'.

Nothing is undertaken by the Gaian process in the interests of satis-fying short-term requirements that can possibly interfere with its con-tinuity or stability, and hence with its perpetuation. In the case of eco-nomic development, or progress, the opposite is true. (see Chapter 64) It is exclusively concerned with immediate political and economic benefits and its promoters show absolutely no interest in the consequences of such behaviour for future generations, for the latter are not players in today's political and economic games. They neither vote, nor save, nor invest, nor produce, nor consume. Why then should they be consulted?

It must follow that if evolution is the Gaian process it cannot be understood by examining the behaviour of that contemporaneous cross-section of the Biosphere of which we are part and that is normally taken to be evolutionary. For such a cross-section does not evolve in order to maintain its stability, but rather the stability of that vast spatio-temporal process-entity, that stretches back to the beginning of life on earth – whose experience is reflected in the information on the basis of which it evolves. It is the latter, in fact, that is evolving, not the former, which on its own has no meaning. From the cybernetic point of view, the total Gaian experience, going back into the mists of time exists, as does the present and as does its future experience, for together they constitute the Gaian process – the unit of evolution. A tribal society is said to be made up of the dead, the living and the yet to be born – that is precisely how Gaia must be seen.

# TWENTY TWO

# Stability rather than change is the basic feature of the living world

●

*Nature, left undisturbed, so fashions her territory as to give it almost unchanging permanence of form, outline and proportion, except when shattered by geologic convulsion; and in these comparatively rare cases of derangement, she sets herself at once to repair the superficial damage, and to restore, as nearly as practicable, the former aspect of her dominion. . . . A condition of equilibrium has been reached which, without the action of man, would remain, with little fluctuation, for countless ages.*
GEORGE PERKINS MARSH

*What is it that holds so many groups of animals to an astonishingly constant form over millions of years? This seems to be the problem now – the problem of constancy, rather than of change.*
W. H. THORPE

The attention of those imbued with the paradigm of science, and hence with the world-view of modernism, is monopolized by change. For them, the world is in perpetual flux, constantly changing in a direction seen as desirable and progressive. This is true of species that are seen to be 'evolving' and societies and economies that are seen to be 'developing'. Reality is quite different. It is continuity or stability that has been the most striking feature of the world of living things.

Charles Darwin himself was highly impressed by the constancy of the natural world and once even suggested that it may be more important than 'the struggle for survival' with which he was so concerned. In a letter to the geologist Charles Lyell he wrote, 'if I had to commence de novo, I would have used "natural preservation".' A similar view has also been expressed by our most eminent neo-Darwinists. Thus Gaylord Simpson, one of the founders of the Synthetic Theory of Evolution, admits that

> heredity is, on the whole, a conservative factor tending to keep succeeding generations within a common pattern. The acorn produces an oak similar to the tree that produced the acorn, except in unessential details, and the egg produces a chicken essentially like the hen that laid it.

But he cannot avoid emphasizing that 'offspring are nevertheless never exactly like their parents' and that 'since evolution is a process of change, these differences are of special concern to us.'

Theodosius Dobzhansky was also struck by the conservatism of nature:

> the bones of Cretaceous opossums are similar to some modern ones ... modern horseshoe crabs (limulus) do not differ greatly from those having lived some 200 million years ago; the brachiopod Lingula changed little if at all for 450 million years.

Both C. H. Waddington, and Jacques Monod were also impressed by the constancy of living things, as was W. H. Thorpe who fully realized that the constancy of certain biological forms is more difficult to explain 'than it is to account for their evolution'. He notes for instance that

> The Wagtail (Motacilla) there in the garden was here before the Himalayas were lifted up! This constancy is so extraordinary, that it seems to demand a special mechanism to account not for the evolution but for the fixity of some groups.

Paul Weiss also realized this. There is so great a preoccupation with change, he noted, that we have totally neglected the less glamorous but more fundamental constancy of the living world. 'In our educational system', he writes, 'we are acting very much like newspaper editors, who highlight the spectacular and neglect the far more constant phenomena.'

Thus we accentuate evolution, but we do not impress on our children that the most fundamental features of all living things are exactly the same and 'have remained the same from the simplest living system that we know, all the way up to man.' They should be told that,

> all the biochemical mechanisms of macromolecular synthesis, energy utilization, respiration, storage, proliferation, cell division, membrane structure and function, contractility, excitability, fibre-formation, pigmentation, and so forth . . . remained unaltered in essence through the ages.

This has been noted by the Harvard palaeontologist Stephen J. Gould and also by his colleagues Steven Stanley and Niles Eldredge, who between them developed the Theory of Punctuated Equilibrium in terms of which long periods of stability are punctuated by short periods of dramatic and rapid evolutionary change. This notion, first put forward in the 1940s by Richard Goldschmidt, is difficult to reconcile with the Darwinian view that evolution occurs as the result of a gradual succession of small changes. Punctuated equilibrium is much easier to reconcile with the fossil record, as has always been known, and fits in much better with our knowledge of life processes.

What then explains this stability? As Dobzhansky asks, 'what caused the living fossils to stop evolving?' A possible answer, he suggests, is that evolution simply stopped when a sufficient degree of adaptiveness was achieved. However, this makes little sense, since he does not consider it obvious that opossums or horseshoe crabs are in any way better adapted than mice, cats or lobsters. His own tentative answer is that ' the living fossils occupy ecological niches that have become perhaps more confining, otherwise not much altered for a long time.' In what way, though, are they more confining? Why should this confinement not imply a better degree of adaptation? Dobzhansky provides no answers to these questions.

For Monod, the answer is to be found in the 'extreme coherence of a teleonomic system, which, during evolution, at once played the role of guide and of break and has preserved, amplified and integrated, but an infinitesimal fraction of the astronomic number of possibilities offered to it.' However, a teleonomic system is one that is programmed to achieve a specific goal – but what is the goal? Monod does not say. He implies that it is to 'preserve, amplify and integrate' the favoured minority of living things – the fittest, in the Darwinian language – but why should this be so? For Monod, as for the rest of the scientific establishment, the explanation must lie in the mysterious workings of 'the roulette of nature'. So randomness is introduced once again, to play the role of the *deus ex machina*.

Waddington more realistically attributes the stability of the living world to the constancy of the genetic material throughout the evolutionary period and to 'the shuffling and recombination of genes that may be present within the population. . . .' These are both critical considerations. None of the scientists mentioned, however, entertains the possibility that it is the overriding goal of all living things to maintain their own stability.

If gradual evolutionary change were the norm, as neo-Darwinists assume, then we would expect that the incidence of random mutations would be high and that it would increase as systems become more highly developed. But the opposite seems to be the case. Random mutations are extremely rare, and this is no coincidence. Indeed, natural systems develop the most elaborate methods to avoid the occurrence of random mutations and reduce their incidence to a minimum. Monod realizes this. 'Because of the conservative nature as well as of the perfection of the mechanism of replication,' he writes, 'individual mutations are very rare events.' What is more, once mutations do occur, special mechanisms that are perfected during the course of evolution exist for assuring their elimination. Thus, as Bryn Bridges points out, cells that have mutated as a result of exposure to radiation or other mutagenic agents are, in normal conditions, eliminated by the body's immune system. If it were not for this, the incidence of cancer would be even higher than it is today.

This must lead us to ask an embarrassing question. If genetic mutations play such an important part in evolutionary change, yet a natural system does everything to prevent their occurrence and indeed seeks desperately to neutralize their effects when they do occur, how can it be considered to be geared to the achievement of such change? Richard Dawkins is fully aware of the contradiction in the neo-Darwinian thesis. How, he asks, 'can we reconcile the idea that copying errors are an essential prerequisite for evolution to occur with the statement that natural selection favours highly copying fidelity'? The answer, he suggests, is that although evolution may seem in some vague sense a 'good thing', especially since we are the product of it, nothing actually 'wants' to evolve. Evolution is something that happens, willy-nilly, in spite of all the efforts of the replicators (and nowadays of the genes) to prevent it happening, a point also made by Jacques Monod in his Herbert Spencer Lecture.

Quite clearly natural systems are not geared towards change but towards the *avoidance of change*. Change occurs, not because it is desirable *per se*, but because in certain conditions it is judged to be necessary, as a means of preventing predictably larger and more disruptive changes. This must be true of social evolution as well as biological evolution. The main feature of vernacular societies, within which man has spent well over 90 per cent of his experience on this planet, has been stability. This is particularly true of hunter-gatherer societies. During the old stone age, for instance, flint-chipping techniques did not change for some 200,000 years. Nor did the lifestyle of Australian Aborigines change for at least 30,000 years. 'The Australian ethos' writes the anthropologist, W. E. H. Stanner,

appears to be continuity, constancy, balance, symmetry, regularity. There are no great conflicts for power, no great contest for place and office. There is no idea of a formal chief, in fact . . . . They do not fight over land. There are no wars or invasions to seize territory. They do not enslave each other. They place a very special value on things remaining unchangingly themselves, on keeping life to a routine which is known and trusted. Absence of change, which means certainty of expectation, seems to them a good thing in itself. The value given

116

to continuity is so high that they are not simply a people 'without history'. They are a people who have been able, in some sense, to 'defeat' history, to become ahistorical in mood, outlook and life.

The same could be said of all hunter-gatherer societies, and tribal societies in general when living in the environment to which they have been adapted by their social evolution.

All this is unlikely to impress anyone. We have all been brainwashed into regarding change as desirable in itself. Hunter gatherers, most of us feel, must have had a very boring life – for they underwent no change, they had no history. But is it so desirable to have had a history? It is very doubtful. Our history books contain little more than the history of wars, invasions, massacres, revolutions, assassinations and intrigues. History makes very depressing reading and does little more than illustrate the extreme squalor of human behaviour once vernacular communities and their cultural patterns have broken down. Indeed, if 'no news is good news' then one can equally well say that 'no history is good history'. The fact that hunter gatherers did not have one reflects above all the orderliness and harmony of their lives, which were not punctuated by the increasingly intolerable discontinuities that are rendering our lives ever less supportable.

One of the problems with the term 'stability' is that it is used differently by different ecologists. Eugene Odum distinguishes between two different types of stability. The first is 'resilience stability' which he defines as 'the ability of an ecosystem to resist perturbations and maintain its structure and function intact.' The second is 'resilience stability' which he takes to be 'a system's ability to recover when a system is disrupted by a perturbation.' An example of the former is provided by the Californian redwood forest which is resistant to fire by virtue of its thick bark and other features, but which, if it happens to burn, will recover very slowly and perhaps never at all. An example of the latter is provided by the Californian chaparral vegetation, which is very easily burned but recovers quickly.

G. H. Orians, who distinguishes between no fewer than seven different types of stability, makes a similar distinction between 'inertia', or the inability of a system to resist external perturbations, and 'amplitude', which he defines as 'the area over which a system is stable' (the extent to which it can be displaced from a previous state and yet return to it). This is very similar to Odum's 'resilience stability'.

The Canadian ecologist C. S. Holling refuses to accept that either Odum's 'resilience stability' or G. H. Orians's 'inertia' is a viable strategy for survival leading to 'persistence'. For him, a stable system is one which returns to 'an equilibrium state' after a temporary disturbance and 'with the least fluctuations'. He includes in this category living things that have not been subjected to change for a long time. These are very vulnerable to environmental changes, and therefore cannot be regarded as 'persistent'. He then contrasts stable systems with resilient systems, which are characterized by large fluctuations and which alone are 'persistent'. He does not seem to notice the irony of classifying as 'non-persistent' such organisms as the horseshoe crab, that has not changed for some five hundred million years, while reserving the term persistent for 'resilient' species like the fruit-fly that is constantly developing new forms.

Holling is a disciple of Ilya Prigogine and thus committed to the most extreme form of the paradigm of science and the world-view of modernism. For him, stability means stagnation, a bad word. In the world in which we live, in any case, it is not an option. Increasingly, he writes, 'we must learn to live with disturbances and live with variability and live with uncertainties.' Discontinuities such as floods, droughts, epidemics, wars, pollution disasters, the erosion of the ozone layer and global warming are desirable, because out of such 'fluctuations' emerge progress and order.

I think we can totally reject Holling's views on stability. Eugene Odum's distinction between 'resistance' and 'resilience stability', on the other hand, seems very sensible; of course, we can refine the concept as Orians sought to do. In particular, we can regard a resilient system as more or less stable, in accordance with the size of the discontinuities that affect the system and from which it must then recover. What is important is that, as a system evolves, so it becomes capable of reducing such discontinuities to a minimum. As this occurs, it comes to enjoy a more cooperative relationship with the other systems that make up the larger system of which it is part. And as this larger system becomes more highly integrated, so resilience stability evolves into resistance stability.

# TWENTY THREE

# Gaia is alive

●

*Man is a self-balancing, 28-jointed adapter-based biped, an electrochemical reduction plant, integral with the segregated storages of special energy extracts in storage batteries, for subsequent actuation of thousands of hydraulic and pneumatic pumps, with motors attached; 62,000 miles of capillaries, millions of warning-signals, railroad and conveyor systems; crushers and cranes . . . and a universally distributed telephone system needing no service for 70 years if well managed; the whole, extraordinary complex mechanism guided with exquisite precision from a turret in which are located telescopic and microscopic self-registering and recording range finders, a spectroscope et cetera.*
BUCKMINSTER FULLER

*A machine is made to realise some conscious human purpose. Its parts work together to secure that purpose, not to secure its own persistence.*
J. H. WOODGER

*I was born a thousand years ago, born in the culture of bows and arrows . . . born in an age when people loved the things of nature and spoke to it as though it had a soul.*
CHIEF DAN GEORGE

For vernacular man, throughout the ages, nature was alive and his religious life was, above all, his relationship with the spirits that inhabited all natural things. Theodore Roszak talks of the Pagan view of nature as 'alive and infused with purpose' and 'aglow with seductively sensuous qualities'. Morris Berman tells us that nature was seen, until the scientific revolution, as 'enchanted', 'alive' and as 'the place of belonging'. Man was not 'an alienated observer' of the cosmos but 'a direct participant in its drama'. His destiny was 'bound up with its destiny' and this gave meaning to his life.

It is no coincidence that vernacular man was an animist for, as the anthropologist Weston La Barre writes, animism 'is deeply linked with the biological nature of the human species.' Indeed, it is part of that intuitive heritage that enabled man to be cognitively adjusted to the world he lived in. However, with the development of the world view of modernism, and in particular of the paradigm of science, the world became 'disenchanted', secularized, and mechanomorphized. The mechanomorphic view of the world, like all the different aspects of the paradigm of science, can be traced back to the sixteenth and seventeenth centuries but it was more explicitly formulated in the eighteenth century by La Mettrie in his *Man a Machine*, Lagrange in *Mécanique Analytique* and Laplace in *Mécanique Céleste*. The mechanomorphic thesis has gone through at least three distinct phases. In the first, with Descartes, Galileo and Newton, life processes were explained in terms of pure mechanics. Scientists sought purely mechanical explanations of digestion, embryogenesis, nerve reactions and even the workings of the mind.

During the next phase, living things were compared to heat engines and life processes to physical burning processes. This notion can be traced to Priestley, who thought that living things like mice and candles emitted a substance which he called 'phlogiston'. When there is no phlogiston left, the candle stops burning and the mice die. Living and burning are one.

Lavoisier replaced phlogiston with oxygen. The process was then reformulated in the language of thermodynamics. It was shown that during metabolism energy is conserved (first law of thermodynamics) and heat is dissipated (second law). It was then noticed that life is more than just the burning up of food to release energy. It also involves synthesis, the switching of potential energy from one state of matter to another. These considerations led to the third phase, called by Peter Calow 'the chemical plant analogy'. Like a chemical plant, an organism makes use of raw materials and adds to them a 'Biological reaction flask' to produce new compounds. This process can also be expressed in the language of thermodynamics: life processes overcome the influence of the second law because the Biosphere within which they occur is an open system, at least from the point of view of energy. (see Appendix 1)

The mechanomorphic thesis suffers from a very serious flaw. Descartes is regarded as the first to have explicitly formulated the thesis that man is a machine – but, officially at least, Descartes remained a Deist. It was God who created man the machine, as He created all the other living machines that make up the Biosphere. The position of mechanistic science, however, is quite different. God has been abolished, and so man and other living things have neither a manufacturer nor an operator.

Mechanistic scientists, as J. H. Woodger notes,

> want to have a machine without a mechanic. Their problem is to show how it is possible to have a machine which comes into existence, runs, repairs and regulates itself, and finally divides into two machines, without a mechanic.

They have, in fact, completely forgotten that 'machines presuppose organisms', and hence all those features of organisms whose very existence the mechanomorphic thesis sets out to deny. Professing to eliminate them, it has merely externalized them on the sly, hoping that no one would notice. In reality, as Woodger notes, 'the choice is not between mechanism and mystery, but between one mystery and another.'

It will be argued that this dogma is no longer entertained by physicists today. Quantum mechanics has revealed that behaviour at the sub-atomic level cannot be understood in terms of Newtonian physics. Quantum physicists, we are told, now view the world in terms of waves and fields. But outside the discipline of quantum mechanics, mainstream science remains very definitely Newtonian. If the sub-atomic constituent is no longer seen as a machine, molecules, organisms and ecosystems still are, and so indeed are human societies.

Why then, we may ask, do mainstream scientists still maintain this untenable thesis? The main reason seems to be that machines are simple and predictable. Their behaviour is explicable in terms of cause and effect, and eminently quantifiable. They can be studied in isolation from other machines and hence in controlled laboratory conditions. Scientists should be honest enough to admit, as Woodger does, that living things are taken to be machines largely because they have to be, if they 'are to be studied by means of scientific method'. In other words, the scientific method can only enable us to understand the behaviour of living things once their most important features, precisely those that distinguish them from mere machines, have been eliminated.

But there is another reason why the mechanomorphic view of life has been adopted by mainstream scientists. If they faced up to the real nature of man as a complex form of life, they would have to face the fact that his real needs – biological, social, ecological, spiritual and cognitive – are ever less adequately satisfied by the progress of economic development. If man is a machine, on the other hand, one can maintain that his only needs are material and technological – precisely those that economic development is capable of satisfying. As Michael Polanyi writes, 'the Laplacean universal mechanics induces the teaching that material welfare and the establishment of an unlimited power for imposing the conditions of material welfare are the supreme good.' And Donald Worster makes the complementary point that 'by reducing plants and animals to insensate matter, mere conglomerates of atomic particles devoid of internal purpose or intelligence', mechanistic science has removed 'the remaining barriers to unrestrained economic exploitation.'

The mechanomorphic view of the world, moreover, is not only alienating but grossly flawed. In his heart, man has always known this, and has constantly reacted against this soul-destroying vision. One of the first to do so was Henry More. He was much influenced by the animism of Plato and Plotinus, who believed in the 'soul of the world' or 'spirit of nature' or *anima mundi*. He described this as a 'substance incorporeal but without sense and animadversion, pervading the whole matter of the universe, and exercising a plastical power therein . . . raising such phenomena in the world . . . as cannot be resolved into mere mechanical powers.' He also posited a vital organizing power in plants and animals. It is because of this power, he maintained, that they are more than 'mere motion of matter'.

The notion of the *anima mundi* was taken up by the romantic poets and writers of the eighteenth and nineteenth centuries in their reaction against mechanistic science and the associated technological ethic. Goethe saw nature 'at work and alive, manifesting herself in her wholeness in every single part of her being.' The Romantics developed a highly ecological world-view. Wordsworth, for instance, talked of 'an intertwined togetherness' and 'a community of existence'. A living thing for the Romantics could not be disassembled, and then reconstructed like a clock. The world was alive, not dead as the scientists were telling them.

Even scientists began to react against the mechanomorphic picture of the world. The highly respected German geneticist Hans Driesch found that he could not explain, in terms of mechanistic science, the ability of the sea-urchin embryo that he studied in his laboratory to develop into a more or less normal phenotype, even after parts of it had been removed. To do so required that he posit a vitalistic principle which he referred to as 'entelechy' from Aristotle's *entelecheia* (from the Greek *en* meaning internal, and *telos* meaning goal). He saw life processes as controlled by a hierarchy of entelechies which were all derived from and controlled by the organism's primary entelechy.

In his *Creative Evolution*, Henri Bergson also insisted that the evolutionary process could not be explained in mechanistic terms but had to be seen as a 'current of life' flowing from one generation to the next and triggered off by a vital impetus or *élan vital*. 'This impetus', he writes, 'sustained right along the lines of evolution, among which it gets divided, is a fundamental cause of variations, at least of those that are regularly passed on, that accumulate and create new species.' The problem with both Driesch's entelechy and Bergson's *élan vital* is that they are very vague notions, so much so that to postulate their existence does not tell us a great deal. Bergson realized this, but argued that at least his *élan vital* could serve as a 'sort of label affixed to our ignorance, so as to remind us of this occasionally, while mechanism invites us to ignore that ignorance.'

Vitalism, however, is not an alternative to the mechanomorphic thesis. It is just something that is added to it to make it more realistic. What is really required is a totally non-mechanistic theory of life and such a theory must by its very nature be holistic. Living things are alive because they are part of a whole. The main features of living things – those that make them alive, their dynamism, creativity, intelligence, purposiveness – are not apparent if one studies them in isolation from the hierarchy of natural systems of which they are part. Living things are alive in a very important sense of the term because they are part of this hierarchy. As Joseph Needham puts it, 'life is a whole in which the parts, instead of going their separate ways, work together.' If they did not, life processes would be chaotic, random, uncoordinated. 'The whole', Needham continues, 'requires its components (of all levels) in order to be "alive", while the parts require the whole in order to make their particular contribution to it by virtue of which it is "alive".' He goes so far as to say that 'a molecule, an atom or an electron, if it belongs to the spatial hierarchy of a living organism, will be just as much "alive" as a cell, while on the contrary, an entity that does not belong to such a spatial hierarchy will be "dead".'

One can see for oneself that if one kills a living thing, it loses its wholeness. The parts, in so far as they can survive, regress to a state of chaos and randomness, and their behaviour can then be understood in the reductionist and mechanomorphic terms of mainstream science. Purposefulness, in the living world, can be identified with the tendency of living things to maintain the whole. Once the whole disintegrates, the parts cease to be purposive and their behaviour can then be explained in terms of the crude mechanistic theory of causality.

Though Needham was only concerned with life up to the level of the biological organism, with some reservations one can apply his criterion of life to higher levels of organization such as that of the society, the ecosystem and Gaia herself. At these levels, living things are not so closely integrated, which means that their separation from the whole does not immediately entail their demise. It will mean nevertheless that their behaviour will cease to be homeotelic, and they will no longer fulfil the task for which they were designed – the maintenance of the critical order of the living world within which their life is sustained. Instead, they will become committed to a course of action that can only lead to their eventual extinction. Homeotely is a condition for homeostasis, so this is consistent with what James Lovelock means when he states that 'Gaia is alive'. 'This notion "alive"', he writes, 'bothers a lot of my scientific colleagues', and he asks them to think of it 'as no more than the capacity of the earth to regulate itself and keep cool, when things are changing adversely.'

In his latest book, *Gaia: The Practical Science of Planetary Medicine*, Lovelock tells us that he sees as alive 'everything that metabolizes and self-regulates . . . so that life is something shared in common by cats and trees, as well as by beehives, forests, coral reefs and Gaia.'

Living things that are integral parts of the Gaian hierarchy and that have the capacity to maintain their homeostasis – within the context of the Gaian hierarchy–display other qualities which distinguish them from mere machines. In the next chapters I shall consider some of them.

---

# TWENTY FOUR

# Natural systems are homeostatic

●

*All the vital mechanisms, varied as they are, have only one object, that of preserving constant the conditions of life in the internal environment.*
CLAUDE BERNARD

*Homeostasis is the totality of steady states maintained in an organism through the coordination of its complex physiological processes.*
WALTER CANNON

*Health is a continuing property, potentially measurable by the individual's ability to rally from insults, whether chemical, physical, infectious, psychological or social.*
J. RALPH AUDY

Biological organisms are self-regulating cybernetic systems capable by their own efforts of maintaining their stability (both resistant and resilient), a quality referred to as homeostasis. A natural system controlled by an external agent, however, cannot be stable. Because an external agent is not part of the Gaian hierarchy, it is not subject to its homearchic control, and so does not behave homeotelically towards it. Instead, it will steer a system towards a random, heterotelic goal – one that satisfies its own specific interests regardless of its effects on biological, social and ecological systems.

Hippocrates (360–77 BC) considered that diseases were cured by the natural actions of the body. As Walter Cannon notes, this 'implies the existence of agencies which are ready to operate correctively when the normal state of the organism is upset.' The nineteenth-century French physiologist Claude Bernard was also impressed by the way in which living cells maintained the constancy of what he was the first to call their 'internal environment' (milieu intérieur). For him, 'this constancy of the internal environment is a condition of free and independent life', a principle still fundamental in physiology. The same principle was noted in 1885 by the German physiologist Eduard Pflüger, and also by his Belgian colleague Leon Fredericq. 'Each disturbing influence', the latter wrote,

> induces by itself the calling forth of compensatory activity to neutralize or repair the disturbance. The higher in the scale of living beings, the more numerous, the more perfect and the more complicated do these regulatory agencies become. They tend to free the organism completely from the unfavourable influences and changes occurring in the environment.

For Claude Bernard, to achieve this state of freedom and well-being must be the fundamental goal of all living things.

The term 'homeostasis' was first coined by the physiologist Walter Cannon in his seminal book The Wisdom of the Body. It is worth considering the concept in some detail. Cannon was struck by the fact that organisms 'composed of material which is characterized by the utmost inconstancy and unsteadiness, have somehow learned the method of maintaining constancy and keeping steady in the presence of conditions which might reasonably be expected to prove profoundly disturbing.' For instance, mammals can maintain the constancy of their body temperature in spite of external changes.

> For a short time men may be exposed to dry heat at 115 to 128 degrees centigrade (239 to 261 degrees Fahrenheit) without an increase of their body temperature above normal. On the other hand, arctic mammals when exposed to cold as low as 35 degrees centigrade below freezing (31 degrees below zero Fahrenheit) do not manifest any noteworthy fall of body temperature.

Resistance to changes induced by external circumstances (what ecologists would call the resistance stability of living things), Cannon notes, is not the 'only evidence of adaptive stabilizing arrangements'. Natural systems are also capable of resisting disturbances from within.

> For instance, the heat produced in maximal muscular effort, continued for twenty minutes, would be so great that, if it were not promptly dissipated, it would cause some of the albuminous substances of the body to become stiff, like a hard-boiled egg. Again continuous and extreme muscular exertion is accompanied by the production of so much lactic acid (the acid of sour milk) in the working muscles that within a short period it would neutralize all the alkali contained in the blood, if other agencies did not appear and prevent that disaster.

The constancy that living things achieve might by some be termed equilibrium. That word, however, has come to have a fairly exact meaning as applied to relatively simple physico-chemical states, in which physico-chemical forces are balanced. Homeostasis is a far more complex condition. It is not 'something set and immobile, a stagnation', but 'a dynamic situation'. What is more, 'the coordinated physiological processes' required to maintain it 'are complex and peculiar to living things – involving as they may the brains and nerves, the heart, the lungs, kidneys and spleen, all working cooperatively.'

Homeostasis is also diachronic. All the cooperating factors can be brought into action successively as well as at the same time. Cannon notes, as did Fredericq, that as an organism evolves, so the homeostatic mechanisms that assure the constancy of its internal environment become correspondingly more elaborate. Thus, 'Lower animals which have not yet achieved the degree of control of stabilization seen in the more highly evolved forms, are limited in their activities and handicapped in the struggle for existence.' A frog, for instance, is not capable of preventing water from evaporating from its body, nor can it regulate its own body temperature. This means that if it leaves the pond in which it normally lives, it soon dries up and, when it gets cold, must seek refuge in the mud at the bottom of the pond and hibernate until spring. Reptiles have developed more effective homeostatic mechanisms against rapid loss of water, which means that they no longer have to remain close to ponds or streams and can even survive in very dry conditions. But, like amphibians, they have no homeostatic mechanisms to insulate their internal environment against changes of temperature. They are still 'cold-blooded', which means that during the winter they too must give up an active existence. 'Only among the higher vertebrates, the birds and mammals, has there been acquired that freedom from the limitations imposed by cold that permits activity even though the rigours of winter may be severe.'

Interestingly enough, Cannon considers the probability that the mechanisms he found in biological organisms may be operative in other natural systems, which could also explain their constancy. A comparative study, he suggests, might show that every complex organization must be capable of 'more or less effective self-righting adjustments in order to prevent a check on its functions, or rapid disintegration of its parts, when it is subjected to stress.' E. P. Odum and B. C. Patten also see homeostatic mechanisms or 'checks and balances (or forces and counter-forces) that dampen oscillations' as operating 'all along the line', and hence not only at the level of the individual where, for instance, they 'keep body temperature . . . fairly constant despite fluctuations in the environment' but also at the level of the population, the community and the ecosystem.

Roy Rappaport was probably one of the first anthropologists to show that tribal societies are capable of such behaviour. In his seminal book *Pigs for the Ancestors* he interpreted the ritual cycle of a small social group in New Guinea in cybernetic terms, showing it to be, above all, a means of controlling the group's impact on its natural environment so as to assure its sustainability or stability. Gerardo Reichel-Dolmatoff, quite independently of Rappaport, interpreted the cultural pattern of the Tukano Indians of Colombia in much the same way. Thomas Harding also sees tribal societies as capable of homeostatic behaviour and thereby of maintaining their stability. 'When acted upon by external forces,' he writes, 'a culture will, if necessary, undergo specific changes only to the extent of, and with the effect of, preserving unchanged, its fundamental structure and character.'

That ecosystems are geared to the maintenance of their homeostasis is denied by mainstream ecologists today, as it is difficult if not impossible to reconcile with the paradigm of science. 'However, if ecosystems are not cybernetic (and hence self-regulating),' Howard Odum asks, 'then by what other means could the perceived harmony of the biosphere have evolved?' Most modern ecologists would give the neo-Darwinist answer – by natural selection from random mutations and hence by a crude and rudimentary mechanism largely determined by external factors such as competition and selection. Thus S. D. Putman and R. J. Wratten insist that self-regulating behaviour at the level of an ecosystem 'is largely due to intra-specific competition for a resource'. They nevertheless admit that such competition seems to achieve an equilibrium 'well before the limiting resource starts to act as a finite shortage'. This suggests that natural systems are capable of foresight and planning (see Chapter 30) but Putman and Wratten deny this.

Odum and Patten see things differently. 'Either the ecosystem is orderly,' they write, 'or its lack of chaos just happened to develop from un-regulated Darwinian struggles between competing populations all alone and uninfluenced except by each other, on the mutual stage of life. The latter seems implausible to us.' Eugene Odum notes how ecosystems are endowed with the necessary mechanisms for self-regulation and hence homeostasis.

> Besides energy flows and material cycles, ecosystems are rich in information networks comprising physical and chemical communication flows that connect all parts and steer or regulate the system as a whole. Accordingly, ecosystems can be considered cybernetic in nature, but control functions are internal and diffuse rather than external and specified as in human-engineered cybernetic devices.

These information networks Odum refers to as 'the invisible wires of nature' or alternatively as 'the hormones of ecosystems.'

A number of experiments have been carried out to determine whether ecosystems display resilience stability and, if so, whether this can be attributed to their own efforts – and hence whether they are cybernetic or self-regulating systems, capable of maintaining their homeostasis. The best-known of such experiments are those conducted by D. S. Simberloff and E. O. L. Wilson. They removed all the fauna from several small mangrove islets and then closely watched the way they were recolonized by terrestrial arthropods. They established that though the islets were eventually populated by very different species from the original ones, the total number of species was very much the same as originally.

Three years later, H. Heatwold and R. Levins examined the same data. Their interest was to classify the different species to be found there in terms of trophic organization, noting the number of species in each of the trophic categories (herbivores, scavengers, detritus feeders, predators, etc.). The results were highly significant. They showed that the trophic structure of the communities on the different islets displayed a remarkable stability even though the species composing each of the trophic levels had undergone a considerable change. This experiment clearly illustrates the principle of homeostasis, though this is denied by Putman and Wratten. They insist that what Heatwold and Levins witnessed was not 'the recovery of a disturbed system' but the creation of a completely new one, which means that there is no evidence for any cybernetic process at work.

Putman and Wratten's error is that they assume that a goal-directed life process (which they refer to as 'deterministic') must, like a machine, display 'microdeterminancy', to use Paul Weiss's term. But as Weiss has taken so much trouble to show, it only displays 'macrodeterminancy'. The parts change, but the whole maintains its constancy; the particularities of life processes change in answer to changing environmental conditions, so that the basic features of the whole can be preserved. What is important, is that the basic trophic structure of the ecosystem studied by Heatwold and Levins was restored. The fact that the actual species that took over the different trophic functions were no longer the same is not important. Indeed, that the same functions can be taken over in this way by different species demonstrates just how adaptive are the mechanisms assuring the homeo-stasis or stability of ecosystems. It provides a perfect illustration of Weiss's 'principle of the conservation of overall pattern' which is really another way of stating the principle of ecological homeostasis.

James Lovelock, in his seminal book *Gaia, a New Look at Life on Earth*, shows that Gaia herself displays homeostasis. Lovelock is struck by the extraordinary stability of the earth's relationship with its environment, the atmosphere. It must have been maintained very much as it is now at least 'since the time that air-breathing animals have been living in forests', or for about 300 million years. Fossil records show that the climate has changed very little since life first appeared on earth about 3500 million years ago. Yet the output of heat from the sun, the surface properties of the earth, and the composition of the atmosphere have almost certainly varied greatly over the same period.

For the incredible stability of world climate to have been the result of pure chance is for Lovelock 'as unlikely as to survive unscathed a drive blindfolded through rush-hour traffic.' Again, the explanation must be that life has developed the capacity for self-regulation, so maintaining its own stability. Lovelock refers to Cannon's work on the homeostasis of bio-logical organisms and considers that there must be a similar homeostatic process regulating the temperature of the planet, a conclusion that has the widest possible implications for our view of the natural world and man's interrelationship with it.

This discussion would be incomplete without the addition of a final proposition. It is that natural systems cannot maintain their own homeo-stasis unless they simultaneously maintain that of Gaia (of which they are integral, constituent parts) by pursuing homeotelic strategies.

# TWENTY FIVE

# Natural systems are homeorhetic

●

*Homeorhesos makes homeostasis possible by assuring the structural development of the organs.*
JEAN PIAGET

In spite of the basic tendency in nature towards relative immobility, living things are changing dynamically all the time. Thus a fertilized egg develops into a foetus, a child into an adult, a pioneer ecosystem into a climax ecosystem, and unicellular organisms (sometimes) into multicellular organisms. How does one reconcile this tendency towards change with the thesis of overall stability?

From the point of view of global evolution, these processes of change do not violate the principle of stability so long as one sees them holistically. Individual generations or ontogenies can be regarded as feelers enabling the long-term evolutionary process – the Gaian process – to monitor its interactions with and thereby permit its adaptation to its spatio-temporal environment.

Seen cybernetically, ontogenetic development occurs along a closely integrated constellation of set paths which C. H. Waddington refers to as 'chreods' (from the Greek root *chre*, it is necessary, and *odos*, a route or path). The total constellation of chreods along which a system develops constitutes what Waddington refers to as the 'epigenetic landscape' – the developmental path the system is constrained to follow by virtue of the instructions with which it is endowed and those with which the systems that make up its environment are endowed. A developing system thereby displays 'a certain lack of flexibility'; its development has

> a strong tendency to proceed to some definite end-point. For instance, the adult tissues such as muscle, nerve, lung, kidney etc., are quite distinct from one another and it is rather difficult to persuade developing cells to differentiate into something intermediate between these main types. Again, the animal as a whole will very often succeed in 'regulating', that is to say, in reaching its normal adult state in spite of injuries or abnormal circumstances it may have met during the course of its development.

This ability has been noticed by many students of development, among them Hans Driesch who reported the remarkable 'equipotentiality' of the sea-urchin embryo. (see Chapter 23) He and others also pointed to the ability of a germ to develop into a normal embryo even after undergoing severe amputations. This goal-seeking behaviour of a developing embryo remains inexplicable in terms of the mechanistic philosophy of science.

The tendency of a developing system to maintain itself on its pre-set path along its constellation of chreods, and to correct any disturbances that might divert it, Waddington refers to as 'homeorhesos' (from the Greek *homo*, meaning same and *rhesos*, meaning flow). Homeorhesos is the principle of homeostasis applied to a predetermined path or trajectory rather than to a fixed point in space-time. G. H. Orians refers to it as 'trajectory stability', which he defines as 'the property of a system to move towards some final end point or zone despite differences in starting points.' This he tells us, is the sort of stability which plants tend to achieve during plant succession, 'where a single "climax" state may be reached from a variety of starting points' (equitinality).

It is reasonably clear that a climax is not a point fixed in space and time. Life processes are dynamic, creative, intelligent and anticipatory. This means that, in changing environmental conditions, a living thing can develop in a new direction so as to achieve a new end state – one which, on the basis of its model of its relationship with its environment would appear to constitute a new climax, a position of still greater stability where discontinuities would be still further reduced.

Of course, this process is subject to homearchic control by the Gaian hierarchy. It is Gaian homeostasis which homeorhetic systems seek to achieve, since this is a precondition of their own stability. During the course of this book, I shall seek to show that all life processes, including evolution or the Gaian process, are homeorhetic regardless of the level of organization at which they occur. (see Chapter 62)

# TWENTY SIX

# The Gaian process is not random

●

*That man is the product of causes which had no prevision of the end they were achieving; that his origin, his growth, his hopes and fears, his loves and beliefs, are but the outcome of accidental collocations of atoms . . . all these things, if not quite beyond dispute, are yet so nearly certain that no philosophy which rejects them can hope to stand. Only within the scaffolding of these truths, only on the firm foundation of unyielding despair, can the soul's habitation henceforth be safely built.*

BERTRAND RUSSELL

*That living things have been brought into being by purely random forces is a gratuitous statement, which we regard as wrong and as irreconcilable with the facts.*

P.-P. GRASSÉ

The notion that the Biosphere and everything in it are the product of pure chance is critical to the paradigm of science. Jacques Monod refers to the mechanism of determining the evolution of life and of culture as 'a gigantic lottery' or as 'Nature's roulette'. 'Chance alone' he sees

> as the source of every innovation, of all creation in the bisosphere. Pure chance, absolutely free but blind, is at the very root of the stupendous edifice of evolution. This central concept of modern biology is no longer one among other conceivable hypotheses. It is the sole conceivable hypothesis, the only one that squares with observed and tested fact. And nothing warrants the supposition – or the hope – that on this score our position is likely ever to be revised.

Many neo-Darwinists, however (including Theodosius Dobzhansky and Julian Huxley), have adopted a less extreme position. Mutations may well be caused by factors that we ignore, though in all cases, as Huxley insists,

> they are random in relation to evolution. Their effects are not related to the needs of the organism, or to the condition in which it is placed. They occur without reference to their biological uses.

This means that though something makes a mother feed her child, that something is unconnected with the child's need to be fed by its mother.

In the real world, however, life processes are not random, even in this less extreme sense of the term. Art styles, for instance, closely reflect the character of the cultures in which they developed. The clothes people wear are indicative of the image of themselves they wish to communicate to others. The way people walk, eat, light a cigarette, blow their noses, do up their shoelaces – all convey something of the personality of the individuals concerned.

Behaviour is indeed so ordered, so little random, that it is questionable whether people are capable of behaving in a random way. This appears to be confirmed by various experiments such as those described by psychologists W. R. Ramsay and Anne Broadhurst, who experimented with a panel of 72 people by asking them to repeat in time to a metronome a series of numbers, 1 to 9, in as random a manner as possible. They found that 'even when subjects try to be random, there is a high degree of stereotype.' It has been suggested that it is even possible to identify a particular individual by his 'random number matrix' and also that the pathological configuration of a matrix may reveal a mental illness and a set of random numbers has actually been used to enable a practitioner to differentiate between brain-damaged patients and normal subjects.

The British cybernetician Stafford Beer also rejects the view that randomness is a natural feature of behaviour in the natural world.

> There are a random number tables on my bookshelf; there are computer tapes for producing pseudo-random numbers next door; there is a large electronic machine for generating noise upstairs; down the road there is a roomful of equipment designed to hurl thousands of little metal balls about in a random way; and I use ten-sided dice as paper-weights. The upkeep of this armoury is considerable; think of all the time we spend trying to ensure that these artefacts produce results which are 'genuinely random' – whatever that may mean. This tremendous practical problem of guaranteeing disorderliness ought to be enough to satisfy any systems man that nothing is more unnatural than chaos.

But how do scientists know that a process is random? How do they know it is not part of an orderly pattern that they simply have not been able to identify? The great French naturalist J. P. Lamarck, who is considered to be the founder of modern biology, is often quoted as stating that 'the word randomness only expresses our ignorance of causes.' The French physicist Jules Poincaré said much the same thing, as did the French theoretical biologist Albert Jacquard and also C. H. Waddington, in particular with regard to the randomness of genetic mutations.

Recent studies have tended to confirm this view. Biologist John Cairns and his colleagues at Harvard University recently conducted studies which suggest that mutations are not random but, on the contrary, highly directive. At first Cairns's studies were dismissed by the scientific establishment; however, Barry Hall of Rochester University has now come up with similar results. He has found that certain mutations in bacteria occur more often when they are useful to the bacteria than when they are not.

Cairns refers to such mutation as directed mutations, while Hall refers to them instead as 'Cairnsian mutations' in honour of their original discoverer.

There is every reason to doubt, too, the concept of 'genetic drift' which has been postulated to explain evolutionary changes that do not appear to have been 'selected'. This concept is used far less today than it was twenty years ago and is increasingly seen as a convenient device for masking our ignorance of the role of such changes. Indeed more and more processes which originally appeared to be random, are found upon closer examination to be highly functional and indeed purposive.

However, one does not need experimental 'evidence' for rejecting the idea that evolution is based on random mutations. We know that single gene mutations can only determine extremely superficial changes. Significant changes can only be brought about by changes occurring to a whole constellation of associated genes (polygeny). This means that for a 'functional unit to make an adapted change' as Rupert Riedl notes, 'requires not just one happy accident, but an accumulation of happy accidents.' Does this seem likely? Waddington did not believe it, in spite of his insistence on remaining within the neo-Darwinian fold. He admitted that to suggest that evolution was based on a selection from random mutations was 'like suggesting that if we went on throwing bricks together into heaps, we should eventually be able to choose ourselves the most desirable house.' Murray Eden rejects the thesis on the grounds of its sheer mathematical improbability. It is as unlikely as it is that 'a child arranging at random a printer's supply of letters could compose the first 20 lines of Virgil's Aeneid.' How then can the absurd notion of the randomness of life processes have been raised to the elated status of 'the central concept of modern biology'? I shall suggest some possible answers.

To begin with, randomness was postulated as an argument against teleology, which was seen as ushering in all sorts of unacceptable supernatural principles, such as God, or various forms of vitalism. Secondly, it is essential in order to rationalize the reductionist nature of modern science. If the biosphere displays order – worse still, if the whole evolutionary process is seen as a single coordinated strategy, involving all life processes at all levels of organization – then the reductionist approach would make no sense. Thirdly, the postulate of randomness is required to justify statistical method which in turn rationalizes other key features of the paradigm of science – the principle of causation, for instance, and reductionism itself.

Finally, randomness is seen as essential because it is impossible to justify the Promethean enterprise to which our industrial society is committed, and which insists on systematically transforming the Biosphere so that it may best satisfy short-term interests, if the Biosphere is seen as organized to achieve a grand overall project of its own. By seeing the Biosphere as random, on the other hand, it is possible to make out that what order there is in the world has been created by science, technology and industry, rather than by God or the evolutionary process. 'The cardinal tendency of progress', as J. D. Bernal writes, 'is the replacement of an indifferent chance environment by a deliberately created one.'

The insistence by mainstream scientists on maintaining the principle of the randomness of life processes in the teeth of all the evidence, both empirical and theoretical, provides an excellent illustration of how scientific theses are formulated to rationalize the paradigm of science, and hence the world-view of modernism which it so faithfully reflects.

# TWENTY SEVEN

# Gaian processes are purposive

●

*Purpose is not imported into nature, and need not be puzzled over as a strange or divine something else that gets inside and makes life go . . . it is simply implicit in the fact of biological organization.*
HERBERT MUELLER

The evidence for the purposefulness of life processes at every level of organization within the hierarchy of the Biosphere is so great that its denial seems inconceivable. Who could deny that the evolution of gills and fins by fish is purposeful to enabling them to breathe and move about in their aquatic environment, or that the development of mammary glands by the females of all species of mammals is purposeful to feeding their babies, or that the human milk provided in this way is designed to satisfy the nutritional needs of their young in the first one or two years of their lives?

To Charles Sherrington it seemed obvious that the embryological process, whereby 'a pin's head ball of cells in the course of some many weeks becomes a child', is purposive. Joseph Barcroft points to

> the levers laid down in gristle, becoming bone when wanted for the heavier pull of muscle which will clothe them. Lungs, solid glands, yet arranged to hollow out at a few minutes' notice when the necessary air shall enter. Limb-buds, futile at their appearing and yet deliberately appearing, in order to become limbs in readiness for existence where they will be all-important.

Barcroft is particularly impressed by the development of such embryonic organs, useless at the time to their possessor, but which will be indispensable later on during the course of its development. 'Organs of skin, ear, eye, nose, tongue,' he writes, 'superfluous all of them in the watery dark where formed, yet each unhaltingly preparing to enter a daylit, airy, object-full manifold world which they will be wanted to report on.'

Purposiveness is also evident in physiology. As Gavin de Beer notes:

> The structure of an animal shows a number of exquisitely delicate adjustments; the splinters inside a bone are situated exactly where they are required to withstand the pressure to which the bone is subjected; the fibres of a tendon lie accurately along the line of strain between a muscle and the bone to which it is attached; centres of nerve cells in the brain are situated close to the ends of the nerve fibres, from which they habitually receive impulses.

The same principle is equally evident in animal behaviour. For Bierens de Haan that the weaving of the web by the spider is purposeful for the catching of insects, and the collecting and storing of caterpillars by the wasp purposeful for the nourishing of its future larva, are facts that are so self-evident that it is not necessary further to elucidate them.

If life processes achieve their purpose it is because they are under control, but they could not be controlled in the first place unless they had a purpose to achieve. Control serves to assure that life processes achieve their pre-existing purpose. This is clear if we consider that a basic ingredient of control is 'negative feedback', which is totally useless to a non-purposive system.

An essential constituent of control is perception and perception is essentially purposive. As Keith Oatley notes, 'the way we see is in terms of our human purpose in the environment.' Or again, what we see 'depends on our particular purpose at the time, what we are trying to do, what aspect of the thing we are seeing that is relevant to what we are trying to achieve.' What is more, it is not just in terms of short-term purposes that we see things, for these are meaningless except in the context of the long-term strategy of which they are part. Nor are our individual strategic purposes meaningful outside the overall context of the purpose of our society, our ecosystem and the Biosphere as a whole.

Thoughtful scientists recognize this as a serious problem. Jacques Monod, for instance, as Gunther Stent notes, insists that 'the cornerstone of scientific method is to postulate that nature is "objective", which means systematically denying the purposive character of life; however, such purposiveness is nevertheless *prima facie* apparent.' Monod admits that 'this self-same contradiction is in fact the central problem of biology.' It is only a problem for modern scientists, however, whose ability to understand the functioning of the Biosphere continues to be seriously hindered by their adherence to the paradigm of science. In the light of the world-view of ecology, on the other hand, purposiveness is seen as a feature of life processes at all levels of organization, and in particular that of the Biosphere whose critical order they seek purposefully to assure.

# TWENTY EIGHT

# Life processes are dynamic

●

*The distinctive aspect of Primitive thought is the accent that it places on the dynamic aspect of living things, while in Western scientific thought, on the other hand, the accent is put on the static aspect of things.*
PLACIDE TEMPELS

*Even under constant external conditions, and in the absence of external stimuli, the organism is not a passive, but a basically active system.*
LUDWIG VON BERTALANFFY

*Almost from the moment a creature is hatched or born it lashes out at the environment, be it liquid or solid, with cilia, flagellae, or muscles; it swims, crawls, glides, pulsates; it kicks, yelps, breathes, feeds on the environment. It does not merely adapt to the environment but adapts the environment to its needs — it eats and drinks its environment, fights and mates with it, burrows and builds in it.*
ARTHUR KOESTLER

That life processes are dynamic was self-evident to vernacular man. For Placide Tempels, author of a seminal book on Bantu philosophy, it is traditional man's accent on the dynamic aspect of living things that characterizes his view of the world. This view contrasts only too starkly with the modern scientific view of living things as essentially static and passive, a view that is consistent with the paradigm of science but not with our knowledge of the real world. (see Chapter 54)

All the different processes involved in adaptive behaviour are necessarily dynamic. Perception is dynamic. Signals are not merely received, they are detected; the organism seeks out those signals that are seen to be relevant to its behaviour pattern in the light of its mental model of its relationship with its environment. Mental activities do not merely occur to interpret external stimuli, they also occur quite spontaneously. Even in the absence of any external stimuli, the brain remains constantly active. We think even when sitting in an armchair in a dark room. Nor does learning merely take place as a reward for a decrease in hunger or thirst, or as a means of escaping from an electric shock. It occurs without reward or punishment. It is an internal activity rather than a reaction to a stimulus.

Erich von Holst has shown that primitive locomotor activities function without the aid of external stimuli. Movements continue to occur even after 'the connection of motoric to sensory nerves has been severed.' Konrad Lorenz has pointed to the existence of what he calls 'innate releasing mechanisms' (IRM) which play a dominant role in our behaviour and can function without the presence of external stimuli. This fits in very well with Ragnar Granit's description of nerve cells that are specified at birth; that are not affected by outside stimuli; and that are subject to the presence of genetically determined instructions whether or not they are operative and whether or not they are triggered off by an environment stimulus.

It must be clear from our own experience that we are not only led to do things by an external need to do them. When I am hungry I shall look for food; it is not just the sight of food which triggers off my food-seeking behaviour. It may undoubtedly stimulate my appetite, but appetite there must be. A good indication that this must be so is furnished by the possibility of recanalizing different behavioural trends, such as aggression, into relatively harmless activities, such as sport, rather than into destructive ones, such as war. (see Chapter 39)

When the normal outlet for a behavioural tendency or urge is unavailable, living things can even imagine it or create it. Thus the Comanche Indians of Nevada, once they were confined to a reservation and deprived of their hereditary enemies, compensated for this by increasing the number and threatening nature of the evil spirits with which they saw themselves surrounded, thereby creating or imagining the stimuli needed to trigger off their aggressive tendencies. In the field of sex, this could not be more evident. If the normal stimulus that triggers off sexual behaviour is not available, others are sought out, and the degree of improvisation seems considerable. In other words, we modify, or even invent the stimuli that alone are supposed to trigger off behavioural responses. This dynamism, what is more, does not occur only at the behavioural level but is a feature of all life processes.

Alister Hardy, like Jean Piaget, has pointed to the close relationship between the dynamism of behaviour and that of evolution. 'It is adaptations which are due to the animal's behaviour, to its restless exploration of its surroundings, to its initiative, that distinguish the main diverging lines of evolution . . . giving the lines of runners, climbers, burrowers, swimmers and conquerors of the air.' Evolving systems are not puppets, controlled by the whims of a distant environmental puppeteer, as Charles Darwin and his successors have implied they must be. On the contrary, it is the dynamism of living things that makes evolution possible.

# TWENTY NINE

# Life processes are creative

●

*I am astonished at the amount of creative force, if such an expression may be used, displayed on these small barren and rocky islands. (The Galapagos)*
CHARLES DARWIN

*Creativity is ultimate. It is not a philosophical postulate but an observed fact, that creative activity or formative process is an intrinsic property of anything in the natural cosmos that is known to man.*
A. N. WHITEHEAD

Clearly, humans have a vast capacity for improvisation and have developed diverse and highly imaginative cultural patterns for dealing with the challenges of life in different environmental conditions. The creative capacity of non-human animals is also well documented as is that of the evolutionary process itself. Living things have developed the most diverse strategies for adapting to different and often highly challenging environments. Thus a warm-blooded animal can learn to survive the rigours of the winter by developing a thick fur coat, by going into hibernation, by migrating to a warmer area, or by lighting a camp fire. Desert plants can learn to avoid desiccation by developing leaves covered with oily substances, or that become spine-like, or that are simply shed during the dry season; or by changing their life cycle so that it is compressed into the wet season.

Not only is nature creative and innovative in the extreme, but creative and innovative changes can occur very quickly, as adaptations to environmental challenges. Consider how mosquitoes have adapted to DDT. Resistance was first reported according to David Merrell in 1946, and by 1965 it had been reported in 165 pest species. More impressive than the speed with which this resistance had developed were the very different mechanisms exploited by the mosquitoes for dealing with this new menace. Some mosquitoes learned not to alight on the walls which had been sprayed with DDT, others developed a thick cuticle which it could not penetrate. Others developed more body fat, thereby increasing their capacity to assimilate fat-soluble DDT. The nerves of others became less sensitive to it. Still others developed an enzyme which breaks it down into a harmless compound. The diversity of different mechanisms made use of by mosquitoes to adapt to DDT spraying programmes, as Merrell notes, bears 'testimony to the opportunism of evolution'.

Mainstream science seeks to explain this extraordinary innovativeness in terms of the neo-Darwinian thesis. The genetic resistance to DDT, Merrell insists, 'already existed in the population and was not induced by exposure to DDT.' But how was this possible? The DDT molecule did not exist in nature before it was produced synthetically in the 1940s. How then could the mosquito's gene pool have prior knowledge that DDT would one day be synthesized by man and released into the environment? The answer we are told, is by chance, by random pre-adaptation. This is the only scientifically respectable explanation of creativity – the only one reconcilable with such essential features of the paradigm of science as causality, mechanomorphism and statistical theory. Chance in the context of evolution means random mutations. Only to such events can evolutionary creativity be imputed. 'Natural selection', Merrell writes, 'has a creative aspect . . . because it has a causal aspect . . . Looking back at a cause we can recognize it as creative; it has brought about something which could not have been predicted – something which cannot be referred back to antecedent events.'

It is like a 'game of chance', he tells us, it is possible to conceive all the possible outcomes of the game – indeed, to calculate the relative probability of each one of them – but it is not possible to foresee exactly which one it will be. The scientific notion of causality is therefore not creative in the true sense of the term – a like cause must create a like effect, and all Merrell is saying is that we cannot predict which particular causal relationship is going to occur, as that will be decided by natural selection.

But natural selection, in spite of what our mainstream scientists tell us, cannot be a source of creative evolutionary change. One can understand that by selecting the most viable living things, and allowing them to reproduce themselves, their characteristics will be transmitted to the next generation which will become correspondingly more viable, but this is only possible if living things can, in the first place, transmit such characteristics to the next generation. Billiard balls cannot, and it is difficult to see how natural selection might help *them* to evolve however much variability they might exhibit. As Ludwig von Bertalanffy notes,

> selection presupposes self-maintenance, adaptability, reproduction, etc. of the living system. These therefore, cannot be the effect of selection. This is the oft discussed circularity of the selectionist argument. Proto-organisms would arise, and organisms further evolve by chance mutations and subsequent selection. But, in order to do so, they must already have had the essential attributes of life.

For J. H. Woodger, the neo-Darwinian thesis is unacceptable on this count alone. 'An explanation of this kind', he writes, 'can only make out a case for itself by begging the fundamental question at issue – the essential characteristics of an organism have to be surreptitiously introduced in vague general language.' They are so introduced largely by attributing to natural selection – the mechanical sorting machine – qualities such as creativity which no machine can possibly display, and that are, in effect, little more than the very 'internal factors' whose role in determining the evolutionary process, neo-Darwinists are at such pains to deny.

That the extraordinary and highly complex Biosphere can be regarded as the product of such a crude process as selection from random mutations has to be seen in the context of other clumsy efforts by mainstream science to maintain the myth of mechanomorphism. But machines cannot create: their output (the effect) is a function of their input (the cause). It was to make sure that embryogenesis, or development, conformed to this principle that the theory of preformation was developed, according to which a fertilized egg contained a miniature replica of a child – the end product of the process. After some time, however, it became clear that the information contained in the fertilized egg was nowhere near sufficient to give rise to the child, and preformation gave rise to epigenesis, a theory that is very difficult to explain in terms of the paradigm of science.

One of the most astonishing feats of creativity in the natural world is the working of the immune system, the most likely explanation for which is the process of genetic recombination. Immunologists tell us that a biological organism can produce $10^7$ or so different antibodies – that is to say, $10^7$ different proteins designed to repel specific threats. All sorts of attempts have been made by mainstream scientists to explain this in the language of the neo-Darwinian orthodoxy. They have failed. Thus it appears that the mosquito populations, for instance, though they were not endowed before the development of DDT with the genes that would confer resistance against that poison, were endowed with cells containing 'bits and pieces of the genes: a kit of components.' As Philip Leder puts it,

> Such components are shuffled in the cells of the immune system called B lymphocytes as those cells develop and mature. The shuffling can lead to a different result in each of millions of lines of cells. Individual mutations amplify the diversity. The result is that in the mature descendants of each line a unique

gene is assembled whose information is expressed in the form of a unique anti-
body.

It is extremely unlikely, what is more, that the mutations referred to
are in any way random. The immune system, like the genome, is self-
regulating and capable of maintaining its homeostasis in the face of external or internal challenges. That mutations are often not random but
highly directive or purposive, has now been established by John Cairns and
others. That such mutations should be brought about by the homearchic
action of the genome, or another cybernism such as that associated with
the functioning of our immune system seems more than likely. Whether
recombinations together with such induced mutations provide a sufficient
explanation for the massive evolutionary leaps that have given rise to meta-
zoans, vertebrates and mammals is uncertain. P.-P. Grassé considers that
this requires the development of new gene loci which previously had no
particular functions – another impressive act of creativity.

All in all, the creativity of the living world is only a problem if we insist
on trying to reconcile it with the paradigm of science. It must, on the
other hand, be an essential principle of the world-view of ecology.

# THIRTY

# Life processes are anticipatory

●

*The essential nature of mind is to govern present action by anticipation of the future in the light of past experiences, to make, in fact, effects precede and determine their causes.*

WILLIAM MCDOUGALL

For natural systems to achieve their goal of maintaining their own and Gaian stability, they must be able to predict changes to which they may have to adapt, as well as the environmental effects of such adaptations. There is every reason to suppose that they are well capable of doing so, providing such changes occur within their tolerance range. (see Chapter 42)

Certain cacti seem able to store in their pores just the amount of water required to tide them over dry periods. It does not stretch the meaning of the word too far to say these cacti must be *predicting* the weather changes involved. Green turtles travel three thousand miles from the coast of South America to Ascension Island in the middle of the Atlantic Ocean, where they lay their eggs. When embarking on such a journey, they can only be seen as *predicting* that their reproductive period is approaching and that by laying their eggs on Ascension Island rather than anywhere else they will give their young the best chance of survival.

Many insects such as Monarch butterflies, Ladybird beetles, hoverflies, Noctuid moths and other species migrate when winter approaches to warmer climes. They do not do so, however, because the cold has become insupportable for, as C. G. Johnson notes, they begin to migrate long before cold weather sets in.

> Neither food shortage nor 'intolerable overcrowding' are evident to the human observer at the time of departure. . . . The migration, therefore, usually comes in advance of any obvious change for the worse in living conditions.

Such examples are not exceptional. As H. Kalmus writes,

> anticipatory actions occur widely in the organic world. A predator catching a moving prey, a tennis player hitting a ball, a spider constructing a web, even a flower displaying its visual and olfactory attractions, all can be said to anticipate future events in their environments.

Prediction is an essential component of perception, the first step in self-regulation. People see very much what they expect to see. They see not a static image, but a hypothesis covering what it implies, its history, why it is there, how it is likely to change and what the consequences will be. Perception, in fact, involves prediction.

Modern science cannot admit that living things predict. They are supposed to be passive and stage-managed by an external agent. In any case, they cannot predict the future for, we are told, knowledge is only acquired by observation and one cannot observe what has not actually occurred. This explains to what lengths mainstream scientists will go to deny that prediction plays a necessary role in adaptive behaviour. Thus the behaviour of dogs in Pavlov's famous experiments has been interpreted in such a way as to avoid having to admit that the dogs are making predictions. When a dog is trained to salivate at the sound of a bell announcing food, it is seen as responding in a blind and unintelligent manner to the ring of a bell *as if the bell were food*. A 'conditioned stimulus' is seen in this way as simply replacing the 'unconditioned stimulus'.

It is becoming increasingly difficult to maintain this myth. Indeed, C. L. Hull, a behaviourist and experimental psychologist inspired by Pavlov, sought towards the end of his life to modify his theories so as to reconcile them with the fact that living things display 'interest, planning, foresight, fore-knowledge, expectancy, purpose and so on' – qualities whose very existence he and his predecessors would previously have denied.

Prediction is not only possible on the basis of the information contained in the brain, but also on that organized in the genome. L. Z. Young has pointed out that the genes have to perform 'a task analogous to prediction.' The genes of the polar bear, for instance, are predicting that this great beast will live in the Arctic snow and that a snow-white coat will camouflage it from its prospective prey. If suddenly there were a radical warming of the Arctic area, these predictions might prove to be wrong and, partly as a result, polar bears might not survive.

W. H. Thorpe is also struck by the ability of the genes to predict the sequence of chemical processes in metabolism. He quotes M. Dixon and E. C. Webb, who ask

> how the gene-forming enzyme 2.4.2.14 'knows' that phosphoribosyl pyrophosphate will be converted by the consecutive action of ten or more different enzymes into a purine nucleotide, or how the gene for the first enzyme of histidine biosynthesis, which acts on the same compound, 'knows' that its product

will be converted into histidine by a different series of enzymes. Even with this information, how do these genes 'know' what amino-acid sequences in their enzymes will act as specific centres combining with purine nucleotides or histidine respectively.

For Dixon and Webb, this ability to predict is only possible if we postulate a mechanism 'whereby information derived from the metabolic processes themselves is transmitted back to the genes and therefore incorporated in the form of polynucleotide sequences.' The existence of such a feedback mechanism violates Francis Crick's central dogma and is irreconcilable with the neo-Darwinian thesis.

C. H. Waddington accepts that evolution must be based on prediction. He tries to reconcile this with the neo-Darwinian thesis by attributing to the environment – which neo-Darwinists have never bothered to define – the capacity to select species for their ability to deal with future as well as present problems, producing 'a system which is stable enough to deal with difficulties that may arise many generations in the future.' However, if it is to selection that we attribute the capacity to achieve this long-term stability, then this mechanical process must be endowed with the ability to predict the future, for how else can it create precisely those genes and gene combinations required to permit an organism to adapt to conditions that have not yet occurred?

Without the capacity to predict, natural selection would, among other things, not be able to bring into being an organ that is still in its embryonic stage and is not yet really functional, for how else could embryonic and non-functional organs have an adaptive function in the short-term, which would justify their selection by the environment? Clearly they could not. For P.-P. Grassé, this provides yet another reason for rejecting the notion that natural selection plays a determinant role in evolution. If it did, then we would have to attribute to natural selection 'the gift of divination, or of prophecy.'

To predict the future for a natural system is only possible on the basis of a model of its relationship with the Gaian hierarchy of which it is part. The accuracy of its predictions will depend not only on the accuracy with which a model represents this relationship, but also on the stability of the

Gaian hierarchy, and hence upon the extent to which the living thing has been adapted to it biologically, socially and cognitively by its evolution.

Chthonic man had no difficulty in predicting the future, for he inhabited a highly stable climax Biosphere, and knew how to earn his living in it without disrupting its critical functioning in any way. In such conditions, he could predict with reasonable certainty that the future would be very much like the present, which in turn would closely resemble the past.

Today, however, we are bringing about the most dramatic possible changes to the living world in which we live. Our scientists have no hope of predicting their consequences, for the methodology which enables them to understand the functioning of the constituents of the Biosphere does not enable them to understand the effects of these changes on the Gaian hierarchy as a whole. Our scientists are capable of producing synthetic organic chemicals, but quite incapable of determining how exposure to them will affect the health of living things. They have developed methods of extracting fossil fuels from the bowels of the earth, using them to generate the power that drives countless devices to achieve all sorts of different and often impressive goals. But they are quite incapable of predicting, with any sort of accuracy, what the effect will be on biological organisms, societies, ecosystems and now on global climate.

# THIRTY ONE

# Living things seek to understand their relationship with their environment

●

*Learning takes place not simply as the emission of a new response when an error occurs. Rather it involves understanding the particular structure of the mistake and deciding what to do next.*

KEITH OATLEY

A living thing apprehends its environment by detecting data that appear relevant to its behaviour pattern and interpreting them in the light of its mental model of its relationship with it. This means that it seeks to establish their meaning and thereby to understand them.

This thesis is irreconcilable with current wisdom on the subject. Behavioural psychologists fall into a number of schools; for a long time, the dominant school was Behaviourism. It is associated with the names of Edward Thorndike and E. R. Guthrie, also with John Broadus Watson particularly and more recently with B. F. Skinner. Though many such as the members of the Gestalt school would not identify themselves with Behaviourism, it remains true that its basic features still underlie most of the thinking in this field. It is the view that best fits in with the paradigm of science underlying the methodology that experimental psychologists and ethologists must use if they are to be taken seriously by the scientific community. This highly reductionistic theory of behaviour is roughly as follows.

Living things apprehend their environment by acquiring sensations or 'sense data' – the atoms of perception – which provide them with measurable atoms of information or 'bits'. (see Appendix 2) It is accepted that living things have a memory, but the memory too is atomized – the atoms of memory being referred to as 'engrams' or memory traces.

The atom of behaviour is the reflex, a mechanism whereby an environmental event referred to as a 'stimulus' triggers off an automatic response. As far back as 1906, Charles Sherrington wrote that the 'simple reflex is probably a purely abstract conception . . . if not a probable fiction.' C. Judson Herrick describes it as pure abstraction, a 'mere manifestation of what is clearly a very coordinated pattern of behaviour.' Such conditions have not deterred others from presenting the process even more mechanistically in terms of inputs and outputs, the stimulus being the input and the response the output, like a machine that switches on when the button is pressed.

Learning has to be explained, of course, and mainstream scientists have developed a most ingenious account with all the random, atomistic and mechanistic features required by the paradigm of science. The learning process is not seen by them as occurring in any necessary order; living things are seen as responding to their environment in a purely random way. A rat trying to find its way out of a maze, for instance, will try out in random order a whole series of trial-and-error moves corresponding to the Darwinist's random variations and the random genetic mutations of the neo-Darwinists. If one such move is crowned with success, it is said to be 'reinforced', the Darwinian equivalent of being 'selected'. In laboratory experiments, rats are given rewards for making what the experimenter judges to be the right moves, and are often also given penalties such as electric shocks for the wrong moves – rewards and penalties being seen in the Benthamite tradition as the only motivations of living things.

Like neo-Darwinists on the subject of selection, behaviourists attribute remarkable powers to reinforcement. Thus Skinner informs his readers that 'a man talks to himself . . . because of the reinforcements he receives'; that thinking is in fact 'behaviour which automatically affects the behaviour and is reinforcing because it does so'; that 'just as the musician plays and composes what he is reinforced by hearing or as the artist paints what reinforces him visually, so the speaker engaged in verbal fantasy says what he is reinforced by hearing or writes what he is reinforced by reading', while the creative artist is 'controlled entirely by the contingencies of reinforcement.'

It is astonishing that serious people can attribute the incredibly subtle and sophisticated behaviour of living things to so crude and rudimentary a mechanism. If we really believed it, as Michael Polanyi points out, we would also have to accept that 'if a dog were consistently offered food whenever it was shown the radiogram of diseased lungs and no food when shown the radiogram of healthy lungs, it should learn to diagnose pulmonary diseases.' Pure trial and error learning, except perhaps in the most rudimentary forms of life, is pure fantasy. This has been realized even within the ranks of experimental psychologists. Thus Karl Lashley has insisted strongly that normal animals do not behave in a random fashion. Keith Oatley agrees: 'In animal or human behaviour', he points out, 'trials are not chosen randomly.' On the contrary, as Herrick notes, 'the learning process is ordinarily directive and it is an organized activity, never a mere random fumbling.' I. Krechevsky considers 'that we must change our description of the learning process so as to recognize the existence of organized and systematic responses at all stages of the process.' Indeed, the rat, 'when placed in an unsolvable situation, does not respond in a helter skelter chance fashion, but makes all sorts of integrated and informed attempts at solution. These systematic responses are, partly at least, initiated by the animal himself and are not altogether merely a resultant of the immediately presented external situation.' Such animals are clearly not just reacting blindly to various stimuli, but seeking to interpret them correctly and thus *understand their meanings*. This means establishing the role of the event that attracts their attention in its relevance to their behaviour, as part of a larger spatio-temporal system.

Some of Lashley's experiments cast considerable light on this question. He showed that rats with large cortical lesions could learn to solve a problem in about the same time as normal rats but their behaviour was simplified. They did so less elegantly. They stumbled on the solutions rather than finding them in a more systematic or logical way. In other words, they did not really *understand* the nature of the problems they had to solve. This reminds one of the behaviour of children brought up in isolation, whose model of the world remains stunted and rudimentary. Peter of Hanover, the celebrated eighteenth-century isolate brought to London as a curiosity, ended up working as a farm labourer. He would perform his tasks well, but could never really *understand* their meaning.

If to understand something is to determine its function within a spatio-temporal system, widening the context in which we study it will increase our knowledge of its function. This is how a detective tries to understand a crime. Each clue is related to an increasingly wider set of events, gradually acquiring ever greater meaning. Other clues are treated in the same way until eventually the crime is reconstituted, at which point the detective can be said to *have understood* exactly what has occurred. There is no other way of proceeding. The clue in isolation from its widening context cannot be interpreted, for it has little meaning. It constitutes data, not information.

When the Tahitians first saw a horse, introduced to the island by de Bougainville's French sailors, they immediately classified it in terms of the mammal they knew most resembled it . . . the pig. It was obviously closer to the horse than the other two mammals of which they had any experience: the dog and the Polynesian rat. Very sensibly, they referred to the horse as a 'man-carrying pig'. This was not a robot-like response; it was a sophisticated attempt to understand a strange beast in the light of their experience of similar beasts. There is no reason to suppose that rats do not do likewise.

Living things, except for the very simplest ones, do not behave like robots. They are intelligent beings and, whether mainstream science likes it or not, they seek desperately to understand their relationship to the world about them.

# THIRTY TWO

# Living systems are intelligent

●

*Existing scientific data indicate a greater degree of intellectual communality among primates and probably a greater communality among all other animals, than has been commonly recognized.*

H. F. HARLOW

The notion that man's mental procedures are categorically distinct from those of other animals is a gratuitous assumption based on no valid knowledge of any kind. It is gratuitous to insist, as mainstream science does today, that only humans are *intelligent* – particularly since the term has never been satisfactorily defined. Science insists that intelligence can be measured by means of tests but, as C. Judson Herrick notes, 'it must be admitted that we do not know just what it is they measure.' Some authors, among them Ashis Nandy, suggest that intelligence is little more than 'that which is tested by intelligence tests'.

A. Binet and T. H. Simon, the pioneers of intelligence testing, consider that 'to judge well, to comprehend well, to reason well, these are the essential activities of intelligence.' For A. W. Heim, 'intelligent activity consists in grasping the essentials in a given situation and responding appropriately to them.' H. F. Harlow defines intelligence as 'all round intellectual ability, to learn, understand, improvise and create' – qualities which all living things, in varying degrees, tend to display. As regards learning, for instance, Harlow considers that

> there is no scientific evidence of a break . . . between primate and non-primate forms. Emergence from the oceans to the land produced no sudden expansion of learning ability. Indeed, there is no evidence that any sharp break ever appeared in the evolutionary development.

Major Hingston would have agreed with Harlow. For seventeen years he observed the behaviour of lowly insects in the tropical forests of India and concluded that they solved their problems in much the same way as we do. The notions 'that insects are nothing but animated machines' and 'that they lead purely reflex lives, these assertions I believe to be quite unfounded.' Regardless of what particular mental qualities we judge as important, Hingston showed, insects seem to display them. They are quite capable of 'reasoning', for instance. Hingston noted how dung-rolling beetles, when their ball was pinned to a long stake, examined the ball, discovered the stake and freed the ball by cutting it in two and putting the separate bits together. They are also quite capable of adapting means to ends. Thus, the wasp *Mellinus arvensis*, Hingston found, can capture flies on pads of dung. It normally does so by sneaking about, but, on one occasion when the flies were particularly active, one of these wasps was seen to lie on the dung, simulating death, and simply waited for the victims to walk into its grasp. 'Is this not a plan perfectly adapted to meet a given end?' Hingston asks.

They are quite able to improvise strategies for dealing with environmental challenges. Hingston describes how Swynnerton's ants dealt with a poisoned spine caterpillar. They ingeniously blocked the poisonous openings with crumbs of earth and then amputated the spine. They are also capable of displaying judgement. Hingston describes the wasp that dragged its large victim to the opening of its nest. Before trying to get it in, the wasp went backwards and forwards between the victim and hole, until, having 'decided' that the victim would not fit, it set about methodically enlarging the hole.

They are able to foresee the effects of their acts. Hingston describes a mason wasp that, in building its nest, did not just build one cell after another in a random way, but started off by laying the foundation plan for all the cells of the finished nest. They are also well able to remember past experiences. A particular ant, Hingston assures us, can remember the place where it has found food after a prolonged period of time. A hive bee can do the same thing. Wasps, he assures us, can not only remember one spot but they can 'keep in their minds a geographical picture of the territory which they work.'

From all this evidence Hingston claims that

> we are not justified in making barriers between insects and human mentality. I mean we have no right to regard their minds as being totally different in kind. In their main essential characteristics, the minds of these humble creatures operate in the same way as the mind of man, and this harmonizes well with those laws of continuity, which, as our knowledge of this world grows, become more and more firmly established.

Mainstream science is unimpressed by these arguments. Non-human living things are indeed capable of very remarkable achievements, but these, it is insisted, are the product of instinct, not intelligence.

Yet man's behaviour is as governed by his instincts as is that of other animals. Our intelligence does not lead us to substitute new goals for those set forth by our instincts. It merely enables us to satisfy them with greater discrimination and in a greater diversity of different conditions than other animals satisfy their instincts. In normal conditions – those that fall within our tolerance range – there is no conflict between our instincts and our intelligence. Our instincts do not lure us into 'primitive types of behaviour against the better judgement of our intelligence', as Paul McLean and Arthur Koestler suggest.

If the term intelligence is to be used in a functional manner, there is no reason why it should be limited to the behaviour of organisms. It should be applied to all life processes. Lucien Cuenot, the Belgian theoretical biologist, goes so far as to attribute to the cell 'a sort of intelligence, and indeed an eminent power equivalent to the purposiveness that is apparent in human behaviour.' Jean Piaget feels that Cuenot has gone too far, and accuses him of 'psychomorphism': but if the function is the same at both levels of organization, why not use the same term? Not to use it is to mislead people into supposing that the processes are different, helping to perpetuate the myth of the uniqueness of man on which the paradigm of science itself depends.

Charles Sherrington was filled with awe at what we could refer to as the intelligence of the ontogenetic process:

> the body is made up of cells, thousands of millions of them, in our own instance about 1000 million. The one cell, the original fertilized cell, grows into two and those two each into two and so forth. When that has gone on in the aggregate some 45 times, there are 26 million million magic bricks, all of a family. That is about the number [of cells] in a human child at birth. They have arranged themselves into a complex, which is a human child. Each has assumed its required form and size in the right place.

How do we explain this? 'It is as if an immanent principle inspired each cell with the knowledge for the carrying out of a design.'

Perhaps the most quoted miracle of nature is the eye. Even the eye of a relatively modest form of life such as an insect is of a degree of sophistication that defies the imagination. The Spanish neurologist Santiago Cajal describes it thus

> From the insect's faceted eye, proceeds an inextricable criss-cross of excessively slender nerve-fibres. These then plunge into a cell-labyrinth which doubtless serves to integrate what forms from the retinal layers. Next follow a countless host of amacrine cells and with them again numberless centrifugal fibres. All these elements are moreover so small the highest powers of the modern microscope hardly avail for following them. The intricacy of the connections defies description. Before it, the mind halts, abased.

The complexity and precision of the eye were an embarrassment to Charles Darwin. As he wrote in *The Origin of Species*,

> to suppose that the eye with all its inimitable contrivances for adjusting the focus to different distances, for admitting different amounts of light, and for the correction of spherical and chromatic aberration, could have been formed by natural selection, seems, I freely confess, absurd in the highest degree.

However, he pointed out, 'when it was first said that the sun stood still, and the world turned round it, the common sense of mankind declared the doctrine false; but the old saying of "Vox Populi, vox Dei", as every philosopher knows, cannot be trusted in science.' Reason, for him, was a better guide, and it told him that the eye, however sophisticated, could still only be the product of natural selection: that crude historical interplay between the generator of randomness and the sorting machine.

It is ironic that in order to explain what in comparison with the eye are the paltry achievements of scientific and technological man, we invoke – his consciousness, his creativity and his intelligence – that he denies to all other living things, let alone to the miraculous process of evolution and morphogenesis that brought them and him into being.

# THIRTY THREE

# Consciousness is not a prerogative of man

●

*Only human beings guide their behaviour by a knowledge of what happened before they were born and a preconception of what may happen after they are dead; thus only human beings find their way by a light that illuminates more than the patch of ground they stand on.*

SIR  PETER  MEDAWAR

*The evidence for some degree of consciousness certainly in the higher animals and perhaps far down the animal scale is overwhelming.*

W.  H.  THORPE

Even if it be admitted that all natural systems are intelligent, thus allowing the term to be used in a meaningful way, it will still be maintained by many that man remains unique as he alone displays consciousness – and if other living things are not 'conscious', how can their behaviour be anything but robot-like, and therefore random unless managed by an external agent? If non-human animals are not conscious, then the extraordinary feats of tropical insects described by Major Hingston can clearly only be the work of blind instinct, not of intelligence.

Sir Peter Medawar considers that only human behaviour can be genuinely purposive because only man is conscious. The same reason is given by Ilya Prigogine and Erich Jantsch to justify the new phase in our 'evolution', as they refer to it, which is to be achieved by genetic engineering, and which along with other élite technologies will ensure the ultimate stages of human progress, enabling the chosen to attain a sort of technological paradise on earth.

That the path dictated by the consciousness of modern man must lead to social, ecological and climatic disasters is seen by Prigogine and Jantsch as an argument in its favour, for these are regarded as 'fluctuations' which alone are capable of giving rise to the 'dissipative structures' that are the constituents of the 'evolving' technological world. Clearly, this demented thesis could not have been entertained were consciousness attributed to all living things and if man's behaviour was seen to be governed by the laws that govern the Gaian hierarchy as a whole. Nor could it have been developed if the term 'consciousness' had been properly defined, which, of course, it has not been, the term being used in all sorts of different ways. (see Chapter 64)

Along with C. Judson Herrick, I think we can best regard consciousness as a state of awareness, associated with enhanced mental activity, which may be required when it is necessary to identify and interpret very carefully an important environmental challenge to which an immediate and often innovative response is required – the unconscious mind being capable of dealing with routine matters that do not require a sophisticated or creative response.

W. H. Thorpe is perfectly willing to accept that man is not the only living thing to possess this faculty. He sees the same degree of consciousness in the higher animals (chimpanzees denote specific states of mind by different facial expressions) and the possibility of its presence far down the animal scale. Conscious awareness, he feels sure, provides some adaptive advantage over the purely unconscious apprehension of the environment. Julian Huxley talks of the 'mind intensifying' organization of animals' brains. He sees this as providing a fuller awareness of both outer and inner situations, and as enabling living things to deal with chaotic and complex situations.

For some authors, all natural systems are endowed with consciousness, or 'bio-conscience'. Teilhard de Chardin goes so far as to attribute a primary consciousness to the atom. This may be going too far. It is probably more realistic to see consciousness as a feature of organisms – embryonic among the simpler organisms, and more highly developed with the evolution of the brain and neo-cortex. It is also important not to overrate the importance of consciousness. As motivation research has revealed, humans themselves are not conscious of their basic underlying motivations, the reasons they give to explain their actions being largely those that best serve to rationalize them.

# THIRTY FOUR

# Gaia is the source of all benefits

●

*Land that is left wholly to nature . . . is called, as indeed it is, waste.*
JOHN LOCKE

*You can gauge a country's wealth, its real wealth, by its tree cover.*
RICHARD ST BARBE-BAKER

*Wilderness is the bank on which all checks are drawn.*
JOHN ASPINALL

*All that great bare belt of country which now stretches south of the Ganges –*
*that vast waste where drought seems to be perennial and famine is as much at*
*home as is Civa in a graveyard – was once an almost impenetrable wood.*
*Luxuriant growth filled it; self-irrigated, it kept the fruit of the summer's rains till*
*winter, while the light winter rains were treasured there in turn till the June*
*monsoon came again. Even as late as the Epic Period, it was a hero's derring-do*
*to wander through that forest-world south of the Nerbudda, which at that time*
*was a great inexhaustible river, its springs conserved by the forest. Now the forest*
*is gone, the hills are bare, the valley is unprotected, and the Nerbudda dries up*
*like a brook, while starved cattle lie down to die on the parched clay that should*
*be a river's bed.*
E. WASHBURN-HOPKINS

It is fundamental to the world-view of modernism that all benefits are man-made – products of scientific, technological and industrial progress, made available via the market system. Thus health is seen as something that is dispensed in hospitals, or at least by the medical profession, with the aid of the latest technological devices and pharmaceutical preparations. Education is seen as a commodity that can only be acquired from schools and universities. Law and order, rather than being natural features of human society, are seen instead as provided by our police force in conjunction with the law courts and the prison system. Even society is seen as man-made, brought into being by the 'social contract'. Not surprisingly, a country's wealth is measured by its per capita Gross National Product (GNP), which provides a rough measure of its ability to provide its citizens with all such man-made commodities, a principle faithfully reflected in modern economics.

For economists trained in these ideas, natural benefits – those provided by the normal workings of biospheric processes, assuring the stability of our climate, the fertility of our soil, the replenishment of our water supplies, and the integrity and cohesion of our families and communities – are not regarded as benefits at all; indeed, our economists attribute to them no value of any kind. It follows that to be deprived of these non-benefits cannot constitute a 'cost' and the natural systems that provide them can therefore be destroyed with economic impunity.

Even economists who can see through this preposterous accounting system still deny that environmental destruction is a problem because they have been taught that the market system, in conjunction with science, technology and industry, can deal with any 'resource shortage'. For instance, the farmers of the San Joaquim valley, in the southern part of the great central valley of California, are faced with a serious water shortage which may put many of them out of business, but they do not seem unduly concerned and are making no effort to adapt highly wasteful water-intensive practices to the new conditions. It is taken for granted that, sooner or later, some massive water diversion scheme will, as in the past, bring them the water they require from some other part of America, or even Canada.

The same argument is used to persuade us that the degradation of our

171

agricultural land is not a problem. For our economists, agricultural land is just another 'resource'. Gale Johnston, a university professor and well-known agricultural economist insists that natural resources play a relatively minor role in determining the wealth of nations. Emery Castle of Resources for the Future, one of the USA's most influential research organizations, told a meeting on the availability of agricultural land in 1980 that the loss of farmland is not a pressing national concern. The agricultural economist Philip Raup tells us that there can be no permanent shortage of agricultural land. To suppose the opposite is an error that stems from wrongly considering the availability of resources in physical rather than economic terms. Indeed, if some land is unsuitable for agriculture, this is only a reflection of current market conditions. If the land were really needed, then the necessary science, technology and capital would make it productive.

This aberrant attitude is further rationalized by mainstream scientists who set out systematically to denigrate natural processes. Sir Peter Medawar talks about nature's 'own artless improvisations'. Lester Ward attacks nature's inefficiency; 'rivers, instead of flowing straight, and so delivering their water to the sea, with minimum expenditure of energy, lazily meander through plains and valleys.' He complains of 'the redundant fertility' of the organic world: the herring lays 10,000 eggs, of which only two will reach maturity, and a large chestnut tree produces up to a ton of pollen. Nature's shortcomings are an invitation to man to become nature's engineer and create a paradise on earth, of his own design, whose functioning he can plan and direct in all its detail.

It is a basic principle of the world-view of ecology that real benefits, and hence real wealth, are derived from the normal functioning of the natural world and of the cosmos itself. Our greatest wealth must be the favourable and stable climate that we have enjoyed for hundreds of millions of years; our forests and savannahs and fertile agricultural lands; our rivers and streams, springs and ground waters; our wetlands and coral reefs; our seas and oceans, and the myriad forms of life that inhabit them all – these are our real wealth.

It is usual today to depict our remote ancestors, who lived off this great wealth without pillaging it, as we are doing today, as being poor and wretched. They are made out to have suffered from chronic malnutrition, living permanently on the edge of famine. Nothing is further from the truth. The incredible biological wealth of the vast area that is now the United States of America is attested by John Bakeless. In the great plains, where modern agriculture has eliminated most of the original vegetation, and where the top-soil is eroding so fast that they will be reduced to low-grade rangeland within the next thirty years, there were

> prairies teeming with buffalo, in herds that would pass all day without end; lordly moose along the lake shores; deer everywhere. Wild grapes roofed much of the eastern forest; there were wild fruits of many kinds; plentiful fish in every lake or stream; oysters nine inches long – or longer – in great clusters, which some fortunate dwellers on Manhattan simply pulled out of the clear waters before their shelters; lobsters beyond 20 pounds, easily caught; wild turkeys in flocks so large their gobbling in the morning might be deafening; passenger pigeons that literally did darken the sky. There were grouse, prairie chicken, ducks of every kind, wild geese so fearless that at times they tried to frighten off approaching hunters.

It is straining one's credulity a little too far to pretend that the dwellers on Manhattan, as it was then, suffered from malnutrition and famine. On the contrary, they were almost certainly considerably better fed than the present inhabitants of that island. In Africa – a continent where famine has now become chronic, and where 27 million people were threatened with starvation in the year 1991 alone – food shortages appear to have been unusual. The anthropologist Richard Lee testifies that Kung Bushmen had an extremely satisfactory diet and rarely suffered food privations. James Woodburn assures us that the same is true of the Hadza, a tribe of hunter-gatherers in Tanzania.

Mungo Park, in his *Travels in Africa*, tells us that the river Gambia abounds with fish and that nature 'with a liberal hand' has bestowed on the inhabitants of that area 'the blessings of fertility and abundance'. Two eighteenth-century French travellers, Poncet and Brevedent, note that in the Gezira area of the Sudan now occupied by eroded cotton fields, there were once 'pleasant forests of flowering acacias full of little green parrots' and 'fruitful and well cultivated plains' and that it was called God's Country (Belad-Allah) 'by reason of the great plenty'. In Kenya, where now an exploding population must be fed from an increasingly degraded environment, food shortages were also uncommon. As B. D. Bowles notes,

> European explorers and Arab traders found little difficulty in obtaining food as they travelled through the area. European conquerors actually burned crops standing in the fields and still survived without the importation of food. They extracted a surplus by force and they would have been unable to do this if no surplus had been available.

Bengal, which includes modern Bangladesh and is now one of the most overpopulated and impoverished areas on our planet, was once known as 'Golden Bengal'. Francois Bernier in his *Travels in the Moghul Empire (1656-1688)* was particularly impressed by its 'richness'. 'Egypt', he writes, 'has been represented in every age as the finest and most fruitful country . . . but the knowledge I have acquired of Bengal, during the two visits paid to that country inclines me to believe that the pre-eminence ascribed to Egypt is rather due to Bengal.' Nor is there any reason to suppose that the Australian Aborigines were short of food. Sir George Grey, who spent a good deal of time with Australian Aborigines in the early part of the nineteenth century, insists that he always 'found the greatest abundance in their huts.'

Even if we are forced to admit that malnutrition and famine were not man's natural lot, we still insist that tribal man was poor because he was deprived of material goods and technological devices. This too is an illusion. For perhaps 95 per cent of man's tenancy of this planet, he pursued a nomadic way of life as a hunter-gatherer, swidden agriculturalist or nomadic pastoralist. For the nomad, material goods which we associate with wealth are, above all, a burden he sees as 'grievously oppressive', the more so the longer they have to be carried around.

When Laurens van der Post wanted to give a present to Bushman friends with whom he had sojourned, as a token of his gratitude for their hospitality, he simply did not know what to give them.

We were humiliated by the realization of how little there was we could give to the Bushmen. Almost everything seemed likely to make his life more difficult for him, by adding to the litter and weight of their daily round. They themselves have practically no possessions: a loin strap, a skin blanket and a leather satchel. There is nothing that they could not assemble in one minute, wrap up in their baskets and carry on their shoulders for a journey of 1000 miles. They had no sense of possession.

To label them as poor, completely misses the point, for Bushmen, living in their natural environment, do not feel in any way deprived by their lack of material goods. Their priorities are simply quite different.

They were even different at the court of the Manchu emperors of China, before that country had been subjected to Western influence. Thus the Emperor Ch'ien Lung was not the least impressed by the gift of manufactured goods presented to him by the British emissaries of King George III, who sought to establish diplomatic links with his country. He rejected the British request and sent a letter to King George, which concluded with the following words:

> Swaying the wide world, I have but one aim in view, namely to maintain a perfect governance and to fulfil the duties of the State. Strange and costly objects do not interest me. . . . As your Ambassador can see for himself, we possess all things. I set no value on objects strange or ingenious, and have no use for your country's manufactures.

This attitude could not be more foreign to us. Our appetite for material goods and technological devices seems insatiable. Indeed, it is in terms of our access to them that our wealth, indeed our welfare, is normally gauged. It is undoubtedly true that today we need a lot of material goods and technological devices, but this is not because we have an *intrinsic* need for them but because, in the aberrant conditions in which we live, they are required for the purpose of satisfying our biological, social, spiritual and aesthetic needs – our real needs. The car, when it was first invented, was undoubtedly a luxury. Slowly, however, it became a necessity: as it came to be assumed that people possessed them, so they were ex-

175

pected to travel ever further to their places of work, to the schools where their children were educated, to shopping centres or for recreational purposes.

It is not religion that is the opiate of the people, as Karl Marx decreed, but materialism. The possession of material goods has only been man's chief preoccupation for a very short time, whereas religion permeated every aspect of the life of vernacular man. Material and technological goods can be regarded indeed, as bribes to induce people to accept the systematic annihilation of their real wealth that inevitably accompanies economic development or progress.

It is unlikely that any man-made commodity, however sophisticated, can adequately replace the natural product that it mimics. The reason is that the latter is designed to satisfy the countless requirements of the smaller systems which compose it, as well as those of the larger systems of which it is part – whereas the man-made commodity is only designed to satisfy a few of these requirements. A good illustration is our attempt, as part of the developmental process, to substitute cow's milk for human milk. Needless to say, it is always easy to find experts, who, on the basis of a simplistic notion of human nutrition, assure us of its superiority. We are assured that cow's milk has a higher protein content, for instance. As the nutritionists Michael and Sheilagh Crawford note, however, a calf needs more protein because, at birth, it grows more quickly than does a human baby. More important still, as S. H. Katz and M. V. Young point out, is the fact that cow's milk contains less polyunsaturated fat, required for building brain tissue, than does human milk, because the brain of a human baby grows more quickly. There are a host of other reasons why cow's milk is a poor substitute for human milk. It contains an almost equal ratio of calcium and phosphorus, unsatisfactory for a human baby which requires more calcium. The level of sodium in cow's milk is too high and may give rise to primary hypertension. The low level of copper in cow's milk has been related to the reduced transportation of iron and hence to the iron deficiency associated with anaemia, common among North American infants. Another advantage of human milk is that it contains the proportion of long-chain fatty acids which most favours their absorption and conversion to energy in the human baby.

176

Furthermore, the gastro-intestinal tract of a baby fed on human milk is colonized by the bacteria *Lactobacillis bifidis*. The important role played by this bacillus appears to have been grossly underestimated. Its presence appears to be essential to the absorption of protein and other nutrients in the milk. There is also growing reason to believe that the contact relationship between mother and infant during breast feeding has a significant effect on the child's digestive capacities. Equally important is the role played by human milk in ensuring immunization to disease. Certain antibodies are transmitted by the placenta which is permeable to them, while other antibodies are excluded. This means that babies are born without immunity to the diseases against which the latter provide protection – including those of gastro-enteric origin which happen to be the leading cause of mortality among babies throughout the world. These antibodies, on the other hand, are present in human milk in sufficient concentrations to provide protection against many gastro-enteric diseases, though it appears that this immunization only occurs if the corresponding antigens are present in the child's immediate environment.

Katz and Young consider that a real synergy is likely to exist among the nutritional, immunological, psychoendocrinological and maternal responses which foster infant development. In fact, if one regards the family as constituting a system of which the mother and child are but interrelated parts, and together with the physical environment in which the family lives as constituting a larger system, it becomes obvious just how naïve it is to suppose that such a natural process which has evolved over hundreds of millions of years can be advantageously replaced by feeding an infant milk designed by evolution to satisfy the requirements of a baby ungulate, contained in a bottle designed to provide but a crude imitation of its mother's teat.

If human milk is one of nature's products that we cannot really do without, so are the natural forests that once covered significant proportions of our planet's land area, in particular the tropical rainforests. One can draw up an almost endless catalogue of the irreplaceable services that rainforests provide us. By means of their elaborate root systems, they literally hold the soil together, preventing erosion from even the steepest slopes. Even in rainforests that are subjected to three hundred inches of rain a year, the water that runs off into the rivers is crystal clear. Their elaborate root system also ensures that the earth beneath it is sponge-like and maximizes its capacity to retain the rains; by the same token, they control run-off to the rivers, releasing only a fraction of what they retain. Once the forests have been cut down, and the roots have rotted, the earth hardens and ceases to be capable of retaining water. Most of the water runs off immediately into the rivers, whose beds have been raised by erosion from the deforested slopes, giving rise to ever-worsening floods. The water table sinks; rivers become torrents that only flow during the rainy season; streams and springs dry up. Forests also provide the perfect habitat for living things – it is said that between 50 and 80 per cent of the tens if not hundreds of millions of different species of living things inhabit the tropical rain-forests. Vernacular man, even after he has become a sedentary cultivator, still derives much of his food from neighbouring forests. He also finds there the materials required for his houses or huts, his artefacts and tools, his medicinal herbs and his vegetable dyes – indeed, they provide the very material basis of his cultural pattern, which necessarily disintegrates once the forests go. Forests also provide an important sink for carbon dioxide and, at the same time, generate the oxygen required for animals to breathe. The wholesale burning of forests that is occurring today is responsible for a significant proportion of the carbon dioxide released into the atmosphere to cause global warming. Forests, via the transpiration from their leaves, give rise to much of the atmospheric moisture that will form into clouds and absorb much of the sun's heat, providing, in this way, a cooling system for the planet. In Amazonia, between 50 and 70 per cent of the rain that falls on the three thousand square kilometres of Amazonian rainforest is generated in this way. Thus over this vast area huge amounts of water are constantly falling and rising, yet another way in which these forests act as a cooling system for our planet. James Lovelock has sought to calculate the annual energy cost of achieving the same degree of cooling by mechanical means.

> If the clouds made by the forests are taken to reduce the heat flats of sunlight received within their canopies by only 1 per cent, then their cooling effect would require a refrigerator with a cooling power of 6 kilowatts per hectare.

The energy needed, assuming complete efficiency and no capital outlay, would cost annually £1,300 per hectare.

On the basis of this calculation, he regards 'the refrigeration system that is the whole of Amazonia' as being worth about one hundred and fifty trillion dollars. This is probably a conservative estimate, and values only one of the large number of different services that the forest provides. Cattle ranching on the same low-grade land would yield a total income of less than one thirteenth of this sum, and even then only for a few years, for by then this highly vulnerable land would have been largely transformed into dust.

Needless to say, we could not afford to install all the technological devices required to perform the free services which the forests once provided for us, even assuming that it was technically possible to do so. Not surprisingly, even after one hundred and fifty years of economic development, the vast bulk of the services required to keep our planet functioning are still provided by the self-regulating processes of the Biosphere. This was stated quite explicitly by Carrol Wilson in his seminal 1967 MIT report *Man's Impact on the Global Environment*.

> Almost all potential plant pests are controlled naturally. Insects pollinate most vegetables, fruits, berries and flowers. Vegetation reduces floods, prevents soil erosion, air-conditions and beautifies the landscape. Fungi and minute organisms work jointly on plant debris and weathered rock to produce soil. Commercial fish are produced almost entirely in natural ecosystems. Natural ecosystems cycle matter through green plants, animals and decomposers to eliminate wastes. Organisms regulate nitrates, ammonia and methane in the environment. On a geological time scale, life regulates the amount of carbon dioxide, oxygen and nitrogen in the atmosphere.

No more than a minute fraction of these essential self-regulating biospheric functions can be taken over – very inadequately, at that – by the externally regulated, technospheric institutions and corporations of our modern world.

Why this must be so is clear if we compare the lot of the Indians of the north-west coast of America, before the arrival of the white man, with that of an astronaut. That region was once covered with luxuriant temperate rainforest, teeming with game and plentifully supplied with all sorts of wild fruits, berries, herbs and roots. At low tide, so abundant were the shellfish on the beaches that the Tlingit, a local Indian tribe, used to say that 'when the tide goes out, the table is laid'; nor, it would seem, was there any need to build bridges across the rivers, for it was said that you could cross them on the backs of the salmon. All this ecological wealth was made available to the Indians, free, by the self-regulating processes of the Biosphere, in what – barring totally unforeseen catastrophes, such as the arrival of the white man – was a totally sustainable manner.

The lot of the astronaut circling our planet in a small metal box, could not be more different. He is deprived of even the most rudimentary eco-logical wealth. No edible plants grow in his space capsule, there is no game to hunt, no fish to catch, no shellfish to gather from the shores. There are no rivers, no streams, no springs from which he can obtain water to drink. Even the oxygen he breathes has to be brought from afar. Indeed, the very conditions required for sustaining life in his capsule can only be main-tained by the most sophisticated technological devices. The cost of sus-taining him in such degraded and highly artificial conditions is beyond cal-culation. The richest man in the world could not afford to enjoy his degraded lifestyle for more than a few days, while only the wealthiest nations at the height of their economic fortunes, could afford to provide it to a handful of their subjects for a few days, weeks or at the most months.

If the US government takes seriously the National Academy of Science's recent publication, *Policy Implications of Greenhouse Warming*, then we may all be condemned to become astronauts on our own planet. In-deed, if we refuse to cut down global emissions of greenhouse gases, by 60–80 per cent as recommended by the United Nations' Intergovern-mental Panel on Climate Change (IPCC), the only method available to us for preventing a global climatic disaster may well be to install the appro-priate technological devices for doing so. Among the 'geo-engineering' strategies suggested by the National Academy of Sciences is the placing of 'fifty thousand, one hundred square kilometre mirrors in the earth's orbit, to reflect incoming sunlight'. Another is to 'use guns or balloons to maintain a dust cloud in the stratosphere, to increase the sunlight reflection'. Other strategies involve using aircraft 'to maintain a cloud of dust in the low stratosphere to reflect sunlight' or decreasing the 'efficiency of burning in engines of aircraft, flying in the low stratosphere, to maintain a thin cloud of soot to intercept sunlight.'

But how do we know that these ludicrously crude geo-engineering strategies would work? Also, what happens if there is a general strike in the country that is responsible for producing them? Or civil war? Or a Chernobyl-type accident to a nuclear installation, which leads to the compulsory evacuation of large numbers of people? Or simply an economic collapse of the sort that occurred in 1929, and which is more than likely to recur in the next decade? Even without an economic collapse, how do we know that the world economy would continue to be capable of sustaining the cost of applying these geo-engineering strategies? How do we know that the resources would always be available, or that our planet could sustain the social and ecological costs? Or even that the climatic degradation caused by carbon dioxide emissions from the burning of fossil fuels required to power so gigantic a geo-engineering enterprise might not neutralize what beneficial climatic effects there were?

That our scientists should even suggest the remote possibility that these absurd technological strategies could provide a substitute for the homeostatic mechanisms of the Biosphere that have so far regulated world climate, indicates to what extent they live in a world of their own – one that seems to be increasingly insulated against social, ecological and even economic realities.

# THIRTY FIVE

# The Biosphere displays order

●

*Order is the condition for understanding the Universe. A world without order would have no meaning. It would be neither recognizable nor conceivable.*
RUPERT RIEDL

*Order is an expression of conformity to Law.*
RUPERT RIEDL

*While for us the order of nature is one thing, and the social order is another, to the Australian (aborigine), they are parts of a single order.*
A. R. RADCLIFFE-BROWN

Order is a basic feature of the Gaian hierarchy, as traditional man fully understood. His own body, his home, his temple, his society, the natural world and the cosmos itself – he saw all as displaying an order which was both universal and critical. The word 'cosmos' itself originally meant order. In many cosmologies, as Mirca Eliade notes, the cosmos came into being once God had succeeded in vanquishing a vast primordial monster, or dragon, that symbolized the original chaos. Often, the monster's body served as the raw material out of which the cosmos was fashioned. Thus Marduk fashioned the cosmos out of the body of the marine monster Tiamat and Yahveh built the cosmos from the body of the primordial monster Rahab. However, so as to prevent the cosmos from reverting to the original chaos, that victory had to be re-enacted every year.

Evolution and its constituent life processes build up order. Individualistic systems become organized, differentiated and hence specialized in the fulfilment of various functions. As this occurs, so competition yields to cooperation, so the incidence and severity of discontinuities is reduced, and so the systems become more stable. Indeed, order implies organization, differentiation, specialization, cooperation, and stability. They are only different ways of looking at the same fundamental feature of the living world. Order cannot increase indefinitely. There is an optimum degree of order at each level of organization in the Gaian hierarchy – as there must be for all its associated features. That degree of order required for best assuring the critical order of the Biosphere can be referred to as homeotelic order.

Order has also been defined as 'the influence of the whole over the parts', though it is often forgotten that this influence takes the form of constraints that are imposed by the whole on the parts. Still less is it admitted that these constraints are best regarded as laws, which the constituent parts must observe if they are to fulfil their homeotelic functions within a larger system, and thereby maintain its integrity and stability. The reason is that this notion cannot be reconciled with the paradigm of science.

Another definition of order invokes the limitation of choice. This makes perfect sense, since to submit systems to constraints or laws, is necessarily to limit their choice by preventing them from undertaking activities which are inconsistent with the maintenance of the integrity and stability of the larger system of which they are part, and by assuring, on the contrary, that they do precisely those things which most favour the achievement of that overriding goal. Thus, as largely autonomous systems are transformed into the differentiated or specialized parts of a larger system, so, by the same token, must the latter's influence over them increase, so must they be subjected to more rigid constraints or laws, and so must their freedom of choice be reduced.

When the slime mould takes the form of a largely autonomous protozoan living in a loose colony, the influence of the whole over the parts is weak and the latter are only subjected to very loose laws or constraints, thereby enjoying a wide range of choices. When, on the other hand, the loose colony is transformed into a multicellular organism, and its parts become more differentiated and specialized in the functions which maintain its integrity and stability, then the influence of the whole over the parts is increased, the constraints or laws to which the latter are subjected become more rigid and their range of choice more limited. The pattern of behaviour which the constituents of such orderly systems are constrained to adopt is that which, in these optimum conditions, they themselves will choose – for it is that which must best satisfy their own needs by providing them with their optimum environment or field.

Natural systems display order whether we see them as spatial entities, as we usually do, or as processes. A disordered or random process can tend in any direction; its behaviour is unpredictable. As order builds up, however, the process is subjected to the influence of the whole of which it is part. Its range of choices is limited as it becomes a differentiated part of the larger Biospheric process, committed to the achievement of a single goal. Hence goal-directedness, or teleology, is just another word for order, applied to life processes.

As Colin Pittendrigh notes, order or organization without purpose

> is an absurdity . . . there is no such thing as organization in any absolute sense, pure and simple. Organization is always relative, and relative to an end. [Thus] an organization of an army is relative to the end of defeating an enemy; and doing so, moreover, in a particular environment or terrain, weapons and politi-

cal system. A room may be organized with respect to relaxation. Certainly, neither a room nor an army can be organized with respect to nothing.

If one states that living systems are organized, then one must be ready to face the question 'with respect to what are they organized?' As Ludwig von Bertalanffy notes, 'the notion of "organ", of visual, auditory, or sexual organ, already involves the notion that this is a "tool" for something.' Animals will eat and drink and breathe and reproduce because these processes are as much part of them as are the organs that assure these functions. Indeed, there are no such things as animals that do not eat and drink, breathe and reproduce, except as photographs, pictures, concepts and words, nor are there such processes as eating, drinking, breathing and reproducing taken apart from the organisms involved. This must follow from the fact that living things are spatio-temporal systems which means that the order they display is spatio-temporal order and this necessarily implies purposiveness.

If the order of the living world, whether seen spatially or temporally, is not apparent to reductionistic mainstream science, it is largely because seeing the world as orderly means looking at it holistically. Indeed, unless one sees a system within its correct field – as part of the hierarchy of larger systems in which it evolved and to whose influence it is subjected, one cannot see that it is orderly or indeed purposive.

Paul Weiss often points out how the parts of a cell are constantly changing, growing, dying, breaking up, recombining, in what appears to be a chaotic manner: but the chaos is illusory; the parts are under cellular control which is essential if the cell is to remain a viable unit of adaptive behaviour. The cell maintains its identity in spite of the apparent disorder of its constituent parts. What is more, it outlives them, for it has greater persistence or stability than they do.

Mainstream scientists would seek to explain this in terms of statistical method. The individual cells, they would maintain, behave in a disorderly manner, but a large number of cells would behave in an orderly manner. For this reason, one cannot make statements about individual cells, but one can about large numbers of them and these statements are necessarily of a statistical nature. Such statistical statements, however, say nothing about the forces that give rise to this order, and hence do not explain why this order comes about. They do not relate order to differentiation, specialization, cooperation, or stability, nor even to the influence of the whole over the parts, nor to the operation of laws or constraints, nor to the reduction of choice, nor to the need for a system to behave in an orderly or purposiveness manner in order to maintain the integrity and stability of the whole. On the contrary, the statistical approach to this subject provides a means of avoiding the many fundamental implications of the orderliness of natural systems, all of which are irreconcilable with the paradigm of science.

Among other things, it makes it possible to avoid recognizing that in the Biosphere a single order prevails. In this way, Edgar Morin can tell us that 'there is order in the universe but not one order.' This is just another way of stating that the Biosphere is atomized and random and that its constituents can therefore be seen as governed by very different sets of laws.

The statistical argument also enables mainstream scientists to avoid recognizing that the order displayed by the Biosphere is not only distinct from but diametrically opposed to that of the technosphere or surrogate world with which modern man is systematically replacing it. To confound Biospheric diversity and complexity with technospheric diversity and complexity is to obscure the essential fact that the expansion of the latter can only occur at the expense of the integrity and stability of the former.

The hierarchy of the Biosphere displays a single order and is governed by a single set of laws whose generalities apply equally well to biological organisms, communities, societies and ecosystems and to Gaia herself. (see Chapter 61) This was fully accepted by tribal man, as is pointed out by Jane Harrison, Radcliffe-Brown and others. Modern man, if he is to have a future, must become aware once more of this fundamental principle.

# THIRTY SIX

# Gaian order is critical

●

*The dominating interest [in tribal society] is to preserve and perpetuate social harmony, stability and welfare. Religious cults and magic practices have chiefly this purpose in view. Everyone who has lived with a 'primitive' people and has tried to immerse his mind in theirs, knows the deep-rooted dread they foster towards any disturbance of the universal and social harmony and equilibrium and the intimate interdependence they assume as existing between these two. A violation of this harmony and equilibrium, whether this issues from the universal sphere – for example, by an unusual occurrence in nature – or from the social – by a dangerous transgression of tradition or by a disturbing event such as the birth of twins – calls forth a corporate and strenuous religious activity towards restoring the harmony and thereby saving the fertility of their fields, their health, the security of their families, the stability and welfare of their tribe from becoming endangered.*

HENDRICK KRAEMER

*The atmospheric concentration of gases such as oxygen and ammonia is found to be kept at an optimum value from which even small departures could have disastrous consequences for life.*

JAMES LOVELOCK

Vernacular man knew that the order of the cosmos was critical, so much so that his overriding preoccupation was to preserve it. The notion of critical order is reflected in such notions as harmony and balance, which were seen by all traditional peoples as essential features of the living world and of the cosmos.

The essential principle, built into the cultural pattern of vernacular people, that everything within the living world has to be recycled (see Chapter 56) was based on the need to maintain its harmony or balance, as was the principle of reciprocity, which governs economic relationships within the vernacular community. The principle of maintaining the balance between two complementary principles, such as the Yin and the Yang among the Taoists, was another means of maintaining the critical order of the living world, while Greek medicine, as W. H. S. Jones notes, sought above all to maintain what was referred to as the 'balance of humours'. For the Natural Theologists of the seventeenth and eighteenth centuries, the 'balance of nature', as Frank Egerton points out, provided incontrovertible evidence of the wisdom of God. The great Swedish naturalist Linnaeus also saw the world as displaying balance and harmony, which to him reflected 'the economy of nature'.

Unfortunately, economic progress cannot occur without disrupting the critical order of the natural world. As the world-view of modernism and the associated paradigm of science slowly developed to rationalize and hence legitimize this anti-evolutionary enterprise, (see Chapter 64) the notion of balance and harmony was increasingly marginalized.

When ecology came into being as a reaction against the paradigm of science, not surprisingly it sought to revive the concept of the balance of nature. Thus S. A. Forbes saw 'an ideal balance of nature as one promotive of the highest good of all the species.' W. C. Allee and the other principle members of the Chicago school of ecology in the 1940s also accepted the principle of the balance of nature according to which 'the community maintains a certain balance, establishes a biotic border, and has a certain unity paralleling the dynamic equilibrium and organization of other living systems.'

In the 1930s and 1940s, however, ecology was systematically transformed so as to make it conform with the paradigm of science. Ecologists sought to discredit the concept of the balance of nature in the same way as they questioned the established ecological principles: that ecological succession leads to a climax, that the whole is more than the sum of the parts and that diversity gives rise to stability. Alfred Russel Wallace, who developed the principle of evolution via natural selection at the same time as Charles Darwin and independently of him, had argued that the occurrence of different types of ecological discontinuities made nonsense of the principle of the balance of nature – a principle which was clearly irreconcilable with his theory.

> Some species exclude all others in particular tracts. Where is the balance? When the locust devastates the vast regions and causes the death of animals and man, what is the meaning of saying the balance is preserved? [Are the devastations of] the Sugar Ants in the West Indies and the locust which Mr. Lyell says have destroyed 800,000 acres an instance of the balance of species? To human apprehension there is no balance but a struggle in which one often exterminates another.

The same argument was put forward again in 1930 by the British ecologist Charles Elton, who argued against the principle of the balance of nature on the grounds that species were constantly being made extinct. This argument, however, takes no account of the fact that such serious discontinuities are unlikely to occur in a climax ecosystem, in which everything conspires to minimize their incidence and severity. Their occurrence thus indicates that an ecosystem is still at a pioneering stage or has been reduced to a neo-pioneering stage – what Eugene Odum calls a 'disclimax' – by an external agent, such as modern man, whose commitment to economic development can only lead to ecological degradation.

This was fully understood more than two hundred years ago, by the famous French naturalist, Bernadin de Saint-Pierre:

> If snails, nay bugs, caterpillars and locusts ravage our plains, it is because we destroy the birds of our groves which live upon them; or because on transporting the trees of foreign countries into our own, such as the great chestnut

of India, the ebony and others, we have transported, with them the eggs of those insects which they nourish, without importing likewise, the birds of the same climate which destroy them. Every country has those peculiar to itself, for the preservation of its plants.

It follows that the occurrence of plagues and other discontinuities, rather than providing evidence that there is no such thing as the balance of nature, must, on the contrary, be seen as part of the price we pay for disrupting this critical balance. Of course, if we insist that there is no such thing as the balance of nature, if the Biosphere has no critical order, then it can be modified with impunity and must be seen as totally malleable. We can then pretend that plagues are *natural* disasters; and rather than treat them by restoring a critical balance of the affected ecosystems, we can justify waging chemical warfare against their vectors – the remedy that best satisfies the requirements of the agro-chemical industry and of the economy in general, though it merely serves to mask the symptoms of disease.

Scientists have sought in all sorts of ways to deny that the order of the natural world is critical. Lamarck believed that the human genetic material, the genome, was so malleable that it could be moulded into any form by environmental influences. That was his principal error. For Descartes, living things in general and for John Locke the human mind itself are but pieces of wax, 'flexible, malleable, ours to shape as we please', as John Passmore puts it. Most modern historians and sociologists also see society in this way. H. A. L. Fisher, for instance, tells us that man does not have a nature, only a history – intimating that human behaviour is infinitely malleable down the random course of history. Edward O. Wilson also talks of the 'extreme plasticity of social behaviour', implying that we can adapt to living in just about any social environment – including, of course, that which economic development or progress imposes upon us.

All this is so much nonsense. Living systems or processes at all levels in the Gaian hierarchy must have a critical structure – that which is consistent with the fulfilment of their homeotelic functions. Thus, clearly the structure of an organism, like that of any other natural system, is critical: its various body fluids, for instance, must have the 'normal' chemical and biological composition, or what would be the point of pharmacological tests? The basic features of a human community are also critical. It must be composed of extended families, and intermediate social groupings which link people together to form cohesive units of social behaviour, all of which, in different societies, will vary in all sorts of relatively superficial ways in order to satisfy the requirements of their specific cultural patterns.

A cultural pattern must also display a critical order and cultural traits can only be understood in accordance with their functions within it. The suppression of vernacular customs and institutions, because they appear undesirable when judged by our particular standard of morality, can have fatal results for the culture involved – very much as the extraction of a key organ can result in the demise of an organism.

Let us take the case of the marital customs of the people of the Comores in the Indian Ocean. They practise polygamy and have a high frequency of divorce, so much so that it is perfectly normal for a woman to have been married five to ten times. On the basis of the experience gained in our culture, we would tend to associate this high divorce rate with an equally high rate of emotional instability, drug addiction, juvenile delinquency and crime. However, things do not work out that way. When I visited the Comores in 1971, I found that the incidence of all these problems was extremely low. This society had thus adapted to marital instability, which ours has not. The reasons are two-fold. Firstly, by virtue of the institution of matriliny and matrilocality, a child is partly the responsibility of the mother's clan, many of the functions of fatherhood being fulfilled by the mother's elder brother (inheritance, being primarily through him rather than through the father). Secondly, by custom, the step-father (or *baba-combo*) also automatically assumes many of the responsibilities of fatherhood vis-à-vis the children that his wife has had with previous husbands. In particular, he is responsible for the payment of the very large expenses involved in the circumcision ceremony of his step-sons.

For all these reasons, divorce does not have the same unsettling effect in the Comores as it does in our society. Now, supposing a busybody missionary or administrator suddenly decided to abolish matriliny and matrilocality – as vestiges of barbarity not to be found in modern advanced societies – the results would be disastrous: delinquency, crime, alienation and other symptoms of social disorder would undoubtedly result, as they do with the break-up of the nuclear family in our society.

If societies have a critical order, so too must ecosystems. They must be made up of green plants that are capable, via photosynthesis, of mobilizing the energy of the sun; herbivores that can feed off the plants; predators that can feed off the herbivores, applying quantitative and qualitative controls on their populations; and decomposers that can break down biological material into its constituent parts to serve as the raw material for the perpetuation of the whole cycle.

Though all terrestrial ecosystems are designed on this same basic plan, they will nevertheless, differ in many respects. Very different species will, in different ecosystems, fulfil the basic ecological roles, and these will also display varying degrees of complexity and diversity, cooperation and competition.

The Biosphere itself, the overall ecosystem, must for the same reason display a critical order. That the earth's atmosphere must do so at a chemical level is clearly noted by James Lovelock. Among other things, its carbon dioxide content is critical: if it were too low, the earth would be too cold; and if too high, its temperature would exceed that which most forms of life could support. Its oxygen content is also critical: if it were too low, then we would not be able to breathe; while if it were too high, the earth's atmosphere would become so inflammable that a single spark would set off uncontrollable fires.

It must follow that adaptive changes occurring to any natural system must be designed either to maintain or to increase its critical order and hence that of the Biosphere itself. Such changes do not occur for their own sake but in order to prevent the occurrence of bigger and more disruptive changes which could seriously disrupt its critical order.

———

# THIRTY SEVEN

# There is no fundamental barrier

# separating man and other living things

●

*The fact that primitive man draws no strict line of cleavage between the animal, vegetable and mineral kingdoms, on the one hand, and human beings on the other, has been so often emphasized, that it can be regarded as an anthropological commonplace.*

RAPHAEL PATAI

*To man in the totemistic stage of thinking, Dike and Themis, natural order and social order, are not distinguished, not even distinguishable. Plants and animals are part of this group, factors in his social structure. It is not that he takes them under his protection; they are his equals, his fellow-tribesmen; naturally they obey the same law.*

JANE HARRISON

———

There is no fundamental difference between the structure and behaviour of vernacular man and that of other living things. Both are governed by the same laws that govern the behaviour of the natural systems which make up the Gaian hierarchy. Vernacular man fully accepted this close relationship with the rest of the animal kingdom.

That the fellowship between man and other animals was strongly felt in classical antiquity, during the middle ages and even as late as the nineteenth century in rural areas of Western Europe is well documented by Edvard Westermarck in his *The Origin and Development of Moral Ideas*. It played an essential part in the world-view of vernacular man, for without it there could be neither animism nor hylozoism. As Raphael Patai notes, it is 'merely a recognition of the true state of things, the perception of the fundamental similarity underlying the apparent diversity of forms.'

It is particularly marked, of course, among 'totemic' societies – those whose members were imbued with a chthonic world-view. For James Frazer, this 'sense of close relationship of man with the lower creatures' is the very essence of totemism. He notes how a Bushman, questioned by a missionary, could not see any difference between man and other animals; for instance, 'he did not know but a buffalo might shoot with bows and arrows as well as a man, if it had them.' The Giliaks of the Amoor attach no importance to the physical differences separating man from other animals:

> in substance every beast is a real man, just like a Giliak himself, only endowed with an intelligence and strength which often surpass those of mere ordinary human beings.

The clans into which many tribal societies are divided are named after specific animals with whom they see themselves as closely related. Indeed, they often actually identify themselves with their totemic animals. F. M. Cornford tells us that among Australian Aborigines, a member of a group that has the kangaroo as its totem, literally believes that he is a kangaroo. 'His belief that he is a kangaroo is so unquestioned that he has no need to pretend that he is one, or to induce a kangaroo to enter into him and possess him for the nonce; all he has to do is to be a kangaroo by behaving as one.' Among the Ojibway, as Frazer notes, the members of the bear clan behave in a surly and pugnacious way, while members of the crane clan affect 'clear ringing voices like cranes'.

Needless to say, tribesmen will desist religiously from killing animals of the species with which they are associated in this way. Frazer tell us how a Mandingo porter offered to forego a whole month's pay in order to save a python, because the python was his totem and to kill it would threaten the survival of his whole family. Such an attitude is a serious impediment to economic development, for if the tribesmen are to participate in this enterprise they cannot have such qualms about killing living creatures. It requires a very different attitude: rather than being our brothers and sisters, non-human animals must be seen as inferior 'beasts' or 'brutes' to whom such qualities as purpose, creativity, intelligence, the ability to predict the results of their actions, consciousness and morality are denied; their behaviour must be judged as blind and robot-like. In this way we can feel justified in exploiting and killing them as much as we like in order to satisfy short-term economic interests.

Some mainstream scientists go further, insisting 'that there is no evidence that animals actually suffer pain'. This is another pretext for exploiting them -- in particular for torturing them in laboratories in order to obtain the 'scientific evidence' that will legitimize the use of new cosmetics, pesticides and pharmaceutical preparations.

Many of those who have sought to justify the colonial enterprise have insisted in a similar way that tribal man was 'little more than an animal', hence little more than a machine. Charles Darwin, for one, wrote in this vein of the Fuegians, the natives of Tierra del Fuego: the domination, indeed the annihilation of tribal cultures was seen by him and the social Darwinists as part of the beneficial working of natural selection. If tribal societies failed to survive, it was that they were not fit to do so. The fact that the colonial powers were capable of dominating and eventually of annihilating them was sufficient proof of the former's superiority. It was fully justified in the name of the 'survival of the fittest' and was seen as a necessary condition for human progress.

All this we must reject. In terms of the world-view of ecology, no fundamental barrier separates us from all the other living things with whom we live on this planet – the particularities of their structure and behaviour may be different, but the basic generalities are the same.

# THIRTY EIGHT

# The Biosphere is a hierarchical

# organization of natural systems

●

*Wholes and parts cannot exist by themselves either at a biological or social level. What we find are intermediary structures on a series of levels in ascending order of complexity, each of which has two faces looking in opposite directions; the face turned towards the lower levels is that of an autonomous whole, the one turned upward that of a dependent part.*

ARTHUR   KOESTLER

Insect societies, human and non-human animal societies, ecosystems, even Gaia herself have all been compared to biological organisms. It would be more accurate, however, to regard them as instances of a more general category of entities. Ralph Gerard referred to them as 'orgs' – not a particularly attractive term – Ludwig von Bertalanffy, Ross Ashby, Paul Weiss and others called them 'systems' or 'natural systems', a term now in general use, while Arthur Koestler and, later, Tom Starr and others named them 'holons'.

Unfortunately, the term 'system', like most other basic terms used by scientists, is defined in many conflicting ways. A. D. Hall and R. E. Fagen originally defined it as 'a set of objects together with the relationships between the objects and between their attributes'. It is more often defined as a set of entities in dynamic interrelationship with each other. However, both of these definitions could apply equally well to a disintegrated or 'atomized' system, such as a cancerous cell, or a modern industrial society, or any of the groupings into which the latter is organised such as state institutions or corporations. But all these systems are necessarily heterotelic rather than homeotelic to the Biosphere.

Koestler defines a 'holon' as 'any stable sub-whole in an organismic, cognitive, or social hierarchy which displays rule-governed behaviour and/or structural Gestalt constancy.' This definition is a little loose. He should specify which rules govern the behaviour of the holon – though, of course, if a 'sub-whole' displays structural constancy, then it can only be that it is subject to the rule of the whole.

Other authors have used the term system in a still more general way. Ilya Prigogine, for instance, includes 'paradigms, the whole system of science, religions, the images we hold of ourselves and our roles in the evolution of the universe' together with cells, organisms, societies and ecosystems in this category. This is simply a device to make it appear that all these things have more in common than they really do. Jacques Monod rightly criticizes the use of the term system as being too loose. 'The trouble with embracing everything is that you can end up holding nothing,' he writes, though he would undoubtedly have used stronger language if he had seen Prigogine's definition.

With Ashby, von Bertalanffy developed an entirely new discipline called

General Systems Theory whose object was to establish the laws governing the behaviour of 'natural systems'. He reserves the use of the term 'system' to complexes of elements in interaction to which systems laws can be applied. Paul Weiss defines a system still more realistically as 'a complex unit in space and in time, whose sub-units cooperate to preserve its integrity and its structure and its behaviour and tend to restore them after a non-destructive disturbance.' In this way, he stresses the major features of the constituents of the Biosphere: their complexity, their existence in space-time, their cooperative, self-regulatory, homeotelic nature, their dynamism, their purposefulness, their dedication to the maintenance of the critical order of the larger systems of which they are part and thus to the preservation of their own integrity and stability.

It is clear that the laws governing the behaviour of natural systems which von Bertalanffy tries to establish would have to be as general as the most general category of systems he describes. Thus the particularities of the behaviour of humans can be seen as governed by a particular set of laws that apply only to humans. More general aspects of their behaviour can be seen to be governed by more general laws that apply to mammals in general, still more general aspects by still more general laws that apply to all organisms in general, and so on. The most general aspects of their behaviour must be governed by laws that apply to natural systems or holons, including Gaia herself.

To determine what are these most general laws must provide the best means of developing a unified science, 'not by the utopian reduction of all the sciences to physics and chemistry,' as von Bertalanffy insists, 'but by virtue of the structural uniformities, which exist between the different levels of the natural world.' Such a unified science would constitute a truly holistic ecology. General Systems Theory also makes it possible to get rid of some of the most misleading dualisms that the paradigm of science has imposed on our understanding of the natural world, such as the great divide between the natural sciences and the social sciences. By defining a natural system in von Bertalanffy's way, one distinguishes it from the components of the technosphere or surrogate world, which satisfy none of these conditions. The failure of many of those involved in General Systems Theory to grasp the significance of this distinction largely explains why this discipline has made remarkably little progress since the death of its founder.

Von Bertalanffy lists two of the laws which he regards as essential and to which systems, in order to be classified as such, must presumably be subjected. The first is the law of 'biological maintenance' which states that 'the organic system tends to preserve itself', another way of saying that it maintains its homeostasis. The second law is that a natural system is organized hierarchically. This he sees as applying both to organic systems and to the inorganic world, 'with its hierarchy of electrons, atoms, molecules, myceas and crystals'. This essential aspect of natural systems is also accentuated very forcefully by Paul Weiss, Arthur Koestler and Eugene Odum. The latter sees all natural systems as organized hierarchically, from the biotic community, to the population, the organism, the organ and the cell. He sees them as forming a spectrum that theoretically, can be extended infinitely in both directions. The upper end of the spectrum, covering populations and the ecosystem, is the concern of ecology.

If every natural system is part of such a hierarchy, regardless of its level of organization, it must have two functions: on the one hand, vis-à-vis the larger systems of which it is part, and on the other vis-à-vis the smaller systems that comprise it. Paul Weiss considers that the cell, which is the main object of his studies, must be seen, 'in a double light; partly as an active worker and partly as a passive subordinate to powers which lie entirely outside of its own competence and control, i.e. supra-cellular powers.' Arthur Koestler sees this as applying to all natural systems or 'holons'. He takes the Roman deity Janus – whose two faces look in opposite directions – as the natural symbol of the holon with its two roles within the hierarchy of nature.

Scientific ecologists tend to ignore this key issue. For instance, there is no mention of hierarchy in S. D. Putman and R. J. Wratten's textbook, nor in the latest ecology textbook to appear in the United Kingdom, that by Michael Begon, John Harper and Colin Townsend. The reason is probably that its many implications are largely unacceptable to those imbued with the paradigm of science. Hierarchy, has to my knowledge been the subject of but two major conferences, one organized by Lancelot Law Whyte and the other by Howard Pattee. Neither was particularly enlightening. M. D. Mesarovic and D. Macko, who attended the first symposium, noted how 'the term "hierarchy" was used to cover a variety of related yet distinct notions' while Majorie Grene, another participant, noted how loosely the term was used. Among ecologists, it is only Eugene Odum it appears whose textbooks take the essentially hierarchical nature of the Biosphere into account.

# THIRTY NINE

# Competition is a secondary Gaian

# interrelationship

●

*From the point of view of the moralist the animal world is on about the same level as a gladiator's show. The creatures are fairly well treated, and set to fight – whereby the strongest, the swiftest and the cunningest live to fight another day. The spectator has no need to turn his thumbs down, as no quarter is given.*
T. H. HUXLEY

*The growth of a large business is merely a survival of the fittest. . . . It is merely the working out of a law of Nature and a law of God.*
JOHN D. ROCKEFELLER SNR

*It is rare to see two animals, particularly animals of different species, tugging at the same piece of meat. And even when competition is observed, it often appears inconsequential. Perhaps a fiddler crab scurries into a hole on a beach only to come running out again, expelled by the current inhabitant. But the crab simply moves off to find another hole. Competition between species – interspecific competition – thus appears to be little more than a minor, temporary inconvenience.*
DANIEL SIMBERLOFF

The industrial revolution transformed our vision of the natural world. Adam Smith sought to show that even the most destructive aspects of industrialism were beneficial. The disintegration of society and the individualism, competitiveness and aggression that are the inevitable concomitants of industrialization he saw as positive factors providing, via the workings of the 'invisible hand', the very basis of economic and hence social prosperity.

Herbert Spencer formulated the principle of 'the struggle for survival' which he took to be the basic feature of human society, and which he regarded as a means of creating a more differentiated and hence a more efficient society. Thomas Malthus insisted that the struggle for food and resources was a mathematical necessity and that poverty, malnutrition and famine were quite normal, indeed desirable, since the victims of the struggle for survival would make way for the victors – the best adapted who alone displayed the qualities required for creating an efficient and prosperous society.

Charles Darwin, highly influenced as he was by Spencer and Malthus, proceeded to show how the struggle for survival, which he loosely identified with competition and natural selection, was the organizing principle in nature and provided the means for achieving evolutionary progress. To do this required considerable imagination, but he was well up to the task as is clear from his treatment in *The Origin of Species* of the metaphor of the tree of life.

> The affinities of all the beings of the same class have sometimes been represented by a great tree. I believe this simile largely speaks the truth. The green and budding twigs may represent existing species: and those produced during former years may represent the long succession of extinct species. At each period of growth, all the growing twigs have tried to branch out of all sides, and to overtop and kill the surrounding twigs and branches, in the same manner as species and groups of species have at all times overmastered other species in the great battle for life.

If he saw competition to be the basic feature of the interrelationships *within* a biological organism, where symbiosis is most highly developed, one can imagine what little room there was, in his scheme of things, for sym-biosis or mutualism *between* organisms within an ecological community, where the role of cooperation in its various forms may not be quite so obvious.

If Adam Smith showed that the competitive principle applied to eco-nomics, and Herbert Spencer did the same for sociology, Malthus for demography and Darwin for evolutionary biology, academic ecologists made sure that they were not left out. As Douglas Boucher notes, 'twen-tieth century ecology, while usually shying away from analogizing the natural and social worlds, has continued the tradition of seeing antagonis-tic interactions as the basis of community organization.' R. E. Ricklefs, author of a famous textbook on ecology, confirms that 'competition as a major organizing principle in ecology is so widely accepted that it has achieved the status of a paradigm.'

Though competition, like natural selection, is a crude and elementary mechanism, ecologists have attributed to it the most sophisticated capac-ities. No feat is considered to be so daunting that competition cannot achieve it. Thus the competitive displacement principle, otherwise known as Gause's principle, tells us that two species with the same lifestyle, and in particular the same diet, cannot occupy the same niche or co-exist on the same territory. In other words, *competition regulates diversity*. Again, common species of plants, referred to by Herbert Gleason as dominants, are declared the most effective competitors, while rare species, or non-domi-nants, are simply less effective competitors. This means, in effect, that *com-petition determines the relative size of populations*. Further, according to S. D. Putman and R. J. Wratten competition for resources entirely *determines eco-logical organization, as well as ecological succession*. Indeed, mainstream ecol-ogists attribute to competition those features of omnipresence, omnipo-tence and hence presumably omniscience that are normally attributed to God.

It is the sociobiologists who have taken up the most extreme position. For them, it is individual self-interest that prevails in every sphere, and it is in terms of this self-interest that any form of cooperation must be inter-preted, no allusion to the larger system's need for such cooperation being regarded as scientific. This leads sociobiologists to see even the humblest of living things making precise cost–benefit calculations, in the manner of modern economists, in order to decide whether or not to cooperate with the members of their community or even with immediate family members. Even the most intimately mutual human relations such as those obtaining between a mother and her child are held to be explicable in such terms: displays of affection mask all sorts of sinister machinations on the part of the child vis-à-vis its unsuspecting mother, and presumably vice versa. Richard Dawkins assures us that

> we can talk about a conflict between parents and young, a battle of the generations. The battle is a subtle one, and no holds are barred on either side. A child will lose no opportunity of cheating. It will pretend to be hungrier than it is, perhaps younger than it is, more in danger than it really is. It is too small and weak to bully its parents physically, but it uses every psychological weapon at its disposal: lying, cheating, deceiving, exploiting, right up to the point where it starts to penalize its relatives more than its genetic relatedness to them should allow. Parents on the other hand, must be alert to the cheating and deceiving and must try not to be fooled by it.

Cheating among the partners of apparently mutualistic relationships is now even regarded as a legitimate and respectable subject of research in those academic circles that take seriously the ideas of sociobiology.

The concept of competition as the ordering principle in nature is not based upon any serious knowledge of any kind. To begin with, there is no standard definition of competition, a term used in many different ways. Darwin, for instance, never established very precisely how he related the notion of competition to those of 'the struggle for existence' or 'the survival of the fittest'. Opinions vary as to how he saw these relationships. David Merrell considers that he regarded competition as one aspect of the struggle for existence. L. C. Birch, on the other hand, considers that he used the two terms in a different way. The former provides a veritable catalogue of the different ways in which the term 'competition' is defined. Summing up, he concludes that 'given these differences of opinion, it may be hazardous to attempt to reach some workable definition of competition.'

Nor are the various applications of the competitive principle to ecology any better defined. The competitive exclusion principle, for instance, has been formulated by different ecologists in literally dozens of ways. Merrell lists many of the formulations. Most of them make reference to limiting resources, but others do not mention resources at all. Furthermore, some definitions state that exclusion occurs if the ecological niches are 'identical'; others only require them to be 'similar'. Worse still, the studies required to justify the thesis that competition is the ordering principle in nature have never really been undertaken. J. H. Connell notes that his review of the literature on the subject yielded only one study involving serious experimental work designed to determine if competition played a significant role in the interaction between species. Peter Price goes so far as to say that 'competition theory lives in a dreamworld where everything can be explained, but the validity of these explanations has not been adequately established in the real world.'

In normal conditions, it would seem that competition is a minor or rare feature of the interrelationship between living things, as E. J. Kormondy and the entomologist E. S. Messenger maintain. The truth seems to be that animals seek to avoid competition, or rather avoid its more destructive manifestations. Thus living things will learn to occupy a different niche from potential competitors, even if it is one to which they may have to adapt by undergoing behavioural and structural modifications.

Robert Augros and George Stanciu also tell us how thousands of different species of living things are known to coexist 'without competing, because they eat different foods, or are active at different times, or otherwise occupy different niches.' Some plant species have learned to live on sandy soil, 'others in rich humus, some prefer acid soil, others alkaline: still others require no soil, such as the lichens; some exploit the early growing season, others the late; some get by only because they are tiny, others only because they are huge.' Some animal species, to avoid competition, will simply move away to occupy an as yet unexploited niche: this is why virtually every Galapagos island now has its own sub-species of finch, tortoise and lizard. In this way, rather than fight to the finish, competing groups spread out and become differentiated.

What is more, when real competition actually occurs it tends to be highly formalized. Intraspecific conflict in the animal kingdom is indeed little more than a ritual conducted according to a set of rules designed, above all, to prevent the occurrence of death or mutilation. Thus rival rattlesnakes, capable of killing with a single bite, never actually bite each other. Their conflict, Konrad Lorenz reports, is a strange ritual resembling Indian wrestling: 'the successful snake pins the loser for a moment with the weight of his body and then lets him escape.' The oryx antelope, with horns capable of putting a lion to flight, does not use them in earnest in an interspecific fight. As Eibl-Eibesfeldt writes,

> a hornless bull observed by Walthe carried out the full ritual of combat as if he still had horns. He struck at his opponent's horns and missed by the precise distance at which his non-existent horns would have made contact. Equally remarkable, his opponent acted as though his horns were in place and responded to his imaginary blows.

Much the same is true of vernacular human societies; for instance, it was the normal procedure in Australian Aboriginal warfare for hostilities to cease at the death of one man. Among the Maori, leadership was all important and hostilities came to an end once the leader of one of the rival groups was put out of action. Andrew Vayda notes that an attacking force of Maoris, even when 'on the verge of victory', might withdraw on the loss of its leader.

Another form of ritualization is the substitution of a match or tournament between two or more champions for a conflict between two armies. The contest between David and Goliath is an obvious example. This strategy was resorted to a great deal during the Middle Ages in Europe. Sport also provides a means of ritualizing conflict between two social groups. Lacrosse was used for this purpose among the Creek Indians of Canada; today, football increasingly takes the form of ritualized conflict between rival groups of fans – often representing rival ethnic groups as in the case of the Celtic and Rangers clubs in Glasgow or the supporters of competing national teams.

Perhaps the most sophisticated of such ritual conflicts is the Palio of Siena, in which the *contrades* – medieval associations, each of which inhabits its own area of the city – compete with each other by means of a horse race round the city's incredibly beautiful Piazza del Campo. Significantly, there is remarkably little crime in this city: people have learned to live with each other and the Palio plays a considerable role in enabling them to do so.

The thesis that competition is the ordering principle in nature is based on the dangerous error made by Malthus, Darwin, the social Darwinists, the sociobiologists (and, indeed, the bulk of mainstream biologists, ecologists and sociologists) of regarding the atomized, individualistic and competitive societies of today as the norm, and seeing them, what is more, as reflecting the basic structure of the natural world. Such societies are, on the contrary, highly aberrant and necessarily short-lived, as is the economic system that they have developed. This was clear to Friedrich Engels when he came to London to study metropolitan societies. He found there 'the war of all against all', and had the wisdom to realize that it was not normal. 'We know well enough', he wrote,

> that this isolation of the individual – the narrow minded egotism – is everywhere the fundamental principle of *modern* society. But nowhere is this selfish egotism so blatantly evident as in the frantic bustle of the great city. The disintegration of society into individuals, each guided by his private principles and each pursuing his own aims, has been pushed to its furthest limits in London. Here, indeed, human society has been split into its component atoms.

Today, London has been seriously outdone. It is in the slums of the larger industrial conurbations of North America that the war of all against all is most in evidence. Here, crime, delinquency and violence of all sorts are the rule and, rather than being seen as normal, they can only be regarded as symptoms of social deprivation and hence of 'eco-deviance' (see Chapter 46) at the social level. If here the community has largely broken down, so has the family; even the nuclear family is no more. Most households are run by a single woman with children whose father no longer has any interest in their upbringing. Such a society, or rather non-society, maintained by a state welfare system which serves to perpetuate the poverty and misery it is supposed to combat, demonstrates social relations as far removed from the norm as they possibly could be.

We have seen that equally deviant relations among baboons in the London Zoo led Lord Zuckerman to conclude that baboons were individualistic and aggressive creatures, which most people believed for a long time afterwards. Yet when ethologists had the opportunity to study baboons in the wild they found them to be, on the contrary, both peaceful and socially integrated. It is important to note, too, that neither in the industrial slums, nor among the baboons of the London Zoo, is there the food shortage that Malthus and Darwin took to be the norm, and that almost all ecologists regard as providing the motivation for competition, including Gause's exclusion principle. Aggression among asocialized and alienated individuals can only be regarded as a symptom of their social isolation and alienation.

Obviously, competition has a role to play in the behaviour of living things, in particular in a pioneer ecosystem. For instance, it serves to eliminate randomness and hence to increase the viability of natural systems, helping to maintain their critical order. Competition also serves in such conditions to space out living things which must, among other things, favour the development of increasing diversity that is adaptive to a greater range of environmental challenges, eliciting more numerous patterns of adaptive behaviour and, eventually, structural forms. As living things evolve, however, as ecosystems develop from their pioneer states towards their climax states, for instance, so such functions are gradually internalized, so does competition give way to cooperation and so is homeostasis correspondingly increased.

# FORTY

# Cooperation is the primary Gaian

# interrelationship

●

*Mutual aid is as much a law of animal life as mutual struggle, but . . . as a factor of evolution, it most probably has a greater importance, inasmuch as it favours the development of such habits and characters as ensure the maintenance and further development of the species, together with the greatest amount of welfare and enjoyment of life for the individual, with the least waste of energy.*
PETER KROPOTKIN

*In nature, the normal way in which trees flourish is by their association in a forest. Each tree may lose something of its individual perfection of growth, but they mutually assist each other in preserving the conditions for survival. The soil is preserved and shaded; and the microbes necessary for its fertility are neither scorched, nor frozen, nor washed away. A forest is the triumph of the organization of mutually dependent species.*
A. N. WHITEHEAD

*Cooperation for mutual benefit, a survival strategy very common in natural systems, is one that humanity needs to emulate.*
EUGENE ODUM

The idea of the world as a 'vast cooperative enterprise' is a very ancient one. It was well understood by traditional man, and, in our Western civilization, it was embodied in the concept of the 'economy of nature' a term first used in 1658 by Sir Kenelm Digby and taken up a century later by the Swedish naturalist Linnaeus when he sought to explain 'the grand organization and governance of life on earth; the rational ordering of all material resources in an interacting whole.' Thirty years later, Gilbert White noted how the cattle standing in the Selborne ponds provided, by their droppings, food for insects and thus indirectly for the fish. White marvelled at the ingenuity of the Creator. 'Nature is a great economist', he wrote, 'for she converts the recreation of one animal to the support of the other.' Charles Darwin himself originally saw nature as 'one grand scheme' of cooperative integration. In his *General Observations* on the ecology of Rio de Janeiro (1832), he writes:

> I could not help noticing how exactly the animals and plants in each region are adapted to each other. Everyone must have noticed how lettuces and cabbages suffer from attacks of Caterpillars and Snails – but when transplanted here in a foreign clime the leaves remain as entire as if they contained poison. – Nature when she formed these animals and these plants knew they must reside together.

Dov Ospovat considers that it was only after reading Malthus that he abandoned these ideas.

The concept of cooperation also played an important part in the thinking of Johannes Warming, one of the earliest scientific ecologists. In particular, he emphasized symbiosis, as in the case of the lichen, a quasi-organism made up of an alga and a fungus. Warming even regarding parasitism as a form of symbiosis, since the parasite and its host eventually become very dependent on each other. The academic discipline of ecology that developed towards the end of the nineteenth century regarded mutualism as a basic feature of ecological organization. Hundreds of articles appeared on this theme in early ecological texts.

The American naturalist Roscoe Pound, for example, described in a celebrated article all the various forms of mutualism that were known to occur in ecosystems, including pollination and the fixation of nitrogen by bacteria living on the root nodules of leguminous plants. Mutualism within ecosystems was even compared to forms of cooperation within organisms – a connection which no academic ecologist would dare to make today. Thus, in the first American book on animal ecology, the ecologist C. C. Adams declared that

> the interactions among the members of an 'association' are to be compared to the similar relations existing between the different cells, organs or activities of a single individual. . . . The physiological needs and states of an association have as real an existence in individual animals as similar needs in the cells which compose the animal body.

As late as the 1940s, Warder C. Allee and the Chicago ecology group continued to regard mutualism as the most basic feature of ecosystems. However, with the development of the world-view of modernism, with its accent on individualism and competition, interest in mutualism rapidly declined.

In 1902, Peter Kropotkin published his classic, *Mutual Aid*, in answer to T. H. Huxley's famous Romanes lecture, perhaps the most extreme statement of what has come to be known as the 'gladiatorial' view of the living world. For Kropotkin, cooperation and mutual aid were in evidence everywhere, among non-human animals and among 'savages', 'barbarians' and 'civilized men': how then could our scientists possibly ignore them, let alone deny their very existence? 'Sociability', he wrote,

> is as much a law of nature as mutual struggle. If we ask nature: 'who are the fittest: those who are continually at war with each other, or those who support one another?' We at once see that those animals which acquire habits of mutual aid are undoubtedly the fittest.

Kropotkin's argument, however, fell on deaf ears, and more recent critics of the gladiatorial view of the natural world have fared no better. Scientists, sociologists and economists, their minds imprisoned within the reigning paradigm, have thus denied basic features of reality clearly evident to observers not conditioned by a mainstream scientific education.

From the 1940s until very recently, ecologists strained to adapt their discipline to the paradigm of science. In the process they lost all interest in mutualism; Eugene and Howard Odum being among the few writers who continued to produce work on the subject. 'Although some of the most spectacular interspecific interactions in nature are obviously mutualistic,' J. H. Vandermeer and Douglas Boucher note, 'relatively little research, empirical or theoretical, has been aimed at understanding this basic and perhaps prevalent form of interaction' – a conclusion amply demonstrated by a close survey of twelve ecology texts (1980–5) undertaken by S. Risch and Boucher.

Worse still, when cooperation or mutualism is admitted to exist at all, it is regarded by some of our most prestigious ecologists as thoroughly counterproductive. For instance, Princeton ecologist Robert May's view that mutualism has a destabilizing effect on ecosystems has gained general acceptance. Though his thesis was no doubt consistent with the mathematical model he built of cooperative relations, it bears little relationship with the real world in which mutualism is a basic condition of stability.

Consider a human family. It is a mutualistic relationship – between husband and wife, parents and children – that holds it together. If mutualism is replaced by competition then the family falls apart: it ceases to remain a stable unit of behaviour. If the cooperative constituents of a human community or of an ecosystem suddenly become competitive, the same thing happens. This is absolutely obvious. If a mathematical model proves the opposite, as May's does, then it must necessarily be wrong, which in any case it must be for at least two additional reasons. The first is that mathematical models of cooperation and competition can only take into account two cooperators or competitors at a time, whereas these relationships necessarily involve a large number of different cooperators and competitors – all those that make up the hierarchy of larger systems of which the systems are part and with which they must necessarily 'cooperate' and 'compete' if they are to ensure their overall stability or survival. Secondly, the only sort of mutualism that can be modelled mathematically is 'facultative' mutualism. 'Obligate' mutualism, which alone is regarded by Odum as true mutualism, is at present very difficult to model.

In the early 1970s, however, there was a sudden resurgence of interest in mutualism. It seemed to manifest itself independently in the work of ecologists at different universities, who were often unaware of each other's work. Well-known ecologists, who had previously downplayed the importance of mutualism, suddenly changed their minds about it. Thus Robert May stated in 1973 that the importance of mutualism 'in populations in general is small.' However, 'in only a few years', to quote Boucher, 'May's appreciation of mutualism changed considerably.' He suddenly announced that mutualism was now seen as 'a conspicuous and ecologically important factor in most tropical communities.' Indeed, in recent years, May has become one of the leaders in encouraging work on mutualism which he sees as 'likely to be one of the growth industries of the 1980s.'

Renewed interest in mutualism has focused attention (in the work of Douglas Boucher, S. James and K. H. Keller, for example) on the role played by micro-organisms in the metabolism of complex organisms. Ecologists have also noted the increasing numbers of parasitic or predatory relationships which, on closer examination, turn out to be mutualistic. Thus S. J. McNaughton has pointed out that the normal view of the relationship between grazers and the grass they graze is false. Whereas 'Ecologists have tended to view plants as relatively passive', it now seems clear that plants are capable of reacting in a much more dynamic manner to grazing, and indeed are capable of 'compensatory growth and assimilate reallocation'. All in all, McNaughton found nine different ways in which the relationship between grazing animals and the grass on which they graze can be regarded as mutualistic. D. F. Owen and R. G. Wiegert carry this analysis a step further. They point to the obvious implication that grazers and the grasses they graze have co-evolved 'to an extent that one would not be possible without the other'. They quote W. I. Mattson and N. D. Addy who consider 'that insects can act as regulators of primary production and nutrient cycling and this performs a vital function in ecosystem dynamics.'

Does this then mean, Boucher asks, that mutualism is 'destined to be part of a new synthesis, in which Newtonian ecology is replaced by a more organicist, integrated, value-laden view of the natural world?' He is not too optimistic on this score. The reason is that 'our present theories of mutualism are still basically mechanistic, mathematical, fitness-maximizing and individualistic.' Unfortunately, this is only too true. D. H. Janzen, for instance, considers that 'mutualisms are the most omnipresent of any organism-to-organism interaction.' However, he still sees mutualism reductionistically in neo-Darwinian terms and insists that 'natural systems larger than the individual cannot be mutualistic.' The reason is that

> a mutualism is an interaction between individual organisms in which the realized or potential genetic fitness of each participant is raised by the actions of the other. The participants are called mutualists. Since a species has no trait that is analogous to the genetic fitness of an individual, mutualism cannot be defined with reference to species.

Boucher considers it inevitable that ecologists should see mutualism in this way:

> While arguing that nature is an integrated whole and that everything is connected to everything else, we continued researching with theories that said that communities are no more than sets of individual organisms. The problem, in other words, is one of cognitive dissonance – the difficulty of working with two sets of ecological ideas, based on different fundamental assumptions and ultimately in conflict.

Mutualism clearly cannot be understood in the light of the paradigm of science, with which it cannot be reconciled. It must be seen in the light of an ecological world-view, which is that of a climax rather than a pioneer society. Such a world-view clearly perceives the role of mutualism in maintaining the critical order of the Gaian hierarchy.

———

# FORTY ONE

# When Gaian control breaks down,

# behaviour becomes heterotelic

●

*Nature has placed man under the governance of two sovereign masters, pain and pleasure. It is for them alone to point out what we ought to do, as well as to determine what we shall do.*
JEREMY   BENTHAM

*We have lived to see a time without order*
*In which everyone is confused in his mind.*
*One cannot bear to join in the madness*
*But if one does not do so, one will not share in the spoils.*
MODERN   JAVANESE   SONG

———

Homeotelic behaviour is normal behaviour, serving the purpose for which it was designed phylogenetically and ontogenetically, which is to maintain the critical order of the Biosphere. (see Chapter 53) Heterotelic behaviour (from the Greek *hetero*, meaning different and *telos*, meaning goal) is behaviour that is misdirected, satisfying up to a point the needs of the individual system but not those of the Gaian hierarchy as a whole. The critical distinction between homeotelic and heterotelic behaviour, between normal and abnormal behaviour, is foreign to the paradigm of science. If behaviour is looked at reductionistically, there is no way in which its purposive and 'whole-maintaining' function can be established, and hence no way of determining whether it is fulfilling this function.

Behaviour can be misdirected if it is based on faulty information. It can also be misdirected if, in new and unpredictable conditions, behaviour based on what has hitherto been sound information ceases to be adaptive. Heterotelic behaviour often occurs when new environmental conditions mimic conditions to which a system is capable of adapting homeotelically, but differ from them in at least one very important respect. Thus, when a developing organism is exposed to the radionuclide Strontium 90, which is chemically very similar to calcium, it treats it as raw material for building up bone. This may serve the immediate requirements of the process in question, but it does not serve its long-term purposes, and hence those of the organism as a whole, since its chances of contracting cancer and other degenerative diseases is considerably increased.

Stephen Boyden establishes the difference between adaptation and what he refers to as 'pseudo-adaptation'. In Scotland today, nearly 40 per cent of people who reach the age of 25 have already lost all their natural teeth. The homeotelic, adaptive or normal response to toothlessness in Scotland, must be to improve the Scottish diet. Only such a response can conceivably solve the problem. The heterotelic or pseudo-adaptive or abnormal response, on the other hand, consists in providing the victims with false teeth. Even if we regard false teeth as a real substitute for real teeth, for the purposes of mastication, to provide them does nothing for all the other consequences of a faulty diet – in particular diabetes, diverticulitis, peptic ulcers, appendicitis, varicose veins, various forms of cancer, and the other diseases of civilization, many of which have been very convincingly linked with the consumption of junk foods.

On the contrary, because the provision of false teeth makes one of the symptoms of a bad diet more tolerable, it will encourage people to maintain poor eating habits, perpetuating the other resulting afflictions. Each of these in turn will be dealt with heterotelically: their symptoms will be suppressed by various patent medicines, all of which have more or less serious side-effects. These will cause further afflictions and the cycle of heterotelically treated illnesses will widen until the victims are consigned to hospitals, where their symptoms are likely to be suppressed by even more drastic methods such as surgical operations, causing still more serious side-effects, etc. There are, of course, exceptions to this rule. Enlightened doctors may well put their patients on a healthier diet, and in general cause them to lead healthier lives which minimize the incidence of disease, but this is likely to be the exception. For as far as medical practitioners are concerned, health is a man-made commodity provided by modern medicines.

The heterotelic use of heterotelic medicines on the present scale assures above all the perpetuation of a massive medical industry, whose sales in the USA account for some 7–8 per cent of gross national product. The medical industry also consumes its share of the non-renewable resources, generating a corresponding proportion of pollution and of social and ecological destruction. The same principle applies in almost every other field of activity in the modern world. In no case are the causes of our problems seriously addressed. All such problems as floods, droughts, epidemics, crime or delinquency are dealt with heterotelically, largely by technological means which our society is geared to providing and which satisfy the immediate economic interests of the corporations and institutions into which it is organized.

Let us consider another example. A man in a stable society will have been designed by his evolution and his cultural upbringing to fulfil those functions within his family that will assure its stability and survival. He fulfils them spontaneously, because it is by doing so that he best satisfies his own individual requirements. Thus the husbandly behaviour he displays towards his wife, which indeed he must display if the family is to survive, will also satisfy his basic individual needs such as sex and companionship.

In aberrant conditions, however, these same needs may be satisfied by displaying similar behaviour towards a woman who is external to the family unit and who may be regarded as mimicking his wife. In this way, one or more husbandly needs are satisfied, but in a way that does not lead to the satisfaction of the needs of the hierarchy of larger systems of which the husband is part. This means that a mechanism designed to hold together the key family unit has been mobilized to do exactly the opposite. We are then left with a one parent family, a highly unstable entity that does not provide a satisfactory environment for the children's upbringing, and which is likely to break down still further, leading to the abandonment of the children as is happening on such a scale in the slums of the major South American cities.

If a man needs a family, so does he need a community. However, with economic development the community, like the family, breaks down and becomes correspondingly atomized, to be replaced by big corporations or institutions (gesseltschaften), which can be regarded as surrogate social groupings that mimic real communities (gemeinschaften). This is particularly so in Japan, where the large corporations usurp most of the functions normally fulfilled by the community – paying for their employees' education, looking after them when they are sick, and even securing their retirement. While this is in many ways admirable, and elicits on the part of the employees a great feeling of loyalty towards the corporation for which they work, it remains true that such behaviour is strictly heterotelic, for though it may serve the interests of the corporations themselves, it does not serve the interests of society as a whole, still less those of the natural world, to whose rapid destruction Japanese corporations are making such a singular contribution.

If the corporation mimics the family and the community, so does the state. This means that the behaviour of modern man towards the state, upon whose many bureaucratic services he has become increasingly dependent, is also heterotelic. For the state is no more a natural constituent of the Gaian hierarchy than is the corporation. It does not seek to provide that environment for its citizens which is required to satisfy their fundamental needs, whether biological, psychological or social, but rather that which best satisfies its own immediate political requirements.

Modern man's religion is also heterotelic, since it diverts human religiosity from fulfilling natural homeotelic religious functions towards the natural world, making the latter corresponding more vulnerable to exploitation and destruction.

Heterotelic behaviour there will always be. It could be regarded as little more than biological, social and ecological randomness. However, in a stable society, it is the exception rather than the rule, and all sorts of social mechanisms exist for reducing its incidence to a minimum. It becomes the rule rather than the exception when a society disintegrates, and the biosphere is replaced by the technosphere. As this occurs, It ceases to be capable of self-regulation or homeostasis, and thereby loses its capacity for counteracting randomness or heterotely. The society is then out of control, as is our modern society today, and set on a course towards social and ecological disaster. All that can then save it is a cultural mega-mutation, an ecologically-based revitalization movement (see Chapter 66), giving rise to a society committed, as were the vernacular societies of the past, to a homeotelic behaviour pattern.

# FORTY TWO

# Natural systems can only behave homeotelically within their 'tolerance range'

●

*It is true that a system in homeostasis is forgiving about disturbance, but only when it is healthy and well within the bounds of its capacity to regulate. When such a system is stressed near the limits of its capacity to regulate, even a small jolt may cause it to jump to a new stable state or even to fail entirely.*
JAMES LOVELOCK

The ecological principle of tolerance holds that natural systems can only function adaptively within an environment whose basic features have not diverged too far from the optimum. As their environment diverges, so adaptive behaviour becomes more difficult and, eventually, impossible. For each particular feature of the environment there are thus limits beyond which, in the words of Robert McIntosh, organisms 'cannot grow, reproduce, or the ultimate extreme, survive.' The same of course, can be said for any other natural systems, whether they be ecosystems or human communities. Today, with global economic development, environments almost everywhere are either reaching these limits or have already passed them. Eugene Odum notes how

> nuclear tests have increased radiation fallout and how the nuclear industry is increasing background levels of radiation which could conceivably exceed our level of tolerance. Our various industrial activities too, are modifying water tables, contaminating groundwater, eroding and desertifying our arable land, and in general modifying our environment to a point that many of its essential features will no longer fall within our tolerance range.

It follows that economic development or progress, which necessarily involves the systematic transformation of the environment of the living things that make up the Biosphere, can only be a temporary phenomenon. Eventually, the tolerance limits of living things will be attained – it is only a question of time – and their survival will then no longer be possible.

The principle of tolerance can be stated in a more subtle way. To begin with, it must be noted – though it rarely is – that the environment most friendly to the needs of living things, that within which their behaviour is most fulfilling and adaptive, can only be the one to which they have been adapted by their evolution and upbringing. Common sense tells us that this must be so. Thus a tiger has been adapted by its evolution and upbringing to living in the jungle, which clearly provides its optimum environment. It is the activities in which it is capable of indulging in the jungle that best satisfy its physical and psychological requirements; it is the food that it finds there that it has best been adapted to eating and digesting; it is the smells encountered there that it has best been adapted to detecting, interpreting, reacting to adaptively and enjoying. There is no reason for supposing that man is in any way exempt from the operation of the fundamental principle that suits the tiger to the jungle.

But what is man's natural environment? To answer this, we must consider that man is by nature a hunter-gatherer. As S. Washburn and C. Lancaster write,

> the common factors that dominate human evolution and produced homo sapiens were pre-agricultural. Agricultural ways of life have dominated less than 1 per cent of human history and there is no evidence of major biological changes during that period of time . . . the origin of all common characteristics must be sought in pre-agricultural times.

As Wes Jackson puts it, if man was designed to be an agriculturalist, 'he would have longer arms'. If he had been designed by his evolution to be an industrialist, Jackson might have added, he would be a robot with no requirement for a family or a community, no feelings for the natural world, no morals and no emotions. He would also be equipped with a physical constitution that enabled him to feed, with impunity, on devitalized and contaminated food, to drink polluted water and breathe polluted air.

It must follow that the optimum environment for man can only be that in which his hunter-gatherer ancestors evolved, one provided by a climax ecosystem. As we transform this environment to satisfy the requirements of economic development or progress, so it satisfies his basic needs ever less satisfactorily. This principle has been formulated very eloquently by the Australian biologist, Stephen Boyden.

> The important corollary to Darwinian theory that I wish to stress has not been given a name. I shall refer to it here as the principle of phylogenetic maladjustment [which he now refers to as 'eco-deviance']. According to this principle, if the conditions of life of an animal deviate from those which prevailed in the environment in which the species evolved, the likelihood is that the animal will be less well suited to the new conditions than to those to which it has become genetically adapted through natural selection and consequently some signs of maladjustment may be anticipated. Obvious though this principle is,

and obvious though its importance is it is seldom referred to in the literature and consequently its significance seems to have been largely overlooked. It relates not only to environmental changes of a physiochemical or material nature, such as changes in the quality of food or air, but also to various non-material environmental influences, such as certain social pressures which may affect behaviour. Furthermore, signs of phylogenetic maladjustments may be physiological, behavioural or both.'

If many of us refuse to face this inescapable principle, it is above all because its implications are so far-reaching. Among other things, it makes nonsense of the very idea of progress, which we have identified with economic development. Far from fulfilling its claim to improve our lives, development brings about changes that must cause our environment and our way of life increasingly to diverge from the conditions to which we have been adapted by our evolution. Progress creates conditions that lie increasingly outside our 'tolerance range' – a process which, if allowed to continue for long enough, must mean the eventual extinction of our species.

FORTY THREE

———

# Living things can only behave

# homeotelically within their field

●

*The fate of a cell is a function of its position.*
HANS DRIESCH

*The Bantu cannot conceive man as an individual, and hence as a force existing by itself, isolated from its relationships with other living things and with the animate and inanimate forces that surround it.*
PLACIDE TEMPELS

*One of the central elements of Buddhism is the concept of 'sunyata' or 'emptiness'. I had difficulty understanding the meaning of this at first, but over the years, in talking to Tashi Rabgyas, things became clearer to me: 'It is something that is not easy to talk about, and impossible to understand through words alone', he told me once. 'It is something you can only fully grasp through a combination of reflection and personal experience. But I'll try to explain it in a simple way. Take any object, like a tree. When you think of a tree you tend to think of it as a distinct, clearly defined object, and on a certain level it is. But on a more important level the tree has no independent existence; rather, it dissolves into a web of relationships. The rain that falls on its leaves, the wind that causes it to sway, the soil which supports it – all form a part of the tree. Ultimately, if you think about it, everything in the universe helps to make the tree what it is. It cannot be isolated; its nature changes from moment to moment – it is never the same. this is what we mean when we say that things are "empty", that they have no substance.'*
HELENA NORBERG HODGE

———

One of the most glaring deficiencies of both modern development theory and modern (neo-Darwinian) evolutionary theory is that the information determining these processes is seen to be exclusively contained within the genes. Such a view fits in with the notion of causality. The phenotype is seen as the product of an external agent or manager, the genes. It fits in, too, with the mechanistic view of life processes, since machines are run in this way by their human operators, but it bears no relationship to what actually happens in the real world.

According to Paul Weiss, the claim that the gene is 'the sole ordering principle in organism . . . rests on sheer assertion, based on blind faith and unqualified reductionistic preconception.' He accuses the proponents of the genetic view of development of glossing over the difficulty of the problem by bestowing on the gene the faculty of spontaneity, the power of 'dictating', 'informing', 'regulating' or 'controlling' the ordering process in its unorganized mileu, 'so as to mould the latter into the coordinated teamwork that is to culminate in an accomplished organism. But they never explain just how this is done.' (see Commoner, 1964)

The organism is a particular type of natural system. It is organized in a specific way and these qualities of the organism can be attributed exclusively neither to the action of the genes nor to the chromosomes of which they are part, nor even to the genome itself. Thus an essential feature of the development of an organism is the differentiation of the cells that compose it. These cells, regardless of whether they are liver cells, pancreatic cells, intestinal cells or cells from the muscles and other tissues, were originally endowed with the same genetic information. Yet they have somehow learned to fulfil very different functions.

It became clear in the 1920s that this could not be explained in terms of mechanistic science, but only in terms of a totally new paradigm. The original inspiration probably came from the New Physics of James Clerk Maxwell. Before Maxwell, the physical world was seen as made up of little bullet-like atoms, or material points, whose change only consisted of motion. Maxwell's work led to the development of a new view of physical reality, which came to be seen as a continuum. An atom could no longer be seen in isolation from other atoms, but was seen instead as a small area of the electric field where strength of the field has a particularly high value, and where there is therefore, an intense concentration of field force. The French physicist Louis de Broglie saw particles as 'wave fields'. For the new physicists, the field, what is more, was not regarded in mechanical or even in material terms. It was 'a concept of relation', as Jerome Ashmore puts it, and was seen as exerting an 'organizing or coordinating action' on its constituents.

In the 1920s, Paul Weiss and A. Gurvitch sought to apply this new concept of the field to biology. Only in terms of this new paradigm, it seemed to them, could scientists explain the notions of form, organization, and the differentiation of the parts of any natural system. 'To me', Weiss writes,

> as an observer of nature, the Universe presents itself naively as an immense cohesive continuum. However, we usually do not look at it as such. We are used to looking at it as a patchwork of discreet fragments. This habit stems partly from a biological heritage, which makes focusing on 'things', such as prey, enemies, or obstacles, a vital necessity; partly from cultural tradition; and partly from sheer curiosity, which draws our attention and interest to limited 'objects'.

It is this 'immense cohesive continuum' of which a natural system is part that Weiss and Gurvitch referred to as its 'field'. C. H. Waddington also adopted this view of the living world. He defined a field as a 'system of order such that the position taken up by unstable entities in one portion of the system bears a definite relation to the position taken up by unstable entities in other portions.' V. Hamberger, one of the original formulators of this view of the living world, saw a field as

> a unit or a whole and not merely the sum of the cellular materials of which it is composed. The field with its organizing capacities remains undisturbed if the cellular material which it controls under normal circumstances is diminished or enlarged. The unit character of the field finds its clearest manifestation in these regulative properties.

In this way, the field controls or coordinates the action of the parts and can maintain its stability in the face of internal or external challenges.

The question we must then ask, is how a system interrelates with its 'field' in order to assure its own differentiated development along a constellation of chreods. Weiss draws attention to the intimate nature of the cybernism's relationship with its specific environment at every level of organization up to that of the individual and the environment.

> Each cell's genes are and always have been, a captive of an ordered environment. While, the genome contributes to the specific properties of that environment in mutual interactions with it during the whole course of embryogenesis, it is only by virtue of the primordial frame of organization of the cytoplasm of the egg that an individual can maintain from the very start the unity of overall design.

In other words, instructions, in this case genetic instructions, are not designed to be transmitted into a random environment. Information, as Louis Brillouin notes, is not something 'that can be poured into an empty vessel like fluid or even energy'. This is one of the most serious flaws in the neo-Darwinian theory of natural selection, in which behaviour is seen as determined by the genes acting in a random environment. The genes do not dictate, as Weiss puts it, but 'interact in cooperation with the whole of which they are part.' The instructions they issue will only be obeyed by systems that have been designed by their evolution and upbringing to receive, understand and believe them. This must be true of the transmission of instructions in all living processes, regardless of the level of organization at which it occurs.

As Waddington writes,

> No transmission system can effectively carry information between a transmitter and a recipient unless the recipient accepts the message as meaningful. . . . As the new born infant develops, for instance, it must be 'moulded' into an information acceptor . . . and an entertainer of beliefs.

But this is not enough. The receiver of a message must also be structured in such a way as to be capable of acting on the information adaptively. 'It is no use pushing the DNA of your sperm', as Waddington points out, 'into an egg unless the egg contains the polymerases capable of transcribing it into a messenger and all the rest of the machinery for turning out a protein according to specification.' In the same way, the cries of a baby in distress provide an important message to its mother who is not only predisposed to hear them and understand their significance but also to respond to them effectively, otherwise there would be no advantage to be gained from the ability to detect them. In other words, the child's message is only likely to be really effective within its immediate field, that of its family, within which the mother is the most essential member. Outside this field the message is likely to lead to a defective response and, if the field is particularly inappropriate, to no response at all.

This is a clear indication of why a child needs to be brought up in a family environment which displays the appropriate degree of order and cooperation. This is particularly important because the experiences of the very early years are the most critical. If a child is not brought up in appropriate conditions during these early years, it is likely to display aberrant psychological traits. Indeed, much of the delinquency and retreatism (drug addiction, alcoholism, schizophrenia) that is a feature of modern society seems to be at least partly due to the breakdown of the family and the community under the impact of economic development. (see Chapter 46) In spite of institutional education or government welfare services, the child deprived of a family is likely to remain emotionally and intellectually stunted. An extreme case is that of the children who have grown up in isolation such as Kasper Hauser or the wild boy of the Aveyron, or those brought up by wild animals who, in spite of all efforts on the part of those who sought to rehabilitate them, could never achieve a mental age of more than two or three.

As children grow older and venture out into the world at large, they undoubtedly require adventure, stimulation and challenges not previously encountered within the family unit. Indeed, living things can suffer not only from deprivation of environmental order but also from saturation by it. Thus a baby brought up in a womb-like family unit, whose every need is anticipated and who is allowed to take no initiative of any kind, is likely to be ill-adapted for dealing with the problems it will encounter when it leaves the family environment and ventures out into the world at large. Living things should develop within an environment or field that displays a specific 'order gradient' or 'gradient of cooperation', one that will vary in different social and ecological conditions.

It is clear that a natural system's 'field' is nothing more than its ordered environment. Indeed, if it had been realized before that an environment is necessarily highly structured rather than random, there would have been no need for the term 'field' or for 'field theory'. Unfortunately, however, neither the term 'field' nor the term 'environment' tend to be seen in the context of the Gaian hierarchy in terms of which their structure and function alone make sense.

---

# FORTY FOUR

# A system's field or its ordered environment is provided by the hierarchy of larger systems of which it is part

●

*Comparative embryology reminds us at every turn that the organism dominates cell formation, using for the same purpose one, several or many cells, massing its material and directing its movements and shaping its organs, as if cells did not exist.*

CHARLES OTIS WHITMAN

Like most of the basic terms used by mainstream scientists today (complexity, organization, competition, hierarchy, stability), the term 'environment' has never been properly defined. It is usually used loosely to refer to little more than 'all that is out there' and no one seems interested in asking what exactly *is* out there. The same can be said for the term 'field'.

Once we realize that every system is part of a larger system, it becomes clear that what is the environment of one system comprises, together with the system itself, the larger system of which it is part, to which it is homeotelic and to whose control it is subjected. Such control I shall refer to as homearchic (from the Greek *homeo* meaning same and *archos* meaning government) as opposed to heterarchic (from the Greek *hetero* meaning different and *archos* meaning government) which I shall apply to control by an external agent such as the state. This was clear to J. H. Woodger with reference to the cytoplasm, which provides the cell with its immediate environment:

> the word cytoplasm can be understood . . . simply in a topographical sense as meaning whatever is left after the removal of the nucleus. Now there is, of course, no such entity as this to be found in nature. What is found in nature, is a certain recurrent mode of organization amid the flux of events. And it is to this important fact that the cell concept gives expression.

B. C. Patten and E. P. Odum also complain that in ecology the term environment is never defined.

> The theory of ecology is not pat for us. We believe that to understand the organism in nature, the other half, environment, will have to be understood as well. At present, 'environment' means environment unspecified, but 'ecosystem' is environment specified.

Of course, it is not sufficient to see a living thing or a life process as part of a system that provides it with its immediate environment: we must see it, as Paul Weiss reminds us, in the context of its total environment, the hierarchy of natural systems of which it is part.

> What has confounded thinking has been that, due to inattention to the hier-
> archical structure of living beings . . . the term 'environment' has mostly been
> used indiscriminately without specifying the respective boundary. Sometimes,
> it meant that natural outer environment of the individual (nutrition, meteor-
> ological and social climate, stress, etc.) sometimes the 'milieu interieur' of
> body fluids and tissue associations, sometimes the cytoplasm around the cell
> nucleus, whereas in reality, as far as the genes are concerned, it comprises all of
> those to the extent to which they are in the last instance relevant for genic
> interactions. From the earliest stages of development on, every cell of the body
> constitutes an environment for all the others; every cytoplasm, for the nucleus
> and the cell organelles; every chromosome for the gene-strings in it.

The same argument applies to other life processes, including the upbringing of a child, day-to-day behaviour and the all-embracing evolutionary process. All involve feedback interactions, directly or indirectly, with every part of their environments, and hence with every system that makes up the hierarchy of the Biosphere, or what Claude Bernard referred to as the *milieu cosmique*.

To see the environment of a natural system in this way enables one to see one of the main defects of the neo-Darwinian theory of natural selection. The undefined and anonymous environment was and still is seen as having mysteriously acquired the capacity to 'select', with the most astonishing discrimination, those individuals that it judges as the 'fittest' – which is taken to mean the most individualistic and competitive. How it is capable of doing this, and indeed *why* it should *want* to do so, has never been explained. It all makes much more sense, once we see the environment or field as the highly organized environment provided by the Biosphere itself, being, like all its constituent sub-systems, endowed with the control mechanism required for controlling and coordinating the homeotelic behaviour of its constituent parts.

Weiss points to the various mechanisms that multicellular organisms develop to control and coordinate the activities of their constituent cells, 'the nervous system, the hormone system, the homeostatic maintenance of the composition of the body fluids'. Eugene Odum also sees ecosystems as possessing very elaborate mechanisms for controlling their constituent parts. (see Chapter 24)

To understand the role of the controlling process we must realize that the sub-systems come into being as relatively homogeneous individuals with great potentialities, but unable to constitute a viable, differentiated, orderly, natural system, capable of maintaining its homeostasis within the Gaian hierarchy. The role of the whole is primarily to oversee the transformation of this potentiality into effectiveness – to assure the differentiation of the parts so that each one is adjusted to its specific environment and to eliminate those that do not adjust and that are therefore random to the whole. Only in this way can the whole constitute a viable and adaptive natural system.

It is particularly important that this function is mediated at the higher cybernismic level where the information contained is plastic, or rapidly modifiable. In the case of human society, the differentiation and mutual adjustment of its individual members are accomplished by the remarkably sophisticated operations of the neo-cortex. It is at this level that general instructions derived from lower levels are differentiated into more particular instructions adapted to specific situations that may arise at any given moment.

Ragnar Granit sees the development of the human brain in order to achieve this essential function as 'true teleological purposiveness'. He quotes Charles Sherrington:

> the dog not only walks, but it walks to greet its master. In a word, the component from the roof-brain alters the character of the motor act from one of generality of purpose to one of narrowed and specific purpose fitting a special occasion. The change is just as if the motor act had suddenly become correlated with the finite mind of the moment.

In other words, potentially adaptive behaviour has been transformed into effectively adaptive behaviour by the process of differentiation involving adaptation to specific and possibly new conditions. The dog no longer walks in any old direction for any old purpose, *it walks to greet its master*.

# FORTY FIVE

# As the environment diverges from the optimum, biological maladjustment increases

●

*Almost all studies that attempt to reconstruct the history of infectious diseases, indicate that the burden of infection has tended to increase, rather than decrease, as human beings adopted civilized life styles.*
MARK NATHAN COHEN

Damage to the biosphere drastically brought about by the economic development we call progress is altering the environment of the living things that make up the Gaian hierarchy. Less and less does it resemble that to which we have been adapted by our evolution and ontogenetic development. For example, we now eat food that is grown by unnatural processes, which make use of a host of chemical substances: hormones, antibiotics, biocides (including insecticides, herbicides, nematocides, fungicides and rodenticides) of which residues are to be found in nearly all food commercially available today. Our food is then processed in vast factories with the result that its molecular structure is often totally different from that of the food we have been adapted to eat during the course of our evolution. It is further contaminated with other chemicals such as emulsifiers, preservatives and anti-oxidants designed to impart to it those qualities required to increase shelf-life and otherwise improve its commercial viability. We drink water contaminated with nitrates, heavy metals and synthetic organic chemicals, including pesticides, which no commercial sewerage works or water purification plants can entirely remove. We breathe air that is polluted with lead from petrol, asbestos particles from brake-linings, carbon monoxide and nitrogen oxides from car exhausts, sulphur dioxides from chimney flues, radioactive iodine, caesium and a host of other radionuclides from the flues of nuclear installations.

It is not surprising that in such conditions we should suffer from a whole range of new diseases, nor that they should be increasingly referred to as 'the diseases of civilization'. Samuel Epstein of the University of Illinois and other scholars attribute a very high proportion of cancers to exposure to chemicals in the food we eat, the water we drink and the air we breathe – a thesis that is, needless to say, fervently contested by the chemical industry and the experts they sponsor. Ischaemic heart disease, diabetes, peptic ulcers, diverticulitis, appendicitis, varicose veins and tooth caries, like cancer, are also diseases of civilization.

The incidence of these diseases is extremely low (in some cases nil) among vernacular people living in their natural habitats, as Albert Darmon and others have shown for the Solomon Islands, and Ian Prior and his colleagues have demonstrated for the Cook and Tokelau Islands over a period of thirty years. Such studies have also shown, however, that as people become exposed to the Western way of life, and in particular as they adopt the modern Western diet, the incidence of the same diseases increases dramatically. Infectious diseases, too, become much more common. This should not surprise us; in many ways, development creates ideal conditions for their transmission.

Thus vast urban conglomerations provide an environmental niche for the vectors of infectious disease in general. Modern agriculture has also put us in close contact with parasites that had previously established a stable relationship with the animals we have domesticated: one example is smallpox, a variant of cowpox; another is brucellosis. Malaria is transmitted by the anopheles mosquito which was originally a parasite of monkeys living on the canopy of tropical forests: well adapted to its hosts, it caused them only mild symptoms of the disease. Once the forests were cut down, the mosquitoes had to find alternative hosts and the most generally available one was man. The cutting down of forests in Amazonia has also brought man into contact with the vectors of leichmanosis, previously a disease of sloths and armadillos. The present pandemic of AIDS, which may once have been a disease of green monkeys or chimpanzees, may well have been transmitted to us in the same manner.

Large-scale irrigation projects have also provided an ideal habitat for water-borne diseases like malaria and schistosomiasis, spreading them to parts of the world where they were previously unknown. Modern highly intensive livestock rearing, in particular the offensive but presumably 'cost-effective' practice of feeding poultry on the carcases of their fellows, or on their own excrement, has caused their meat and eggs to be increasingly contaminated with such pathogenic bacteria as salmonella. The equally offensive practice of incorporating offal and other animal wastes in the feed of dairy cattle has led to an increase in the contamination of milk products with another pathogenic bacterium, listeria, and to the contamination of beef offal and possibly also beef with the vectors of Bovine Spongiform Encephalitis (BSE) which may or may not be transferable to man.

Ironically, the modern preoccupation with hygiene also gives rise to ideal conditions for the proliferation of pathogens. Pasteurized milk products can easily be colonized by micro-organisms, some of which could be pathogens, since in the sterile conditions provided they do not encounter any competition from other micro-organisms. This is the favoured explanation for the epidemic of listeria poisoning in Switzerland a few years ago. Poliomyelitis is also a disease of hygiene. Vernacular people, who as children were exposed to the micro-organisms present in soil and perhaps to animal excrement, and who were at the same time fed on their mother's milk, do not get it – but they become vulnerable once they are brought up in a hygenic environment and fed on cow's milk.

Greatly increased human mobility has also contributed to the spread of diseases: in a matter of weeks, if not days, any new outbreak will reach the major population centres of the world. Under such conditions, it is not surprising that the incidence of just about every infectious disease, with the exception of smallpox and poliomyelitis, is increasing worldwide. Meanwhile new diseases, such as AIDS, are appearing and there will undoubtedly be more of them, especially once genetic engineering really gets into its stride. It can only be a matter of time before our scientists release into the environment a genetically engineered pathogen, of which our species has had no evolutionary experience of any sort, with potentially disastrous consequences.

As ozone depletion increases over the next ten to fifteen years, which will happen even if we stop producing CFCs and other ozone-depleting chemicals today, we will be subjected to increasing ultra-violet radiation which will not only dramatically increase the incidence of skin cancer but also disrupt the functioning of our immune systems, making us correspondingly more vulnerable to both degenerative and infectious diseases. The health consequences of global warming are likely to be serious for the inhabitants of temperate areas, who will now be exposed to the vectors and pathogens that transmit a host of tropical diseases that make life very much more difficult and more precarious in the tropics than in the cooler areas of our planet. Lacking evolutionary experience of these diseases, they are likely to be all the more seriously affected by them.

To these problems, there is no effective technological solution. Medicine can certainly do little to help since it is largely concerned with treating symptoms of diseases, while to control their incidence would mean taking measures which lie outside the brief of the medical profession, (see

Chapter 65) and which would in any case be unacceptable both politically and economically, since it would mean reversing many of the essential processes of economic development or progress.

The molecular biologist and Nobel laureate Peter Watson suggests that if man cannot adapt to the world that science is bringing into being, then he must be changed. A new genetically engineered man must presumably be mass-produced, one who can adapt to and perhaps even thrive in the polluted and ecologically degraded world which modern man is substituting for the world to which we have been adapted by our evolution. Such a suggestion can only demonstrate to what extent mainstream science has lost touch with the real world in which we continue to live so precariously.

# FORTY SIX

# As the environment diverges from the optimum, social maladjustment increases

●

*The poverty in the black Puerto Rican neighbourhoods on the west side of Chicago is worse than any poverty I saw in West Africa. The people there are guided by strong traditional values. They do not live in constant fear of violence, vermin and fire. We don't find the same sense of desperation and hopelessness that you find in the American ghetto.*

ROBERT WURMSTEDT

Economic development causes our social as well as our physical environment to diverge from the optimum. Man evolved in the extended family, the lineage group and the small community, together with a host of 'intermediary associations' such as age-grades and secret societies. In other words, he evolved within a highly structured social environment, which we can regard as his social field (see Durkheim, 1964). (see Chapter 44)

With economic development, however, the community and the intermediary associations disintegrate. Edward Banfield, who made a sociological study of a South Italian village, was particularly struck by the alienation and demoralization of its inhabitants, a phenomenon known locally as *la miseria*. This, he found, was not basically attributable to the lack of material goods – what is normally regarded as poverty – but to the isolation of the families from each other, the absence of any wider social groupings. This, as we shall see, (see Chapter 60) he attributed to the usurpation by the state of the basic functions which the village should normally assume.

With the development of modern industry, the extended family itself disintegrates until we get an atomized society of which all that is left of the original social structure is a truncated nuclear family. Even that is eventually subject to further degradation and we end up with the one parent family, which in the worse case disintegrates still further into its individual members. (see Chapter 60)

There is yet another form of alienation. Families, communities and societies exist in time as well as in space. To be isolated from them thus makes of us temporal as well as spatial isolates – isolated from our ancestors and our children as we are from our contemporaries. This is reflected in our world-view. Whereas in a vernacular society a man sees his life as but a link in a long chain of being, a man in an atomized society such as ours sees it as something unique. When a man dies, all is over. That is one of the reasons why we in the West have so great a fear of death, a fear that is not shared by man in a vernacular society, who sees himself as living on in the person of his children. Concerned with the short term of a single life, we are less interested in the world we will leave to children, grandchildren and great-grandchildren. The notion that we owe nothing to posterity seems to justify, in the eyes of many people, our terrible egotism, the deliberate pillaging of the world's natural resources to which our society is so committed in order to maintain our present standard of material consumption.

Not surprisingly, people in such conditions become increasingly unhappy and depressed. A study undertaken by the Alcohol, Drug Abuse and Mental Health Administration of the United States Government documented how people 'born after 1945 are ten times more likely to suffer depression than people born 50 years earlier'; a second study found that people born after 1950 were twenty times more likely to suffer depression than those born before 1910. What is more, such depressions are afflicting much younger people than before.

Émile Durkheim referred to the alienation suffered by people deprived of a satisfactory social environment as 'anomie'. Robert McIver sees people as suffering from anomie 'when their lives are empty and purposeless, and deprived of meaningful human relations.' The disintegration of the family is possibly the most serious source of alienation or anomie and it is proceeding today at an unprecedented rate. In the USA, one parent families were a little more than 10 per cent of the total in 1970; the figure is more than 23 per cent in 1988. In the UK, the proportion of babies born to unmarried mothers was 28 per cent in 1990, up from 12.8 per cent in 1981. This is consistent with a 1990 report which predicted that by the end of the century 50 per cent of children in the UK would be brought up outside the family, which must inevitably bring about a further massive increase in social alienation. Significantly, the number of abandoned children in the UK is increasing. In South America it has already reached epidemic proportions, with about 10 million abandoned children at present roaming the streets of the major cities of Brazil and an estimated 30 million in South America as a whole, a figure that is expected to increase to 100 million by the end of the century. (see Brindle, 1990)

There is increasing evidence that deprivation of a satisfactory family environment will affect children profoundly and colour every aspect of their later lives. Such children are often referred to as emotionally disturbed. However bright they may be, they will tend to find it very difficult to fit into their social environment, the reason being that the early and most important stages of socialization were badly impaired. The earlier family deprivation occurred, the more will this be the case, as D. O. Hebb shows. School education cannot do much for emotionally disturbed children. They tend to have a short concentration span and are particularly concerned with the present and the short term, are loath to accept social constraints, and are predisposed to all pathological forms of behaviour such as delinquency, drug addiction, alcoholism and schizophrenia. When these young people are forced, at the same time, to live in squalid modern housing estates and are largely unemployed, as is increasingly the case today, their lot becomes hopeless. Theodore Dalrymple, a doctor on one such estate in the UK, describes the sheer hopelessness of the world in which he lives:

> I live in a wasteland. In the council estate the glass of many of the windows has been replaced by ply-wood; such gardens as there are have reverted to grey-green scrub, with empty beer and soft drink cans, used condoms and loose sheets of tabloid newspaper in place of flowers; and the people trudge through the desolation as disconsolately as in any communist city.

Dalrymple refers to the young men of the housing estates as 'bodily mature, but with the mind and inclinations of juvenile barbarians'. They

> eye the world with solemn hostility, which the tattoos on their knuckles, necks and forearms not infrequently express in words. They are unemployed and often profoundly unemployable; they are intolerant of any external restraint on their behaviour, and cannot fix their minds upon anything for more than a few moments. What job could one give them?

What makes matters even more hopeless is that these young people live in a moral and cultural void. 'In the absence of a system of values,' Dalrymple writes, 'adolescent revolt has become a permanent state of mind. Lack of belief in anything is compensated for by shrillness, as if mere noise could fill the inner void.'

The same hopelessness has been a feature of the welfare-maintained ghettos of the larger American cities for decades. Oscar Lewis describes the inhabitants of such areas as having a strong feeling of fatalism, helplessness, dependence and inferiority. Other traits include a high incidence of weak ego-structure, morality and confusion of sexual identification, or reflecting internal deprivation, a strong present time orientation, with relatively little disposition to dearer gratification and plan for the future, and high tolerance of psychological pathology of all kinds. There is widespread belief in male superiority, and among men, a strong preoccupation with machismo, their masculinity.

He refers to this situation as 'the culture of poverty' and sees it as a feature of the welfare-maintained slums of the industrial world. Today, however, it is spreading to other sectors of society and, at the current rate, it will probably not be long before the culture of poverty becomes the culture of industrial society as a whole. That economic development would lead to this state of affairs was intuited by Adam Smith himself. According to Lawrence Dickey, 'towards the end of the 1780s, Smith was becoming increasingly alarmed by what he referred to as "the depleting moral legacy" of commercial society.' Today, the breakdown in public morality is particularly alarming. A recent report by James Pattison and Peter Kerr, *The Day America Told the Truth*, shows that Americans live in a virtual moral vacuum. The authors of the report found

that 91 per cent of Americans lie regularly both at work and at home; 68 per cent believe there are no American heroes; 47 per cent are not certain that they would marry the same person again; 31 per cent of married people have had, or are having, an affair; 20 per cent lost their virginity before the age of 13; and 33 per cent of AIDS victims have not told their partners that they are infected.

Equally illustrative is the aberrant behaviour of people when the elaborate mechanisms of the law break down temporarily for some technical reason. In Montreal, during a 24-hour police strike, shops were pillaged, women raped, and houses burgled. In London, during a power strike, theft increased to such an extent in shops and department stores that many had to close until the light came on again. In San Croix, the capital of the American Virgin Islands, members of the Police and National

Guard were among those who took advantage of the chaos that followed a hurricane by looting stores and terrorizing island residents, many of whom barricaded themselves into their homes.

Crime is increasing at a record rate in the UK, in America and elsewhere. A study by Humberside Police Superintendent John Taylor predicts that by the year 2000 the number of recorded crimes in the UK will have increased from 4 to 6 million per year, and that only one in four is likely to be solved. Taylor considers that recorded crimes are merely 'the tip of an iceberg', no more than a quarter of those actually committed. If this is so, then in the UK by the end of this century, there would be 24 million crimes, nearly one for every two inhabitants. The crime rate in the US is even higher and it is worse still in many South American countries, especially in the cities where frequently order has simply broken down.

The victims of social alienation react in a number of different ways to their plight. One reaction among young slum dwellers is to organize themselves into street gangs – a rudimentary community that provides them at once with an identity, a goal structure, an embryonic cultural pattern and a means of achieving recognition and success, at least within their particular group. This gives rise to what Richard Cloward and Lloyd Ohlin refer to as the 'violent gang sub-culture'.

Another reaction to social alienation, more common among middle-class youths, is to indulge in some form of retreatism, isolating oneself from a way of life and an environment that increasingly fail to satisfy basic psychological needs. For American sociologist, Robert Merton,

> Defeatism, quietism and resignation are manifested in escape mechanisms, which ultimately lead him to 'escape' from the requirements of the society. It is thus an expedient which arises from the continued failure to near the goal by legitimate measures and from an inability to use the illegitimate route because of internalized prohibitions, this process occurring while the supreme value of the success-goal has not yet been renounced.

One obvious form of retreatism is alcoholism. Another is drug addiction, and the incidence of both these aberrations increases dramatically with social disintegration. Another form of retreatism is schizophrenia, which involves building up and seeking refuge in one's own world of fantasy. This and other forms of mental disease tend to increase with social disintegration, and are particularly in evidence among the members of a society undergoing acculturation (when a culture is breaking down under the influence of an alien one).

Durkheim regarded suicide as the ultimate manifestation of anomie. In one study he found that the suicide rate was particularly low in poor rural communities where social structures were intact and high in disintegrated affluent societies, especially among the working classes and even more so among Italian immigrants to the cities of Lorraine. He goes so far as to say that 'suicide varies in inverse proportion to the degree of integration of the social groups to which the individual belongs.'

The reaction of our political establishment to the increased incidence of all these social aberrations is to blame the victims. They are seen to be deficient in one way or another or 'unfit', in the terminology of social Darwinism. Often this is seen as an inherited problem and attributed to a faulty gene; numerous studies have been conducted to explain why this should be so. Thus the US government study on depression, cited above, attributed its growing incidence to a genetic cause. Criminals are often made out to be men with an X and two Y chromosomes, rather than single X and Y chromosomes, which is a more normal arrangement. Another ploy is to attribute these social aberrations to purely economic factors. They are seen to be caused by poverty, interpreted in purely economic and material terms, or to unemployment. Such interpretations conveniently rationalize further economic development which is inevitably seen as providing the only means of combating an economic problem. That economic development has itself brought these problems into being is suggested neither in political nor academic circles, for it would make nonsense of what remains the overriding goal of government policies throughout the world in which we live today – a goal which serves the immediate political and economic interests of politicians and their allies within the industrial community.

———

# FORTY SEVEN

# As the environment diverges from the optimum, cognitive maladjustment increases

●

*Man has been driven out of the paradise in which he could trust his instincts.*
KONRAD LORENZ

Our perceptive apparatus is admirably suited to providing us with the subjective knowledge of our relationship with our environment that we require for adaptive purposes, so long as we remain within the broad limits of the environment to which we have been adapted phylogenetically and ontogenetically. (see Chapter 13 and 43) As our environment moves beyond these limits, however, our perceptions become ever less useful for understanding it and for helping us to adapt to it: the condition of cognitive maladjustment.

Ross Hume Hall points out that we are cognitively maladjusted to eating modern processed foods and, as a result, are incapable of behaving adaptively towards them.

> Nature endowed us with the capacity to determine nutritional quality and safety of food so long as it was natural . . . But all this changes in the modern era . . . the taste of fabricated food is no reliable guide to freshness, nutritional quality, or whether the food will eventually kill you. The responsibility for safety and nutritional quality of what we eat has passed into the hands of scientists and administrators.

It is not only our senses, but our very intuitive faculties that cease to provide us with adaptive knowledge concerning our relationship with our environment. The problems that confront us become increasingly 'counter-intuitive', to use Jay Forrester's expression – though this is not because the environment is too complex, as he suggests, but because we have no evolutionary experience of it.

Whereas our ancestors had no difficulty in understanding their relationship with the living world, we have no means of understanding our relationship with the surrogate world we have created. What are the implications, for instance, of subjecting our children to X-rays; or permitting a nuclear power station to be built in the vicinity of our homes; of using CFC-emitting cosmetic sprays that erode the ozone layer which shields our planet from ultra-violet radiation; of cutting down the world's tropical forests; or indeed of countenancing the industrialization process itself? We depend for counsel on experts who are rarely objective and, even if they were, are unlikely to have been trained to take into account all the relevant factors involved.

It is not only our senses and our intuitive faculties that fail us before the brave new world to which economic development is giving rise; our very instincts cease to serve as a guide to adaptive behaviour. The instinctive behaviour of a child in a vernacular society is controlled via the socialization process and continues to be influenced by public opinion reflecting the traditional law that is homeotelic to the Gaian hierarchy. (see Chapter 53) Once social and ecological systems have disintegrated, however, bereft of these influences the child's behaviour becomes heterotelic to what remains of the Gaian hierarchy.

A typical example is our aggressivity. In a vernacular society, like all other forms of competitiveness it is ritualized and serves social ends. Its destructiveness is considerably reduced because vernacular technology is also under social control, which means that wars are fought with traditional and hence not particularly lethal weapons. (see Chapter 57) All this changes dramatically with economic development, when the associated social and cultural destruction removes the means of controlling our aggressivity and constraining the development of the most lethal and destructive armaments.

Thus we bring into being a world that has diverged so drastically from that to which we have been adapted by our evolution that the very mechanisms with which evolution has endowed us for maintaining the stability of our societies, and hence our own survival, now serve to achieve the opposite end. Edward O. Wilson, the founder of sociobiology, and other proponents of perpetual progress consider for that reason that we must suppress our instinctive drives, our emotions, our intuitive values and everything else that makes us human, in the interests of 'adapting' to the new world that progress is creating for us.

Undoubtedly the most alarming instance of cognitive maladjustment must be our failure to grasp the critical nature of the global environmental problems that confront us – deforestation, soil erosion, salinization and desertification, the general chemicalization of the environment, the depletion of the ozone layer and global warming. Only a tiny minority of our academics – not to mention our industrialists or politicians – show any concern at all for these daunting problems, and no measures of any consequence have been undertaken to solve them. At recent conferences held by the Conservative, Labour and Social Democratic Parties in the UK (1991), politicians discussed the usual vote-catching topics, obstinately refusing even to mention (save perhaps in a most cursory manner) the real issues that must determine our future and that of our children.

It may not be irrelevant to note that even very modest forms of life, like earthworms, dung beetles and fiddler crabs, have no trouble identifying the real problems they must deal with if they are to survive.

———

# FORTY EIGHT

# Man is psychically maladjusted to the world depicted by the paradigm of science

●

*Science has substituted for our world of quality and sense perception, the world in which we live and love and die, another world – the world of quantity, of rectified geometry, a world in which, though there is a place for everything, there is no place for man.*

ALEXANDER KOYRE

*It is time that man awakens from his millennial dreams, to face the reality of his isolation and of his solitude. He must realize that, like the gypsy, he lives on the margins of the cosmos – cosmos that is deaf to his music and indifferent to his aspirations, as it is to his sufferings and to his crimes.*

JACQUES MONOD

The world that progress is bringing into being is ever less tolerable to us psychically. Ethically and emotionally, it has no meaning. The Austrian psychologist Victor Frankl bases many of his observations on the concept of 'the will to meaning', which he contrasts with Adler's 'will to power' and Freud's 'will to pleasure'. For Frankl, one in four neuroses are of noogenic origin (originating in thought) and most of these, he believes, can be traced to our 'existential vacuum', the meaninglessness of life and the world about us.

This 'existential vacuum' is deepened by the modern scientific view of man as no more than a machine, responding robot-like to environmental stimuli. His innermost feelings, values and beliefs are little more than illusions; his family, community, society, even the natural world itself are no more than a seething mass of atoms and molecules, random, purposeless and uncaring. Frankl recalls his reaction to being told by his science teacher that life is nothing but combustion, an oxidation process. On hearing this, the schoolboy jumped indignantly to his feet. 'Dr Fritz,' he asked, 'if this is true, what meaning then does life have?' To which question the teacher presumably had no better answer that today's mainstream scientists.

Man is psychically adjusted to entertaining the chthonic world-view, or the 'old-Gnosis' as Theodore Roszak refers to it, in terms of which all the constituents of the natural world, whether they be 'animal, plant, mineral – radiate meanings: are intelligible beings' and integral parts of the cosmic hierarchy. Vernacular man did not have to be cajoled or coerced into accepting such a world-view. It came to him naturally, and it evolved as he was socialized into the culture of his ancestors.

Jacques Monod admits that vernacular man, or 'animistic man' as he refers to him, could see himself as an integral part of the natural world. 'Animism', he writes, 'established a covenant between man and nature, a profound alliance outside of which seems to stretch only terrifying solitude.' But today, science has revealed to us the terrible truth. 'The ancient covenant has been broken,' he tells us, 'man knows at last that he is alone in the immensity of the universe – a universe in which he has no function, to which he has no duties and in which he emerged by pure hazard.' Monod nevertheless considers that we have no choice but to continue along our present path. This is not the view of Gunther Stent. 'The dissolution of the covenant', he writes, 'presages the end of science, since there is little use in continuing to push the limits of our knowledge further and further, if the results have less and less meaning to man's psyche.'

# FORTY NINE

# The internalization of control increases

# stability

●

*The operation of rituals among the Tsembaga and other Maring helps to maintain an undegraded environment, limits fighting to frequencies which do not endanger the existence of original populations, adjusts man–land ratios, facilitates trade, distributes local surpluses of pig throughout the regional population in the form of pork and assures people of high quality protein when they are most in need of it.*

ROY RAPPAPORT

As systems develop, their homeostatic mechanisms become more sophisticated, their relationship with their environment more stable. In this process, controls become internalized. In the early stages of development, controls are crude and applied externally (heterarchically). The limit to the expansion of a population, for instance, will be set directly by the resources of its environment. If it expands beyond that limit, the population will be reduced by starvation and disease to a level that the environment can support. This is the only sort of population control that is reconcilable with the paradigm of science, which sees living things other than modern man as passive and robot-like, manipulated by some external agent.

One method of internalizing behavioural controls is through ritualization, a principle alien to industrial society's emphasis on bringing about the maximum environmental change with the minimum human effort. Ritualization does the opposite: it minimizes environmental change with the maximum effort. Contrary to what we have all been taught, it is the latter strategy which is usually most adaptive.

V. C. Wynne Edwards describes in detail how different living things have internalized population control. He notes that external factors – disease, starvation, accidents – play an insignificant role in controlling animal populations and concludes that they 'themselves must exercise the necessary restraints'. It is thus 'the threat of starvation tomorrow, not hunger itself today, that seems to be the factor that decides what the density of a population ought to be.'

The territorial system of birds, and also of some animals, helps to make this possible. Wynne Edwards notes that in the breeding season the male of many species of birds

> lays claim to an area of not less than a certain minimum size and keeps out all other males of the species; in this way a group of males will parcel out the available ground as individual territories and put a limit on crowding. It is a perfect example of an artificial mechanism geared to adjusting the density of population to the food resources. Instead of competing directly for the food itself, the members compete furiously for pieces of ground, each of which then becomes the exclusive food preserve of its owner. If the standard territory is large enough to feed a family, the entire group is safe from the danger of overtaxing the food supply.

There are many variations on this theme, some of which are more sophisticated. Wynne Edwards refers to them as 'social conventions' and sees them as providing the 'homeostatic machinery that prevents the growth of the population from departing too far from the optimal density.'

In vernacular human societies, these internal controls are even more sophisticated. Every tribal society, for instance, exploits a whole constellation of population control strategies built into its cultural patterns and imposed homearchically by public opinion and by the councils of elders. Many societies have taboos against sexual activity during lactation, or during the first year of widowhood, or before taking part in all sorts of different rituals and ceremonies. In India, among the Brahmins and related castes, widow remarriage is not permitted. This was, at one time, of considerable significance since it was customary for children to get married at the age of five or six: if the bridegroom were to die a few years later, his widow would never be allowed to remarry. Indeed, when the British first went to India they were horrified to find that there were literally hundreds of thousands of widows under the age of eight or nine. In Tibet, a considerable proportion of young people entered monasteries or nunneries. There is every reason to suppose that all traditional societies exploited a constellation of population control strategies that fitted into their particular cultural behaviour patterns (see Chapter 57) and were justified by their mythological and religious beliefs. Malthus was obviously unaware that in climax societies population control is internalized in this way, or he would not have declared that populations necessarily expanded until they were reduced by food shortages.

Gerardo Reichel-Dolmatoff explains how the mythology of the Tukano Indians of Colombia serves to rationalize a whole system of prohibitions against such undesirable trends as 'population growth, the exploitation of the physical environment, and aggression in inter-personal relations', which could otherwise destroy their ecological balance and threaten their survival. In their mythology, the superior forces of the earth frequently punish animal species that have become over-indulgent, aggressive or improvident. They serve as examples, not only to other animal species but to humans as well. 'Animals . . . are metaphors for survival. By analysing animal behaviour, the Indians try to discover an order in the physical world, a world order to which human activities can then be adjusted.' The prohibitions against eating different types of food and indulging in different types of sexual activity are very elaborate; as are the prohibitions on over-hunting and over-fishing. All animals are governed by the 'Master of Animals', who jealously guards his flock of deer, tapir, peccary, agouti, paca, monkeys and other species that the Tukano rely on for food.

Before anyone can go out hunting, he must first obtain permission from the Master of Animals, and this will only be granted if he undergoes a rigorous preparation which consists of sexual continence, a restricted diet and purification rites including cleansing the body by bathing and emetics. For some days before going on a hunting excursion, the man should not have had any dream with an erotic content. Moreover, it is necessary that none of the women who live in his household be menstruating. To make things even more difficult, a species can only be hunted after the constellation with which it is associated in the Tukano mythology has risen over the horizon. Even then, Reichel-Dolmatoff notes, the hunt is not a purely utilitarian affair, devoid of internalized controls. Highly ritualized, it is best regarded as 'a courtship, in which the prey has to be seduced to submit to the hunter'.

When game is scarce it becomes even more difficult to obtain permission. The prospective hunter must visit the Master of Animals 'in a narcotic trance' and promise to send to the Master's abode the souls of persons who, at their death, must return to this great storehouse to replenish the energy of those animals the supernatural gamekeeper gives to the hunters. In this way, the necessary controls for preventing over-hunting and over-fishing are built into the cultural pattern of the Tukano. What is more, fear of retribution from the superior powers of the earth – which usually takes the form of illness or misfortune in hunting – further secures the prohibitions against violation. (see Chapter 65)

With the breakdown of traditional societies under the impact of economic development, culturally internalized constraints of this sort cease to be operative. Unfortunately, external controls applied by the state and its specialized agencies are no substitute, which means that behaviour gets out of control and increasingly heterotelic. This will lead to the society's collapse, unless control is reasserted by some sort of social mega-mutation. (see Chapter 66)

---

# FIFTY

# Life processes are sequential and tend towards the most stable state

●

*That ecological succession is a developmental process and not just a succession of species each acting alone is one of the most important unifying theories in ecology.*
EUGENE ODUM

---

All life processes are sequential. This implies that their various stages must occur in the right order, so much so that if one stage is left out then the succeeding stages will not occur, or will occur imperfectly. It also implies that each stage must occur in the spatio-temporal environment or field to which behaviour at that stage is adaptive. Let me make this a little clearer.

All behaviour must be seen as modifying the environment, not in a random way but as part of a wider strategy. Thus the new environment will be that which will best serve to elicit the behaviour that leads to the next stage in the strategy. This does not mean that the whole process is predetermined in a precise way, for at each stage there may be a large number of variants of a basic behavioural response: the given conditions will determine which of these (whether one or more) will be adopted.

Jean Piaget is struck by the 'sequential character of development' which exhibits 'a series of stages, of which each one necessarily results from the preceding one'. Embryological development, because it occurs within a highly protected and ordered environment and so obviously constitutes a planned strategy, is quite clearly sequential in nature. Piaget and Bärbel Inhelder pointed out at Arthur Koestler's famous Ansbach symposium that

> learning is definitely dependent upon the subject's development level. Generally, in all this research, it has been shown that the child never manages to accomplish more than the passage from one sub-stage to the next without ever jumping a stage.

Another feature of sequential development is that it must occur at the appropriate rate. If it is speeded up or slowed down, the end product is unlikely to be optimum. The reason is that any behavioural process or strategy, because of the hierarchical nature of the Biosphere, is likely to be part of a larger process or strategy with which it must be synchronized. Rupert Riedl refers to the inertia caused by the need to synchronize a process with a host of others as its 'burden'. Piaget and Inhelder note the impossibility of accelerating the passage from one stage to the next. Indeed,

> if mechanisms in mental development can be compared to what Waddington

in embryology calls 'chreods' or necessary paths with a 'time-tally' it appears obvious that development always has an optimum rate, neither too slow nor too fast.

The sequential principle in ecology is known as 'ecological succession'. Succession was regarded by Frederick Clements as fundamental to the developing science of ecology. Nature, he considered, did not move aimlessly but in a steady flow toward stability. In a specific environment, a clear progression could be plotted through what Clements called a 'sere' that begins in the pioneering stages with an unbalanced and relatively unstable assemblage and ends with a complex and stable equilibrium community, capable of sustaining itself indefinitely. Clements accentuated the role of climate in determining the nature of the sere and also established the principle that in any given habitat the sere could only end in a single climax (monoclimax). Both these positions later came under serious attack.

Clements's theory of succession to the climax, as Donald Worster notes, undoubtedly reflected his 'underlying, almost metaphysical faith that the development of vegetation must resemble the growth process of an individual plant or animal organism.' This view is unacceptable to modern science and hence to modern scientific ecology on a number of counts. Firstly, it tends to confirm the scientifically unacceptable idea that an ecosystem is a 'superorganism' as Clements maintained, or at least that it resembles an organism in a significant way. Secondly, it implies that the development of an ecosystem is not the result of random changes selected by an undefined environmental 'invisible hand' in accordance with the Neo-Darwinian thesis, but occurs instead according to an orderly strategy. Thirdly, it implies that this strategy is carefully coordinated by the ecosystem, which means that ecological development is at once teleological and holistic, which is doubly anathema to mainstream scientists and scientific ecologists for whom life processes are random and atomized.

It is unacceptable for another closely associated reason, which is that it implies that the goal of ecological development is the achievement of stability, whereas our modern industrial society is committed to perpetual change in a single direction. This requires the reversal of the successional process or sere and the artificial maintenance of an ecosystem at its most productive pioneering stage, marked by discontinuities such as floods, droughts, epidemics, population explosions and wars, a highly desirable situation that justifies continuous technological interventions that add up to GNP.

To accept the principle of ecological succession to a climax is thus to accept the destructive nature of economic development, and so modernist ecologists eventually had to reject Clements's thesis and succession came to be seen instead as largely random. As Herbert Gleason, who first formulated the new view of succession in 1927, wrote: 'In the centre of an association we see only the fluctuations in structure from year to year.' He even suggested that succession might be retrogressive. (see McKintosh, 1975)

The whole question of succession to a climax came to a head during the debate over the great dustbowl in the late 1930s. Ecologists, at the time, showed that the crisis was man-made. Ploughing the delicate southern plains, ecologists maintained, should never have been undertaken. It caused the land to diverge from its climax state and the dustbowl was the inevitable consequence. During the debate that followed, the very notion of a 'climax' came under attack. Arthur Tansley was particularly keen to discredit the concept. He insisted that man, with his great ingenuity, was capable of creating his own climax, an 'anthropogenic climax' as he called it, which he insisted could even be superior to the natural variety.

Clements's climax was also attacked very bitterly by the agricultural historian, James Malin. For him the large-scale mechanized agriculture, which was seen by ecologists as responsible for the dustbowl, was another step in the march of progress. The plains had benefited from it, nature needed to be ploughed up, and 'blowing dirt around was necessary for it to remain vigorous and fertile.' Frederick Clements was the bogey man. His writings provided the rationale for the 'hysterical' conspiracy against progress and had to be discredited. Indeed, 'the conventional and traditional concept of the state of nature must be abandoned – the mythical, idealised condition, in which natural forces, biological and physical, were supposed to exist in a state of virtual equilibrium, undisturbed by man.' Malin never bothered to disguise his motives. The idea of a climax 'assumed the end of change', and hence of economic development, which they saw as a panacea for every possible problem.

Ironically, it is the anti-ecological ideas of Gleason, Tansley and Malin that have come to be regarded as the ecological orthodoxy. It is the view of R. E. Ricklefs that 'in recent years the concept of the climax as an organism or unit has been greatly modified to the point of outright rejection by many ecologists, with the recognition of communities as open systems whose composition varies continuously over environmental gradients.' In line with current scientific dogma, ecological succession is explained in terms of competition and related to the properties of populations rather than whole ecosystems. S. D. Putman and R. J. Wratten tell us that pioneering species are replaced 'not just because the environment does not suit them but because they are poor competitors and competition is more intense in climax ecosystems.'

It is difficult to see how they can really believe this. The operation of all sorts of internally generated negative-feedback mechanisms (Eugene Odum's 'environmental hormones') which inhibit the growth of species that are displaced in the succession towards a climax is clearly visible to all but the most prejudiced eye. Ricklefs alludes to the operation of such a mechanism when describing the process of succession on abandoned farmland in the piedmont region of North Carolina. He describes how

> decaying horseweed roots stunt the growth of horseweed seedlings: this self-inhibiting effect, whose function and origin is not understood, cuts short the life of horseweed in the sere. Such growth inhibitors presumably are the byproduct of other adaptations that increase the fitness of horseweed during the first year of succession. If horseweed plants had little chance of persisting during the second year, owing to invasion of the sere by superior competitors, self-inhibition would have little negative selective value.

Putman and Wratten also refuse to accept that the development of an ecosystem towards a climax is part of a long-term strategy. This means that the climax cannot be taken to its logical outcome; instead it must be seen as 'thrust upon' the system from the outside. For this reason they suggest that we abandon the use of the term climax altogether and use instead the term 'end community'.

How then does their version of succession occur? Putman and Wratten offer the sort of simplistic explanation that can be quantified and modelled by systems ecologists. They suggest that succession is the result of 'an accumulation of biomass' which stops when the process comes up against gross features of the environment that are immutable, such as a shortage of resources for further growth. Alternatively, they see it in purely energetic terms as 'an imbalance within the energy relations of the community resulting in the accumulation of biomass by the community.' Both these explanations are based on the notion that the behaviour of an ecosystem is random, mechanistic and individualistic: it is thus uncoordinated, passive and externally controlled like all the life processes that have been made to fit the Procrustean paradigm of science.

Putman and Wratten go further. Productivity, they tell us, is often low in a climax compared to earlier stages in the succession: 'due to the complexity of web-design, cycling of materials through the system is extremely slow.' Such features of a climax have traditionally been regarded as beneficial. But Putman and Wratten wonder if they really are. They point out that there are 'many examples of far more productive, indeed far more diverse communities characteristic of earlier pre-climax seral stages.' They then ask whether a climax is, in fact, tantamount to over-maturity? The argument assumes that productivity is the yardstick for judging ecosystems – the position taken by Tansley and Malin when they opposed the application of any constraints on man's ecologically destructive agricultural activities in the southern plains. Unfortunately, Putman and Wratten are thoroughly representative of modern ecologists whose work serves to rationalize technological progress. Inevitably, they wonder whether a biological explanation of succession towards a climax is even necessary. All we are witnessing, they suggest, is an example of a 'statistical process known as a "regular Markov chain".' (see Chapter 11)

Eugene Odum is one of the few modern scientific ecologists to retain a holistic view of succession. For him the main features of the process are the 'more or less directional and predictable sequence of populations', its ability to correct divergences from its optimum course (C. H. Waddington's chreod) which will lead to the requisite climax, and its achievement of an increasingly sophisticated and stable state as it reaches its climax, thereby converting 'an inorganic environment to a more organic one' (see Odum, Eugene, 1969). (see Chapter 64)

---

# FIFTY ONE

# Increased complexity leads to greater stability

●

*The term 'complex' (as used by modern ecologists) need imply no more than a haphazard conglomeration, whereas in the living system, we find distinctive orderliness of the complexes.*
PAUL WEISS

Until recently ecologists have tended, along with Charles Elton, to assume that as a system becomes more complex it also becomes more stable – though Eugene Odum considers that complexity tapers off some time before a climax, the most stable state, is achieved. Today, however, the link between complexity and stability is denied by most mainstream ecologists.

One of the books that has played an important role in changing this view is R. M. May's *Stability and Complexity in Model Ecosystems*. Influenced by those built by A. S. Lotka and Vito Volterra, May's model is seriously flawed. Underlying it is the assumption that a system's complexity can be measured by the number of its constitutent parts without considering the way they are organized, let alone their wider role within the Gaian hierarchy.

This notion of complexity does not help us to understand the structure and function of the Biosphere. To state that a system is 'complex', in this sense of the term, does not tell us whether it is healthy or unhealthy, stable or unstable. Thus a highly destructive ecological invasion, such as that brought about by the introduction of the rabbit into Australia, or the walking catfish into Florida, *increases* the number of the consistent parts of these ecosystems; and the fact that it tends to reduce their health, integrity and stability can, of course, be construed as confirming May's thesis that complexity reduces stability. May actually admits this.

> The stability of complex continental ecosystems was no armour against the Japanese beetle, the European gypsy moth or the Oriental chestnut blight *Edothia parasitica* in North America. It is trivial but not irrelevant to observe that stability was hardly enhanced by the extra links added to the trophic web in these instances.

Indeed, to introduce into an ecosystem a living thing that has been designed by its evolution to fulfil a very different role as a constituent of a very different ecosystem, can only increase randomness and reduce its organized 'complexity'.

Ilya Prigogine also insists that increased 'complexity' is associated with growing instability. This for him is confirmed by the fact that the world is becoming ever more complex, yet, at the same time, increasingly unstable. It is this instability, in fact, that is reflected in the ever-growing fluctuations – floods, droughts, epidemics and wars – that are everywhere apparent. In his particular scheme of things, however, these fluctuations are highly desirable because they justify economic development or progress. The complexity that Prigogine refers to is again of the random kind, which offers no basis for distinguishing between the *Biospheric complexity* required to maintain the integrity and stability of the real world and the *technospheric complexity* created by economic development, which is heterotelic to the Biosphere and necessarily disrupts its critical order and stability.

The fact is that neither Prigogine nor May can handle organized complexity for it is extremely difficult to quantify and hence to model. Not surprisingly, the model that May builds to prove that complexity reduces stability bears little relationship with the real world. Among other things, the underlying assumptions are totally unrealistic. (see Chapter 12) Thus May admits that his model only applies to systems with an even number of species, a 'disquieting' thought, he agrees, but not one that leads him to question its intrinsic value because, for his purposes, 'whether or not the Lotka-Volterra equations are applicable to real-world situations is beside the point being made here, which is that simple mathematical models are in general less stable than the corresponding simple mathematical models with few species.' In order words, he is not concerned with the relationships between complexity and stability in the real world, but only in his mathematical model. In the real world, May admits (though only as an afterthought), things may be different.

In the real world, complexity is not random but organized and purposive. The various parts of a complex system do not come into being by random proliferation, but by the coordinated integration and differentiation of its adaptive functions to increase its stability or homeostasis in the face of specific environmental conditions. Thus in a simple ecosystem, for instance, different species of herbivores are relatively undifferentiated eaters. A mountain goat must be able to eat practically anything if it is to survive its inhospitable habitat, so much so that a slight increase in the population of other species is sufficient to cause a shortage of the basic foodstuffs they have in common. Complex ecosystems however, are far less vulnerable to such discontinuities. Impala and eland in the African savannah, for instance, have a much more specific diet. They will not only eat different plants but often different parts of the same plants. This means that a population explosion of one species will not necessarily reduce the availability of food for the other species. An increase in the number of predator species must also further refine the quantitative and qualitative controls they apply on prey populations. In these, and a host of other ways, a system becomes more stable as it becomes more complex.

There is a cost, however: the greater the specialization and the commitment to specific environmental conditions, the smaller the range of possible responses which a system is capable of mediating, and hence the fewer the environmental challenges to which it can respond adaptively. This means that the more highly integrated a system, the less capable it is of tolerating serious internal or external challenges.

Thus a tropical rainforest is a highly integrated and complex system judged by the standard of other ecosystems (though clearly it displays nothing like the degree of integration of a biological organism). For this reason it does not withstand improbable external disturbances. Cut down its trees, for instance, and it does not really recover, whereas a simpler and less integrated system such as a savannah can recover from similar treatment much more readily. That is why Clifford Geertz wrongly regards a tropical rainforest as being less stable than a paddy field. The human organism, being still more highly integrated, is correspondingly more vulnerable to a disturbance. Deprive it of the organs that ensure essential metabolic functions, such as the liver or the kidneys, and it too will fail to recover.

Natural systems can only function adaptively (maintain their homeostasis) within specific conditions. (see Chapter 43) In the case of complex integrated systems, these conditions are often very specialized. For this reason, certain ecologists have maintained that such systems are nonpersistent. But this is not so, for on the basis of a very long experience such living things can assume, usually with justification, that these specialized conditions will be maintained. (see Chapter 30)

What is more, why such conditions have been maintained can very easily be explained. A system together with its environment constitute a larger system. This larger system, by maintaining its own stability, assures the orderliness of the environment to which its sub-systems are submitted and hence the stability of their relationship with their environment. Thus an embryo will tolerate only minor changes in the highly ordered environment or field it requires. However, it cannot on this account be regarded as unstable. The requisite orderliness of its internal environment is assured by virtue of its being an integral part of the hierarchy of natural systems whose goal it is to maintain overall stability. Similarly, a child can only function in an environment or field displaying a certain measure of order, that of the family. This does not mean that it is unstable or non-persistent, as this orderly environment is preserved by the normal behaviour of the various members of the family unit. The family itself is designed to function in an environment or field that also displays a certain measure of order, and this is provided by the community. This pattern of integration extends all the way up the hierarchy of the Biosphere. In other words, though a complex integrated system may only be able to adapt to a limited range of environmental conditions, changes that are outside this range are unlikely to occur, because of the orderly and predictable environment provided by the hierarchy of natural systems of which it is part. In other words, it displays high *resistance* stability. (see Chapter 22)

A less complex and less integrated system may be able to adapt to a wider range of environmental conditions, but it is not insulated in the same way from these conditions, which are correspondingly more likely to occur. For this reason the system must be more capable of dealing with them, displaying the requisite level of *resilience* stability. In both cases, the system's capacity to deal with change in the environment to which it has been adapted by its evolution seems commensurate with the probability of the occurrence of such change. This must be so, if the system is to maintain its stability and hence survive.

---

# FIFTY TWO

# By increasing its diversity a system increases the range of environmental challenges with which it is capable of dealing

●

*No single organism can make use of all forms of energy and nutrient resources, attack all host genotypes, survive in all temperatures and moisture conditions, or self resist all forms of predation.*
DAVID PIMENTEL

*Monocultures are almost invariably prone to disease.*
MIGUEL ALTIERI

There does not seem to be any generally accepted distinction between complexity and diversity. In the ecological literature these terms tend to be used almost synonymously. Diversity is generally considered as having two components. The first is 'species richness', also referred to as 'species density', a measure of the total number of species present in an ecosystem. The second is 'species evenness', a measure of the relative abundance of the different species present and of the extent to which the most abundant ones dominate. It is difficult to see what is to be gained by including these two different and not necessarily connected notions under the same heading of 'diversity'. How can such a concept help us to understand the role of natural systems within the Biosphere, let alone their role in maintaining its critical order? (see Chapter 53)

There is considerable apparent redundancy in the natural world. Flies, ticks, herrings and many other forms of life produce a vast number of offspring, of which but a minute fraction will survive and reproduce. Only a very small proportion of the genes that make up the human genome are made use of in protein-synthesis. The others, often referred to as 'junk genes', are regarded as redundant. A human can lead an apparently normal life even when deprived of half the neurons that make up his neo-cortex. The rest might also be regarded as redundant 'junk neurons'. A population, too, can be reduced drastically without its ability to survive being impaired, at least in the short-term.

It would be presumptuous, however, to suppose that the systems involved have not been affected in some way by the reduction in the number of their constituents. Eugene Odum obviously thinks they have, for he considers that to increase an ecosystem's redundancy must also increase its stability. There would then be more than one species capable of fulfilling a specific function, and hence if one became extinct the others could take over.

Redundancy is a misleading term to use. One of the basic techniques used in biotechnology is cloning. This means growing large numbers of plants that are all genetically identical. However, as Patrick Mooney puts it, 'genetic uniformity in crops amounts to an invitation for an epidemic to destroy that crop.' The world has already experienced the terrible consequences of an agricultural system's dependence on too narrow a genetic base. The best known consequence is Ireland's nineteenth-century potato economy. The bulk of the population of that country lived off the potato, cereals being produced largely for export to England. Since the potatoes were of a single variety, it was only a matter of time before the whole crop would be struck by a disease. When this happened, 2 million people died and several million more were forced to seek a new life in North America. In 1970, the world was reminded of this danger when the USA lost 15 per cent of its maize crop to corn blight. Fortunately the superpower did not depend on maize for its sustenance; in many Third World countries, such a blight would have been a catastrophe.

Genetic uniformity also reduces a population's adaptive capacity. Thus D. J. Merrell and J. C. Underhill failed to induce resistance to DDT among inbred strains of the fruit-fly (*Drosophila melanogaster*) after two and half years' exposure to that poison. In contrast to this, resistance to DDT was induced in normal wild populations in less than six months. C. H. Waddington also found that genetic assimilation (see Appendix 4) 'fails completely, at least over periods of fairly small numbers of generations, in inbred strains lacking genetic variability.'

Not surprisingly, 'uniform redundancy' does not occur in the natural world. It is not part of the strategy of Nature. Natural redundancy is highly diversified and the Biosphere's capacity to create this diversity is stupendous. We all know just how many different words can be constructed by using an alphabet of 26 letters. Similarly, it would seem that an almost limitless number of instructions can be issued by using the genetic code of four basic nucleotides; and that an almost limitless number of different forms of life can be generated from the twenty different amino acids required to make proteins. Not surprisingly, the Biosphere is not only capable of generating an incredible number of different species, but also of different sub-species, varieties and individuals.

This diversity enables a natural system to deal with a very wide range of both internal and external challenges – not a random but a specific range – that which in the light of the system's phylogenetic and ontogenetic experience, is most threatening and most likely to materialize. The more diversity a system displays, the more unthreatening and the more improbable the challenges it is capable of dealing with. In such conditions the sub-systems must be able to act very much more on their own. Each must be specialized in dealing with different possible challenges. On the other hand a complex system, displaying very little diversity and organized to adapt with great accuracy to very specific environmental conditions, would only be capable of dealing with the most threatening and the most probable challenges.

It might be useful to think of the role of diversity as one of insurance against discontinuities. Thus the most significant feature of tribal agriculture is the incredible diversity of the crops (and varieties of the same crop) that are grown. According to the ecologist Peter Freeman, among Central African farmers

> fields of sorghum and millet are commonly composed not only of different varieties, but even of different species of the same genera. As for rice, maize, groundnuts and voandzu, it is more a matter of mixtures of different types than of varieties distinguished one from another.

In peasant societies the same principle applies. Peasants are imbued with what has been termed the 'subsistence ethic'. Their concern is not to maximize yields but to reduce vulnerability and hence discontinuities such as droughts, floods or plant epidemics. As James Scott writes,

> the tradition of seed varieties, planting techniques and timing was designed over centuries of trial and error to produce the most stable and reliable yield possible under the circumstances. . . . Typically, the peasant seeks to avoid the failure that will ruin him rather than attempting a big, but risky, killing.

Such prudence is, however, inimical to the development of the market and hence to the interests of industrialists and politicians. To satisfy them, production and consumption must be maximized and insurance sought via market mechanisms. This motivates farmers to adopt precisely those methods – biologically, socially and ecologically disruptive – that will maximize rather than minimize risk. There is no effective substitute for diversity as an insurance against discontinuities.

It is often very difficult to determine which of the constituents of a natural system contribute to its complexity, and which contribute to its diversity. Many must contribute to both. The planting of a large number of different crops by traditional agriculturalists increases not only the diversity but also the complexity of the agricultural ecosystem. In a well-planned intercropping system, early established plants tend to reduce soil temperature and produce the appropriate micro-climate for other plants. Plants also complement each other in terms of nutrient cycling: thus deep-rooted plants can act as 'nutrient pumps', bringing up minerals from deep down in the sub-soil. Minerals released by the decomposition of annuals are taken up by perennials. The nutrient intensity of some plants is compensated for by the addition of organic matter to the soil by others. Thus cereals benefit by being grown in conjunction with legumes, which have deeper roots permitting a better use of nutrients and soil moisture, and root nodules which host bacteria specialized in fixing nitrogen. All these crops thus play a significant role in the metabolism of the agricultural ecosystem and thereby contribute to its complexity. On the other hand, such crops retain their ability to react individually to many environmental challenges. Because the system is not too highly integrated they can fulfil two roles, contributing to both the complexity and the diversity of the ecosystem.

It is interesting to note that some natural systems that are organized to display great diversity can, if required to deal with new environmental changes, transform this diversity into complexity and vice versa. A typical example is the slime mould, a small amoeba-like creature which normally lives in colonies that display considerable diversity. When there is a shortage of *Enterechia coli* – the bacteria on which they feed – they undergo an impressive metamorphosis, joining together to form a highly differentiated multicellular organism displaying a corresponding degree of complexity. As soon as their food supply increases this organism breaks down once more into its constituent parts, complexity yielding to diversity.

The same thing occurs among vernacular human communities. When faced with an external challenge, they organize themselves to form larger social groupings – as did the Bushmen in their struggle against the Bantu invaders, and as occasionally did the Indians of North America in their struggle against the colonial invaders. There is every reason to suppose that had these native peoples won their struggle, and kept out the invaders, they would afterwards have resumed their normal lifestyles in the traditional social groupings within which such lifestyles are best led – complexity once more giving way to diversity.

# FIFTY THREE

# Natural systems are homeotelic to Gaia

●

*One cannot help being struck by the way in which the cells in an organism not only cooperate but cooperate in a specific direction towards the fulfilment and maintenance of the type of the particular organism which they constitute.*
JAN SMUTS

*The land is one organism. Its parts, like our own parts, compete with each other and cooperate with each other. The competitions are as much a part of the inner workings as the cooperations.*
ALDO LEOPOLD

All cooperation implies goal-directedness or purposiveness. Natural systems, as differentiated parts of the Gaian hierarchy, share the common goal of maintaining its critical order or stability, for only in this way can they maintain their own critical order and hence their own stability. It is significant that there is no term in the English language for this essential type of cooperation which must necessarily underlie all other forms of cooperation within the natural world. So I have had to coin a new word – homeotely, from the Greek *homeo* (same) and *telos* (goal).

At the level of a biological organism, the operation of this principle is clear. As Lucien Cuenot notes, 'birds that fly can do so because a thousand details converge; long wing and tail feathers; pneumatic bones; airsacs; breast bone and pectoral muscles; design of the ribs; necks; feet; spinal column; pelvis; automatic hooking of feather barbules etc.' All the features of a bird conspire to enable it to fly. All are homeotelic to its flying activities, while flying is itself homeotelic to the maintenance unit of the critical order of the birds within the Gaian hierarchy.

The same principle applies to a community and a society. Anthropologists of the 'functional' school saw cultural behaviour as ensuring the integrity and stability of social systems. For A. R. Radcliffe-Brown, the function of a behavioural trait is the contribution which it makes 'to the total activity of which it is part' while, 'the function of a particular social usage is the contribution it makes to the total social life as a functioning unit of the total social system.'

The principle of homeotely must clearly apply to all natural systems. Thus Ludwig von Bertalanffy accentuates the 'whole-maintaining character' of life processes:

> The most convinced representative of an ateleological point of view must admit that actually an enormous preponderance of vital processes and mechanisms have a whole-maintaining character; were this not so, the organism could not exist at all. But if this is so, then the establishment of the significance of the processes for the life of the organism is a necessary branch of investigation.

He cites E. Ungerer as another who was so impressed by the 'whole-maintaining' function of life processes that he decided to replace the biological 'consideration of purpose' with that of 'wholeness'.

If we accentuate the temporal rather than the spatial aspect of a natural system, seeing it as a process rather than an entity, it is apparent that it is a strategy made up of a number of closely associated steps which must occur in the right order. Only when these successive steps are seen in terms of their specific contributions to the process as a whole do they have any meaning. The development of an embryo in the womb is not a series of ad hoc moves, but part of a carefully coordinated strategy designed to give rise to an end-product, the human child; every step in an ecological succession contributes to the achievement of the ecosystem's goal, a climax state. Each step could be seen superficially as cooperating with others, but in reality it cooperates with the process as a whole, for what is happening only makes sense if it is seen teleologically.

The coordination of homeotelic processes is particularly impressive. The processes occurring within an organism, for instance, clearly do not interfere with each other's functioning. Thus food cannot be properly digested if the blood does not circulate adequately, nor can the circulation of the blood take place in an organism that is no longer capable of digesting its food and which, as a consequence, is wasting away from starvation. In other words, the sort of trade-offs encountered in a modern society do not occur.

It is not so obvious but equally true that this coordination of homeotelic activities occurs in all natural systems, whether they be stable societies, climax ecosystems or Gaia herself. This was fully understood by Radcliffe-Brown. He saw a society's social structure as depending for its continued existence on the 'totality of social usages', which provides it with its 'functional unity', a concept which he defines as 'a condition in which all parts of the social system work together with a sufficient degree of harmony or internal consistency, i.e. without producing persistent conflicts which could neither be resolved nor regulated.' He notes that this view of society is in direct conflict with the view that culture is no more than a collection of 'shreds and patches' for which there are 'no discoverable significant social laws'.

Competitive as well as cooperative behaviour serves to maintain the critical order of the cosmos, and can therefore be regarded as homeotelic.

Thus the competitive activity that serves to eliminate randomness within any natural system must be homeotelic to that system and to the hierarchy of natural systems of which it is part. Competitive strategies that serve to space out populations and increase diversity are similarly homeotelic.

Predators have an obviously homeotelic function to fulfil within an ecosystem. Their role is to apply qualitative and quantitative controls on the prey populations, maintaining their optimum size, organization and viability, and helping to maintain at the same time the optimum structure of the ecosystem of which they are part. An individual zebra does not see the lion that is stalking it as a benefactor, yet its behaviour is undoubtedly beneficial to the zebra population as a whole. It is thus only if one sees predator/prey relations holistically that their homeotelic nature becomes apparent. Significantly, predatory behaviour is encouraged by the prey species itself. Thus, behind a herd of Cape buffalo there is often a much smaller herd of stragglers, made up of the old and weak. If one of the stragglers tries to join the main herd, it is pushed out. It is on the stragglers, of course, that the lions will concentrate, for to attack the main herd would be too daunting a prospect. In a sense, both predator and prey cooperate to ensure that it is the old and weak – one might say the random elements – that are eliminated, so as to maintain the viability of prey populations required to assure the critical order of the Biosphere. (see Chapter 40)

The homeotelic nature of predatory behaviour becomes clearer still when one is faced with the ecological consequences of removing predators from the ecosystems in which they would normally live. In Bangladesh, for instance, frogs were being caught in vast numbers and exported to satisfy the very considerable market for frogs' legs in France and elsewhere. The result was a population explosion for all the insects on which the frogs fed, leading to a massive increase in the use of pesticides required for controlling them. Eventually, it is said the cost in pesticides became greater than the income derived from selling the frogs.

The removal of predators has also led to a reduction in the ecological diversity required to maintain an ecosystem's stability. S. D. Putman and R. J. Wratten note that the removal of the starfish *(Pisasta ochracens)* in the intertidal ecosystem in California caused a dramatic ecological change. Instead of the original fourteen species, only eight remained; of those, only four were among the eleven species preyed upon by the starfish. They admit that predators therefore seem to 'enhance production of individual prey populations' and 'create and maintain diversity within a community.'

Why do living things behave homeotelically to the hierarchy of natural systems of which they are part? The reason must be that they are the differentiated parts of larger systems, in isolation from which they have no meaning, cannot survive, or, in the case of a loosely integrated system, can survive only imperfectly and precariously. As Eugene Odum writes,

> because each level in the biosystem's spectrum is 'integrated' or interdependent with other levels, there can be no sharp lines or breaks, in a functional sense, not even between organism and population. The individual organism, for example, cannot survive for long without its population, any more than the organ would be able to survive for long as a self-perpetuating unit without its organism.

From another perspective, they must behave homeotelically because the hierarchy of larger systems provides them with their field, the environment to which they have been adapted by their evolution and upbringing and which, as Stephen Boyden points out, must best satisfy their most fundamental needs.

The dependence of the parts on the whole cannot be better illustrated than by the tendency of parts of a natural system to reorganize themselves, after separation and even after having been shuffled like a deck of cards, into something approaching their original configuration. Paul Weiss notes how this is true of a virus, the bacteriophague T4. When its parts are mixed *in vitro*, they reassemble of their own accord and the reconstituted virus is quite capable of fulfilling its normal functions. Michael Polanyi notes that freely floating cells form disassociated embryonic skins; cartilage and kidney tissue, if thrown together at random, reassociated themselves to form 'higher stages of the tissue in question'.

Perhaps the most striking example of this phenomenon could be obtained if one were to shuffle the members of a family or of a climax community in such a way as to create a random assemblage of individuals. Like the parts of the bacteriophague or the embryonic kidney tissue, they would quickly reorganize themselves into their natural groupings. Indeed, one can imagine the frenzied efforts that mothers would make to locate their children; children to find their mothers; fathers to search for their wives and children; elderly grandparents to reintegrate themselves into their families. Members of different lineage groups and village communities also seek each other out, as they do when they migrate to big cities which, in Africa, tend to be clearly divided up into distinct tribal areas. Much the same thing occurs in Western cities. In New York, for instance, different ethnic groups such as the Jews, Irish, Italians, Germans, Puerto Ricans and Blacks live very largely in separate ethnic communities, even when, as is usually the case, the state is committed to integrating such separate groups into the vast anonymous mass society that best suits its heterarchical purposes.

---

# FIFTY FOUR

# In a vernacular, society education is

# homeotelic to Gaia

●

*Education is the cultural process . . . in which each new born individual is transformed into a full member of a specific human society, sharing with the other members a specific human culture.*

MARGARET MEAD

*By definition children are pupils and learning is a human activity which least needs manipulation by others. Most learning is not the result of instruction. It is rather the result of unhampered participation in a meaningful setting.*

IVAN ILLICH

Education in a vernacular society is but another word for socialization, a process whereby a child born with a potential for becoming a member of almost any family, community or society learns to become a member of a specific family, community and society. (see Chapter 44) In other words, from the point of view of the society itself, it is the means for renewing itself, or progressively reproducing itself, by integrating successive generations into its critical structure.

A functionally similar process occurs at all levels of organization. Thus a cell, immediately after division, is also endowed with the potential for becoming a member of a large number of possible tissues or organs, and slowly learns to fulfil its specialized functions within that tissue or organ in which it is situated. (see Chapter 43) The process of cell development or differentiation is also the means whereby the organ or tissue, and indeed the organism itself, can reconcile the necessarily short lifespan of its constituent cells with its overall goal of maintaining its stability and that of the Biospheric hierarchy of which it is part.

Not surprisingly, the educational process is governed by precisely the same general laws which govern the differentiation of a cell, the development of an embryo and indeed all other homeorhetic (see Chapter 25) life processes at different levels of organization. One such law is that behaviour proceeds from the general to the particular. It is during the earlier phases that the generalities of a child's behaviour pattern will be determined. It is these earlier stages which are the most important and that is why the mother is the most important educator and the quality of the family environment the most significant factor in determining a child's character and capabilities. Another complementary law is that behavioural processes are sequential, their various stages occurring in a specific order. If one is left out, it must follow that the subsequent ones will either not be able to occur at all, or will occur at best imperfectly. Thus what a child learns during its formal institutionalized education cannot make up for any deficiency in the earlier phases of its upbringing. This is the conclusion that most serious studies have revealed. J. S. Coleman, for instance, whose massive study led him to examine the careers of 600,000 children, 6000 teachers and 4000 schools, reported in 1966 'that family background differences account for much more variation in achievement than do school differences.'

This is also the conclusion to the US government study *Equality of Education Opportunities*, published in 1964, which stated that 'variations in the facilities and curriculum of the schools account for relatively little variation in pupil achievement', the most important factor measured being the home background of the individual child. If their educational upbringing is deficient then the incidence of the symptoms of faulty socialization – emotional instability, delinquency, drug addiction and alcoholism – are likely to increase correspondingly.

Like all life processes, education in a vernacular society is highly dynamic, the child being an active participant rather than a consumer of educational merchandise. In such conditions, institutions are largely unnecessary. It suffices to introduce a child into the dynamic social process so admirably described by O. F. Raum in his seminal book *Chaga Childhood*.

> The child is not a passive object of education. He is a very active agent in it. There is an irrepressible tendency in the child to become an adult, to rise to the status of being allowed to enjoy the privileges of a grown up. . . . The child attempts to force the pace of his 'social promotion'.

All homeorhetic life processes are closely integrated. C. H. Waddington emphasizes the close integration of individual chreods within the constellation of chreods that makes up the epigenetic landscape, noting that 'the sequence of changes by which the fertilized egg becomes an adult animal always involves considerable interactions between neighbouring parts of the embryo.' The development of a child into an adult in a vernacular society proceeds in the same way. The child develops a close interaction with the different members of various social groups – its lineage group, its age grade, its clan, the secret society to which it may belong – and hence with the community that these different social groups constitute.

If education is identified with socialization, then each society must require a different type of education. Thus the programme which will transform a Chaga child into an adult member of society, capable of fulfilling specific functions within a very distinctive African tribe, cannot conceivably be the same as that which will enable a baby Eskimo to learn equally specialized but very different functions as a member of a family and small community geared to survival in the inhospitable Arctic regions. A Chaga with the education of an Eskimo is, from the point of view of Chaga society, uneducated, as he would be were he to have been educated in a Western school or university.

The colonial powers sought to destroy the cultural patterns of traditional societies largely because many of their essential features prevented traditional people from subordinating social, ecological and spiritual imperatives to the short-term economic ends served by participation in the colonial economy. There is no better way of destroying a society than by undermining its educational system. Thus, as John Middleton tells us, 'the learning of genealogies of the families and clans as among the Ashanti and the Baganda, the recognition of social groupings in hierarchical tribal settings and of their reciprocal relationships, the hearing of tribal history in praise songs and legends told at tribal gatherings' – none of these essential socializing activities were deemed worthy of the curriculums of institutionalized Western schools. They had little contribution to make towards the achievement of the overriding economic goals of colonial regimes. This meant, however, that the young were deprived of that traditional knowledge which alone could make them effective members of their societies. Unable to renew themselves, traditional societies were doomed to annihilation and their citizens to becoming isolates in an anonymous mass society in which they usually fulfilled menial functions.

In the modern world we have lost sight of the true role of education. The main reason is that our society has disintegrated – and if there is no society, then of course there can be no socialization. In these conditions education must mean something quite different. Among other things, it requires that children be educated in specialized institutions instead of in their families and communities. Indeed, the isolation of education has dramatic consequences. For one thing it ceases to be a spontaneous vernacular process and becomes instead an institutional one. The results are dramatic. As Coleman writes,

> this setting-apart of our children in schools which take on ever more func-

tions, ever more extra curricular activities for ever longer periods of training has a singular impact on the child of high school age. He is 'cut off' from the rest of society, forced inward towards his own age group, made to carry out his whole social life with others of his own age. With his fellows, he comes to constitute a small society, one that has most of its important interactions within itself, and maintains only a few threads of connection with the outside adult society. Consequently, our society has within its midst a set of small teenage societies, which focus teenage interests and attitudes on things far removed from adult responsibilities and which may develop standards that lead away from those goals established by the larger society.

The child is cut off from society for another reason. It is that modern education is concerned with training people for a career in the predominantly urban industrial world – the technosphere. It is said in India that when a young person gets a high school diploma, he leaves his ancestral village for the nearest town; when he gets a university degree, he moves to the city; and when he gets a PhD, he leaves the country for Europe or America. Instead of providing the village with a means of renewing itself, education thereby provides instead a means of assuring its inevitable demise.

---

# FIFTY FIVE

# In a vernacular society, settlements are

# homeotelic to Gaia

●

We need our *marae* [the traditional Maori meeting compound] for a
host of reasons:
That we may rise tall in oratory.
That we may weep for our dead.
That we may pray to God.
That we may have our feasts.
That we may house our guests.
That we may have our meetings.
That we may have our weddings.
That we may have our reunions.
That we may sing.
That we may dance.
And there know the richness of life.
And the proud heritage that is truly ours.
MAORI   GREETING   CHANT

Vernacular settlements, through the ages, were designed to satisfy the needs of the whole Gaian hierarchy. To begin with, they were small. Vernacular man usually lived in communities of between fifty and a thousand people. Aristotle considered that a city should not contain more than 5400 people – the number that could comfortably gather into the Athens marketplace.

Ecologically the temporary settlements of nomads are the most desirable, because they have the smallest impact on the environment. The anthropologist W. E. H. Stanner goes so far as to say that Australian Aborigines probably had less impact on their environment than do many non-human animals, like beavers who build dams and termites who build nests; an Aborigine encampment, a year or so after its abandonment, is almost impossible to identify.

Even when fixed, the needs of small settlements for timber and firewood can be met without annihilating local forests; their need for food does not overtax the soil; and their wastes can be absorbed by the local ecosystem without degrading it.

This clearly cannot be said of even the cities of antiquity. It is no coincidence that the sites of most of the capital cities of the civilizations that once thrived in tropical and sub-tropical areas are now occupied by deserts. The decline and fall of these cities has been attributed to a number of factors, but among them must surely be reckoned the fatal impact of these massive conurbations on fragile ecosystems. Thus in about 1500 BC, the great Indus civilization drew to an end. Its principal city, Mohenjo Daro, was built of kiln-baked bricks. Its demise could have been predicted on purely ecological grounds, for among other things it has been estimated that 400 square miles of forest would have had to be cleared just to fire the bricks for a city of this size. If this process had continued for centuries, it would have led to such serious soil deterioration that the surrounding area would no longer have been able to support the city (see Wheeler, 1959). The impact of our modern industrial cities on their environment is very much greater and correspondingly more destructive.

From the health point of view, the small settlement is also desirable. Its inhabitants will be exposed to relatively low levels of pollution, and it does not provide the niche required to sustain a viable population of some of the principal pathogens affecting human populations. George Armelagos considers that

> Small, isolated populations are incapable of the continuous transmission of disease, and outbreaks of endemic infectious disease, where they do occur, are likely to be periodic or sporadic. This is a consequence of the lack of potential hosts in a small population. If the disease pathogen cannot survive until it comes into contact with a new host, the disease will not be maintained in the population. Many infectious diseases, amongst them measles and influenza, require an interacting population of 500,000 individuals in order to be maintained.

The American historian William McNeil has shown how infectious diseases throughout history have spread in one direction: from the urbanized countries of the West to areas where people still lived in small and much healthier settlements.

Settlements must also be small so that each man can have contact with nature. Man has evolved as part of the world of living things. It is doubtful if he can live in the totally artificial environment that we have created in our cities with biological and psychological impunity. René Dubos, that great microbiologist and ecologist, went so far as to question whether 'man can retain his physical and mental health if he loses contact with the natural forces that have shaped his biological and mental nature.' Not surprisingly, urban man often tries desperately to create something of nature in the concrete jungle in which he lives. Thus we see balconies in urban apartment blocks shrouded in vegetation, sprouting from rows of plastic pots. In the background, we can sometimes even hear recorded versions of the sounds of nature, the wind blowing through the trees, a bubbling brook, or the song of the humpback whale.

Settlements must also be small in order to satisfy social requirements, for the structure of human settlements must reflect that of the societies whose physical infrastructure they provide (see Rappaport, Amos, 1978). The basic social unit is undoubtedly the extended family and it is this that must first of all be accommodated. The settlement must also accommodate the lineage group and the community. Each, moreover, must have its requisite element of privacy.

In an Australian Aboriginal encampment, for instance, we find that each family has its own space – the area that the family sweeps several times a day. This place is protected by a windbreak (*wiltja*) and at the edge of it there is a fire. The family spaces are grouped around a larger central space. In the darkness of the night they cannot see each other and thereby have the privacy they require, further enhanced by the custom that once it is dark people do not leave their family space for fear of malignant spirits that lurk around it.

In a traditional Zulu village, according to Eileen Jensen Krige, the huts are arranged in a circle around the cattle kraal; the chief's hut is always situated in the same position and those of the wives are arranged in order of seniority. The kinship group (whose blood relationship may be real or fictitious) that inhabits such a village also has the necessary privacy, with a considerable space between the grouped huts of each family.

The Motilone Indians of the Amazon forests, according to Robert Janlin, live in settlements called *bohios*, which accommodate ten to thirty families under a single roof. Inside the *bohio*, there is semi-darkness. Each family has a space partitioned off from other families. Each, too, has a fire in front of its space, blocking the view from the central circular public space.

According to Paul Stirling, the traditional Turkish village is made up of households organized into groups that tend to occupy the same quarters or wards (*mohalle*). The cities of the Yoruba of Western Nigeria are also divided into areas inhabited by different extended families, which are further organized into neighbourhoods inhabited by closely related families. Those inhabiting adjoining areas are also related, although less closely. The city is thus a hierarchical system of houses, compounds, neighbourhoods and clusters of neighbourhoods of related people: these are closely built and larger spaces separate less closely related groups. In this way the settlement pattern reflects the society's social structure.

The evidence suggests that it is by following these principles that social problems in modern conurbations are reduced to a minimum. Thus Valerius Geist points out that successful modern building designs have been those that limited people to social groups close in number to those found in primitive societies. We can recognize three limits, one of about eight persons mimicking the size of an extended family, one of about twenty-five, mimicking a hunting band; one of about two hundred which is the limit of people that any one individual can recognize . . . .

A successful building should have less than 200 inhabitants, and should be broken into units housing clusters of about 25 people of five families. Had architects designed public housing units keeping these 'magic numbers' in mind, they would have taken one step towards reducing anonymity.

Conversely, a number of anthropological studies have shown the consequences of modernizing the settlements of stable societies to satisfy market requirements. Robert Janlin has shown how such changes led to the disintegration of the society of the Motilone Indians. The French anthropologist Claude Lévi-Strauss has also described this process as it affected the Bori Indians of Brazil.

A village or small town must also be arranged so as to confer on it a feeling of wholeness and oneness. In south-west France, the two neighbouring towns of Marmande and Villeneuve-sur-Lot are said to exert very different influences on their inhabitants. The former is stretched out along a main road, the latter, an ancient *bastide*, is built round a central square. Of the two, it is the latter which is known for its spirited community.

Cities, if we are to have them, should also be designed on similar principles if they are to satisfy social needs. The central square is a very important feature, offering a place where the citizens can gather to run their affairs. The Greeks could not conceive of a city without its *agora*. Significantly, in the industrial cities of the West, as economic concerns take over from social ones, it is the shopping precinct with its multi-storied carpark that is the focal point.

Houses, squares and other parts of the settlement should serve as many purposes as possible so as to maximize social contacts. As Nicholas Hildyard notes, it is when the whole spectrum of classes, ages, occupations and activities are concentrated into one localized area

that the tight mesh of relationships, which form the basis of a community, can develop. Dissect the community, and like a dissected body, it eventually dies. Instead of one community, one gets a series of disjointed, fluid, and highly unstable groupings. By fragmenting activities, one quite simply fragments social relations.

That is precisely what we are doing today. 'Work belongs to the industrial estate; play to the playground; leisure to the leisure centre; sleeping and eating to the housing estate; shopping to the shopping centre; growing old to the old peoples' home; being ill and dying to the hospital; being rich to one area; and being poor to another.'

A settlement should also be compact, the houses close together. Instead of expanses of lawn and concrete there should be narrow streets, maximizing social contact. As Peter Blake writes:

> What the city needs is not wide open spaces, but tightly structured spaces full of shops, restaurants, markets and all the rest. The one sure way to kill cities is to turn their ground floors into great spacious expanses of nothing – 'into a sort of social no man's land'.

A society's monuments are also important in that they confer on a settlement its identity, as do its language and customs which help to differentiate it from its neighbours. More than that, they are associated with the community's heroes, its founders, its religious leaders, all those who symbolize the city and serve to sanctify it. This contributes to its identity and its continuity, and helps make people proud of it – which they need to be, if it is to be a real community.

A settlement must be aesthetically satisfying, which means providing an interesting and also a diverse environment, as vernacular settlements succeed in doing. Psychologically, this diversity is as necessary as its absence in the faceless conurbations where more and more people live is intolerable. Indeed, as Lewis Mumford writes,

> If man had originally inhabited a world as blankly uniform as a 'highrise' housing development, as featureless as a parking lot, as destitute of life as an automated factory, it is doubtful that he would have had a sufficiently varied ex-

perience to retain images, mould language, or acquire ideas.

The depressing effect of living in such conditions was brought home to us during an electoral campaign in Walsall, a suburb of Birmingham, some years ago. My wife, Katherine, and I, together with a number of our friends, had come from Cornwall to help Jonathan Tyler, then Chairman of the Ecology Party (now the Green Party), to contest a parliamentary seat. In a bar, Katherine met a group of young men with whom she tried to discuss the town in which they lived. They showed little interest in doing so: 'We are ashamed of our town', they told her.

There could be no starker contrast with the attitude of young people in Siena towards their beautiful city. This could not be more evident than after the Palio, when the young people of the winning Contrade strut triumphantly through the streets all night – and indeed, for several days and nights afterwards – singing the traditional Palio song:

> In the Piazza del Campo
> Where the verbena grows
> Long live our Siena
> The most beautiful of all cities.

> Long live our square
> The town and the chapel
> Long live our Siena
> the most beautiful of all cities,

Significantly, Siena is socially an ideal city, with an extremely low incidence of crime and other social aberrations.

Needless to say, during the industrial age, those who have planned and built our cities have almost totally ignored all these considerations. Over the last fifty years, particularly, our settlements have been designed almost exclusively with economic and utilitarian ends in view, and the results, as we all know, have been catastrophic.

Finally, another essential feature of a settlement is its sanctity. Vernacular man could not consider living in a house or settlement that had

not been sanctified and hence ritually integrated into the cosmic hierarchy. Thus before a wild and uninhabited area could be inhabited, sacred
rites had to be performed so as to 'cosmicize' it. Ananda Coomaraswamy
tells us that in the *Rig Veda* the word *vima*, meaning 'measure out' or 'lay
out', is used to refer to 'the bringing into being of inhabitable space' or the
laying out of 'abodes of cosmic order'.

To build a new village or city meant first building a holy house, or
temple, on the cosmic model (see Chapter 61). In this way, the settlement
that surrounded it was integrated into the cosmic hierarchy. The traditional ceremony performed to dedicate the site was a re-enactment of the
original creation, or cosmogenesis. Thus when Romulus founded Rome,
he dug a small ditch in the form of a circle. He threw into it some sacred
earth that he had brought with him from the town where his ancestors
were buried, and each of his companions did likewise. In this way, Rome
remained *terra patrum*. The ditch was always known as Mundus, which
apparently referred to the place the *Manes* or ancestors lived, and which
also meant the world or cosmos. (see Eliade, 1971)

Believing that he, his artefacts and his settlements were integral parts
of the cosmic hierarchy, chthonic man saw them all as designed according
to the same basic plan. According to Fred Eiseman, an authority on
Balinese culture, man

> is a tiny part of the overall Hindu-Balinese universe but he contains its struc-
> ture in microcosm. Man's body has three parts – head, body and feet – just as
> the universe, macrocosm, has three parts: the upper world of God and heaven,
> the middle world of man, and the underworld. Man is a kind of scale-model of
> the universe, with exactly the same structure – as is the island of Bali and each
> village, temple, house, compound, building and occupant of it.

Titus Burckhardt, too, notes how 'in vernacular societies, every dwelling is
seen as an image of the cosmos, for every house or tent "contains" and
"envelops" man on the model of the great world.'

The great Colombian anthropologist Gerardo Reichel-Dolmatoff shows
how true this still is of the temples built by the Kogi Indians of Colombia.

Kogi temples are meant to be cosmic models, models that convey a sense of world order and, simultaneously are interpreted as the body of the Mother. Each post, beam or rafter, up to the smallest detail of roof constructions, thatch or vines, used in tying together the different parts, has its specific symbolic values. A temple construction can be read as an anatomical model, a geographical model, a model of social structure and organization, or priestly ritual, or of the upper and netherworlds; it also is an instrument for astronomical observation.

This was also true of the ancient Jewish temple. According to the *Midrash Tadische* (see Patai, 1947), it 'corresponds to the whole world and to the creation of man who is a small world.' In an ancient Jewish legend, Yahveh asks Moses to build him the temple.

'How shall I know how to make it?' Yahveh answered, 'Do not get frightened; just as I created the world and your body, even so will you make the Tabernacle. You find in the Tabernacle that the beams were fixed into sockets, and in the body the ribs are fixed into the vertebra and so in the world the mountains are fixed into the fundaments of the earth. In the Tabernacle there were bolts in the beams to keep them upright and in the body limbs and sinews are drawn to keep man upright and in the world trees and grasses are drawn in the earth. In the Tabernacle there were hangings to cover its top and both its sides, and in the body the skin of man covers his limbs, and his ribs on both his sides, and in the world the heavens cover the earth on both its sides. In the Tabernacle the veil is divided between the Holy Place and the Holy of Holies, and in the body the diaphragm divides the heart from the stomach, and in the world it is the firmament which divides between the upper waters and the lower waters.'

That the settlement itself is seen as reflecting the same cosmic structure is well established, and vividly demonstrated by the encampments of the Omaha People of North America, whose overall pattern was that of a wide circle – a tribal circle called Hu-dhu-ga. This cosmic representation was divided into two halves. One, called In-shta-sun-da, represented the heavens; the other, Hun-ga-she-nu, the earth. These divisions were in turn subdivided into clans, and each of the (ten) clans had its particular symbol or totem. Each totem, in turn, represented a cosmic force, one of the various forms of life on earth.

By seeing his body, his house and his settlement as reflecting the same critical order, which is also that of his society of the natural world and of the cosmos itself, vernacular man confirms that his life is subject to the same single law that governs the cosmic hierarchy, and that he is a participant in the great Gaian enterprise, whose goal it is to maintain the critical order of the cosmos.

# FIFTY SIX

# In a vernacular society, economic activity

# is homeotelic to Gaia

●

*I owe the public nothing.*
JOHN PIERPONT MORGAN

*The outstanding discovery of recent historical and ethnographic research is that man's economy, as a rule, is submerged in his social relationships. He does not act so as to safeguard his individual interest in the possession of material goods; he acts so as to safeguard his social standing, his social claims, his social assets. He values material goods only in so far as they serve this end.*
KARL POLANYI

*Economics is based on* homo economicus *as a self-interested individual who commends policies that inevitably disrupt existing social relationships. These social costs can be considered only as externalities and are actually little considered even under that heading. For the most part they are hardly noticed. We believe these social costs are of enormous importance, that the increase of gross global product at the expense of human well-being should cease. We believe human beings are fundamentally social and that economics should be refounded on the recognition of this reality. We call for rethinking economics on the basis of a new concept of* homo economicus *as person-in-community.*
HERMAN DALY AND JOHN COBB

Modern economics is supposed to determine how scarce resources should be distributed within a society. Its basic assumption, which is never questioned, is that such resources should be distributed so as to maximize wealth. Wealth is measured in terms of per capita Gross National Product (GNP), which is the sum of all economic transactions within a nation state. This means that to maximize wealth means maximizing transactions, or trade.

Neither of these two assumptions can be accepted. If economics concerns itself with the distribution of scarce resources, this is largely because it is only when resources are scarce that they can be sold at a profit, which is when corporations find it worth their while to produce and distribute them. This is so much the case that much of their work involves creating artificial scarcities, firstly by creating a market that did not exist previously for goods which they have developed or plan to develop, and secondly, by building into these goods what is generally referred to as 'planned obsolescence'. However, for thousands of years prior to the development of the formal economy, the food and artefacts required to satisfy human needs were not necessarily in short supply. Scarcity was not a feature of the economy of vernacular man R. B. Lee and I. Devore insist and Marshall Sahlins agrees with them.

Thus it would be more appropriate to adopt George Dalton's view of economics as dealing with the provision of material goods to satisfy biological and social needs. This is what Karl Polanyi refers to as the 'substantive' use of the term economics as opposed to the 'formal' use of the term. I propose a still more general meaning, to refer simply to the study of how resources are distributed within a natural system. In this way we could expand our study to include the economics of biological organisms, ecosystems, vernacular society and the Biosphere itself. Clearly all require resources of various sorts, such as nutrients, to ensure their sustenance and hence preserve their critical order or stability. If we accept the thesis of General Systems Theory, (see Chapter 38) we may also suppose that the same fundamental laws govern the distribution of resources in all natural systems, regardless of their level of organization.

The most fundamental of such laws is that resources are distributed so as to maintain the integrity and stability of the system within the Gaian hierarchy of which the system is part. This aim imposes the necessary consideration that our planet's resources are finite, for the Biosphere is a closed system from the point of view of materials though it is an open system from the point of view of energy. This means that materials must be constantly recycled, the waste products of one process serving as the raw materials of other processes. Recycling materials is necessary, too, in order to avoid their accumulation in any given area, which would give rise to randomness or pollution. Thus, during photosynthesis, carbon is extracted from carbon dioxide in the atmosphere and the oxygen is released. Oxygen is a waste product of this particular process, but it is the essential raw material for another process, that of breathing by animals. Recycled from one living process to another, oxygen is thereby regarded from one living process to another as are all the chemicals required to sustain the living systems that make up the Biosphere and to maintain the critical chemical composition of the Biosphere and its atmosphere.

Another essential cyclic process is the food chain, which should really be referred to as the 'food cycle': the primary producers (grass, algae, phytoplankton), which alone can harness the energy of the sun, are eaten by herbivores, who in turn are preyed on by carnivores; their dead bodies, together with other dead matter, being eaten by scavengers; and what remains being broken down by micro-organisms into the nutrients required by the primary producers, so that the cycle can renew itself. All living things, including vernacular man, cooperate in assuring the success of this cycle, without which life would not be possible.

The need to recycle materials was built into the cultural pattern of all traditional peoples. It was not seen as a scientific requirement but as a moral one. Interestingly enough, the principle is formulated in the sole surviving fragment of the writings of the philosopher Anaximander. 'Things perish into those thing out of which they have their birth', he writes, 'according to that which is ordained; for they give reparation to one another and pay the penalty of their injustice according to the disposition of time.' Anaximander intimates here that the development of living things is an injustice – a violation of both fate (Moira) and righteousness (Dike) or morality. 'Birth was seen as a crime,' as F. M. Cornford puts it, and growth as 'an aggravated robbery'. It must follow that reparations had to be made to the natural world; the living things that committed the offence must return to the dust from which they came. Martin von Hilde-brand shows that a very similar notion is built into the cultural pattern of certain Amazonian Indian tribes of Colombia.

Modern man violates this fundamental law of natural economics in everything he does; in doing so, he is spelling his own doom. Human waste, instead of being carefully returned to the soil – the practice of end-less generations of traditional farmers – is simply consigned to the nearest waterways. Twenty billion tons of it, every year, deprives the soil of its fer-tility and poisons our waterways, reducing their capacity to support fish life. Agricultural produce, instead of being consumed locally by those who produce it, is exported as systematically as the timber from our woodlands – a one-way process stripping the land of essential minerals and organic matter. The American agronomist F. H. King, noted in his classic *Farmers of Forty Centuries* (1904) how traditional farmers in Japan, Korea and China – countries which he visited at that time – meticulously returned all organic matter to the soil, as a result of which its fertility had been maintained for more than 4000 years. In his words, he had travelled 'from practices [in the USA] by which three generations had exhausted strong virgin fields . . . to others still fertile after thirty centuries of cropping.'

The economic activities of modern man are interfering ever more dra-matically with the most fundamental Gaian cycles – water, carbon, sul-phur, phosphorus – thus disrupting the critical order of the Biosphere and reducing its capacity to support life. This is unfortunately inevitable if eco-nomic development remains modern man's overriding goal. For it is a one-way process, in which the Biosphere is systematically transformed into the technosphere and technospheric waste – a process that cannot continue indefinitely.

That resources within a natural system are distributed for the purpose of maintaining its integrity and stability is clear at the level of a biological organism. Thus, oxygen is transported via the red corpuscles to all parts of the body in accordance with its requirements; so are the various nutrients that the body requires. This principle is even clearer when a scarcity occurs. In such conditions, the natural system is perfectly capable of set-ting up its own rationing system. Nutrients are provided to the parts in accordance with the importance of their contribution to the preservation and hence the stability of the living whole. Not surprisingly, the last parts of the organism to be deprived of nutrients are the nervous system and the heart. As Ralph Gerard points out, 'One can get along without a digestive system quite well under starvation conditions, a great wasting of muscles can be tolerated, the reproductive system isn't important, and so on; but if the heart stops pumping or the brain functioning, the whole system is gone.' In the same way, in cold weather, a rationing system becomes operative in preserving the necessary temperature of the critical parts of the body. To begin with, there is a reduction in the blood flow to the surface of the skin, reducing radiation and conduction. This may proceed so far that the skin is frozen and dies, the subordinate unit sacrificed 'for the protection of the larger unit'. Such behaviour is an essential part of an organism's homeostatic mechanism. The same principle applies within a vernacular society. It is well known that in times of food scarcity, hunter-gatherer groups will make food available to the adults who are necessary for assuring the continuity of the society – the old, who are more dispensable, and the very young, who can be replaced, are sometimes sacrificed.

If the economic system of vernacular society is subject to the same laws that govern the economics of other systems, then it cannot be governed by the laws that our modern economists have formulated and that they assume to be of universal application. This was first pointed out by the economic historian Karl Polanyi, who showed that in the vernacular world *homo economicus* was conspicuous by his absence, and economic activities were largely conducted to satisfy social rather than commercial goals.

> The outstanding discovery of recent historical and anthropological research is that man's economy, as a rule, is submerged in his social relationships. He does not act so as to safeguard his individual interest in the possession of material goods; he acts so as to safeguard his social standing, his social claims, his social assets. He values material goods only in so far as they serve this end. Neither the process of production nor that of distribution is linked to specific economic interests attached to the possession of goods; but every single step in that process is geared to a number of social interests which eventually ensure

that the required step be taken. These interests will be very different in a small hunting or fishing community from those in a vast despotic society, but in either case, the economic system will be run on non-economic motives.

Polanyi also notes that in behaving in this way vernacular man was serving his own immediate interests, for vernacular society

> keeps all its members from starving unless it is itself borne down by catastrophe, in which case interests are again threatened collectively, not individually. The maintenance of social ties, on the other hand, is crucial. First, because by disregarding the accepted code of honour, or generosity, the individual cuts himself off from the community and becomes an outcast; second, because in the long run, all social obligations are reciprocal, and their fulfilment serves also the individual's give-and-take interests best.

The vernacular economy is embedded in social relations. Its unit of economic activity is not the corporation but the family and the community. There are no purely economic activities, for a man produces, as Sahlins writes, 'in his capacity as a social person, as husband and father, brother and lineage mate, member of a clan and village.' He works as an integral member of these social groups, as *a whole man*. One can go further and say that in a vernacular society there is no work in our sense of the word. Economic activities are undertaken by unspoken agreement, just as a mother looks after her children without payment or any other external inducement. Production is part of everyday life, as are the fulfilment of ritual and ceremonial duties and all those activities which, in the modern world, we associate with leisure.

Mungo Park wrote towards the end of the eighteenth century, that 'paid service is unknown to the negro, indeed, the African language ignores the word', as do the languages of vernacular people throughout the world. Jean Liedloff tells us that though the Yequana Indians of Venezuelan Amazonia do have a word for work – *tarabajo* – it obviously comes from the Spanish *trabajo*, thereby pointing to its relatively recent origin.

Sahlins concludes that vernacular economic behaviour is 'organized by means completely different from capitalist production and market transaction' – and, one might add, from socialist production and distribution via a state bureaucracy. That in a vernacular society there is sufficient motivation to perform 'work' with enthusiasm and skill is attested by many anthropologists. Richard Thurnwald notes, for instance, that among tribes 'labour always tends beyond that which is strictly necessary' and again that 'work is never limited to the unavoidable minimum but exceeds the absolutely necessary amount, owing to a natural or acquired functional urge to activity.' Neither is vernacular man alienated from the product of his work as Karl Marx saw the worker to be in a capitalist economy. Tribesmen, Sahlins tells us,

> are not alienated from the means of production or from the products. Indeed, the tribesmen's relation to productive means and finished products often exceeds ownership as we understand it, moving beyond mundane possession to a mystic attachment. The land is a spiritual value, a beneficient source – the home of his ancestors, 'the plain of one's bones', Hawaians say. And the things man makes and habitually uses are expressions of himself, perhaps so imbued with his genius, that their ultimate disposition can be only his own grave.

It is hardly surprising that members of vernacular societies strongly resisted being transformed into units of wage labour. Thus J. Akpapa describes the difficulties encountered by the Enugu coal mining industry in Nigeria in obtaining labour for its mines. Labourers, it appears, could only be obtained by press gangs. Every day 700 of them disappeared, not to be seen again unless they had the misfortune to be 'grabbed' a second time. Eventually, the chiefs were employed to force their subjects into working for the mining company, and paid for each wage labourer they provided. At first those who refused to obey their chiefs were fined; eventually it became necessary to sentence them to varying periods of hard labour. This gives some idea of the difficulty of persuading people leading a self-fulfilling vernacular life to leave their families and communities for monotonous, soul-destroying work in some large enterprise. Ironically, such enterprises have always been justified on the grounds of relieving unemployment in tribal areas.

Vernacular economic behaviour is best demonstrated by horticulture and agriculture, a family and community activity to which people contribute largely in accordance with their status within the society, the produce then being distributed by individual gardeners according to their obligations to different members of the family and community. The anthropologist Peter Huber, who has studied the agriculture of the Anggor people of New Guinea, goes so far as to argue that they do not just organize themselves in order to produce food; on the contrary, they 'produce food in order to organize themselves.' He sees 'the problems of creating and maintaining sociality' as being 'the central element' in their agricultural system. Social organization is produced among the Anggor by the hunting and communal distribution of feral pigs. 'These pigs are not valued simply as meat', he writes,

> or even simply as pigs, but rather in terms of a complex system of association which links religion, land tenure, daily life and social classification. It is because of these associations that the Anggor can produce organization by killing and distributing feral pigs.

This is not an isolated example – on the contrary, Huber tells us that the ethnographic record is 'replete with instances in which agricultural production is quite explicitly linked – directly and/or indirectly – with ritual events which organize communities on various levels.'

Polanyi sees the distribution of food and other products in a vernacular society as governed by two basic principles, of which the first is reciprocity. When a hunter kills a game animal he will not sell it or even store it for a rainy day; instead, he will give a feast. In a sense this will provide him with all the advantages he could have derived from selling or storing it, because he knows that his hospitality will one day be reciprocated. Giving a feast is like putting money in the bank or using one's friends as a deep freeze but it enables one to get fresh instead of frozen food in exchange, and a party to boot. At the same time, the system creates a veritable network of mutual obligations which help knit together the members of the society, and increase its cohesion and viability.

Once people are provided with the equipment for storing perishable food, the most basic motive for holding feasts is removed. In one of the

Pacific islands administered by New Zealand, deep freezes have been installed at the main population centres: as a result reciprocity has ceased to be the favoured means of storing surplus food. There are far fewer feasts and social life has suffered, with a loss of cohesion in local communities.

The second basic principle underlying vernacular distribution of food and other products is what Polanyi refers to as redistribution. This occurs within the extended family and lineage group, providing its needier members with food and artefacts to build up family bonds, while simultaneously increasing the social prestige of the donor. Such redistribution may be very exacting: Phyllis Kaberry describes what it involves among the Lunga of Australia.

> The husband must from time to time give kangaroo to his wife's parents and brothers; besides this, he always distributes a little among his blood relatives. Most of what the women has obtained is consumed by herself, husband and children; if she has a little extra, she takes some to her mother, sister, mother's mother, father, in fact to any close relative. She on another occasion receives similar offerings from them, and also meat from her male relatives, which she shares with her husband and children. These gifts are not compulsory as are her husband's to her people. They are dictated by tribal sentiment and her own affection for these individuals; by kinship system which finds concrete expression not only in attitudes and linguistic usage but also in exchange of the limited food resources and the material and ritual objects which are found in the community.

Kaberry regards such behaviour as motivated by 'enlightened self-interest'. The donor may not get anything material in exchange, as elderly relatives do not go hunting and may not have enough strength to do much gathering, but he gets in exchange their esteem and also that of the larger community at large. He is, thereby, building up 'social wealth' for which, in many cases, money in the bank may be but a poor substitute.

There is also a redistributive element in many apparently reciprocal transactions. In the Comores, for instance, loans of oxen and foodstuffs (djelileo) are made to a young man by members of his age grade on the occasion of his 'grand marriage' – the most important ceremony of his life, on the lavishness of which his subsequent status within the community will in great measure depend. When a lender subsequently prepares his 'grand marriage' he will expect repayment of any loans he previously made. He will not, however, get goods of exactly the same value. Some previous borrowers may return less than they borrowed; most, however, will try desperately to return goods whose value exceeds by as much as possible that of the goods they once borrowed. The reason is obvious; their status will depend on their generosity. The more the value of the goods they return exceeds that of the goods they borrowed, the greater the prestige they acquire and the more social wealth they build up.

This brings us to redistribution as the term is normally used. In some societies, important men (big men as they are referred to in Melanasia) give large feasts which other members of the society may never be in a position to reciprocate. It is social prestige that they obtain in exchange. The best-known example of this sort of redistribution is the legendary potlatch of the Indians of the north-west coast of North America, a practice that satisfies many social requirements. As Bronislaw Malinowski writes, 'the chief everywhere acts as a tribal banker, collecting food, storing it, protecting it and then using it for the benefit of the whole community.' Malinowski sees this process as 'the prototype of the public finance system and the organization of state treasuries today.' At the same time it contributes, as does reciprocity, to the building up of social bonds. An economic system based on reciprocity and redistribution also prevents the accumulation of goods that might otherwise be translated into capital, leading to the development of large-scale economic enterprises that are no longer subject to effective social control, and to the development of the market with the corresponding reorganization of the Biosphere to satisfy market rather than Biospheric exigencies.

In other words, economic behaviour in a stable society does not interfere with social and ecological priorities, as it does in our modern industrial society; instead, it serves to fulfil essential social and ecological functions. Malinowski came to this conclusion after his exhaustive study of the life of the Trobriand Islanders. He regarded its elaborate system of reciprocity and redistribution as 'one of the main instruments of social organization, of the power of the chief, of the bonds of kinship and of relationships in law.'

That the vernacular economy is 'embedded', to use Polanyi's word, in 'social relations' is critical. What this means is that such an economy is under *social control*, hence designed to satisfy the society's basic requirements: the maintenance of its integrity and stability. Once economic life ceases to be embedded in social relations – and, worse still, social relations become 'embedded in the economic system' – then it ceases to be under control, becoming random to the society and the Biosphere and disrupting their critical order.

# FIFTY SEVEN

# In a vernacular society, technology is

# homeotelic to Gaia

●

*At the heart of the Industrial Revolution of the eighteenth century there was an almost miraculous improvement in the tools of production, which was accomplished by a catastrophic dislocation of the lives of the common people.*
KARL POLANYI

*Technology, as we know it today, is a historical phenomenon born of a certain idea of nature, of a certain idea of progress, of a certain preconception about the deterministic structure of the world and also related to specific social ideals and specific visions of the ends of human life.*
HENRYK SKOLIMOWSKI

*High technology is merely an instrument for making the plundering of our planet more effective.*
PAUL BLAU

In a vernacular society, technology is 'embedded' in social relations – in other words, it is under social and hence ecological control. The technology used by a vernacular society in the production of its artefacts, or in the cultivation of its fields, is not that which maximizes productivity but that which best suits the strategies that the society exploits for achieving its goal of maintaining its homeostasis and hence that of the Biosphere itself. This technology is also rationalized and legitimized by its mythology.

All economic activities in vernacular society are highly ritualized. Every stage in an economic activity is marked by a ceremony that gives a cosmic meaning to it, enabling it to contribute to maintaining that wider critical order on which the survival of every society depends. That this was the case among the ancient Greeks is made clear by Hesiod in his *Works and Days*. (see Chapter 61) The art of agriculture, in order to be effective, must above all be in keeping with the Nomos, or the traditional law, and hence with nature's course. As F. M. Cornford notes, 'man must keep straight upon the path of custom (Nomos) or right (Dike), or else the answering processes of natural life would likewise leave the track.' His productive activities and the technology he made use of were designed to satisfy his real needs, without disrupting the social and ecological systems, which he rightly saw as his only source of real wealth and security. (see Chapter 34)

Thus the technology of vernacular man was not designed to transform or master the environment but rather to enable him to live with it. Gerardo Reichel-Dolmatoff notes how the Tukano Indians of Colombia have

little interest in new knowledge that might be used for exploiting the environment more effectively and there is little concern for maximizing short-term gains or for obtaining more food or raw materials than are actually needed. But there is always a great deal of interest in accumulating more factual knowledge about biological reality and, above all, about knowing what the physical world requires from man. This knowledge, the Indians believe, is essential for survival because man must bring himself into conformity with nature if he wants to exist as part of nature's unity, and must fit his demands to nature's availabilities.

He notes how highly developed is the Indians' knowledge of ecology and animal behaviour. 'Such phenomena as parasitism, symbiosis, commensalism and other relationships between co-occurring species have been well observed by them and are pointed out as possible methods of adaptation.' They are also well aware of what would be the consequences for them of violating basic ecological laws. Thus their mythology describes how various animal species have been punished and occasionally made extinct

> for not obeying certain prescribed rules of adaptive significance. Thus, gluttony, improvidence, aggressiveness and all forms of overindulgence are punished by the superior forces to serve as examples not only to the animal community, but also to human society. Animals, then, are metaphors for survival. By analysing animal behaviour the Indians try to discover an order in the physical world, a world-order to which human activities can then be adjusted.

It follows that a society's technology is very much its own, part of its cultural heritage and frequently sacred to it. For this reason there is very little 'technology transfer' among vernacular people. Mary Douglas describes how the Lele, who live on one bank of the Congo River, persist in making use of their own relatively simple technologies although they are well acquainted with the more sophisticated technologies of the Bushong, who live on the opposite bank of the river. It does not occur to the Lele to make use of Bushong technology because it does not fit in with their own cultural pattern, nor is its use rationalized and validated by their metaphysical beliefs and mythology. Similarly, according to I. de Garine (see de Garine, 1979), The Massa of the North Cameroons and of Chad have refused to cultivate sorghum during the dry season even though to do so would enable them to double their food production. This is not because they do not know about its cultivation, since their neighbours the Tupuri cultivate it very successfully. It is simply that the Massa regard it as more important to maintain their cultural identity than to increase their food production.

When the Portugese introduced the musket into sixteenth-century Japan, its use was frowned upon and it took a very long time before it was allowed to replace traditional weapons. Its efficacy as an instrument of war was unquestioned, but it simply did not fit in with the Japanese cultural traditions, in terms of which the use of a device which enabled a small child to kill an experienced Samurai who had devoted his life to mastering the martial arts was totally unacceptable. The musket had no part to play in their traditional lifestyle.

Similarly the wheel, which we regard as one of the most basic of technologies, was not seen by the Yequana Indians of Venezuelan Amazonia as having a part to play in their lives. Jean Liedloff, who lived among them for two and a half years, claims that she has seen the wheel being invented at least eleven times. Children played with it, and it was a source of great amusement for all, but it never occurred to them that it could be put to any sensible use and they soon got bored with it, relegating it to the rubbish heap. It was no different in the Golden Age of ancient Athens when, as Henryk Skolimowski notes, all sorts of ingenious gadgets were developed not for utilitarian purposes, but purely for entertainment. According to Plutarch, even Archimedes attached little importance to technological innovations and did not bother to leave any commentary on his inventions.

It is because vernacular societies have learned to live with their environments that they are sustainable, unlike modern industrial societies. Robert Fernea, who describes the traditional irrigation system of the El Shabana tribe of Mesopotamia, contrasts its sustainability with modern irrigation methods. He believes that all the ancient tribal societies who once practised irrigated agriculture in Mesopotamia achieved a 'congruence of fit' between their methods of cultivation, their land-tenure systems and 'the nature of land, water and climate' which modern society cannot begin to emulate.

It is often assumed that sustainability can only be achieved at the cost of reduced efficiency but this is an error of perspective. At the turn of the century, the British government sent an agricultural expert, Augustus Voelcker, to study Indian agriculture with a view to modernizing it. He was surprised, and extremely impressed by what he saw:

> I do not share the opinions which have been expressed as to Indian agriculture being, as a whole, primitive and backward, but I believe that in many parts there is little or nothing that can be improved. I make bold to say that it is a

much easier task to propose improvements in English agriculture than to make really valuable suggestions for that of India.

He was particularly impressed by their traditional technology.

Anyone, who has watched the clever devices of the native cultivators in the implements which they use, for harrowing, levelling, drilling, raising water, etc. will see that if anything is to replace the existing implements it must be simple, cheap and effective. He will indeed be a clever man who introduces something really practical.

A. O. Hume, another British agronomist of that period, formed the same impression.

I believe that the implements in ordinary use are entirely suitable for the conditions of Indian agriculture. To those who are sceptical I can show in parts of the Bombay Presidency cultivation by means of indigenous tillage implements only, which in respect of neatness, thoroughness and profitableness cannot be excelled by the best gardeners or the best farmers in any part of the world. That statement I deliberately make and am quite prepared to substantiate.

The same is true of African agriculture. For example, Robert Mann considers that the Ethiopian ard plough cannot be improved upon for the conditions under which it has been designed to work:

it produces a ridged tilth, does not invert the soil, leaves dead vegetation on the surface, and the unique pivot action between furrow-openers and beam enables the plough point to be lifted up and over obstacles. Yet there have been many attempts to introduce ploughs of foreign origin into Ethiopia contrary to that accumulated local wisdom.

If traditional agriculture was so eminently satisfactory, one might ask, why has it been systematically abandoned and replaced by obviously non-sustainable modern agricultural methods? The reason is, that it does not fit in with the atomized, corporation-dominated consumer society that economic development has brought into being. Its existence is not compatible with the achievement of such a society's overall goal, the maximization of economic activity and hence of economic growth. The World Bank, which had a hand in financing this process in Kenya, is quite honest about its motives:

> over much of the country nature's bounty produces enough to eat with relatively little expenditure of effort. . . . Until enough subsistence farmers have their traditional lifestyles changed by the growth of new consumption wants, this labour constraint may make it difficult to introduce new crops.

And new crops must be introduced – the new hybrids in particular that are particularly sensitive to inputs of fertilizer, pesticides and irrigation water, and whose introduction is essential to the powerful agrochemical industry, and that are specifically designed for export to the industrial world to earn the foreign exchange required to finance the purchase of still more of our manufactured products.

Even in the World Bank's iniquitous Berg report, it is acknowledged that smallholders 'are outstanding managers of their own resources – their land and capital, fertilizer and water.' However, the dominance of this type of agriculture or 'subsistence production' 'presented obstacles to agricultural development. The farmers had to be induced to produce for the market, adopt new crops and undertake new risks.' Economic development rapidly puts the small farmers out of business, as it does the artisans, and they are replaced by ever bigger, ever more influential corporations. As this process occurs, so technology is disembedded from its social and ecological context and grows increasingly out of control.

Nowhere is the destructive nature of modern technology more apparent than when we introduce it into vernacular societies in the Third World. Lauriston Sharp tells a story that has been repeated over and over again in the anthropological literature. It shows how a minute and seemingly inoffensive technological innovation – in this case the substitution of steel axes for stone axes in an Australian Aboriginal tribe – is sometimes enough to spell a society's rapid disintegration. The elders of the tribe in question had a virtual monopoly of the use of stone axes and only lent them out in accordance with a very strict set of rules which ensured that they returned into their possession. The power of the elders, and indeed the whole structure of the society, is shown by Sharp to have depended on the maintenance of these arrangements. Missionaries, eager to modernize this tribal society and reduce the workload of its members, introduced steel axes which were distributed indiscriminately within the tribe: in this way, the elders were deprived of one of their most important means of maintaining the critical order of their society. It soon disintegrated, and it was not long before its now alienated members began to drift to the shanty towns and the mission stations.

Wolfgang Sachs also notes the social implications of the generalized use of as seemingly innocent a technological device as the electric mixer:

> Whirring and slightly vibrating, it makes juice from solid fruit in next to no time. A wonderful tool! So it seems. But a quick look at cord and wall-socket shows that what we have before us is rather the domestic terminal of a national, indeed, worldwide system.
>
> The electricity arrives via a network of cables and overhead utility lines, which are fed by power stations that depend on water pressures, pipelines or tanker consignments, which in turn require dams, off-shore platforms or derricks in distant deserts. The whole chain only guarantees an adequate and prompt delivery if every one of its parts is staffed by armies of engineers, planners and financial experts, who themselves can fall back on administrations, universities, indeed, entire industries (and sometimes even the military) . . . . Whoever flicks a switch on is not using a tool. He or she is plugging into a combine of functioning systems. Between the use of simple techniques and that of modern equipment lies the reorganization of a whole society.

As Ralph Keyes notes, 'Our household conveniences – our whole drive for a convenient life – has cut us off from each other. The cooperation and communication that used to accompany life's chores is being built out of our social system.' Technologies, as J. C. Mathes and Donald H. Gray put it, 'make us independent of community and social restraints and tradition, but dependent on the technological system.'

It may well be, as Mathes and Gray believe, that the engineer – rather than the bureaucrat, the politician or the economist – is the true architect of our brave new world. Indeed, no government edict could possibly have changed society as drastically as did the introduction of the automobile or the television set. There is irony in this, for the engineer tends to be a conservative in the true sense of the term, who cherishes such institutions as the family, the community and their traditional values – all of which his professional activities must inevitably destroy.

Jerry Ravetz, the well-known philosopher of science, considers that even Francis Bacon and Descartes retained some moral sense. For them the development of science and technology would still be subject to moral constraints. Thus, the sages of 'Solomon's House' in Bacon's *New Atlantis* decided which knowledge should be revealed to the state and which should remain secret, while Descartes took a 'scientist's oath' not to engage on projects which could be useful to some only by harming others. Galileo, however, was uncompromising. He saw himself as having the right to state what he took to be the philosophical truth without any concern for its possible social consequences, and denied any responsibility for his actions.

This has increasingly become the standpoint of today's scientists, in spite of the terrifying nature of the new technologies they have unleashed on the world. Nuclear power is a case in point. When nuclear fission was discovered in 1938, its military applications were rapidly understood. Some of the atomic scientists – Leo Szilard, for example – wanted to keep the discovery a secret but others, such as Jean Joliot-Curie, refused. For him, one could not stop scientific progress. Besides, he insisted, scientists were not responsible for the use to which their discoveries were put. Most mainstream scientists join him in protesting that science and technology are neutral. As Sir Peter Medawar writes, 'it is the height of folly to blame the weapon for the crime.' And as Dorothy Nelkin notes, many scientists feel that 'freedom of scientific enquiry is a constitutional right – like freedom of speech.'

In 1973 Arthur Tamplin and John Goffman resigned their important posts at the Lawrence Livermore Laboratories in Berkeley, California. They had reached the conclusion that there was no peaceful atom, and that the building of nuclear installations to provide electricity was just as much a threat to human survival as the building of nuclear weapons. Very few members of the nuclear establishment have displayed that sort of responsibility, however.

James Shapiro and his colleagues have refused to participate any further in what is perhaps the most threatening of all technological enterprises so far – genetic engineering, the creation of evolutionary new forms of life. Even if this technology were neutral, they argued, the basic control over scientific work in the United States was in the hands of a small minority of industrialists and bureaucrats who have always exploited science for harmful purposes so as to increase their own power. They believe that scientists, and everyone else for that matter, should actively work for radical political changes and that if this means that the progress of science itself may be interrupted that is something we will have to accept. Shapiro resigned from his post, but few have followed his lead. So far, all attempts to bring genetic engineering under social control have failed. To quote the Nobel laureate David Baltimore,

> Contemporary research in molecular biology has grown up in an era of almost complete permissiveness. Its practitioners have been allowed to decide their own priorities and have met with virtually no restraints on the types of work they can do.

A few eminent scientists continue to warn us of the perils of genetic engineering. Erwin Chargaff of Columbia University writes of the

> awesome irreversibility of what is being contemplated. . . . You can stop splitting the atom, you can stop visiting the moon; you can stop using aerosols; you may even decide not to kill entire populations by the use of a few bombs, but you cannot recall a new form of life. . . . An irreversible attack on the Biosphere is something so unheard-of, so unthinkable to previous generations, that I could only wish that mine had not been guilty of it.

Liebe Cavalieri of Cornell University warns that 'a single unrecognized accident could contaminate the entire earth with an ineradicable and dangerous agent that might not reveal its presence until its deadly work was done.' But Chargaff and Cavalieri represent only a small minority of the scientists involved in genetic engineering, which provides the basis of an increasingly big and powerful industry whose irresponsible activities are spinning out of control.

Our inability to control technological intrusions into the workings of the Biosphere constitutes an ever-growing threat to human survival as the scale of the interventions increases. Already scientists have exploded a nuclear bomb in the Van Allen belt, without bothering to find out its exact function in assuring the habitability of our planet. In the mid 1960s, nearly a hundred million dollars was spent on the Mohole project, which consisted of drilling a hole through the earth's crust – a project which, fortunately, came to naught. Pentagon officials also talked seriously, some years ago, of using the moon as a missile testing target.

They have recently been outdone, however, by Alexander Abian, a professor at Iowa State University. The learned professor considers the moon to be responsible for the bad weather on our planet. It apparently exerts a pull on the earth that helps tilt it on a 23° axis, which alters the angle at which it is hit by the sun's rays. This is seen as causing hot summers in parts of the world and stormy winters elsewhere. If only the moon could be got rid of, the earth would rotate more evenly, the sun would warm the planet more temperately and we would all enjoy what the professor refers to as 'eternal spring'. Abian seriously proposes that the moon be blasted with nuclear-powered rockets. If certain romantics really wanted the moon back again, then this could easily be arranged. 'Once human beings learn the secrets to re-arranging the Universe, scientists will be able to pluck moons from other planets and bring them closer to earth – but not so close that they interfere with the weather.' The professor is shocked that no-one has yet sought to do so. 'From the earliest traces of primate fossils, some 70 million years ago,' he writes, 'no-one – but no-one – has ever raised a finger of defiance at the celestial organization.' To defy the 'celestial organization' of the universe is obviously the duty of technological man. God obviously did a bad job, and it is incumbent on our scientists to rearrange the universe according to their vastly superior design. What is particularly terrifying is that this suggestion is apparently being taken seriously by various scientific bodies – the Czechoslovak Academy of Sciences, for instance.

These and similar tales should make it clear just how urgent it is that science and technology be brought back under social control – embedded once again in social relations. To those who fear that this might compromise our ability to solve real social and ecological problems, it must be pointed out that technology, though it has many uses, cannot solve the most pressing problems that confront our society today. The root of our crisis is the disruption of natural systems, whose proper functioning no technology can restore. There is no technology, for instance, that will re-create a tropical rainforest; none that will bring back into being the hundreds of thousands, if not millions, of species that are made extinct every year and of which only a fraction have even been catalogued by our scientists. There is no gadgetry that will reconstitute a disintegrated family or community, or restore its degraded cultural pattern. Only nature can do this, and the most our technologists can do is develop – as a matter of urgency – less destructive technologies that exert a much smaller impact on our environment, creating conditions in which nature can do its work.

# FIFTY EIGHT

# In an ecological economy, money is

# homeotelic to Gaia

●

*Our money is impersonal and commercial while primitive money frequently has
pedigree and personality, sacred uses, or moral and emotional connotations.*
GEORGE DALTON

In our world, money is a medium of exchange in terms of which the value of all commodities designed for exchange on the market can be expressed. It clearly serves to facilitate trade in goods and services, regardless of whether such trade is desirable on social, ecological, spiritual or moral grounds. Money, in this sense of the term, does not exist in a stable society. In the first place, goods are not produced for exchange, except in special circumstances, but for use. Secondly, the system of valuation is different: things are not valued in accordance with what they can be exchanged for, but for their importance in maintaining the stability of the social system, the Biosphere and the cosmos itself.

Some form of money is used in vernacular societies, but rather than being designed, as is our money, to facilitate economic exchange, it is designed instead to serve social ends, maintain social structures, strengthen social bonds and hence build up social wealth. Not surprisingly, modern economists inevitably criticize what they regard as the irrational nature of primitive money. They find it too bulky and difficult to carry about; worse still, it is not divisible in the way pounds can be divided into pennies. Thus the Rossel islanders use two different types of shells, Ndap and Nka. There are actually twenty-two different classes of the Ndap and only a limited number of actual shells in each class, probably no more than a thousand of each of the first thirteen classes. Each shell is known and has a veritable identity of its own and a different value. There is no means of changing a shell of one class into one of another. This means that something which is priced in terms of shells of class 20, for example, must be paid for in shells of that class. Thus, under the existing arrangements, if a man wants to buy an object priced in terms of number 20 class Ndap shells, he has to borrow an object also priced in terms of this currency. W. E. Armstrong, an economist who studied Rossel Island money, was keen to show the islanders how their currency could be 'rationalized' so as greatly to facilitate the conduct of their commercial transactions. He pointed out that this elaborate borrowing could be avoided, or much reduced, if the value of the different shells could be related. What he completely failed to grasp was that their unsuitability for use in a modern market economy was irrelevant, for they were designed to fulfil a very different purpose.

The Kula armbands used in the famous Kula trade described by Marcel

Mauss and Bronislaw Malinowski, the coppers (great ceremonial copper discs) used by north-west coast Indian chiefs at a potlatch, Rossel Island shells and all the other currencies in use in tribal societies may not be convenient, portable or divisible, but neither, as George Dalton points out, are they the media of commercial exchange. Instead, they should be regarded as treasure items or heirlooms, crown jewels or sports trophies, as Malinowski suggests. According to George Dalton,

> such treasures can take on special roles as non-commercial money; their acquisition and disposition are carefully structured and regarded as extremely important events; they change hands in specified ways, in transactions which have strong moral implications. Often they are used to create social relationships (marriage; entrance into secret societies), prevent a break in social relationships (bloodwealth; mortuary payments), or keep or elevate one's social position (potlatch). Their 'money-ness' consists in their being required means of (reciprocal or redistributive) payment.

Mary Douglas regards primitive money as more like coupons than modern commercial money. Their role 'is not to expedite the transformation of goods and services, as is money', but instead to control the drive to satisfy individual wants.

> The essence of money is to be transferable. It circulates, but coupons when spent return to an issuing point and their acquisition is continually under survey and control. Admittedly, there is a big difference between modern and primitive coupons. In a modern economy, paper coupons once spent are returned to the office of issue, counted and destroyed. But primitive commodity coupons simply return at each transfer into the hands of the senior members of the community who become by this fact to all intents and purposes the issuing authority. This makes it almost impossible to acquire coupons without being acceptable to the senior old men who hold them. Coupons do not circulate; they are continually issued and returned and re-issued.

Going further, she suggests that they provide a means of licensing rather than rationing. The object of rationing is to assure equal distribution of scarce resources. The object of licensing, on the contrary, is protective. One of its uses is

> to ensure the responsible use of possibly dangerous powers, so we have licensing of guns and liquor sales. Licensing pins responsibility so we have marriage licences and pet licences, licensing protects vulnerable areas of economy so we have import licensing etc.

But licensing, of course, creates monopoly advantages both for those who issue licences and those to whom they are issued, both parties becoming 'bound in a patron/client relation sustained by the strong interest of each in the continuance of the system.'

Mary Douglas shows that this is precisely what occurs among the Lele of Zaire. The old men of the tribe, by the workings of the system, obtain a monopoly of the issue of raffia cloth which is the currency used for paying bridewealth. Because of their monopoly, the older men establish a patron/client relationship with the younger men, who acquire the raffia from them if they wish to get married. This serves as a means of licensing marriage, and hence of controlling population, whose increase can lead to the degradation of the biotic environment; as a means, too, of maintaining the society's basic structure and hence the integrity of its cultural pattern, of which this marriage licensing system is an essential part.

# FIFTY NINE

# The vernacular community is largely

# self-sufficient

●

*Free trade for a country which has become industrial, whose population can and
does live in cities, whose people do not mind preying upon other nations and,
therefore, sustain the biggest navy to protect their unnatural commerce, may be
economically sound (though, as the reader perceives, I question its morality). Free
trade for India has proved her curse and held her in bondage.*

M.   K.   GANDHI

*Free traders, having freed themselves from the restraints of community at the
national level and having moved into the cosmopolitan world, which is not a
community, have effectively freed themselves of all community obligations.*

HERMAN   DALY   AND   JOHN   COBB

*Whenever the timber trade is good, permanent famine reigns in the Ogowe region.*

ALBERT   SCHWEITZER

As evolution proceeds, natural systems become increasingly self-sufficient, reducing their dependence on forces outside their control. This is an essential strategy for increasing their capacity for homeostasis and hence their stability. Thus Eugene Odum notes that as ecological succession occurs, ecosystems become increasingly self-sufficient and less dependent for their maintenance on resources derived from the outside. Thus food chains become more complex, with detritus providing an increasingly important source of nutrients. 'In a mature forest, less than 10 per cent of annual net production is consumed (that is, grazed) in the living state: most is utilized as dead matter (detritus) through delayed and complex pathways involving as yet little understood animal–micro-organism inter-actions.' Similarly, inorganic nutrients which were originally derived from outside the ecosystem slowly become 'intrabiotic', being constantly re-cycled within it.

A similar arrangement prevails within a vernacular community. Food and artefacts are largely distributed via procedures that observe the rules of reciprocity and redistribution, and are entirely under social control. In many vernacular societies, what appear to be commercial transactions are in reality highly ritualized exchanges, embedded in social relations. Thus certain goods are often traded with goods of another sort, and even with socially valuable objects which closely resemble what we would regard as money. But even such trade is not conducted for 'economic' motives, as Bronislaw Malinowski points out with reference to the Trobriand Islands:

> there is not even a trace of gain, nor is there any reason for looking at it from the purely utilitarian and economic standpoint, since there is no enhancement of material utility through the exchange. . . . Thus it is quite a usual thing in the Trobriands for a type of transaction to take place in which 'A' gives twenty baskets of yams to 'B', receiving for it a small polished blade, only to have the whole transaction reversed in a few weeks time.

The same applies to trade with other related social groups. Thus both Marcel Mauss and Malinowski have described the large trading expeditions periodically undertaken by natives of the Trobriand Islands. They trans-ported certain types of valuable objects to people living in distant islands visited in a clockwise sequence, while other expeditions carried other kinds of valuable objects to islands lying counter clockwise. The object of these expeditions was not an economic one. 'We describe it as trade', Karl Polanyi writes, 'though no profit is involved; either in money or in kind.'

Even in the vernacular Indian village where social structure has diverted somewhat from the tribal norm, what one might regard as commercial transactions were until recently under social control. A farmer obtained his pots from the village potter and his tools from the village blacksmith, giving them an amount of food in exchange – all at a rate established by tradition. What is more, if the local potter was an indifferent craftsman and better pots could be bought elsewhere, this is not regarded as a reason for abandoning him. Judged by the values of modern economics such a system provided no inducement to producers to increase production or to improve the quality of their produce, but this objection misses the point. The trading relations between the different members of a traditional Indian village were primarily designed to satisfy social rather than purely economic goals. After all, the quality of the available pots is not the primary consideration. The maintenance of social cohesion and stability is much more important.

Mahatma Gandhi understood this well. One of the basic concepts of his philosophy was that of *swadeshi* which he describes as that 'spirit in us which restricts us to the use and service of our immediate surroundings to the exclusion of the more remote.' Sunderlal Bahuguna, the leader of the Chipko movement in the Himalayas, regards *swadeshi* as the most fundamental of Mahatma Gandhi's teachings. However, it is totally undermined by economic development, which rests on the principle that all considerations, whether moral, social or ecological, must be ruthlessly subordinated to short-term economics. The village community is sacrificed to ever greater quantities of bigger and better pots. Production and consumption are no longer under social control.

In tribal societies, it is only when dealing with complete strangers that commercial transactions are allowed to occur and the laws of the market are allowed to operate free of social constraints. As Paul and Laura Bohannan put it,

> A 'market' is a transaction which in itself calls up no long-term personal relationship, and which is therefore to be exploited to as great a degree as possible. In fact, the presence of a previous relationship makes a 'good market' impossible. People do not like to sell to kinsmen since it is bad form to demand as high a price from a kinsman as one might from a stranger. Market behaviour and kinship behaviour are incompatible in a single relationship and the individual must give way to one or the other.

This is very much in keeping with the Old Testament precept that 'Unto a stranger thou mayest lend upon usury; but unto thy brother, thou shalt not lend upon usury.'

Marshall Sahlins shows that it is possible to distinguish between the economic relations within different sectors such as the house, the lineage, the village, the tribe and those outside the tribe. As we proceed along the social order gradient, so reciprocity and solidarity are slowly replaced by haggling and profit-making, while economic relations become increasingly commercial. That is why the development of the market system within a society could only occur once solidarity and reciprocity within the inner social groupings had waned and the essential difference between social relations within and without these groupings had become sufficiently blurred. Before economic wealth could become man's principal preoccupation, he had first to be deprived of his social wealth.

Though all societies have possessed an economy of some sort, no economy previous to our time, as Karl Polanyi notes, 'has ever existed that, even in principle, was controlled by markets.' This is not surprising, since only by resisting the power of market forces could 'the integrity of our social and ecological systems . . . be maintained for so long.' Once markets become more than incidental to economic life, the societies in which they operated, together with the ecosystems in which the societies existed, were condemned to rapid disintegration.

During the Middle Ages in Europe, only resources of secondary social and ecological importance – spices, candle wax, oriental silks and luxury articles primarily of interest to the Church and aristocracy – were traded via the market, at annual fairs held in a few major European cities. In the twelfth and thirteenth centuries, however, an economic revolution

326

occurred: the market expanded rapidly until it came to dominate the economic life of many European societies. Essential to this revolution was the transformation of key resources – labour and land – into commodities, as Polanyi points out: 'Labour is only another name for human activity that goes with life itself, which is not produced for sale but for entirely different reasons, nor can that activity be detached from the rest of life, be stored or mobilized: land is only another name for nature.' In medieval Europe neither labour nor land had previously been exchanged via the market. Medieval serfs were bound to their land: whatever were the abuses of the feudal system, this arrangement nevertheless normally provided them with security of tenure.

Once human life came to be treated as a mere commodity, work ceased to be embedded in social relation – and the 'whole man' was replaced by the worker, a new human category altogether. Whereas vernacular man – the whole man – is a member of his family and community, the worker lives in a largely atomized society and can be mobilized to fulfil any function – however socially and ecologically disruptive or morally repulsive it might be – so long as it provides the wage on which he becomes increasingly dependent for the satisfaction of his most basic biological and social needs.

The transformation of land into a commodity had enormous social and economic implications. Contract – established via the market system – rather than status – established by tradition and reflecting the society's social structure – now determined where individual families lived and worked the land. (see Chapter 60) The resulting pattern of land-ownership may well have satisfied the requirements of the new economic system, but it set in train the disintegration of society into mere congeries of strangers. The disintegrated community, what is more, was often deprived of its livelihood, since its food was sold via the market, and was bought by whoever paid the most for it, regardless of the community or society to which he belonged.

Polanyi attributes the severe famines that occurred in India under the British Raj to the operation of the newly established market system. The Indian peasant starved, he writes, 'according to the rules of the game', for it is the very basis of the market system that goods should be bought as cheaply as possible and sold at the highest price. This means that there must be a steady one-way traffic of the essentials of life from the poor to the rich countries, regardless of the malnutrition and famine caused among the local people when they are deprived in this way of their food supplies. Thus Redcliffe Salaman notes how, in Ireland during the great famine, corn continued to be exported to England in spite of the millions of people who were dying of hunger. 'If it was not available to the local people, it was partly because it was being shipped to England at the rate of 16,000 quarters a week and also because, even if it were not, the Irish could not have afforded it.'

Today, this traffic is one of the major causes of malnutrition and famine in the Third World, where a high proportuion of arable land – up to 70 per cent in certain countries – is used for export crops, marginalizing the staple food crops on which the local population depends for its sustenance. Today, according to the rules established by the General Agreement on Tariffs and Trade (GATT), the crops that a country produces must be exported so long as a market demand exists. Only when malnutrition and hunger prevail can an exception be made, and US delegates at the current Uruguay Round of GATT insist that even in such dire circumstances food must continue to be exported. If they have their way, it will then be 'GATT-illegal' for a country to feed its starving people, rather than export it to the already overfed. It is only by doing so that it can maximize its expenditure on the manufactured goods of the industrial countries that control GATT.

This illustrates a principle: production governed by 'market forces' is not designed to satisfy biological, social or ecological needs. Kenneth Lux points out that economists must deny the very existence of such needs if modern economic theory is to make any sense at all. The market is seen as catering only for our 'wants' which, when backed up by solid cash, are reflected in 'effective demand'; a country is seen as becoming 'self-sufficient' once 'effective demand' is satisfied. Thus the modernization of agriculture through the adoption of the 'Green Revolution' is said to have enabled India to achieve food self-sufficiency. This sounds very impressive, because it suggests that all the citizens of that country are now properly fed; but nothing could be further from the truth. A recent report by the United

Nations Children's Fund (UNICEF) reveals that about 85 per cent of India's children are now affected by malnutrition; many will be stunted physically and mentally as a result. To state that India is self-sufficient in food means only that more food in the shops would not lead to further sales, for those who are malnourished do not have the money to buy food: their biological needs are not reflected in the 'effective demand' that they exert.

Once the market rules our economic life, the natural world is seen to be no more than a source of resources to be commoditized and trans-formed into cash on the global market. The process is a malignant one. By means of it, everywhere, forests, wetlands, coral reefs, rivers, estuaries and seas, together with all the living things that inhabit them, are system-atically cashed in. What happens when all these are gone, and the countries are transformed into virtual deserts, does not seem to concern our politicians, industrialists or economists.

Any resource that can be cashed in is at risk, and can only be preserved by keeping it outside the orbit of the global market. In New Zealand, it is now illegal to sell trout in shops. They are reserved for anglers, and it is for this reason that there are still trout to be caught in the country's lakes and rivers. Only by setting up national parks in which living things are kept out of the orbit of the market can many species be preserved, though one can unfortunately predict that if economic development proceeds for very much longer, the pressures on these parks will become irresistible. Today too, in certain parts of Tanzania where the economy has largely collapsed and there is not enough money to repair the roads, people are now begin-ning to eat properly again: no longer able to export their food on the global market, they are free once more to eat it themselves.

The export process is often as destructive to the importer as to the ex-porter: 'a process of mutual poisoning' in E. F. Schumacher's phrase. For the import of cheap food from areas where it can be grown particularly cheaply, or is heavily subsidized by the state, to areas where, for various reasons, it is more expensive to produce has ruined countless farmers throughout the Third World. The adoption of modern agricultural methods – imposed by international agencies such as the International Monetary Fund (IMF) on its debtor countries – increases their dependence on imported off-farm inputs such as farm machinery, hybrid seeds, fertilizers and pesticides which they can ill afford, especially as their price increases while the land that their previous use has served to degrade becomes ever less productive. The farmers become increasingly impoverished until eventually they must leave the land and make for the slums that surround the nearest conurbation, a fate which awaits the bulk of the Third World's rural population.

The lot of the traditional craftsman or artisan is very similar. Mahatma Gandhi's constant theme was how Lancashire's mass-produced textiles had destroyed India's artisanal, village-based textile industry, bringing on the degradation of rural life. Carders, dyers, spinners and weavers – droves of them, who kept the village economy going – were all ruined, and the Indian village was deprived of its economic and social life.

It is for the same reasons that the small farmer and the artisan have been virtually eliminated in Britain and North America, and are rapidly disappearing in the rest of Europe. Even the medium-sized farmer and the medium-sized company are everywhere under stress. During the present recession (1991), the European agricultural community has entered a state of near bankruptcy, and only the biggest farms have any prospect of survival. In the USA agriculture is in similar straits. The plight of small to medium businesses is scarcely better, with nine hundred or so going bankrupt every week in the UK at the time of writing.

That the future lies with the large corporations – in particular the multinational corporations – no one familiar with current trends can doubt. As the market expands to encompass the entire world and becomes progressively 'freer', the greater must be the niche it provides for the multinational corporatiions. Free trade sounds highly desirable; its proponents make it appear that it frees the oppressed individual of yet another set of shackles previously imposed on him and on his ancestors by tyrannical rulers and governments. But the multinational corporation is the 'individual' who benefits from free trade; and the freedom it provides is the freedom to cut down virgin forests in order to produce plywood, lavatory paper and the Sunday edition of the *New York Times*. It is the freedom to erode, salinize, waterlog, compact and desertify agricultural land so as to produce the cheap raw materials for the food-processing industry; it is the freedom to pillage the oceans with vast trawlers that literally annihilate fish populations with 'wall of death' drift nets that are often 60 miles long. It is the freedom to grub up the world's remaining coral reefs that protect vulnerable islands from the waves, and that are among the most productive of all ecosystems, in order to provide specimens for souvenir shops. It is the freedom to drain the pathetic remains of the world's once extensive wetlands, in order to provide more pastureland for the world's over-inflated livestock population, or to make available more building land for the developers. It is the freedom to churn out ever greater amounts of ever more toxic chemicals to spread on our fields, release into our rivers and groundwaters, dump into holes in the ground, or inject under pressure into deep boreholes – from where they find their way into our food and drinking water, increasing the incidence of mutations, cancers and child malformations. It is the freedom to destroy the ozone layer, which protects us from lethal ultraviolet radiation, in the interests of using patented CFCs in cosmetic sprays, refrigerators and air conditioners, rather than non-patentable substitutes which would reduce the profits of the main producers, Du Pont and ICI. It is the freedom to increase poverty and misery, malnutrition and disease, to extinguish hundreds of thousands if not millions of species of living things every year, all in order to satisfy the short-term financial interests of a few utterly irresponsible industrialists and the bureaucrats and politicians who live off them. This is the freedom that free trade provides, and these are the interests the current GATT proposals are designed to serve. If approved, they will have delivered the world to its pillagers, on a plate, to do with it as they like.

What is required is just the opposite – a transition to a world of largely self-sufficient communities, carrying out their economic activities at the level of the family, the small artisanal enterprise and the community itself, largely to satisfy local needs via local markets.

Only in this way can economic activity be subordinated, as it must be if we are to survive for long on this beleaguered planet, to biological, social, ecological and moral imperatives.

# SIXTY

# The vernacular community is the unit of

# homeotelic behaviour

●

*Men may make kingdoms, but the community seems to come from the hand of God.*
ALEXIS DE TOCQUEVILLE

*The ideal of a future based on ecological principles must have, as a fundamental prerequisite, the re-emergence of* Gemeinschaft *in social relationships.*
ALWYN JONES

The world-view of modernism regards the state as the only possible instrument of government. People are seen as the individualistic, competitive, aggressive and disorderly units of an atomized society. The notion that society is a natural system, capable of governing itself and securing its own homeostasis, is foreign to modern sociologists, let alone modern political circles. Margaret Thatcher, when she was Prime Minister, stated quite explicitly that a human society was no more than the sum of the individuals and families that inhabited it. Such a society, or rather non-society, cannot govern itself and must depend on the state and its specialized services to maintain any semblance or order – a situation we are taught to regard as normal. Indeed, we are told, where there is no state there can only be 'a war of everyone against everyone' and life must necessarily be in Thomas Hobbes's consecrated phrase, 'solitary, nasty, brutish and short'.

This distorted view of human society can only be entertained by one who has had no experience of a vernacular society of the type within which our ancestors once lived, and which still survives somewhat precariously in those areas that have succeeded in remaining outside the orbit of international trade.

A succession of scholars have noted the essential difference between these two types of society. Sir Henry Sumner Maine, in his *Ancient Society* (1861), traced the transition from the 'familial' to the 'individuated' society, from one governed by personal and sacred law to one governed by impersonal and secular law. For him, behaviour in the former society was based on 'status', while in the latter it was based on 'contract'.

John Locke's 'social contract', entered into by the citizens of an originally chaotic and disorderly non-society, in order to set up a government that would provide them with order and security, is still a generally accepted notion. The contract is seen as having been entered into consciously and rationally by individual people; implicit in it is the idea of management by an external agency, just as in a corporation.

On the other hand, the notion of a society as a natural and spontaneous Biospheric creation is unacceptable to the modernist world-view. Such a society could only be held together by irrational forces such as emotion or sentiment, which in the view of William Graham Sumner, the best known and most outspoken of American Social Darwinists, have no role to play in public affairs and should be limited to the field of personal relations.

The French historian and social philosopher, Fustel de Coulanges, in his seminal *La Cité Antique* (1927), stressed the religious nature of the family, community and larger society, which he saw as providing their cohesion and stability. Of the ancient Greek city state, he wrote: 'This state and its religion were so totally fused that it was impossible not only to imagine the conflict between them, but even to distinguish one from the other.' For him, the ancient society died once its law was separated from its religion.

The early American ethnographer Lewis H. Morgan published his *Ancient Society* in 1877. He distinguished between *societas* and *civitas*, the former based on kinship and the latter on territorial connection. This is an important distinction. Real vernacular communities are based on consanguinity, real or fictitious. With the development of trade and industry, however, normal rules of residence reflecting the kinship structures of communities, and their relationships with other key groupings such as the clan, are subordinated to new, economic considerations. Among the Hebrews, as Adolphe Lods writes,

> the early groupings, based originally on consanguinity (natural or artificial), tended to become territorial aggregations. The clan finally became synonymous with the population of a town. . . . Membership of a tribe consisted not in descent from a particular individual but in belonging by birth to a particular territory.

As this change occurred, contiguity become the main bond holding together the members of a community. Today, even this bond has been systematically eroded, people live wherever they can find a job and in the US it is said that less than 15 per cent of the population now live where they were born. In this way a country's population is shuffled like a deck of cards to satisfy the requirements of the economy, and the community is transformed into a mere congery of strangers incapable of governing themselves or fulfilling their homeotelic functions.

Perhaps the best-known distinction between these two types of society is that proposed by the German sociologist Ferdinand Tonnies in *Gemein-schaft and Gesellschaft* (1920). He saw the *gemeinschaft* or community as constituting a single coherent social unit whose members are bound together by intimate social bonds and common values, whereas the members of a *gesellschaft*, on the contrary, are linked by superficial and self-motivated considerations. F. Pappenheim states this very clearly:

> Individuals who enter a Gesellschaft do so with only a fraction of their being, that is, with that part of their existence which corresponds to the specific purpose of the organization. Members of a tax-payers' association, or individuals who own stock in a company, are related to each other, not as whole persons, but with only that part of themselves which is concerned with being a taxpayer or shareholder. . . . Thus they remain loosely connected and essentially remote from each other. . . . So deep is the separation between man and man in Gesellschaft that . . . it becomes a social world in which latent hostility and potential war are inherent in the relationship of one to another.

Roy Rappaport contrasts the community with what he calls the 'special purpose association'. Whereas the community seeks to satisfy social and ecological requirements, the special purpose association – in which category he includes corporations and governmental institutions, and which corresponds very closely to Tonnies's *gesellschaft* – only seeks to achieve the purpose for which it was set up. Even then it is subject to what he calls 'goal displacement', at which point its one preoccupation is to perpetuate itself and if possible increase its power and influence, which can often mean becoming an obstacle to the realization of its original goal.

In the case of government agencies set up to control the activities of unscrupulous industrialists, goal-displacement occurs very rapidly. They are nearly always subverted, indeed often completely taken over by the industrialists whose activities they have been set up to control – a process known as 'regulatory capture' or 'agency capture'. In the UK the Advisory Committee on Pesticides, which is supposed to advise the government on the control of the use of pesticides, is largely made up of representatives of the agrochemical industry and various academics whose research grants they pay or otherwise control. The UK's Ministry of Agriculture, Forestry and Fisheries (MAFF), like the United States Department of Agriculture (USDA) is dominated by the agrochemical industry, the thousands of agricultural extension offices throughout the country being little more than agencies for the sale of fertilizers and pesticides. The same can be said of the Food and Agricultural Organization of the United Nations (FAO), to which subject *The Ecologist* recently devoted a special issue.

When the Reagan administration came to power in the USA, Anne Gorsuch, an attorney specialized in defending polluting industries against litigation by the Environmental Protection Agency (EPA), was actually made head of that agency and proceeded to dismiss the scientists engaged during the Carter administration – not, on her own admission, because they were incompetent, but because they were 'their scientists' (or scientists with real environmental concerns) and had to be replaced by 'our scientists' (representing the interest of the polluters).

In general, governments will take no measures that go against the interest of any important industry, however destructive its activities, unless it is forced to do so by public opinion. The main reason is that governments have an insatiable appetite for money. In a 'democracy' it is money that will enable them to get re-elected by providing material advantages to those sectors of society whose electoral support they particularly require, and by selling themselves to the electorate through elaborate publicity campaigns at election times. In a dictatorship, money will buy the arms and pay the police and troops that maintain the dictator in power. Unfortunately, big corporations have a virtual monopoly of money – hence the inevitable alliance between government and industry, and policies that are not adopted because they are desirable on human, social or ecological grounds, but because they serve the purpose of powerful special purpose associations. It is these heterotelic policies that are rapidly making our planet uninhabitable.

For the French anthropologist Pierre Clastres the most basic feature of the vernacular society is probably its capacity to run its own affairs without the aid of formal state institutions.

> There is on the one hand the primitive society, or the society without the state, and on the other, the society with the state. It is the presence or absence of the

state (which can take many forms) which separates these two fundamentally different types of society from each other.

That the vernacular society can run itself without the aid of formal state institutions is well documented. As the American anthropologist Robert Lowie writes:

> the legislative function in most primitive communities seems strangely curtailed when compared with that exercised in the more complex civilizations. All the exigencies of normal social intercourse are covered by customary law, and the business of such governmental machinery as exists is rather to exact obedience to traditional usage than to create new products.

The power of public opinion, reflecting traditional values, is enough to bring disorderly elements to heel. Often a miscreant is simply laughed at; if this is not enough, people will no longer attend his feasts and his company will be avoided. This is usually sufficient; if it is not, he will be ostracized – the worst possible penalty, since a man in a vernacular community cannot conceive of life outside it, away from the land where his ancestors are buried and where alone he can perform his essential religious rites. As Edward Tyler notes, 'one of the most essential things that we can learn from the life of crude tribes is how society can function without the policeman to keep order.' A vernacular society is also fully capable of bringing up its own children, looking after the sick and the old, and dealing with any psychiatric disorders. The social psychiatrist Marvin Opler has shown that a vernacular society will automatically provide a cathartic outlet for the particular tensions that, by its specific nature, it must generate.

Vernacular society coordinates all these activities so that they contribute to the society's stability in the face of change. Above all, this means maintaining the critical order of the hierarchy of larger systems of which it is part and on whose preservation its stability must ultimately depend. For this to be possible, the vernacular community, families and individuals must cooperate in the achievement of this goal, seeking among other things to avoid interfering with each other's activities. As a result, the conflict of interests that we are often faced with in the modern world – say, between the use of land for agriculture or for urban development – tend not to occur.

A member of a vernacular society, in Stanley Diamond's words, is

> an integrated person. His society is neither compartmentalized nor fragmented, and none of its parts is in fatal conflict with the others. Thus he does not perceive himself as divided into 'homo economicus', 'homo religiosus', 'homo politicus' and so forth. On the contrary, he performs his various economic, religious and political tasks as part of a coordinated strategy that is embodied in the cultural pattern with which he has been imbued, and which has regulated his relationship with his fellow men and with his natural environment from time immemorial.

In such conditions, there is clearly no need for the state. The intrusion of such a foreign body into a society's affairs would usurp its most fundamental functions and prerogatives, generating initiatives beyond the control of traditional law as laid down by the ancestors. In a vernacular society, as Clastres puts it, 'there is no state because the state is an impossibility.'

The state can only come into being once social structures have been destroyed. This is a central theme of Aristotle's *Politics*. He notes that tyrants like Pisistratus of Athens and Dionysius of Syracuse could only come to power once the social structures of their respective cities had broken down, with the emergence of an anonymous proletariat incapable of governing itself. This explains the title of Clastres's seminal essay, 'La Société contre l'État'. In every country, the state seeks purposefully to destroy the vernacular institutions of society. In India, it wages war against the caste system which, in spite of its obvious abuses, provides the very basis of Indian social structure. It also attacks 'linguism', the preservation of the languages spoken by the different ethnic groups that inhabit modern India and even rounds on 'statism' where this refers to the residual autonomy of what were once ethnically based Indian states.

In Africa, the governments of the artificial nations states whose arbitrary boundaries have been inherited from the colonial period strive to eradicate 'tribalism' in the interest of creating 'national unity', which really means bringing into being vast homogeneous masses of anonymous and alienated people totally dependent, as we in the West have become, on the specialized services provided by an increasingly powerful state.

The close relationship between the development of the state and the disintegration of self-regulating society is described by Edward Banfield in a study of peasant society in southern Italy. The village, he finds, has been relieved of responsibility for organizing its own religious life by the centralized bureaucracy of the Vatican. It has also lost control of its own educational system, since its school has been built for it and teachers are appointed by the state. It no longer maintains law and order; the state's police are supposed to do that. As a result, the community has begun to disintegrate, the largest unit of organization now being the family, with no effective cooperation above that level. In such a society, Banfield writes,

> No-one will further the interests of the group or community except as it is to his private advantage to do so. In other words, the hope of material gain in the short run will be the only motive for concern of public affairs . . . the law will be disregarded when there is no reason to fear punishment . . . an office holder will take bribes when he can . . . but whether he takes bribes or not, it will be assumed by society that he does.

Clearly, such a society can only exist because the state provides it with all the services it once provided itself. 'Except for the intervention of the state', Banfield writes, 'the war of all against all would sooner or later erupt into open violence, and the local society would either perish or produce new cultural forms – precisely the state of affairs that Hobbes and later the Social Darwinists took to be the norm.

A peasant society is still only in the early stages of disintegration, since the extended family is still intact. But as economic development proceeds, the extended family breaks down into the very unstable nuclear family with which we are all acquainted today. Eventually even that disintegrates until, in the growing slums of the industrial world's conurbations, the one-parent family becomes the rule. In such a society, there is still less cooperation. It is each one for himself; individualism and competition are the rule. (see Chapter 46) People are so alienated that they are no longer capable of looking after their affairs, and the state takes over more and more of the functions that they and their now disintegrated families and communities can no longer fulfil. As a Pomo Indian pointed out to a white North American (see Diamond, 1974):

> the police and soldiers take care of protecting you, the courts give you justice, the Post Office carries messages for you, the school teaches you. Everything is taken care of, even your children, if you should die, but with us the family must do all that. Without the family, we are nothing, and in the old days before white people came, the family was given first consideration by anyone who was about to do anything at all. That is why we got along.

Unfortunately, we have been taught to regard the proliferation of a country's state services as a sign of social and economic progress. The more of them a government provides to its citizens, the higher their perceived standard of living. This notion is consistent with the dogma that all benefits are man-made, the product of economic development or progress. (see Chapter 34) It is consistent, too, with the modern belief in scientific and technical expertise and professionalism, for the services provided by the state are seen to be superior in these terms to those provided by the family and the community in a vernacular society. In Sweden, according to David Popenoe, the bourgeois family is seen as a major cause of social problems: 'in order to destroy it, some welfare state ideologues are eager to promote alternatives not only to the bourgeois family, but to the nuclear family, and to turn over most child-rearing to the state.' Even family members in Sweden are apparently succumbing to this propaganda, and coming to accept that care is best provided by government-employed professionals. After all, they are scientifically trained to look after children and must therefore be capable of doing so better than their amateurish parents.

As people delegate their prerogatives to experts, John McKnight notes, they act less as citizens and more as clients. This is occurring in just about every field of activity – in medicine, in education, and in the case of old people, and it is affecting every aspect of social policy. At the same time, normal people as members of their families and communities are prevented from fulfilling the basic functions for which they were equipped by their evolution, and which they must fulfil to maintain the integrity and stability of families, communities, societies and the rest of the Gaian hierarchy.

The state is foreign to society. It is a *gesellschaft* – a single-purpose association concerned almost exclusively with its own short-term interests and almost invariably oblivious to the real needs of those it has been called upon to govern. There is no place for the state or its specialized institutions in a society that seeks to recreate for itself a sustainable existence on a sustainable planet. Instead, we must recreate the extended family and the vernacular community within which we have evolved and which, throughout our evolutionary experience, have been the effective units of homeotelic social and ecological behaviour.

------

# SIXTY ONE

# Vernacular man follows the Way

●

*Tao is like Dike, the Way, the way of nature; and man's whole religion, his whole moral effort is to bring himself into accordance with Tao.*
JANE HARRISON

*When the world has the Way, ambling horses are retired to fertilize fields. When the world lacks the Way, war horses are reared in the suburbs.*
LAO-TZU

*Humankind's greatest priority is to reintegrate with the natural world.*
JONATHON PORRITT

*The earth dries and withers,
the world languishes and withers,
the heavens languish together with the earth.
The earth lies polluted
under its inhabitants,
for they have transgressed the laws,
violated the statutes,
broken the everlasting covenant.*
ISAIAH 24:4-5

Like the developing embryo in the womb each life process must follow an appointed constellation of chreods, or path, if it is to achieve its end-state and thereby contribute to maintaining the critical order of the cosmos. Thus one can talk – as does Rupert Sheldrake – of a 'behavioural chreod' and also of a cultural chreod: a society, by means of its specific cultural pattern, is capable of maintaining itself on its chreod by correcting any diversions from it – so long as they occur within its tolerance range and hence its field. The Way a society must follow is that which conforms to its traditional law (see Chapter 2) which the ancient Greeks referred to as the *Nomos*. The Way was also referred to by them as *Dike*, which meant justice, righteousness or morality. Jane Harrison tells us that *Dike* was also 'the Way of the world, the way things happen'.

The Way was also referred to as *Themis*, which Jane Harrison regards as 'that specialized way for human beings which is sanctioned by the collective conscience'. *Themis* was also taken to be the way of the earth, and sometimes the Way of the cosmos itself, that which governed the behaviour of the gods. Later, when these concepts were personalized, *Themis* became the goddess of law and of justice, and hence of morality. The Way was also seen to coincide with *Moira*, the path of destiny or fate. The chthonic gods were subordinated to *Moira*, as they were to *Dike*, the two actually coinciding with each other. Thus, for Anaximander, basic elements are attributed to different provinces that provide the basis of the critical order of the natural world 'according to what is ordained', a concept in which, according to F. M. Cornford, 'necessity and right are united.' In Homer, the gods are seen as subordinate to *Moira*, and indeed to *Dike* – cosmic forces that are older than the gods themselves and that are moral. Against fate, and hence against the moral law, the gods can do nothing. As Homer tells us in the *Odyssey*, the gods cannot even save a man whom they love, if the 'dread fate of death' is upon him. Herodotus tells us that 'it is impossible even for a god to avoid the fate that is ordained.'

The Way to be followed by all human beings was the same as that which must be followed by society as a whole, by the natural world, by the cosmos and therefore by the gods themselves. There is thus a single law which governs the behaviour of the whole cosmic hierarchy. 'Themis in the world of Zeus', as Pythagoras writes (see Iamblichus), 'and Dike in the world below, hold the same place and rank as Nomos in the cities of men; so that he who does not justly perform his appointed duty may appear as a violator of the whole order of the universe.' The higher the status of an individual, and hence the greater the vital force with which he was endowed, the more important it was that he should rigorously follow the Way. Thus Odysseus tells us that when a blameless king maintains the *Dike*, 'The black earth bears wheat and barley, and the trees are laden with fruit, and the sheep bring forth and fail not, and the sea gives store of fish and all out of his good guidance, and the people prosper under him.'

The concept of the Way was probably entertained, explicitly or implicitly, by all vernacular societies. The Chinese concept of *Tao* refers at once to the order and to the Way of the cosmos. The term is applied to the daily and yearly 'revolution of the heavens' and of the two powers of light and darkness, day and night, summer and winter, heat and cold. E. de Groot tells us that,

> It represents all that is correct, normal or right (*ching* or *twan*) in the universe; it does, indeed, never deviate from its course. It consequently includes all correct and righteous dealings of men and spirits, which alone promote universal happiness and life.

*Tao* represents the natural course of things. It was considered, Joseph Needham writes, 'not only as vaguely informing of all things, but as being the naturalness, the very structure of particular and individual things.' Feng Yu-Lan sees the *Tao* as 'the all-embracing first principle of things'. All living things, including humans, are enfolded in this natural order, subject to the *Tao* which is its governing principle. '*Tao*, as the order of nature . . . governs their very action', Feng Yu-Lan writes. Humans follow the *Tao* or Way, by behaving naturally. In Taoist terms, this means abiding by Lao-Tzu's principle of *Wu Wei*, for 'when all things obey the laws of the *Tao*,' as Wing-Tsit Chan writes, 'they will form a harmonious whole, and the universe will become an integrated organism.'

In ancient Egypt, we learn from Siegfried Morenz, that the concept of *Maat* fulfilled a similar role. *Maat* meant 'the right order in nature and society as established by the act of creation . . . what is right, what is correct, law, order, justice and trust' – not only in society but in the cosmos as a whole. Significantly, Re was at once Lord of the cosmos, Lord of the judgement of the dead and Lord of *Maat*. Later when Osiris came into his own, he also became the Lord of *Maat*. *Maat*, though it came into being with creation, nevertheless had to be renewed and preserved. It follows that '*Maat* is . . . not only right order but also the object of human activity. *Maat* is both the task which man sets himself and, also, as righteousness, the promise and reward which awaits him on fulfilling it.'

Because ancient Egypt was a centralized kingdom, run by a divine king, it was he in particular whose role it was to maintain *Maat* and hence the order of the cosmos. Thus we read in contemporary texts edited by Morenz that 'the sky is at peace, the earth is in joy, for they have heard that (the deceased king) will set right in the place of disorder (*Isft*, the opposite of *Maat*).' And again, Tutankhamum 'drove out disorder (*Isft*) from the two lands and *Maat* is firmly established in its place: he made lying (*Grg*) an abomination and the land is as it was at the first time.' It was the king's close association with *Maat* that gave authority to his edicts. What he ordered was necessarily part of the *Maat* that his subject must follow.

A similar concept existed in Vedic India. 'The processes whose perpetual sameness or regular recurrence give rise to the representation of order', writes Maurice Bloomfield, 'obey *R'ta* or their occurrence is *R'ta*.' We read in the Vedas that

> The rivers flow *R'ta*. According to the *R'ta* the light of the heavenborn morning has come. . . . The year is the path of *R'ta*. The Gods themselves are born of the *R'ta* or in the *R'ta*; they show by the acts that they know, observe and love the *R'ta*. In man's activity, the *R'ta* manifests itself as the moral law.

*R'ta* also stands for truth, though in a philosophical context truth is usually *Satya*. Untruth, though it is sometimes *Asatya*, is usually expressed as *An-R'ta*, hence as a divergence from the Way.

The Vedic poet, as Krishna Chaitanya notes, fully realizes that to obtain nature's bounty, man must obey *R'ta*: 'for one who lives according to Eternal Law, the winds are full of sweetness, the rivers pour sweets. So may the plants be full of sweetness for us.' The great Vedic *Hymn to Earth* clearly expresses the belief in human dependence on the order of the cosmos and the human role in maintaining it by observing the ancient law. The poet expresses his faith in the eternal order and in the human duty to preserve it. It is this order which has bound 'rock, soil, stone and dust' in such a way that 'trees, Lords of the Forest, stand very firm.' It is this order that maintains in 'unfailing flow, day and night, the waters that are common to all' and nurtures 'cornfields that nourish quadrupeds and bipeds.' In all this the poet displays a respect that unites the spiritual and the practical: 'Whatever I dig from thee, Earth, may it have quick growth again. O purifier, may we not injure thy vitals or thy heart.'

In the Persian Avestas, the Way is also referred to as *Asha*, the celestial representative of justice on earth. According to Chantepie de la Saussaye; 'Justice is the rule of the world's life, as *Asha* is the principle of all well-ordered existence, and the establishment or accomplishment of justice is the end of the evolution of the universe.' Later, the concept of *Dharma* was also used by the Hindus in the same way: 'that regularity, that normality of the universe, which produces good crops, fat cattle, peace and contentment,' A. M. Hocart writes, 'is expressed by the word *Dharma* which means etymologically "support", "upholding".' It describes the way in which animals, men or things are expected to behave; it is natural law. The sun is sometimes identified with *Dharma* because it regulates the seasons; sometimes it is considered to be regulated by it. Among the gods, Varuna is the 'Lord of Right', who lays down ordinances for the universe. The king on his accession is seen to have become to his people what Varuna is to the gods. For that reason, he, too, is known as the 'Lord of Right'. In Balinese Hinduism, Fred Eiseman writes, *Dharma* is seen as 'the organizing force that maintains order, the organization that governs the universe as a whole, the relationships between various parts of the universe and actions within the various parts of the universe.'

The concept of *Dharma* was also taken up by the Buddhists, who brought it to China where the *Dharma* of Mahayana Buddhism was identified with the *Tao*. De Groot describes the Buddhist *Dharma* as the universal law which embraces the world in its entirety. 'It exists for the benefit of all beings, for does not its chief manifestation, the light of the world, shine its blessing on all men and all things?' When a Buddhist Lama sets his prayer wheel turning, he is performing a ritual that has deep meaning both in terms of the *Dharma* and the *R'ta*. Not only are the prayers printed on it repeated by his audience, but, as Jane Harrison notes,

> He finds himself in sympathetic touch with the Wheel of the Universe; he performs the act *Dharma-Chakra-Pravartana*, 'Justice-Wheel-Setting in motion'. He dare not turn the wheel contrariwise; lest that were to upset the whole order of nature.

If there is a notion of the right way to follow in order to maintain the order of the cosmos, there is, in all traditional societies, a notion of the *wrong way*, or anti-way, which threatens the order of the cosmos and must thereby give rise to the worst possible discontinuities. In the Vedas, as Chaitanya notes, we read that *R'ta*, though benign, can also be 'stern and fierce' when it comes to transgressions. 'Brihaspati rides a fearsome chariot of *R'ta* for destroying the wicked', meaning those who violate the eternal laws and so threaten the critical order of the cosmos.

Among the ancient Egyptians, the wrong way was referred to as *Isft*. Among the Greeks, it was often referred to as *ou Themis*, the opposite of *Themis* (which occasionally was used to mean 'social order' and occasionally 'the order of the pantheon' as well as the path to be followed to achieve such order). Among the Indians of the Vedic period, the anti-Way was referred to as *An-R'ta*, the opposite of *R'ta*, and among the Buddhists as *Adharma*, the opposite of *Dharma*.

To follow the *ou Themis* could not be done with impunity. Among the Greeks, Themis (or Dike) was seen on such occasions as taking on a very different form, that of Nemesis, which is seen by Cornford as related to *Nomos* – in turn related to Nemos, the sacred grove which was almost certainly the original place of worship of the ancient Greeks, as it was of the Celts. Nemos, or Nemesis, inhabited such a grove. She may originally have been the woodland goddess, identified with Artemis, or Diana of the woods. She was also a goddess of fertility, closely allied with Fortuna, 'the Lady who brings forth the fruits of the earth'. However, as Cornford notes,

'She who dispenses good things can withhold them or dispense blights instead of blessings, the awful power which haunts the *Nemos* may blast the profane invader of her sanctuary.'

In the earliest times, when Nemos was a sacred grove, Nemesis, as Donald Hughes notes, would have wrought vengeance on those who trespassed. Eventually, once the sacred groves fell into disuse, Nemesis would have become the guardian of the law, that is of *Nomos* and hence of *Dike*.

Classical mythology abounds in stories of the earth taking her revenge on those who destroy the natural world. Thus Erysichthon, whose name means 'tearer of earth', cut down a tree inhabited by a dryad, in spite of the tree-spirit's protests. She complained to Mother Earth, who afflicted him with insatiable hunger. Orion boasted that he would kill all the animals in the world. This, too, was reported to Mother Earth, who sent a monstrous scorpion to sting him to death. Today they are constellations opposite one another in the sky.

Our modern society has quite clearly set out systematically to deviate from the Way. Its overriding goal is economic development or progress, which can only be achieved by methodically disrupting the critical order of the Biosphere, indeed *destroying* the Biosphere so as to replace it with a totally different organization – the technosphere – which derives its resources from the Biosphere and consigns there its ever more voluminous and more toxic wastes. Technospheric expansion is another way of looking at Biospheric disintegration and contraction, and the pattern of behaviour that must be adopted to achieve the goal of modern society can only be the anti-Way. (see Chapter 64)

# SIXTY TWO

# For vernacular man, to increase his stock

# of 'vital force' is to follow the Way

●

*The ultimate goal of the Bantu is to possess as much vital force as possible, while what he fears most, is to see a reduction in his stock of this inestimable commodity. Every disease, wound or suffering or depression, every injustice and every failure is interpreted by the Bantu as a sure sign that there has been a reduction in his stock of vital force.*

PLACIDE TEMPELS

*What is required is restoring the category of the sacred, the category most thoroughly destroyed by the scientific establishment.*

HANS JONAS

Vernacular man follows the Way even in those societies in which the concept has not been clearly articulated. F. M. Cornford tells us that, in the classical world, a place was regarded as sacred because of the presence in it of a dangerous power, which made it sacrosanct – 'not to be set foot on by the profane'. Thus things that were sacred had to be treated with great respect, indeed, with trepidation. They were the source of every benefit and also of all misfortunes, for sacred things contain a dangerous energy or 'vital force'. Every traditional society has its word for it: *mana* among the Melanesians and Polynesians, *orenda* among the Sioux, *muntu* among the Baluba.

Émile Durkheim regards vital force as 'the source of all religiosity'. He sees 'spirits, demons, genii and gods of every sort' as 'the concrete forms taken by this energy'. It is partly, as least, because they are endowed with this vital force that they are sacred and have become objects of religious cults. The sun, the moon and the stars are also worshipped for this reason. 'They have not owed this honour to their intrinsic nature or their distinctive properties, but to the fact that they are thought to participate in this force which alone is able to give things a sacred character, and which is also found in a multitude of other beings even the smallest.' Adolphe Lods considers that 'the very ancient term which is found in all Semitic languages to express the idea of "god", one of the various forms of *el* (Hebrew), *ilu* (Babylonian), *ilah* (Arab), originally denoted the vague force which was the source of all strength and life.'

Vital force is seen as powering the whole living world. To acquire it personally is the only sure avenue to success. Placide Tempels, in his seminal work on Bantu philosophy, tells us that for them 'supreme happiness, the only form of good fortune is to possess the greatest possible amount of vital force, while the worst adversity and indeed the only real misfortune is to see a reduction in one's stock of this power.' Among the Baluba, vital force is referred to as *muntu*. A powerful man is described as *Muntu mukulumpe*, a man with a great deal of *muntu*, whereas a man of no social significance is referred to as a *Muntu mutupu*, or one who has but a small amount of *muntu*. A complex vocabulary is used to describe all the changes that can affect a man's stock of *muntu*. All illnesses, depressions or failures in any field of activity are taken to be evidence of a reduction in this vital force and can be avoided by maintaining one's stock of it. A man with none left at all is known as *Mufu*. He is as good as dead.

Not surprisingly, tribal man's overriding preoccupation is to increase his stock of 'vital force'. According to Robert Codrington, 'all Melanesian religion consists in getting this *mana* for one's self, or getting it used for one's benefit.' Tempels considers the same to be true of the Bantu. 'The goal of all efforts among the Bantu,' Tempels insists, 'can only be to intensify this vital force.' And indeed, their customs only make sense if one interprets them 'as a means of preserving or increasing one's stock of vital force.' Leopold Senghor, the poet, philosopher and former president of Senegal, considers that the goal of all religious ceremonies, all rituals and indeed all artistic endeavour in Africa is 'to increase the stock of vital force.'

Vital force is not just accumulated by individuals. It is usually seen as flowing through the cosmos and concentrating in certain things and beings, and, in doing so, forming a pattern of power and hence of sanctity – a philosophy known as Hylozoism. Paul Schebesta tells us that for the Pygmies of the Ituri forest in Zaire, vital force or *megbe*

> is spread out everywhere, but its power does not manifest itself everywhere with the same force nor in the same way. Certain animals are richly endowed with it. Humans possess a lot more of some types of *megbe* but less of other types. Able men are precisely those who have accumulated a lot of *megbe*: this is true of witch-doctors.

For the Comanches of the Nevada desert, the constituents of the natural world are imbued with different sorts of vital force. The greatest is variously personified by the eagle, the earth, the sky and the sun. The highest force is God. After him come the first fathers who founded various clans, and next comes the head of the tribe. The living also form a hierarchy in accordance with the vital power which they possess, and animals, plants and minerals are organized in the same way (see Kardiner, 1945).

It seems clear that vital force is organized within society, the natural world and the cosmos itself in a way which reflects its hierarchical structure. This is confirmed by Alassane Ndaw's account of vital force in the world-view of Bantu society: 'all the forces are organized hierarchically: first come the demigods or genii, then the original mythical ancestors, then the ordinary ancestors, then living men, in order of primogeniture, then animals, plants and minerals. In this way, the distribution of vital force serves to sanctify the cosmic hierarchy, preserving it from human depredations. Significantly, the amount of vital force at the different levels of social organization reflects the extent to which the society is integrated or centralized. Thus, in a very loose society, individuals and families are endowed with a considerable proportion of the society's vital force. On the other hand, in a highly centralized traditional kingdom such as ancient Egypt, Dahomey, or Benin in West Africa, the vital force becomes concentrated in the person of the divine king, who is divine precisely for that reason. In such a society, the welfare of all the inhabitants is regarded as totally dependent on the fulfilment of the important rituals and ceremonies designed to preserve and increase the king's stock of vital force, and on the observance of the many taboos surrounding his person.

The relationship between things and beings at different echelons in the hierarchy of the cosmos is not symmetrical. Vital power flows downwards to vitalize and hence sanctify things and beings at the lower echelons, though it will only do so if the latter fulfil their obligations towards the higher echelons and hence towards the cosmos as a whole. It is thus understandable that the rituals and ceremonies of a traditional people – and, indeed, their whole way of life – should be designed to maintain the correct distribution of vital force at each level in the cosmic hierarchy. Only thus can they serve to maintain the critical order and stability of the cosmos, and thereby follow the Way.

To neglect the performance of these sacred rituals and ceremonies – worse still, to break the sacred laws that govern their performance – is to violate a taboo. This leads to a change in the distribution of vital force within the cosmic hierarchy. An act is taboo, according to Roger Caillois, because it disrupts 'the universal order, which is at once that of nature and society' and, as a result, 'the Earth might no longer yield a harvest, the cattle might be struck with infertility, the stars might no longer follow their appointed course, death and disease could stalk the land.'

This all-pervading fear of disrupting the critical order of the cosmos is reflected in the taboos set up in all tribal societies against mixing things that belong to the different classes or provinces into which the cosmos is seen to be divided. This goes a long way towards explaining food taboos. If it is taboo to eat pork among the Hebrews, this is because the pig, as Mary Douglas notes,

> is put into the class of abominable, unclean creatures, along with the hare, the Hyrax and the camel. The grounds alleged are that these creatures either cleave the hoof or chew the cud, but do not do both. In other words, they don't quite make it into the class of ungulates.

To eat water creatures that do not have fins and scales is also taboo, for they do not fall into natural cosmic categories either. Nor do air creatures that do not fly or hop on the earth, and do not have wings and two legs. To eat such creatures can only reduce a person's vital force and simultaneously threaten the critical order of the cosmos. Mixed marriages between naturally exogamous social groups are seen in the same light; they threaten the critical order of society and thereby that of the cosmos of which it is part.

Among the Igbo of Nigeria, according to Victor Uchendu, 'deviations which disrupt the natural order are called *Aru*, literally, abominations.' The word *aru*, however, also means 'crime against nature'. Such crimes include a number of unnatural acts that defy normal behavioural categories, such as a man having sexual intercourse with his father's wife, or with an animal. The birth of twins and the hen hatching but one chick also fall into this category. These taboo events are *aru* because the Igbo believe 'that they transgress the laws guiding the ontological order, and will therefore bring disaster to the community.'

Once we abandon tribal man's notion of vital force, we go a long way towards desanctifying society and the natural world; in doing so, we leave it wide open to the depredations of modern industrial man, who follows the anti-Way.

———

# SIXTY THREE

# For vernacular man, to serve his gods is
# to follow the Way

●

*There is no better way to please the Buddha than to please all sentient beings.*
LADAKHI SAYING (HELENA NORBERG HODGE)

*The religious behaviour of man contributes to maintaining the sanctity of the world.*
MIRCA ELIADE

*And God saw everything that He had made, and found it very good.*
*And He said: This is a beautiful world that I have given you.*
*Take good care of it; do not ruin it.*
JEWISH PRAYER

———

If the term religion is to be used in the narrow sense of man's relationship with his gods and spirits, then the principal religion of chthonic man is ancestor worship – or 'communion with the ancestors' as Jomo Kenyatta prefers to call it on the grounds that the relationship is much more informal than 'worship' suggests. Underlying this form of religion is the principle that a dead ancestor or a deity remains a member of his family, his community and his society rather than inhabiting some distant paradise, a concept unknown to chthonic man.

In this way, the ancestral gods are as much part of society as are the living, as William Robertson-Smith pointed out many years ago in a famous passage:

> The circle into which a man was born was not simply a group of kinsfolk and fellow-citizens, but embraced also certain divine beings, the gods of the state, which to the ancient mind were as much a part of the particular community with which they stood connected as the human members of the social circle. The relationship between the gods of antiquity and their worshippers was expressed in the language of human relationship, and this language was not taken in a figurative sense but with strict literality.
>
> Thus a man was born into a fixed relation to certain gods as surely as he was born into relation to his fellow-men; and his religion, that is, the part of conduct which was determined by his relation to the gods, was simply one side of the general scheme of conduct prescribed for him by his position as a member of society. There was no separation between the spheres of religion and of ordinary life. Every social act had a reference to the gods as well as to men, for the social body was not made up of men only, but of gods and men.

Significantly, the gods of vernacular man, like his vital force, were seen as reflecting faithfully the hierarchical structure of his society. Thus Lafcadio Hearn writes of Japan:

> The three forms of the Shinto worship of ancestors are the Domestic Cult, the Communal Cult and the State Cult; or, in other words, the worship of family ancestors, the worship of clan or tribal ancestors and the worship of imperial ancestors. The first is the religion of the home; the second is the religion of the

local divinity, or titular god; the third is the national religion.

E. Driver shows how differences in the organization of the gods among North American Indian societies could be explained in terms of their degree of integration or centralization:

> There was a strong tendency to arrange gods in a ranked hierarchy in areas where people were ranked in a similar manner, and to ignore such ranking where egalitarianism dominated human societies. Thus the people of Meso-America carefully ranked their gods, while those in the Sub-Arctic Plateau and Great Basin believed in large numbers of spirits of about equal rank. Other areas tended to be intermediate in this respect. Among the Pueblos where many spiritual personalities were widely recognized to be designated as gods, there was little tendency towards ranking, just as there was more equality among human beings.

The people of Alor, as described by Cora Dubois, have a very loosely organized society. Few constraints are applied at a level higher than that of the family and the family itself is very weak. The average Alorese is undisciplined and self-indulgent, and has little regard for authority of any kind. Not surprisingly, the Alorese pantheon reflects this disorderly state of affairs. 'They have a culture hero and supreme deity,' writes Cora Dubois,

> but these play a very small part in their thought. Ancestral spirits are more important, but behaviour to them is loose and undisciplined, just as it is towards their parents. . . . The dead are merely pressing and insistent predators who can enforce their demands through supernatural powers. This is precisely the experience of the child with his parents. Hence he obeys reluctantly and grudgingly.

The Swazi, on the other hand, have developed a cohesive and hierarchically organized society, and, according to Hilda Kuper, their gods are organized in exactly the same way:

> In the ancestral cult the world of the living is projected onto a world of spirit

(*emadloti*). Men and women, old and young, aristocrats and commoners, continued the patterns of superiority and inferiority established by earthly experiences. Paternal and maternal spirits exercise complementary roles, similar to those operating in daily life on earth; the paternal role reinforces legal and economic obligations; the maternal exercises a less formalized protective influence. Although the cult is set in a kinship framework, it is extended to the nation through the king, who is regarded as the father of all Swazi. His ancestors are the most powerful of all the spirits.'

The ancestral gods, and thus the vital force which they personify, are organized in such a way as to reflect the critical order of vernacular society. This means, above all, that the structure of society is sanctified and its members forced, for fear of incurring the most terrible penalties, to preserve it come what may. By sanctifying the critical order of society, the ancestral gods simultaneously sanctify the natural world of which it is an integral part and which, as we have seen, is organized in accordance with the same basic plan. Significantly, the original chthonic gods had animal forms. Thus among the Greeks, according to Jane Harrison, Zeus Ktesios was once a snake, while 'Zeus Olbios, in local worship, long preserved his bull's head. . . . The Sun god of Crete, in Bull form, wooed the Moon Goddess, herself a cow; their child is a young bull-god, the Minos-Bull, the Minotaur.'

Because chthonic people made no radical distinction between themselves and other animals, there was no reason, in their scheme of things, to distinguish between man and his gods and the animals and the spirits that represented them, for all were part of the same cosmos. Significantly, among the ancient Greeks and Romans the original worshipping place was the sacred grove, known to the Greeks as the *Temene* and to the Romans as the Temple. 'The woods', as Pliny writes, 'were formerly temples of the deities, and even now simple country folk dedicate a tall tree to a God with the ritual of olden times; and we adore sacred groves and the very silence that reigns in them no less devoutly than images that gleam in gold and ivory.' The sacred groves could not be desecrated with impunity. It was Agamemnon's crime not just to kill a deer, but to do so in a *Temene*. Trees, as Donald Hughes tells us, were sacred to the Gods, 'the oak to Zeus, the laurel to Apollo, the willow to Hera, the pine tree (or perhaps the oak) to Pan.' Robert T. Parsons, writing about the Kono of Nigeria, sums up the nature and function of vernacular religion. It is not only

> an organization of human relationships, but includes also the relationships of people with the earth as a whole, with their own land and with the unseen world of constructive forces and beings in which they believe. Religion brings them all into a consistent whole.

The relationship between chthonic people and their gods was one of mutual obligations. The gods had needs, and their principal need was for the living to fulfil their ritual and ceremonial obligations, observing the laws that the ancestors themselves had enacted *in illo tempore*. For their part, the living – families, clans and tribes – needed the gods to protect them from malnutrition, disease, enemy invasions and other disasters. As Lafcadio Hearn puts it, 'the happiness of the dead depends upon the respectful service rendered them by the living; and the happiness of the living depends upon the fulfilment of pious duty to the dead' – a clear case of hierarchical mutualism.

Observing their obligations and obeying the cosmic law, chthonic people followed the behaviour pattern which best preserved the critical order of the cosmos, reflected and sanctified in their pantheon. However, chthonic religion dies as society disintegrates. The Olympian gods were the products of this social disintegration. Whereas the behaviour of the original chthonic deities was subjected to the great powers that governed the cosmos (the *Moira*, or fate, which once also referred to the spatial order of the cosmos, and *Dike*, or justice, which was responsible for assuring its temporal order) – the Olympian gods were set above these cosmic powers. Their behaviour, and indeed that of the disintegrating society whose organization they reflected, was no longer subject to the constraints that previously served to maintain the critical order of the cosmos.

Jane Harrison sees the shift from the chthonic to the Olympian gods as a move from the holistic view of society and of the cosmos to the individualized view. 'The Olympian has clear form', she writes, he is the *principium individuationis* incarnate . . . the mystery (or chthonic) god is the life of the whole of things, he can only be felt – as soon as he is thought and individualized he passes, as Dionysos had to pass, into the thin, rare ether of the Olympian. The Olympians are of conscious thinking, divided, distinct, departmental; the mystery god is the impulse of life through all things, perennial, indivisible.

As social disintegration proceeded still further, the Olympian gods ceased to have any relationship with society, for society was no more. The accent was then on the cult of a national God and eventually on that of the universal God. As society further disintegrated; the only remaining vernacular social grouping was the nuclear family and, not surprisingly, the universal god acquired a wife and a child so that the now truncated pantheon reflected the newly atomized society.

The Christian Trinity finds its counterpart in the religion of other disintegrated societies. The cult of Osiris and Isis and the baby Horus, for example, developed during the breakdown of ancient Egyptian society and was most popular during the Ptolemaic age. As the role of religion ceases to be social, it serves instead to provide solace to the individual and the nuclear family, beyond which lies an undifferentiated mass of humanity from which individuals feel increasingly alienated, as they are from the natural world and from the cosmos. It is then only to the universal God, who like him is a temporal as well as a spatial isolate, that he feels any duty. As Theodore Roszak puts it, such a God, having become 'infinitely removed from falling nature, becomes that cosmic bouillon cube, in which all holiness is now to be concentrated for safe keeping.' The 'revealed' religions of today, such as Christianity, Islam and modern Judaism, have desanctified society and the natural world, leaving them open to exploitation and destruction. For Nicholas Berdyaev, 'Christianity alone made possible both positive science and technique. The reason is that it severed man from nature emotionally.' But the same is true of Islam and modern Judaism.

As society disintegrates and religion becomes increasingly 'otherworldly', as man is severed from nature and indeed from the entire Gaian hierarchy, so his attitude and behaviour towards his gods ceases to occur within its correct field, that provided by the Gaian hierarchy of which he is part. Instead, it becomes heterotelic to the Gaian hierarchy and ceases to fulfil its true social, ecological and cosmic role, leading man to follow the anti-Way.

# SIXTY FOUR

# Progress is anti-evolutionary and is the

# anti-Way

●

*. . . Such is my awful Vision:*
*I see the Four-fold Man, The Humanity in deadly sleep*
*And its fallen Emanation, The Spectre and its cruel Shadow.*
*I see the Past, Present and Future existing all at once*
*Before me. O Divine Spirit, sustain me on thy wings,*
*That I may awake Albion from her long and cold repose;*
*For Bacon and Newton, sheath'd in dismal steel, their terrors hang*
*Like iron scourges over Albion: Reasonings like vast Serpents*
*Infold around my limbs, bruising my minute articulations.*
*I turn my eyes to the Schools and Universities of Europe*
*And there behold the Loom of Locke, whose Woof rages dire,*
*Wash'd by the Water-wheels of Newton; black the cloth*
*In heavy wreathes folds over every nation: cruel Works*
*Of many Wheels I view, wheel without wheel, with cogs tyrannic*
*Moving by compulsion each other, not as those in Eden, which Wheel within*
*Wheel, in freedom revolve in harmony and peace.*
WILLIAM BLAKE

In terms of the world-view of modernism and of the associated paradigm of science, progress – the changes brought to the Biosphere by modern man, with the aid of science, technology and industry – are part and parcel of the evolutionary process. No distinction is made between the process that leads to the development of the world of living things, or the Biosphere, and that which leads instead to the development of the technosphere.

If these two obviously very different and indeed conflicting processes are distinguished at all, it is only in the distinction between 'endosomatic' and 'exosomatic' types of evolution. The former involves the modification of organs and behaviour, or the emergence of new organs and behaviour in the development of an organism, while the latter proceeds largely by the technical construction of new 'organs' outside the organism (or person). Sir Peter Medawar illustrates this position when he makes fun of a student who asked him if humans 'might not evolve to possess wings and so make it possible to fly.' 'This is a foolish question', he insists, since 'it is obvious that human beings have already acquired some of the capabilities of both birds and fish – capabilities which they owe to their own special style of evolution, the "exosomatic".'

In the view of Julian Huxley and other eminent biologists, the historical era, and particularly the industrial age, have created a heightening of human evolution in psychological and social terms, although there is no evidence that such a development has in any way changed the human organism or resulted in a creature better adapted psychologically and socially than it was in the prehistoric environment. Even ecologists lend support to this fallacy. Ramon Margalef, the celebrated Spanish ecologist, tells us that 'industrialization has brought mankind a marked acceleration of evolutionary processes.' Erich Jantsch goes further. For him, progress or economic development 'forms a meaningful and integral part of a universal evolution . . . mankind is an agent of this universal evolution, and even an important one.'

Another ardent supporter of this view is Peter Russell, who invites us to 'sit here and wonder at the whole evolutionary process, which has, step by step, resulted in me and you, in farms, automobiles and computers, in men walking on the moon, in the Taj Mahal, the Emperor Concerto and the Theory of Relativity.' For Russell, one of the most powerful tools that modern science makes available to this version of evolution is genetic engineering. This will enable us to create 'completely new species' and, as a result, evolution will no longer have to follow 'the slow process of trial and error, and natural selection'. Instead, new species can be 'consciously designed and created within a matter of months.' Atomic physics, we are assured, will also contribute to our further evolution.

> With the advent of particle accelerators, scientists once again became more than just passive observers. They were now able to change some elements into others, or even create completely new elements, by bombarding the nucleus with atomic particles and thereby changing its structure.

The invention of the solar cells, he also tells us, 'represents an evolutionary development as significant as that of photosynthesis 3.5 billion years ago.' Moreover we shall soon be able to influence our evolution by means of our growing ability to colonize space, 'a development as significant as the colonization of land by the first amphibians 400 million years ago.' Russell is so impressed by all these technological developments that he is led to ask whether 'the rapid acceleration so characteristic of today is heading us towards an evolutionary leap.' Indeed, he asks, 'could we be on the threshold of a leap as significant as the evolution of life from inanimate matter?'

Those who support the notion that technological progress is part and parcel of the evolutionary process usually regard the early stages of evolution as instinctive, while the later stages that we associate with technological progress are taken to be conscious and purposive. This seems to be the standard position of today's mainstream scientists. Erich Jantsch, for example, argues that evolution is usually seen as the history of the organization of matter and energy. However, it can also be viewed as 'the organization of information into complexity of knowledge'. This 'may be understood as the evolution of consciousness', the highest state of evolution corresponding to Teilhard de Chardin's noosphere. 'Once this state is achieved', he writes, 'the whole universe can be identified with consciousness and it is this consciousness that determines the course of further evolution.' If human consciousness alone determines evolution, then man is *free to determine his own evolution*. As Jantsch puts it, the 'evolution of consciousness' is also the evolution of 'autonomy and emancipation'. Man is thereby deified. Indeed, 'it is because man possesses consciousness', Jantsch tells us, 'that mankind is not redeemed by God, but redeems itself.'

Some of our most brilliant theoretical biologists, among them Julian Huxley and C. H. Waddington, see progress in a similar light. For them 'human evolution', as they refer to it, is also the latest phase of evolution, and it is principally the product of the development of mind, consciousness and reason. Because they consider man to be endowed with these three unique attributes, he is free to determine his own evolution – unencumbered, they clearly intimate, by any obligation to subject his progressive activities to any social, ecological or cosmic constraints.

In the light of the analysis provided in this book, however, human evolution, or progress, is the very negation of evolution, or the Gaian process, and is best referred to as anti-evolution. Since evolution or the Gaian process can be equated with the Way, serving as it does to maintain the critical order and hence the stability of the Biosphere, progress or anti-evolution can be equated with the anti-Way – serving as it does to disrupt the critical order of the Biosphere and reduce its stability.

In terms of the neo-Darwinian view of evolution as a random process, heading in no particular direction, and hence just as capable of giving rise to a climax Biosphere as to a highly developed industrial technosphere, the very notion of anti-evolution is meaningless. It is also contradictory to see the Gaian process as directive but then insist, as some leading scientists do, that its goal is to increase its complexity or its diversity. For none of .these concepts have been defined in a sufficiently discriminatory way to enable one to distinguish between the sort of complexity or diversity serves to preserve the critical order of the Biosphere and that which serves instead to build up the technosphere – an organization of resources that is in direct competition with the Biosphere, from which it derives its resources and to which it consigns its ever more voluminous and toxic waste products. It is because this critical distinction has not been made that it is still possible for mainstream scientists and economists to pretend that evolution and economic development or progress are part and parcel of the same process, whereas in fact they are antithetical to each other.

Thus as biological, ecological and social systems evolve, they become more complex and also more diverse, though in ecosystems complexity and diversity tend to stop increasing a little before a climax state is reached. Increasing complexity enables a system to assure its homeostasis in the specific conditions in which it lives, whereas increasing diversity enables it to hold its own in a wide range of conditions, dealing with challenges that are less probable in terms of its evolutionary experience. Progress or economic development, on the other hand, simplifies and degrades interrelationships between the constituent parts of natural systems. Human families and communities are atomized and largely replaced by institutions and corporations which are in competition with them. Primary forest ecosystems are destroyed and replaced by a series of ever less complex and diverse systems: secondary forests, then plantations of fast-growing exotics, then pasture and finally cement to accommodate urban development.

The reduction of genetic diversity occurring as a result of the destruction of tropical rainforests is stupendous. There may be as many as 300 million different species of living things, between 50 and 80 per cent of which probably live in the world's remaining tropical rainforests, now being destroyed at such a rate that within a matter of 20 or 30 years only the most inaccessible will remain. During that period, the march of progress-logging, mining, road building, dam building and the conversion of forest to rangeland and agricultural land – will lead to the extinction of thousands of species if not more every day: a global biological holocaust of unthinkable proportions.

Social evolution has also led to the development of a wide diversity of different ethnic groups, each perfectly adapted to the specialized environment in which it lives. There are said to have been at least 120 different tribes in California alone, and 700 in New Guinea. With progress, or anti-evolution, their cultures are beomg disrupted and their members are transformed into a vast homogeneous mass of alienated people – most of whom are condemned, within a decade or two, to living in the growing slums that will soon accommodate half of humanity.

Increasing complexity and diversity are closely associated with increasing cooperation between the constituents of a natural system. Indeed, with evolution, competition gives way to cooperation, or what ecologists call mutualism. However, as the anti-evolutionary process gets under way, and complexity is dramatically reduced, so mutualism gives way to competition. In a human society the same is true. The cooperation that obtains among the members of an extended family and the vernacular community of which they are part is so great, and contributes so much to the quality of their lives and indeed to their survival, that it is best regarded as 'social wealth'. With progress, social wealth is rapidly dissipated as social cooperation is replaced by interpersonal competition and aggression. The social wealth lost in this way cannot be compensated for by state services or economic wealth, which can only satisfy superficial human needs precariously at that.

As evolution proceeds, there is a reduction in randomness and a corresponding increase in order. This order is possible because the constituent parts behave homeotelically or in such a way as to maintain the order of the whole. In a climax society, for instance, education is homeotelic to society, to the natural world and to the cosmos itself. So are settlement patterns, technology, economic activities, and government itself.

The units of homeotelic activity are the natural social units within which human beings evolved: the family, the community and the society. When these units disintegrate under the impact of economic development or progress, and are replaced by corporations and institutions, the activities they formerly supported become increasingly heterotelic or random to the goal of maintaining the critical order of society and of the Gaian hierarchy. Thus education no longer serves its basic function of socializing young people so they can become homeotelic members of their families and communities, settlement patterns cease to be designed to reflect social structure and the structure of the cosmos, technology and economic activities in general cease to be embedded 'in social relations' and rapidly spin out of control, eventually becoming the principle agents of social and ecological destruction. Religion becomes universal and otherworldly and no longer serves to sanctify social structure or the structure of the natural world, leaving them open to exploitation and destruction. Government, instead of being a normal communal function, is fulfilled by an external body preoccupied with its own short-term interests which are necessarily in conflict with both those of the society it is called upon to govern, and of the natural world.

As evolution proceeds, systems also become increasingly self-sufficient: Eugene Odum notes that the perfecting of a system's recycling mechanisms is an essential means of increasing self-sufficiency. As ecosystems develop, they are endowed with ever more elaborate methods for recycling precious materials: this is particularly true of tropical rainforests. A vernacular society, too, becomes increasingly committed to the careful recycling of all materials.

Again, progress or anti-evolution puts this process into reverse. The waste products of one process, rather than serving as raw materials for the next, are simply released into the environment in the cheapest way possible, without considering pollution or the long-run shortages this will cause. Worse still, xenobiotic materials of which the biosphere has had no experience, and thus cannot be recycled homeotelically, are released into the environment in ever greater quantities.

With evolution vernacular communities also learn to become self-sufficient, at least in the basic resources on which they must depend for their survival. Thus trade – which brings dependence on external sources of supply as well as on external markets for the sale of produce – is limited to products that are of secondary importance. In this way economic activities remain under communal control and homeotelic to Gaian needs. Reversing this process, economic development or progress turns the world into one vast 'global supermarket' and the resulting growth in social and economic dependence on an ever less sustainable technosphere can only maximize global instability.

On the one hand, therefore, a range of evolutionary trends make the Biosphere ever more stable and more homeostatic, with a corresponding reduction in the incidence and severity of discontinuities. On the other hand, economic development or progress degrades and destabilizes the Biosphere, with a corresponding increase in the incidence and severity of ecological discontinuities such as pollution accidents, droughts, floods, epidemics and climatic changes.

Significantly, both Margalef and Odum compare evolution with eco-

logical succession. Odum notes that the changes brought about by industrial man are reversing ecological succession. Margalef also points out
that man's interference with the functioning of ecosystems must return
them to a lower and more unstable successional stage – one Odum refers
to as a 'disclimax' (a disturbance climax) or an 'anthropogenic sub-climax'.
This is difficult to reconcile with Arthur Tansley's notion of the superiority of the anthropogenic climax over the natural climax; it is also incompatible with the very notion of economic development or progress as a
means of improving human welfare.

Today, with the globalization of progress, we are rapidly heading
towards a global Biospheric disclimax in which modern man will have
effectively reversed three thousand million years of evolution to create an
impoverished and degraded world that is ever less capable of sustaining
complex forms of life such as man. Sir Peter Medawar admits that our
hopes have not worked out: 'every folly, every enormity we look back on
with repugnance can find its equivalent in contemporary life.' But still, for
him, this does not invalidate the principle of progress. 'There is no need',
he writes, 'to be dismayed by the fact that we cannot yet envisage a defin-
itive solution of our problems, we can obviously do better than this.' In
any case, 'it is a bit too early to expect our grander ambitions to be fulfilled.' We must remember that 'human history is only just beginning.' We
have known that 'there has always been room for improvement; now we
know that there is time for improvement too.'

But is there really time? Is history only just beginning, or is it in reality
coming to an end? Is there really any reason to suppose that 'we can do
better' if we continue to move in this anti-evolutionary direction? This is a
pure act of faith – one that is irreconcilable with all our relevant knowledge.

# SIXTY FIVE

# To keep to the Way, society must be able

# to correct any divergence from it

●

*Man has lost his way in the jungle of chemistry and engineering and will have to retrace his steps, however painful this may be. He will have to discover where he went wrong and make his peace with nature. In so doing, perhaps he may be able to recapture the rhythm of life and the love of the simple things of life, which will be an ever-unfolding joy to him.*
RICHARD ST BARBE-BAKER

*Grandfather,*
*Look at our brokenness.*
*We know that in all creation*
*Only the human family*
*Has strayed from the Sacred Way.*
*We know that we are the ones*
*Who are divided*
*And we are the ones*
*Who must come back together*
*To walk in the Sacred Way.*
*Grandfather,*
*Sacred One,*
*Teach us love, compassion, and honour*
*That we may heal the earth*
*And heal each other.*
OJIBWAY PRAYER

Developing natural systems can only maintain their course or chreod if they can deal effectively with external or internal challenges that might divert them from it. To do this, they must either isolate themselves from challenges (resistance stability) or, alternatively, correct divergences from their path or Way (resilience stability) which requires that they interpret the problems caused by such divergences correctly.

Vernacular man in the classical world understood, as Donald Hughes notes, that 'hunger, ill-health, erosion, poverty and general ruin' were only different forms 'that the earth's revenge could take for the terrible mistreatment meted out to her by man' – punishments for having diverted from the Way in pursuit of the anti-Way or what the ancient Greeks would have called the *ou themis*. The only way to combat these ills, therefore, was to treat the earth with greater care, which meant to return to the Way of the ancestors who lived in the Golden Age when such ills were unknown.

Vernacular people invariably interpreted disease in particular in this way. Thus among the Tukanos of Colombia, as Gerardo Reichel-Dolmatoff notes,

> illness is taken to be the consequence of a person's upsetting a certain aspect of the ecological balance. Overhunting is a common cause and so are harvesting activities in which some relatively scarce natural resource has been wasted. The delicate balance existing within the natural environment between nature and society, and within society itself, is bound to affect the whole.'

In other words,

> The shaman as a healer of illness does not so much interfere on the individual level, but operates on the level of those supra-individual structures that have been disturbed by the person. To be effective, he has to apply his treatment to the disturbed part of the ecosystem. It might be said then that a Tukano shaman does not have individual patients: his task is to cure a social malfunctioning.

He does this by re-establishing the rules that 'will avoid overhunting, the depletion of certain plant resources and unchecked population increase.'

Quite clearly, then, the shaman is more than a medical practitioner. He is a 'truly powerful source in the control and management of resources' for he can really affect the incidence and severity of diseases over which the modern medical practitioner has no control whatsoever.

Victor Turner shows that among the Ndembu of East Africa the doctor 'sees his task in very much the same way.' It is

> less as curing an individual patient than as remedying the ills of a corporate group. The sickness of a patient is mainly a sign that 'something is rotten' in the corporate body. The patient will not get better until all the tensions and aggressions in the group's interrelations have been brought to light and exposed to ritual treatment. The doctor's task is to tap the various streams of affect associated with these conflicts and with the social and interpersonal disputes in which they are manifested – and to channel them in a socially positive direction. The raw energies of conflict are thus domesticated in the service of the traditional social order.

The philosophy underlying this interpretation and treatment of disease is even more explicit in the case of the Qollahuaya diviners of the community of Kaata in the Bolivian Andes. They see their community as an integral part of an *Ayllu* – conceptualizing their mountainous territory as a human body with communities living on the high ground, the central areas and in the lowlands. According to Joseph W. Bastien, the head of the *Ayllu* is the 'moist *puna* area' where herders graze alpacas, llamas, sheep and pigs; the grasses that grow there are its hair, its eyes are the lakes of Apacheta. Its trunk is formed by the sloping terraced fields of potatoes, *oca* and barley.

The *Ayllu* also has a heart and a liver, which produce blood and fat and are the 'principles of life and power'. They are circulated by the diviners throughout the community and in particular into the 'earth shrines' by means of rituals and ceremonies in which the sick people 'eat with the mountain'. For the people of Kaata, human health is thereby identified with the integrity of their *Ayllu*: it follows that when people, society and environment 'work together to form one body, the bodies of sick individuals become whole' and the sick are thus restored to health. The body metaphor provides in this way 'a systemic model in which there is an analogy between the human body and the environmental and social bodies.' Diseases are diagnosed as 'signs of disorders between man and his land, or between his vertical *Ayllu* and *Ayllu* Kaata.' The disease is then combated 'not by isolating the individual in a hospital away from his land' but instead 'by gathering the members of his social group in ritual and together feeding all the parts of *Ayllu* Kaata.'

Bastien sees this as typical of the approach to disease of the people of the Andes in general. For them, disease

> is an organic, cultural, environmental and social phenomenon. . . . By means of the body metaphor, diviners not only examine, but also interrelate the complex networks of environmental factors and social structure with physical distress. This often prevents subsequent illness because action is taken to change social and environmental causes of the sickness.

In this manner, vernacular man diagnoses heterotelic diseases as the symptoms of social and ecological maladjustments brought about by diverging from the Way, thereby violating the laws of the cosmos and disrupting its critical order: maladjustments that can only be eliminated by correcting the divergence and returning to the Way.

Modern man, on the other hand, interprets problems in terms of cause and effect relationships on the basis of which a disease is attributed to a discreet event such as the action of a bacterium, virus or other pathogen – which must then be eliminated, usually by waging chemical warfare against it. To do this, we build factories for manufacturing the chemicals, shops in which to sell them, hospitals in which to administer them and universities in which we train the chemical engineers, pharmacists, doctors and other specialists involved in manufacturing, selling and administering them. Thus we put our faith in scientific, technological and industrial development, or progress – precisely what our society is organized to provide. This may occasionally serve to cure individual sufferers; it will always serve the interests of industrialists and their political allies; but it will do nothing to reduce the incidence of the disease.

All the other ever more daunting problems which confront our society today are interpreted in much the same way. Each one is made to appear soluble by the expedients that science, technology and industry can provide, rationalized and legitimized by the world-view of modernism. Thus poverty is seen to be primarily a shortage of material goods and technological devices, and of the money required to purchase them. Economic development can solve this problem, since it will enable us to build factories which can manufacture these commodities, and provide jobs to enable people to earn the money required to pay for them.

The World Bank and other Multinational Development Banks (MDBs) insist that the object of the destructive economic development that they finance is the eradication of poverty. Thus, in the President of the World Bank's 1987 address to his Board of Governors, he stated that his purpose that day was to

> outline the Bank's strategy for steady advance towards restored global economic growth, for steady progress in the fight against poverty.

Bilateral aid agencies seek to maintain the same fiction. 'The principal purpose' of US aid, a former US Secretary of State told his country's Senate foreign affairs committee, is 'to meet the basic needs of poor people in the developing countries' – which is difficult to reconcile with the fact that about 75 per cent of American bilateral aid is 'tied' to the purchase of American manufactured goods, and serves principally to subsidize American exports.

The rapid degradation of the world's remaining agricultural lands is invariably attributed by governments and international agencies to traditional agricultural techniques. Thus US aid attributes the rapid deterioration of 'the soil resource base' in arid lands to mismanagement, based on the use of 'traditional technology and agricultural practices' – though these techniques have been used sustainably for thousands of years. Broske G. Schoepf also notes how a scientist sent to Zaire to work on the Man and the Biosphere programme (MAB) saw peasant cultivators as 'enemies of the environment'. On the other hand, corporations operating large plantations were viewed by him as 'progressive in their contributions to development – as forces with whom alliance and accommodation are to be sought.' Margaret Thatcher, in her 1989 address to the United Nations General Assembly, attributes the degradation of agricultural land to what she calls 'cut-and-burn' agriculture, and recommends action 'to improve agricultural methods – good husbandry, that ploughs back nourishment into the soil', a rather rosy view of modern agriculture.

Malnutrition and famine are also attributed to archaic agricultural practices and, in particular, to low inputs of fertilizer. A report based on a 20-year study jointly undertaken by the Food and Agricultural Organization (FAO) and other organizations insists that the amount of food produced in the world is a direct function of fertilizer use, without mentioning the diminishing returns on successive applications of fertilizer experienced wherever farmers have adopted modern agriculture methods. According to the FAO, malnutrition and famine are also due to poverty. People starve because they do not have the money required to buy food; it follows that 'the income of the poor must be increased so that their basic food requirements can be translated into effective demand.' Hence more economic development – even though, in spite of the unprecedented economic development of the post-war years, more people than ever before now lack the money to buy food.

The population explosion is also primarily attributed to poverty. Poor people are insecure, which leads them to produce more children, who can be put to work to earn money for their parents. This means that to bring population growth under control requires rapid economic development which will provide them with the money they require to assure their security, assuring in this way 'a demographic transition' as has already occurred in the industrial world. No mention is made of the fact that this transition only occurred in the industrial world once per-capita income had reached a much higher level than Third World people can hope to achieve. Nor is it noted that economic development, by destroying families and communities, annihilating their natural environment and forcing them off the land and into the slums, is the greatest source of their present insecurity.

The population explosion is seen above all to be the result of a shortage of family planning devices – also so much so, that the World Bank estimates that to achieve 'a rapid fertility decline goal' in sub-Saharan Africa, would mean increasing the amount of money spent on 'family planning' twenty times by the end of the century – an extremely convenient approach to the problem from the point of view of manufacturers of birth-control pills, condoms and IUDs.

So it is, with all the other problems that confront us, whether it be unemployment, crime, delinquency, drug-addiction, alcoholism, pollution and resource depletion, global deforestation and global warming. Each of these problems is interpreted in a way that rationalizes policies we have already decided to adopt: those that make the greatest contribution to economic development and hence best satisfy the requirements of the corporations and institutions that dominate our society. In other words, instead of interpreting our problems as the inevitable consequence of economic development or progress – that anti-evolutionary process that diverts us ever further from the Way – we interpret them instead as providing evidence that economic development has not proceeded far or fast enough – that, in effect, we have not deviated sufficiently from the Way.

This is the essence of the Great Misinterpretation – the ultimate manifestation of modern man's cognitive maladjustment to the industrial world that he has created. It has drawn us into a chain reaction of ever greater social and environmental destruction, from which we must waste no time in extracting ourselves if we are to have any future on this planet.

# SIXTY SIX

# The Great Reinterpretation requires a

# conversion to the world-view of ecology

●

*The quest for a communal reality assumes the shape of a massive salvage operation, reaching out in many unlikely directions. I think this is the great adventure of our age and far more humanly valuable than the 'race for space'. It is the reclamation and renewal of the Old Gnosis. For those who respond to the call, what happens within the world of science, though still consequential in public policy, will have less and less existential meaning. The scientists and their many imitators will become for them an arcane priesthood carrying on obscure professional ceremonies and exchanging their 'public knowledge' within the inner sanctum of the state temple.*

THEODORE ROSZAK

*This generation may either be the last to exist in any semblance of a civilized world or it will be the first to have the vision, the bearing and the greatness to say 'I will have nothing to do with this destruction of life, I will play no part in this devastation of the land, I am determined to live and work for peaceful construction for I am morally responsible for the world of today and the generations of tomorrow'.*

RICHARD ST BARBE-BAKER

No amount of empirical or theoretical evidence is likely to persuade mainstream scientists or other protagonists of the world-view of modernism to accept any of the principles set out in this book. If eventually they are to be accepted, it will not be because they will by then have been 'proved' to be true in the scientific sense of the term, but because the reigning paradigm or canon of knowledge will have changed to such an extent that they have become consistent with it. Until this occurs, these principles are, in the words of Gunther Stent, 'premature' in that 'its implications cannot be connected by a series of simple logical steps to "canonical" or "generally accepted knowledge" within the current paradigm.' In this way, Gleason's 'individualistic concept of the plant association' was rejected when ecology was still a holistic discipline only to be adopted once it had been brought into line with the paradigm of science.

At the same time, no amount of empirical or theoretical 'evidence' as to the untenability of a hypothesis can lead scientists to abandon it if it is part of current wisdom, the reigning paradigm, or the canon of knowledge. However, once it has ceased to enjoy that status, because it has been transferred to another paradigm, then the hypothesis will simply die a natural death. In this way, hypotheses that have achieved the status of 'scientific facts' have, in the space of a few years, been 'completely discredited and committed to oblivion, without ever having been disproved or even newly tested.' This is, as Michael Polanyi points out, 'simply because the conceptual framework of science had, meanwhile, so altered that the facts no longer appeared credible.'

Clearly then, so long as we argue within the accepted 'conceptual framework' of the reigning paradigm, or the canonical knowledge of the day, we can never persuade people either to accept a new idea or to abandon an old one. 'Demonstration', Polanyi insists, 'must be supplemented . . . by forms of persuasion which can induce a conversion.' This is the crux of the matter. It is the conceptual framework itself that must be changed, and this, as Polanyi suggests, means converting people to a new conceptual framework. For people to accept the principles listed in this book, it is the paradigm of science itself that must be abandoned, and hence the world-view of modernism which it faithfully reflects; and they must be replaced by the world-view of ecology. Such a conversion, or generalized paradigm shift, involves a profound rearrangement or recombination of the knowledge that makes up our world-view. It must affect its very metaphysical, ethical and aesthetic foundations. It must, in fact, involve a change akin to a religious conversion, which – as Thomas S. Kuhn, Polanyi and, more recently, Rupert Sheldrake have noted – is also true of a paradigm shift occurring in a purely scientific context.

One must distinguish between a real religious conversion and a nominal one. All too often, a religious conversion is of a very superficial nature; it is largely the terminology used in addressing the world of gods and spirits that changes, and little else. Real conversion seems to occur in quite specific conditions, which the psychologist William Sergeant has compared to those that lead, more stressfully, to a nervous breakdown, and also to the brainwashing to which prisoners of war are often subjected in order to make them confess to crimes they have not committed. It seems probable that electric shock treatment in psychiatric hospitals fulfils a similar function. This explains why religious conversions are often preceded by physically and mentally exhausting ceremonies, the taking of alcohol and drugs, and the achievement of trance-like states as in the famous Dionysian rites. All this gives rise to a state of mind that may well be functionally analogous to a nervous breakdown, in which people can be inculcated with a new world-view.

It may be that the same process occurs – though in a less dramatic way – in new environmental conditions such as those created by economic development, or when a traditional cultural pattern proves to be unadaptive, causing people to question and eventually abandon the world view with which they and their ancestors have been imbued for centuries or even millennia. They pass through a highly stressful – indeed, psychically intolerable – experience, for the human psyche abhors a cultural vacuum as it does the terrible social disorder to which it must give rise.

Such a situation occurred with the breakdown of Paganism – as we refer to the traditional religion or world-view of early Roman society. In the chaos that ensued, there was a frantic search to replace Paganism with a different world-view, one that could at least satisfy the psychic requirements of the increasingly atomized and alienated masses that inhabited the growing conurbations of the Roman Empire. Not surprisingly, they turned eastwards for inspiration, to where similar social conditions had already existed for millennia. Franz Cumont describes the proliferation of eastern cults among the culturally deprived Roman masses. Eastern gods such as Attis, Adonis, Mithra, Osiris and Isis all had their devotees. But it was the religion preached by St Paul, the religion of Jesus Christ, that was to prevail.

Anthony Wallace seeks to explain the process involved. He sees every person in society as 'maintaining a mental image of the society and its culture, as well as of his own body and its behavioural regularities, in order to act in ways which reduce stress at all levels of the system.' This mental image or model, he refers to as 'a mazeway'. However, when a person under stress receives repeated information indicating 'that his mazeway does not lead to action which reduces the level of stress, he must choose between maintaining his present maze-way and tolerating the stress, or changing the maze-way in an attempt to reduce the stress.' This involves 'changing his total gestalt, of his image of self, society and culture, of nature and body, and of ways of action' – in this way, a new culture comes into being. Such a culture is generally referred to as millenarist, largely because they proliferated in Europe during the tenth century, a period of socio-economic change that caused very serious social stresses. Many of the movements which sought to establish new cultural patterns during those troubled times were convinced that the year 1000 presaged the end of the world and called upon their adepts to prepare themselves spiritually for this momentous event. Such movements are also referred to as 'Messianic' in that they are often led by a prophet who sees himself as divinely inspired – as the reincarnation of a great religious figure, or, in the case of movements of this sort occurring among the Jews, as the Messiah himself. Such movements have proliferated throughout the Third World during the colonial period in particular. In Lagos, there has been such a proliferation of messianic cults that the Messiahs have gone so far as to create their own trade union, introducing in this way a little humour into what is otherwise a tragic situation. Wallace refers to such movements as 'revitalist', and defines a revitalization movement as

a deliberate, organized, conscious effort by members of a society to construct a more satisfying culture. Revitalization is thus, from a cultural standpoint, a special kind of culture-change phenomenon: the persons involved in a process of revitalization must perceive their culture, or some major areas of it, as a system (whether accurately or not); they must feel this cultural system as unsatisfactory; and they must innovate not merely discreet items, but a new cultural system, specifying new relationships as well as, in some cases, new traits.

Wallace considers that both Christianity and Mohammedanism, and possibly Buddhism too, originated in revitalization movements. Indeed, it seems that all organized religions are 'relics' of old revitalization movements, 'surviving in routinized form in stabilized cultures.'

The increasing failure of all policies based on the world-view of modernism and its derivative paradigms – those of science and of modern economics – to satisfy our most fundamental psychological needs, or indeed to solve any of the problems that threaten our very survival on this planet, gives rise to conditions increasingly propitious to the emergence of revitalist movements. The chances are that many such movements will be affected by ecological ideas that are increasingly in the air and whose relevance is becoming ever more apparent even to the blindest among us. There are signs, too, that such movements could preach a return to the vernacular way of life. Thus while the rise of Islamic fundamentalism in the Moslem world and of Hindu fundamentalism in India can be seen as a particularly unpleasant trend towards chauvinism, bigotry and intolerance, it is clearly also a reaction against Western economic imperialism and the disruption of the cultures and traditions of Moslems and Hindus by Western science, technology and industrial development.

Significantly, too, a considerable proportion of the revitalist movements that have so far sprung up in the Third World have been 'nativistic' – which is to say that they correctly attributed the ills against which they were reacting to the way of life imposed upon them by their colonial masters, and preached a return to the Way of their ancestors. Many such movements have been violent and unpleasant, of that there is no doubt. Usually, too, they are put down with equal violence and unpleasantness, as their ideas are seen as a threat to the established order. However, there is reason to hope that the ecology-based revitalist movements of the future will seek to achieve their ends by peaceful means, in the true Gandhian tradition. It could be that Deep Ecology, with its ethical and metaphysical preoccupations, might well develop into such a movement. So could the Earth First movement in the USA, whose religious and metaphysical basis has recently been described by Bron Taylor.

We cannot afford to wait and see whether such movements will develop into revitalist cults that are powerful enough to transform our society. Instead, we should work towards their development, by helping to create the conditions in which they are likely to emerge. Let us remember that the world-view of ecology is very much that of a vernacular, community-based society, whereas the world-view of modernism is that of a corporation-based industrial society. We must set out to combat and systematically weaken the main institutions of the industrial system – the state, the corporations and the science and technology which they use to transform society and the natural world. At the same time, we must do everything to recreate the family and the community, and above all an economy based on them, reducing in this way an almost universal dependence on a destructive economic system that in any case is certainly in decline and may well be close to collapse.

As we multiply our efforts in these directions, so we must create the terrain in which ecological ideas can take root and flourish. May they inspire those who will lead us back to the Way, and thereby to restore and preserve what still remains of the beautiful world we have been privileged to inherit.

# APPENDIX 1

# Does the entropy law apply to the real world?

There is a set of laws that have a privileged status. They are the laws of thermodynamics, in particular the second law, usually referred to as the entropy law.

The term 'entropy' was coined by Rudolph Clausius in 1868. He observed that within a closed receptacle heat differences tended to even out. The evening-out continued until total heat uniformity was obtained. This uniformity could thus be regarded as a position of 'equilibrium', at least from the thermodynamic point of view, and he referred to it as 'entropy'.

However, the concept itself is much older. Sadi Carnot, a French engineer, first made use of it in 1827. In trying to understand the workings of a steam engine, he realized that it was exploiting the heat difference between that part of the system which was hot and that which was cold. It was this difference in temperature that enabled the system 'to do the work'. The difference tended to even out, however, reducing the system's ability to do work. In such conditions, energy is said to have been dissipated, which means that it has degraded to a more homogeneous state identified with equilibrium or what Clausius called 'entropy'.

This, in essence, is the entropy law, and it would be quite acceptable if it were applied strictly to the field of thermodynamics. The trouble, however, is that its use has been extended to apply to fields of behaviour that are very distant from thermodynamics and would appear to most sensible people to be governed by very different laws from those that govern the behaviour of hot air in a closed receptacle, or of steam in the boiler of a locomotive.

The entropy law has suffered the fate of many other scientific theories. It has become the object of a cult, worshipped as the key which will unravel the secrets of the universe. The same thing has happened to Claude Shannon and Warren Weaver's Information Theory (see Appendix 2) which is also perfectly acceptable so long as it is applied to the field of communications for which it was designed, but has only served to confuse everybody after being hailed as a great scientific discovery that would, among other things, provide a means of measuring Biospheric complexity or organization.

How, then, do we know that the entropy law does not apply to behaviour within the Biosphere? To begin with, it is easy to see that it does not. Life probably began on this planet three throusand million years ago and since then – that is, until the beginning of the historical era a mere ten thousand years ago – it has not ceased to develop in complexity, diversity and stability. In other words it has behaved, over what most sensible people would regard as a sufficient sample of time, in a manner diametrically opposed to that in which it should have behaved had it been governed by the entropy law.

This is a source of great embarrassment to our scientists. 'How is it possible to understand life,' asks Louis Brillouin, 'when the whole world is ruled by such a rule as the second principle of thermodynamics which points towards death and annihilation?' Indeed, either we are all mad and there has not been such a thing as evolution, and the Biosphere with its myriad forms of life is an illusion, or else the entropy law does not apply to the behaviour of living things – only to that of hot air in a closed receptacle or steam in a locomotive.

Some of the more thoughtful philosophers of biology, such as Arthur Koestler, seem to realize this:

the Second Law applies only in the special case of so-called 'closed systems' (such as a gas enclosed in a perfectly isolated container). But no such closed systems exist even in inanimate nature, and whether or not the universe as a whole is a closed system in this sense is anybody's guess. All living organisms, however, are 'open systems', that is to say, they maintain exchanges of energies and material with their environment. Instead of 'running down' like a mechanical clock that dissipates its energies through friction, the living organism is constantly 'building up' more complex substances from the substance it feeds on, more complex forms of energies from the energies it aborbs, and more complex patterns of information – perceptions, feelings, thoughts – from the input of its receptor organs.

Brillouin makes the same point. 'Both principles of thermodynamics,' he writes, 'apply only to an isolated system, which is contained in an enclosure through which no heat can be transferred, no work can be done and no matter nor radiation can be exchanged.' The world, on the other hand, is not a closed system. 'It is constantly receiving energy and negative entropy from outside – radiant heat from the sun, gravitational energy from the sun and moon (provoking sea tides), cosmic radiation from unknown origin, and so on.' In this way, 'the sentence to "death by confinement" is avoided by living in a world that is not a confined and closed system.'

C. H. Waddington questions the applicability of the entropy law to Biospheric processes. He notes that the embryo increases its complexity as it develops and for this and other reasons he cannot believe that 'any serious embryologists have considered that the second law of thermodynamics could be applied in any simple way to their subject matter, in spite of what classical physicists might say.' Indeed, Waddington assures us that the most creative physicists of his day would not have been tempted to impose the entropy law 'as a rigid dogma of biology'. Is it only because the earth receives energy from the sun (and is therefore an open system) that the entropy law does not apply? There seem to be other reasons. After all, other celestial bodies are open systems just as is the planet earth. They are all bombarded with energy, 'radiant heat from the sun, gravitational energy from the sun and moon, cosmic radiation etc.' Yet this has not enabled them to develop life as our planet has done.

Another consideration leads one to the same conclusion. Even in a closed system, behaviour does not always occur as it should do were it governed by the entropy law. Thus, if one puts a corpse in a closed receptacle, one would expect it to decompose into its component parts, and hence move towards that state of disorder which our aristoscientists indentify with entropy. However, it may not do so unless we open our closed receptacle and let in some oxygen.

It is not altogether surprising that other conditions should have to be satisfied, for it is difficult to believe that the development of the Biosphere can be explained, as the entropy law implies, simply in terms of energy. This is an old myth which we can refer to as 'energy reductionism'. It originally appears to have come into being as a way of getting round the problems associated with the understanding of matter. The atomic theory of matter was controversial. Thermodynamics was supposed to be based on it. Carnot, however, showed that this science was independent of such a theory. It only involved energy changes. As Stephen Mason points out, this meant that 'thermodynamics could proceed without a theoretical model of the nature of matter, indeed, it could proceed without the supposition that matter existed objectively.' Hence the development of the 'Energetik' school which taught that the phenomena of nature were explicable in terms of the transformation of energy.

Of course, other writers have told us that everything is number, while atomic reductionists like Francis Crick tell us that the world is exclusively made up of atoms. In reality, it is the way these atoms are organized that is critical, and there is no reason to believe that atoms have any greater reality than the tables, chairs, dung beetles or fiddler crabs into which they are organized. It is only possible to maintain these various forms of reductionism if we limit our study to very simple inanimate objects like gases and billiard balls. As soon as we look at the behaviour of complex forms of life in the real world, the illusory character of these theories is quickly revealed. As Brillouin points out:

> for inert matter it suffices to know energy and entropy. For living organisms
> we have to introduce the 'food value' of products. Calories contained in coal
> and calories in wheat and meat do not have the same function. Food value

must itself be considered separately for different categories of living organisms. Cellulose is a food for some animals, but others cannot use it. When it comes to vitamins or hormones, new properties of chemical compounds are observed, which cannot be reduced to energy or entropy. All these data remain rather vague, but they all seem to point towards the need for a new leading idea (call it principle or law) in addition to current thermodynamics, before these new classifications can be understood and typical properties of living organisms can be logically connected together. ....

It is easy to show that if a complex natural system is deprived of any of its basic constituents – energy, information or any of the the basic chemicals of life – it will cease to function properly and will slowly disintegrate, moving in the direction of disorder or what mainstream scientists would call entropy. Thus it would be more accurate to talk of 'energy entropy', which would enable us to distinguish this notion from 'information entropy' and 'materials entropy'. We could then have a whole set of entropy laws, each one stating that, in the absence of a specific constituent of life, movement will be towards 'general' entropy. Such a law is implicit in Shannon and Weaver's theory of information. Nicholas Georgescu-Roegen also formulated such a law with regard to materials – the Fourth Law of Thermodynamics. We can, of course, go much further still and subdivide materials entropy into carbon entropy, phosphorous entropy, water entropy and so on, conferring a different sort of energy on each of the essential ingredients of living things. All such concepts would be as valid as that of energy entropy about which people make so much fuss, but they would be equally invalid once all the other conditions favouring Biospheric development were satisfied, for then systems are either able to synthesize their own constituents or derive them from elsewhere in the quantities required.

The availability of these constituents then leads to a very strange, indeed apparently unique phenomenon. They tend to organize themselves not in a random or haphazard way, as is suggested by Alfred Lotka, V. Volterra, R. M. May, Ilya Prigogine and many others, but in a highly directive way, for random organization does not exist in the real world. As living things develop, successive thresholds are achieved which are referred to as levels of organization. Each time one is achieved new forms of behaviour appear that are governed by laws not previously operative. At the most sophisticated levels of organization, behaviour displays those features we associate with life and is governed by a set of laws quite unknown to the physicist and the chemist, whose knowledge is derived from the study of behaviour at lower levels of organization. What is particularly relevant to the thesis of this appendix is that living things are capable of overcoming many of the constraints applying to the behaviour of simpler things. 'Consider a living organism,' writes Brillouin,

> It has special properties which enable it to resist destruction, to heal its wounds, and to cure occasional sickness. This is very strange behaviour, and nothing similar can be observed about inert matter. Is such behaviour an exception to the second principle? It appears so, at least superficially, and we must be prepared to accept a 'life principle' that would allow for some exceptions to the second principle. When life ceases and death occurs, the 'life principle' stops working and the second principle regains its full power, implying demolition of the living structure. There is no more healing, no more resistance to sickness; the destruction of the former organism goes on unchecked and is completed in a very short time. Thus the conclusion or question: what about life and the second principle? Is there not, in living organisms, some power that prevents the action of the second principle?

The notion that living things have some property that distinguishes them from inanimate things is referred to as 'vitalism'. This property was once taken to be of a supernatural nature, as in the case of Aristotle's 'entelechy' or Bergson's *élan vital*. Vitalism is condemned because it implies that the world cannot be understood purely in terms of physics, which our physicists – who want to maintain their dominion over science, indeed over knowledge in general – cannot conceivably accept. But we do not have to appeal to vitalism to show that the second law is irrelevant to an understanding of the real world.

Because of the way living things are organized, they are capable of providing themselves with the energy they require to maintain their stability – green plants via photosynthesis and predators by consuming green plants.

A physicist might tell us that the sun's energy has been dissipated, but the answer to this is 'So what?' As far as a student of the Biosphere is concerned, this dissipation is required to power the development of living things and to increase their stability and that of the Biosphere. The case of Georgescu-Roegen's fourth law is, superficially at least, a stronger one than his case for the second law, since though the world is an open system from the point of view of energy, it is closed from the point of view of materials. But once more living things can overcome this constraint by developing the means of recycling the materials they require, the waste products of specific Biospheric processes serving as the raw materials of the next.

The question we must now ask ourselves is why our scientists so stubbornly refuse to face both the theoretical and empirical evidence against the applicability of the entropy law to the world of living things. To understand their obstinacy, one must consider the world-view or paradigm of the physical sciences in the middle and towards the end of the nineteenth century. In terms of it, the world was seen as an enormous machine, whose components behaved largely like planets and billiard balls. It was just the world-view required to rationalize the trend initiated by the industrial revolution towards materialism, individualism, utilitarianism and economism – the closely associated values of the industrial age. Science then was largely identified with physics, as indeed it is today. All other sciences were, and still are, considered very inferior, so much so that their practitioners are largely preoccupied with raising their status by slavishly imitating the methodology of the physical sciences. If physics was to be the fundamental science governing everything else, then the behaviour of physical things – billiard balls and the like – must be shown to provide a model for that of living things.

The trouble was that in terms of the neo-Newtonian world-view it failed to do so on two counts. The first and most important obstacle was that Newtonian time was reversible. It could move backwards or forwards just as a billiard ball can, while in the real world, time is irreverisble: one cannot eradicate experience nor restore the past exactly as it once was. As Brillouin puts it, one of the most important things about time is its irreversibility. Time flows on and never comes back. When the physicist is confronted with this fact he is greatly disturbed. All the laws of physics in their elementary forms are reversible.

The Newtonian paradigm also failed to explain the direction of time. Newton formulated laws governing the movement of bodies but did not tell us that they moved in one direction rather than any other. This, again, did not tally with the behaviour of living things.

The entropy law remedied all this. Since energy could only be degraded, it must follow that the time during which its degradation took place was irreversible. As Brillouin notes, 'it is a strange coincidence that life and the second law represent the two most important examples of the importance of time's running backwards.' All this was just what our physicists were looking for: incontrovertible evidence, as they saw it, that the entropy law underlay the behaviour of living processes. This was further confirmed by the fact that, as in living processes, energy did not move in a random but in a specific direction.

Ludwig Boltzmann's formulation of the entropy law as a statistical law further confirmed the entropy thesis, since the behaviour of living things was also held to be governed by such laws. Of course, a limitless number of processes can be shown to tend statistically in an irreversible direction. Even a game of snakes and ladders, for instance, satisfies these conditions, yet nobody suggests that this great nursery game provides a model for life processes. Why the behaviour of gas in a closed receptacle should provide a better model is not at all clear, but what is clear is the stake our aristo-scientists have in proving that it does.

Another reason why our scientists are so keen to preserve the entropy law, contrary to all the theoretical and empirical evidence, is that it is easily quantifiable. This is a critical consideration for it is a dogma of aristoscience that only a quantifiable proposition can be regarded as scientific. The 'statistical method' is, of course, very convenient. Indeed, if the entropy law is seen only as a statistical law, then the development of the Biosphere over the last three thousand million years, rather than providing a clear violation of the entropy law, can be interpreted as nothing more than an exception to this law which does not invalidate it.

Georgescu-Roegen realizes how unsatisfactory Boltzmann's compromise is. 'According to this new discipline', he notes,

> a pile of ashes may very well become capable of heating the boiler. Also a corpse may resuscitate to lead a second life in exactly reverse order of the first. Only the probability of such events is fantastically small.

In other words, the second law, once it is seen to be no more than a statistical law, tells us nothing about the real world, which is then no more than a freak event. Nor does it help us to understand the biological, social and ecological laws that govern evolution, for those are so statistically improbable as not to be worth considering, and the fact that the laws of thermodynamics are irreconcilable with them is of no importance whatsover.

A second device for sustaining the entropy law in the face of all the evidence to the contrary, is to postulate that though the earth may be an open system, the universe itself is a closed one, which means that life on earth can only develop at the cost of increasing the entropy of the universe. The trouble with this argument is that there is no reason whatsoever for supposing that the universe is a closed system. Mark Braham points out that a completely closed system 'is a theoretical construct' and that 'we have no way of determining whether the universe is closed or not', while to say that the universe is an open system raises a number of difficult problems. It would mean for instance, that it is exchanging energy with its environment, but we know nothing about such an environment; if it exists, then it must be part of another universe, a 'mega-universe' of which we are but a sub-system.

'What then,' Braham asks, 'are the limits to the other universe, or to the mega-universe and so on?' Since we are quite incapable of answering such questions, it may be convenient to postulate that the universe is closed. But would this help us very much? As Braham points out,

> to assume closure is to assume a boundary. By definition, a boundary is be-

tween something and something else; there must therefore be something on the 'other side'. If we were to speculate meaningfully about this boundary, we would require information about the 'other side' and this would clearly require a leak in the system and hence no closure at all.

But even if we can find a way round this objection and accept that the system is a closed one, and that one day the sun's energy will be entirely dissipated, is this consideration of any practical significance? The terrible problems we face today (such as global warming, the depletion of the ozone layer, the population explosion, social disintegration, deforestation, desertification, the chemical contamination of groundwater, rivers, seas and estuaries) have not been caused by any reduction in the amount of energy generated by the sun. To preoccupy ourselves unduly with the possibility that such a reduction may eventually occur is to divert attention from these immediate problems to an exceedingly long-term one (for no one suggests that the sun is likely to stop shining for a few million years or so). It is to misdirect precious time and energy from problems that can be solved to one about which we can do strictly nothing – for not even our most fanatical technomaniacs have yet offered to devise a substitute for the sun.

# APPENDIX 2

# What is information?

The term 'information', in a scientific context, refers to Claude Shannon and Warren Weaver's Information Theory, developed in 1948. Since then, other theories of information have been proposed, but they seem to constitute little more than minor variations on the original theme. In any case, they do not appear to have earned any general acceptance among scientists. They are listed, together with their most salient features, by Everett Rogers and Lawrence Kincaid.

Both Shannon and Weaver, when they developed their theory, were working for the Bell Telephone Company. Their chief concern was to determine how to maximize the amount of 'information' – not just the number of signs – that could be transmitted via a communications channel with limited capacity. They found it convenient to define information in such a way that it could be measured in terms of Ludwig Boltzmann's mathematical formula for the measurement of entropy. Information is thereby equated with entropy, with the difference that whereas entropy is seen as the most probably arrangement of molecules in a particular energy state, information measures the most probable arrangement of signs in a message; probability in both cases being equated with randomness in accordance with the Second Law of Thermodynamics, or the entropy law.

It is difficult to understand this notion unless one realizes that, for the communications engineer, randomness (and thus the absence of any organization or constraints on the order in which the signs appear) is equated with the freedom he enjoys in choosing the message he wishes to send, and hence the order in which the signs must appear so as to satisfy his professional requirements. Randomness, or entropy, is thus for him the 'ideal' and must therefore, for his purposes, be associated with the highest information.

> Information is highest when the probabilities of the various choices are as nearly equal as circumstances permit – when one has as much freedom of choice, being driven as little as possible towards some certain choices which have more than their share of probability.

On the other hand, when a 'situation is highly organized, it is not characterized by a large degree of randomness or of choice' and in these conditions, 'the information (or the entropy) is low'.

The sort of constraints that Shannon and Weaver regard as reducing this freedom of choice (and hence the information content of a message) are linguistic constraints. Each language has a particular structure or organization, in terms of which one can predict that certain words are more or less likely to follow other words. Thus, 'after the three words "in the event" the probability for "that" as the next word is fairly high, and for "elephant" as the next word is very low.' These linguistic constraints reduce the information content of a message by forcing the sender to include signs in his message not because he wants to but because they are imposed on him by the structure of the language in which the message is formulated. These signs are regarded as redundant and each language is said to have a quantifiable built-in redundancy, that of the English language being about 50 per cent. Thus one can say that the higher the organization, and hence the lower the entropy, the greater must be the constraints, the higher the redundancy and the lower the information contained.

The amount of information in a message is calculated in terms of the logarithm (Base 2) of the number of choices. The result is formulated in terms of 'bits' (the term 'bit') was first suggested by John W. Tukey, as an abbreviation for 'binary digit'). When numbers are expressed in the binary system there are only two digits, zero and one. These may be taken symbolically to represent any two alternative choices. In a situation in which there are only two choices, there is said to be one bit of information. The greater the number of free unconstrained choices, the greater the amount of information. If there are sixteen choices from among which we are equally free to choose, there are four 'bits' of information.

The greater the freedom enjoyed by the sender in the selection of signs or messages for emission, the greater must be the improbability that a particular sign or message will be sent. To illustrate this, I shall assume that Shannon and Weaver's 'information' takes 'meaning' into account. Thus a message that told us that a horse called Green Crocodile would win a race in which there were sixteen contestants of unknown breeding and with no previous form (all in theory having the same chance of winning) would communicate four 'bits' of information. If we knew something about their breeding and form, and, on this basis, could classify the horses in accordance with what appeared to be their chances of winning the race, the information communicated would be correspondingly reduced. If one horse was backed down to even money on the theory that it had one chance out of two of winning the race, then a message informing us that it would win would communicate still less information, in fact no more than one 'bit' – the same amount of information as it would communicate were Green Crocodile to have but a single other contestant to deal with rather than fifteen others. This is clearly a very sensible way of calculating the value of information from the point of view of communications. The greater the number of 'bits' ascribed to a message, the more valuable the information must be. This is certainly so in the case cited, in any case to both the bookmaker and the punter.

In reality it does not quite work this way, since Shannon and Weaver are not concerned with the probability or improbability of a statement being true or false. This is the concern of the epistemologist, not the communications engineer. The latter is not even preoccupied with the probability or improbability of a particular statement, nor even of a particular word, but only of particular signs being emitted – regardless of whether these signs make up intelligible words or whether such words make up intelligible sentences. In other words, the information content of a message, for them, does not take into account its meaning. 'Information must not be confused with meaning,' they write, and 'the semantic aspects of communication are irrelevant to the engineering aspect.' This means, as they freely admit, that their use of the term 'information' is very different from its normal use in the English language.

An essential feature of Shannon and Weaver's theory is that during the emission of a message its information content is reduced. The reason is that as a message is spelled out along a channel, so does the probability or improbability of specific signs occurring become easier to calculate. Linguistic organization is seen to build up – as does 'redundancy', which means that 'entropy' and 'information' are correspondingly reduced. Another reason why the amount of information contained in a message must fall as it is spelled out, is that communication channels are subject to 'noise' or 'randomness'. Noise, of course, increases uncertainty or improbability. One might think that it would thereby lead to increased (rather than decreased) information; however, Shannon and Weaver distinguish between the type of uncertainty caused by noise, which they regard as undesirable, and desirable types of uncertainty, which they identify with 'freedom of choice' and hence with information. The information content of a message is therefore not equal to uncertainty but to 'desirable' uncertainty minus 'undesirable' uncertainty or noise.

That the equations used to measure entropy and information are the same holds great significance for Shannon and Weaver. They point out that for Sir Arthur Stanley Eddington 'the law that entropy always increases – the second law of Thermodynamics – holds, I think, the supreme position among the laws of Nature.' Thus, Shannon and Weaver note, when the engineer 'meets the concept of entropy in communications theory, he has a right to be rather excited – a right to suspect that one has hold of something that may turn out to be basic and important.'

Another aspect of the Theory of Information that makes it so attractive to the scientist is its quantifiability. However for quantification to be possible, as Michael Apter points out, we must know the exact number of possible messages that could be transmitted at any one time. This may well be possible in the field of communications but not in the field of behaviour. It is for this reason, as Louis Brillouin points out, that

> the modest but, we think, significant applications of information theory to various psychological experiments have occurred in precisely those situations in which the set in question was strictly defined: a list of syllables to be memorized, associations to be formed, responses selected from etc. There was therefore no difficulty in quantifying the associated 'amounts of information' and relating such amounts to certain aspects of performance.

But, as he points out, such situations are 'banal'. We can add to this that they do not normally occur in the living world.

In any case, the notion of a passive source of information (whether it displays order or disorder) from which messages are selected by an external agent does not correspond to anything that exists in the world of living things. The natural systems that make up the Biosphere are dynamic not static, active not passive; what is more, they are self-regulating, not regulated from the outside (heterarchically) by an external agent such as a communications engineer. The source of information and the sender of the message in the world of living things are, in fact, part and parcel of the same self-regulating system.

If we integrate Shannon and Weaver's sender of messages and the source of the messages in the same system, however, it must cease to display entropy – for one of the basic features of entropy is randomness and hence non-purposiveness, whereas the sender of messages acts purposefully since, as we are told, he selects for emission those messages that display the minimum redundancy, and hence the maximum information content. What is more, if the system is to achieve its goal efficiently, then the information it contains must be organized in the manner most favourable to the achievement of that goal. This we can predict with confidence on the basis of our empirical knowledge of the way patterns of information or cybernisms (brains, genes, genomes, gene pools, etc.) are organized in the world of living things.

Another consideration is that the sort of improbability that Shannon and Weaver write about is not a useful concept for understanding the working of the Biosphere. For Shannon and Weaver, improbability is either improbability vis-à-vis the workings of the entropy law, which as we have seen does not apply to the world of living things, or else it is improbability on the basis of probability theory, which they wrongly take to be the same thing. In the world of living things, improbability, if we are to use this concept, means improbability vis-à-vis a system's model or image of its relationship with its environment. This reflects its experience and that of its cultural group (if a human animal) and its species for a specific purpose – that of assuring the system's stability in relation to its environment, and hence its survival.

Thus as living things evolve they develop the capacity to discriminate between an increasing range of different environmental situations, to interpret them correctly and to react to them adaptively. A very simple organism, the *Dyonea* flytrap that so fascinated Darwin, can do one of two things when something lands in its trap: close it or not, and it does so with the minimum powers of discrimination since it cannot discriminate between an edible insect and and inedible pebble. At the other end of the scale is a human animal that can handle a vast number of different signals and interpret them correctly, and thus has at its disposal an exceptionally large repertoire of adaptive responses. In the language of Shannon and Weaver, one can say that the human animal is capable of handling messages with a high degree of improbability and hence of high information value – thousands of bits of information in contrast to the mere one bit that the *Dyonea* flytrap can handle.

The ease with which a living thing can handle messages seems to be a function of their importance or relevance to its behaviour pattern and also of the probability, in terms of its own experience and that of its species, that such a message will actually be received. In other words, information in the brain and nervous system is not arranged at random and hence does not display entropy; on the contrary, it is highly organized, as is all information used by natural systems within the Biosphere (genetic information, for instance).

If information is organized, partly at least, in accordance with the probability of its being required, then systems living in a protected environment, in which only probable things occur, will need to react adaptively to a correspondingly limited range of different environmental situations. Those that live in a less well protected environment in which improbable things occur, however, will need to react adaptively to a wider range of ever more improbable environmental situations – and hence will have to make use of information displaying a greater diversity or organized redundancy.

Shannon and Weaver rightly regard a certain amount of redundancy as useful for counteracting the effects of noise. However, they take it to be otherwise undesirable in that it reduces the information content of a message by reducing the freedom of choice of the sender, and hence the variety of messages he can send. But in the world of living things, as already mentioned, organized redundancy, or diversity, has a positive value. It increases rather than reduces a message's information content since it permits the mediation of an essential aspect of behaviour, its ability to adapt to improbable events.

An even more serious criticism of the extension of Shannon and Weaver's concept of information to the world of living things is that information, as I have already intimated, is very much more than improbability. This is also the view of Donald Mackay:

> To dress improbability up as a definition of information, as some exponents do, seems the most unfortunate obscurantism. Unexpectedness is a measurable quality or attribute of information – not a definition of it.

Brillouin agrees: 'It is naive,' he writes,

> to take simply the flux of signals per second, to multiply it by bits per signal in the communication engineering sense, and call the result 'amount of information' in the sense of transmission of knowledge (labelling everything one does not like 'noise').

In the world of living things, a message is not emitted because it is improbable or, for that matter, probable. It is emitted because it is of some relevance to the relationship between the sender and the receiver. Shannon and Weaver, however, are not in the least concerned with whether the receiver is interested in receiving a message, let alone whether he can understand it or is likely to believe it. Again, this may make sense in the world of communications engineering, but not in the world of living things, where these considerations are critical.

As C. H. Waddington points out, information in the real world largely consists of instructions (programmes or 'algorithms'). Thus genes combine to provide instructions for protein-synthesis. A gene pool provides instructions for the renewal of a viable population. The brain and central nervous system provide instructions for the proper functioning of an individual's metabolism and day-to-day adaptive relationships with his environment. A culture provides instructions for the mediation of a society's adaptive behaviour pattern.

Such instructions will only be obeyed by systems that have been programmed by their evolution and upbringing to receive, understand and believe. This must be true of the transmission of instructions and hence of information in all living processes, and the receiver of a message must also be capable of acting on the information adaptively. (see Chapter 43) The cries of a baby in distress provide an important message to its mother, who is not only disposed to hear them and understand their significance, but also to respond effectively. Otherwise there would be no advantage to be gained from the ability to detect them.

The quality of a message that will determine whether it will be detected and interpreted by a natural system is its relevance to the system's behaviour pattern. Since information in a natural system is organized hierarchically, from the general to the particular, the importance of a message can be determined in accordance with its relevance to the most general and important information contained within a pattern of information or cybernism. This in turn will reflect its relevance to the most important or general phases of the system's behavioural strategy. As natural systems evolve, they develop the capacity to deal with messages of lesser importance as well. This enables them to develop a more subtle behaviour pattern and thus adapt with greater precision to their specific environment. Nevertheless, the more important messages will remain their primary concern.

The final reason why Shannon and Weaver's theory is inapplicable to the world of living things is that they see the amount of information contained in a message as it is being emitted as decreasing (because of the accumulation of linguistic constraints and noise). In the world of living things, however, the opposite is true: there, the information content of a message can only increase. It is fairly evident, as Waddington points out, that an adult rabbit running around a field contains a very much greater 'amount or variety' of information than a newly fertilized rabbit's egg. How then, Waddington asks, can one explain such a situation 'in terms of an information theory whose basic tenet is that information cannot be gained'?

That the information content of a natural system increases as it becomes more complex seems clear to a number of writers who have, nevertheless, sought to measure a system's complexity in terms of its information content, using Shannon and Weaver's concept of information. Thus S. M. Dancoff and H. Quastler postulate that the larger the number of different components in a system, and hence the greater its complexity, the greater must be the amount of information it contains, since the higher must be the improbability of building up such a system by assembling its components in a random manner.

Unfortunately, what Dancoff and Quastler actually measure has nothing in common with the sort of complexity encountered in the Biosphere. This cannot be measured by adding up its component parts, because it derives its essential features, above all, from the way these parts are organized. (see Chapter 51) For Shannon and Weaver, however, organization and the constraints associated with it reduce rather than increase information. Thus, unless increasing complexity is associated with reduced information and the nemotode *Ascaris* is taken to contain more information than man, Dancoff and Quastler have to ignore the all-important organizational component of complexity.

Significantly, Dancoff and Quastler themselves admit that their work yields but 'crude approximations and vague hypotheses' and that their estimates are 'extremely coarse'. Nevertheless, they insist that this is 'better than no estimates at all'. I do not think this is so. Mathematical calculations based on false premises and making use of inappropriate concepts can only, by virtue of the impression of great scientific accuracy that they convey, serve to mislead people and to obscure the real issues at stake.

I have tried to show that the use of the communications concept of information for understanding behaviour in the world of living things cannot conceivably be justified on either theoretical or empirical grounds. This is not altogether surprising, since it was not designed for this purpose, any more, for that matter, than was the associated concept of entropy. This is Waddington's view. Information theory, he points out, 'was developed in connection with a particular type of process and has limitations which make it extremely difficult if not impossible to use in many of the biological contexts to which people have been tempted to apply it.' Apter makes much the same point. 'Information theory based on statistical considerations,' he writes, 'is concerned with how data are transmitted, ignoring however, any human factors involved.' Brillouin, as we have seen, also criticizes the extension of this theory to the study of the world of living things.

Yet in spite of these criticisms, all these writers, with the exception of Apter, still explicitly justify its use for this purpose. Waddington, for instance, argues that it allows the concept 'to be clearly expressed' though what I think he really means is 'quantified'. But what, one might ask, is to be gained by quantifying a concept that corresponds to nothing in the world of living things to which it is supposed to apply? It can only serve to give an air of spurious accuracy to what is, in effect, little more than a fiction.

Brillouin's argument for the extension of Shannon and Weaver's theory is that if it is 'to break out' of 'its original habitat of bandwidths and modulation', then a proper beginning must be made, 'which usually means a modest beginning'. But why *not* allow the concept of information to remain 'in its original habitat of bandwidths and modulation'? What evidence does Brillouin or anybody else provide to suggest that its use can profitably be extended to other fields for which it was not designed? The answer, I am afraid, is none whatsoever.

On the contrary, the only function that the extension of the theory is likely to serve is to perpetuate the myth that behaviour is mechanistic, passive, atomized and random, since the theory attributes precisely such features to the information on the basis of which behaviour is mediated.

This can only serve to obscure the most important features of the be-haviour of living things, which is, on the contrary, dynamic, creative, organized and purposeful. Applied to the world of living things, this theory is simply an instrument of scientific obscurantism and mystification.

# APPENDIX 3

# The artificialistic fallacy

The best-known objection to a Biospheric or naturalistic ethic is a logical one. In his *Treatise on Human Nature* (1740), David Hume wrote the now famous passage:

> In every system of morality which I have hitherto met with, I have always remarked that the author proceeds for some time in the ordinary way of reasoning, and establishes the being of a God, or makes observations concerning human affairs; whereon of a sudden, I am surprised to find, that instead of the usual copulations of proposition, 'is' and 'is not', I meet with no proposition that is not connected with an 'ought' or 'ought not'.
>
> The change is imperceptible; but, however, of the last consequence. For this 'ought' or 'ought not' expresses some new relation or affirmation, it is necessary that it should be observed and explained; and at the same time, a reason should be given for what seems altogether inconceivable, how this new relation can be a deduction from others, which are entirely different from it.'

To argue in this way from 'is' to 'ought' is to be guilty of what G. E. Moore called the 'naturalistic fallacy', which no philosopher or scientist wishes to be accused of. My aim is to show that Hume's argument is invalid. The reason is that though it may well be true that an 'ought' statement cannot be deduced from an 'is' statement, no one is in fact suggesting that it can.

In its widest sense, Hume's argument does little more than state the perceived division between knowledge and values that is still taken to be fundamental to modern science – though Karl Popper, Michael Polanyi and many other modern epistemologists have shown that it is illusory and that there is no such thing as value-free knowledge. This finding is not altogether surprising since objective information (and knowledge is clearly some type of information) plays no role in the strategy of the natural world.

Objective knowledge may be impossible, but, as Theodore Roszak notes, the psychology of objectivism continues to wield its influence. It leads, above all, to a separation of man from the real world of nature, of which he is an integral part and outside of which he is meaningless.

If man cannot entertain objective knowledge, he clearly cannot be motivated by it. It is thus not reason that motivates him, but his largely unconscious values – the non-plastic general instructions that reflect the long-term experience of our society and of our species, and which control those differentiated instructions that reflect our own short-term experience.

Man, as Anatol Rapoport puts it, is a rationalizing rather than a rational animal. He has always cherished values and then sought some authority to rationalize and hence, in his eyes, to legitimize them: so much so that, as Donald Worster puts it, '*ought* has been shaping *is*, not vice versa'. Such an authority is science, which, in the modern world, is constantly appealed to in order to legitimize a subjective value. Such an appeal, as A. N. White-head points out, 'follows rather than precedes the conviction of rightness, and the ultimate source of the moral impulse remains hidden in the human heart.' This leads one to the inescapable conclusion that an 'is' proposition is little more than the explicit and seemingly objective and value-free tip of a vast implicit, quite clearly subjective and value-laden, cognitive iceberg. It is this underlying world-view that Michael Polanyi calls a 'cognitive framework' and that Thomas Kuhn refers to (in the very much more restricted field of science) as a 'paradigm'.

It is only in terms of this implicit, subjective and value-laden world-view that an explicit, apparently objective and value-free proposition has any meaning. What is more, it is only in terms of its ability to fit into a world-view that the validity of a proposition can be established. This is undoubtedly C. H. Waddington's conclusion. 'The validity of Hume's argument', he writes,

> depends entirely on what is the content of the notion conveyed by 'is'. If one conceives of existence as, to put it crudely, Newtonian space-time with some billiard balls flying round in it, then clearly neither 'ought' nor 'owed' nor many other concepts can be logically deduced. But if, to take another extreme, existence is considered as the manifestation of the nature of a beneficient deity, quite other consequences would follow. In fact, any invocation of 'is' other than as a logical copula, involves an epistemology, and it is impossible to reduce the relation of 'is' to 'ought' to a matter of pure logic.

Now, quite clearly, still 'other consequences would follow' if we saw Hume's statement in the light of the world-view of modernism, which is clearly reflected in just about all the knowledge imparted today in our universities.

For modern man, the argument from 'is' to 'ought', when used to justify the naturalistic ethic, is judged to be false, not because it is deemed unverifiable, unfalsifiable, illogical or meaningless, but because it is incompatible with his world-view. In terms of that world-view, an earthly paradise can be achieved with the help of science, technology and industry, by systematically replacing the natural world – that which has developed as a result of three thousand million years of evolution – with a totally different organization – the artificial world of human artefacts. This process is known as economic development and is equated with progress. This world-view reflects an ethic that is in total opposition to the naturalistic ethic – one that we could call the artificialistic ethic. This ethic and the world-view that it underlies, serve above all to rationalize and hence to legitimize the enterprise of economic development to which our society is geared.

It seems clear that the artificialistic ethic is implicit to mainstream science today. Thus Edward O. Wilson, the father of sociobiology, warns against the trap of the naturalistic fallacy of ethics which uncritically concludes that 'what is', 'should be'. The 'what is' in human nature is the legacy of a long heritage as hunter-gatherers. Even when we can identify genetically determined behaviour it cannot be used to justify a continuing practice in present and future societies. As we live in a radically new and changing environment of our own making, such a practice would invite disaster. For example, the tendency under certain conditions to indulge in warfare against competing groups may well be in our genes, having been advantageous to our Neolithic ancestors, but it would be global suicide now.

Implicit in Wilson's warning is the admonition that we 'ought' to adapt to the brave new world that science, technology and industry are conspiring to create for us – even if this means behaving in a way that is contrary to our nature as determined by our genes. This may or may not be possible. However, neither Wilson nor any other writers who preach this 'anti-nature ethic' bother to determine whether it is.

Stephen Boyden has convincingly argued that it is not. As we have seen, he regards the diseases of civilization, whose incidence increases with per capita GNP (a measure of the extent to which our lifestyle and environment have diverged from those to which we have been adapted by our evolution), as the symptoms of 'phylogenetic (or evolutionary) maladjustment'. In his view, attempts by our modern society to combat such maladjustments by largely technological means do not constitute adaptations in the true sense of the term, but rather 'pseudo-adaptations' (or heterotelic adaptions), whose role it is to mask the symptoms of these maladjustments at the cost of perpetuating them.

The strongest objection to Wilson's argument is that he is, in effect, arguing from 'is not' to 'ought'. But why, we might ask, should this be more legitimate than to argue from 'is' to 'ought'? Is the 'ought' logically contained in the 'is not' in a way that it is not in the 'is'? Clearly not. Indeed, if a legitimate argument must be one that observes the laws of deductive logic, then Hume, Moore and Wilson are not arguing legitimately. The artificialistic fallacy violates the laws of deductive logic, just as the naturalistic fallacy does, but its principal failing is quite different: to argue from 'is not' to 'ought' is to argue for the morality of economic development or progress, a process that can only occur by disrupting the critical order of the Biosphere; whereas to argue from 'is' to 'ought' is to argue for the preservation of the Biosphere and hence for maximizing the welfare of humans and other forms of life – the only truly moral enterprise. (see Chapter 17)

# APPENDIX 4

# The need for a feedback mechanism linking behaviour to evolution

Mainstream science sees evolutionary change as exclusively the result of changes affecting the genes of individual living things. No other process – neither its morphogenesis nor the development of a child into an adult, nor physiological nor behavioural experience – are regarded as affecting the genetic material in any way. These processes are seen as external to evolution, unable to play an evolutionary role.

Charles Darwin never said this. For him, natural selection from random mutations (or random variations as he referred to them) was not the only mechanism of evolution – only the principle one. Indeed, towards the end of his life, he actually accepted Lamarck's ideas on the inheritance of acquired characteristics in order to dispose of Fleeming Jenkin's criticism. It was not Darwin but August Weismann who formulated the preposterous dogma that natural selection is the only mechanism of evolution, thereby denying that behaviour could affect evolution through the inheritance of 'acquired characteristics'. This thesis, another of science's gratuitous dogmas, is based on no serious theoretical or ecological considerations. Weismann's main argument for it is that he could not conceive of a mechanism whereby acquired characteristics could be translated into the language of the gene, and it was for this reason alone that he insisted – as P. Wintrebert points out – that all biologists had to agree that it did not exist.

It can be argued that Weismann proved his point experimentally – but his experiments were little more than a farce. He cut off the tails of rats, let them breed, repeated the experience on their progeny and went on doing this for twenty-two generations. The fact that a tailless breed of rats did not arise he held to be proof that acquired characteristics were not transmitted. However, as Wintrebert notes, Lamarck never suggested that living things passed on their *mutilations* to their progeny but only the characteristics that they developed as a result of their *own efforts*. Indeed, the rats, as Arthur Koestler put it, were no more likely to transmit their mutilated tails than a mutilated man is likely to transmit his wooden leg.

Such experiments are, in any case, deeply flawed for another reason. Though the genetic material is indeed plastic – contrary to what we are told – it is only slightly so. As J. B. S. Haldane notes, it is always possible that such experiments will fail, because the effects of acquired characters may not become apparent at a rate that makes them observable, though they may be rapid enough to be significant in geological time.

There are countless reasons why the genetic material in the genome cannot be isolated from the genes of the soma. To begin with, no life process can maintain its homeostasis without acquiring information concerning its relationship with its environment in order to monitor its actions and correct any divergences from the appropriate course on which it is set. The only possible sources of such information are morphogenesis and behaviour (ontogeny). Secondly, genetic material is not external to a living system but part of it. The genes do not dictate epigenesis, which, as Barry Commoner has shown so convincingly, can only be understood in terms of the interaction between the genetic material and the cytoplasm which forms its environment. Nor, for similar reasons, do the genes dictate evolution.

In addition, as P. P. Grassé points out, if we accept the Weismann-Crick thesis, how do we explain the creation of new genes? The first living thing itself would have been endowed with all the genes which have made possible the evolution of plants and animals in their infinite variety. Since no information can have come from outside, DNA must have been the unique source of information. This means, surely, attributing miraculous properties to this chemical substance, which is simply not a serious position to take.

It has always been quite clear to serious students of evolution that there had to be a feedback between behaviour, ontogeny and evolution. In 1896 the American psychologist, J. M. Baldwin, published the famous article in which he described his principles of 'functional and organic selection'. In adapting to its environment, Baldwin maintained, an organism can affect its congenital characteristics by 'accommodating' them to new environmental conditions. These accommodations, he argued, can eventually become fixed genetically. Forty years later, the theoretical biologist Richard Goldschmidt suggested that information contained in the phenotype which is acquired by a living thing during the course of its life can, in certain conditions, be 'copied' by the genome and then become fixed genetically as a 'phenocopy'.

C. H. Waddington proposed an analogous mechanism which he referred to as 'genetic assimilation'. He saw organisms as being able to respond to stress by changing their behaviour and sometimes by bringing about corresponding structural changes. To do this, they must be able to defy the pressure on them to resist divergences from their pre-ordained course, or constellation of chreods. This can only mean affecting, in some way, the genes that control the stability or flexibility of these chreods and eventually – perhaps after a few generations – modifying them. Once this has happened, the altered phenotype can occur with or without the environmental stress, and it would then be said to have been 'assimilated by the genotype'.

At the same time as Waddington developed the theory of genetic assimilation, the Russian theoretical biologist I. L. Schmalhausen worked out a slightly different way in which negative feedback could occur. He referred to it as 'stabilizing selection'. Later, Jean Piaget revived Goldschmidt's phenocopy, which he modified considerably. The resulting mechanism is the most interesting, in that it diverges the most from the neo-Darwinist position, as the acquired changes are not seen to be the product of natural selection.

In any case, recent experiments conducted by John Cairns and others now seem to have established empirically that information flows in both directions. This means that mainstream scientists no longer have any argument for opposing the essential and unescapable principle that morphology, physiology and behaviour are integral parts of the evolutionary process, providing it with a highly effective feedback mechanism to ensure that it remains adaptive to changing environmental conditions.

# Bibliography

Abian, Alexander, 1991, 'Hate Winter? Here's One Man's Solution: Blow Up the Moon', *Wall Street Journal, Europe,* April 22nd. *317*

Ackoff, Russell L., 1963, 'General systems theory and systems research: contrasting conceptions of systems science', *General Systems Yearbook,* Vol. V III. *3, 3a*

Adams, C. C., 1917, 'The new natural history ecology', *American Museum Journal,* 27th April. *16, 212*

Akpapa, J., 1973, 'Problems in initiating industrial labour in a pre-industrial community', *Cahiers d'Etudes Africaines,* Spring. *35*

'Alcohol, Drug Abuse and Mental Health', Administration of the US Government, quoted by Lux, 1990, *Adam Smith's Mistake. 242*

Allee, W. C., Emerson, W. C. E. A., Park, O., Park, T., Schmidt, K. P., *Principles of Animal Ecology,* Philadelphia, W. B. Saunders, 1949. *212*

Anaximander, fragment, quoted by Cornford, 1957, *From Religion to Philosophy. 299, 343*

Apter, Michael, 1966, *Cybernetics and Development,* Pergamon Press, Oxford. *395, 401*

Armelagos, George, and McArdle, Alan, 1976, 'The Role of culture in the control of infectious diseases', *The Ecologist,* Vol. 6, No. 5, June. *289*

Armstrong, W. E., 1925, 'Rossel Island money. A unique monetary system', *The Economic Journal,* 34. *320*

Asch S. E., 1955, 'Opinions and social pressure', *Scientific American,* November. *66*

Ashmore, Jerome, 1966, 'Technology and the humanities', *Main Currents in Modern Thought,* Vol. 22. *227*

Atlan, Henri, 1979, *Entre le Cristal et la Fumée,* Edition du Seuil, Paris. *26*

Augros Robert and Stanciu George, 1987, *The New Biology: Discovering the Wisdom in Nature,* New Science Library, Boston, Mass. *206*

Ayala, F. J. and Dobzhansky, Theodosius, eds. 1971, *Studies in the Philosophy of Biology,* University of California Press, Los Angeles. *72*

Bacon, Francis, *Novum Organcum,* quoted by Bajaj, 1988, 'Francis Bacon, The first philosopher of modern science: a non-western view'. *63*

Bajaj Jatinder, 1988, 'Francis Bacon, the first philosopher of modern science: a non-western view' in Nandy ed., *Science, Hegemony and Violence. 63*

Bakeless, John, 1977, 'Our land as it was', *The Ecologist,* Vol. 7, No. 2. *173*

Baldwin, J. M., 1896, 'A New factor in evolution', *American Naturalist. 410*

Baltimore, David, 1979, 'Limiting science: A biologist's perspective' in Holton and Morison eds., *Limits of Scientific Inquiry. 316*

Banfield, Edward C., 1958, *The Moral Basis of a Backward Society,* The Free Press, New York. *241, 339*

Barcroft, Joseph, 1938, *The Brain and its Environment,* Yale University Press, New Haven. *142, 142b*

Barker, Jonathan ed., 1984 *The Politics of Agriculture in Tropical Africa,* Sage, London. *373*

Bartlett, Frederic C., 1977, *Remembering. A Study in Experimental and Social Psychology,* Cambridge University Press, Cambridge. *48-49*

Barre La, Weston, see under La Barre.

Bastien, Joseph E., 1981, 'Metaphorical relations between sickness, society and land in a Qollahuaya ritual', *American Anthropological Association Bulletin,* No. 12. *371-372*

Bean, William B., 1980, quoted by Graham, 'The Witch-hunt of Rachel Carson'. *75*

Beer, Stafford, 1969, 'Beyond the twilight arch', *General Systems Yearbook,* Vol. V. *138*

Begon, Michael, Harper, John L., Townsend, Colin R., 1986, *Ecology,* Basil Blackwell, Oxford. *200*

Berdyaev, Nicholai Aleksandrovich, 1936, *The Meaning of History,* trans. George Reavey, Geoffrey Bles, London. *359*

Bergson, Henri, quoted by Krishna Chaitanya, 1975 in *The Biology of Freedom*, Somaiya Publishing, Bombay. *104*

Bergson, Henri, 1981 (original edition 1970), *L'Evolution Creatice*, Presses Universitaires de France, Paris. *123, 123b*

Berman, Morris, 1981, *The Re-Enchantment of the World*, Cornell University Press, Ithaca. *120*

Bernal, J. D., 1969, *The World, The Flesh and The Devil*, Indiana University Press, Bloomington. *140*

Bernard, Claude, *Leçons sur les Phenomenes de la Vie communs aux Animaux et aux Vegetaux*, ed. A. Dastre, Cours de Physiologie Generale du Museum d'Histoire Naturelle, Paris. *127, 127b*

Bernier, François, 1699, *Voyages de François Bernier*, (ed. in English: Archibald Constable, London 1841), Contenant la Description des Etats du Grand Mogul, de l'Hindoustan, du Royaume de Kachemire, Amsterdam, Paul Marret. *174*

Bethwell, A. and Ogot, A., eds. 1976, *Ecology and History in East Africa*, Nairobi. *174*

Bettelheim, Bruno, 1979, *Surviving and Other Essays*, Knopf, New York. *76*

Binet, A. and Simon, T. H., 1916, 'The Development of Intelligence in Children', in Chaitanya, 1976, *The Psychology of Freedom*, Williams and Williams, London. *163*

Blake, Peter, 1975, 'Can technology solve the housing crisis?', *The Atlantic Monthly*, October. *292*

Bloomfield, Maurice, 1908, *The Religion of the Veda, The Ancient Religion of India from Rig-Veda to Upanishads*, 1957, quoted by Cornford, *From Religion to Philosophy*, G. P. Putnams and Sons, London and New York. *345*

Blyth, R. H., 1979, quoted by Bolen, *The Tao of Psychology*. *39*

Bodenheimer, F. S., ed. 1978, *The Concept of Biotic Organization in Synecology*, Studies in Biology and its History, Biological Studies Publishers, Jersualem. *16*

Bohannan, Paul, ed. 1967, *Law and Warfare*, Natural History Press, New York. *207*

Bohannan, Paul and Laura, 1968, *Tiv Economy*, Longmans, London. *325-6*

Bolen, Jean Shinoda, 1979, *The Tao of Psychology, Synchronicity and the Self*, Harper and Row, New York. *39*

---

414

Bortoft, Henri O., 1986, *Goethe's Scientific Consciousness,* Institute for Cultural Research Monograph, 22, The Institute for Cultural Research, Tunbridge Wells. *71*

Boucher, D. H., James S., and Keeler, K. H., 1982, 'The ecology of mutualism', *Annual Review of Ecology and Systematics 13. 213, 214*

Boucher, D. H., 'The Idea of Mutualism' in D. H. Boucher, ed. 1985, *The Biology of Mutualism,* Croom Helm, London. *205, 214, 215*

Boucher, D. H. and Vandermeer, J. H., 1978, 'Varieties of mutualistic interactions in population models', *Journal of Theoretical Biology 74. 213*

Boucher, D. H. and Risch, S., 1976, 'What ecologists look for', *Bulletin of The Ecological Society of America, 57. 213*

Bowles, B. D., 1976, 'Underdevelopment in agriculture in colonial Kenya. Some ecological and dietary aspects', in Bethwell and Ogot eds., *Ecology and History in East Africa. 174*

Boyden, Stephen, 1973, 'Evolution and health', *The Ecologist,* Vol. 3, No. 8. *217, 223-4*

Boyle, Robert, see More L. T., 1944

Braham, Mark, 1973, 'A General theory of organisation', *General Systems Yearbook,* Volume XVIII. *390*

Bridges, Bryn, 1971, 'Environmental genetic hazards. The impossible problem?' *The Ecologist,* Vol. 1, No. 12, June. *115*

Brillouin, L., 1968, 'Information, communication and meaning', in Buckley and Rapoport eds., *Modern Systems Research for the Behavioral Scientist,* Aldine, Chicago. *228, 387, 396, 398, 401*

Brillouin, L., 1968, 'Life, thermodynamics and cybernetics' in Buckley ed., *Modern Systems Research for the Behavioral Scientist,* Aldine, Chicago. *383, 384, 385-6, 387, 388-9*

Brindle, David, 1990, 'Rate of divorce and births outside marriage increases', *The Guardian,* July 5th. *242*

Broadhurst, Anne, and Ramsay, W. R., 1968, 'The non-randomness of attempts at random responses: relationships with personality variables in psychiatric disorders', in *British Journal of Psychology,* Vol. 59, August. *137-138*

Brown, Harold I., 1979, *Perception, Theory and Commitment,* University of Chicago Press, Chicago. *75, 89, 89b*

Buckley, Walter and Rapoport, Anatol, 1968, *Modern Systems Research for the Behavioral Scientist*, Aldine, Chicago. *387*

Bunyard, Peter and Goldsmith, Edward, eds. 1988, *Gaia, the Thesis, the Mechanisms and the Implications*, Wadebridge Ecological Centre, Wadebridge. *98, 99, 125, 300*

Burckhardt, Titus, 1967, *Sacred Art in East and West*, trans. Lord Northbourne, Perennial Books, London. *294*

Caillois, Roger, 1988, *L'Homme et la Sacré*, Gallimard, Paris.

Cajal, see Santiago

Castle, Emery, 1981, quoted by Sampson, *Farmland or Wasteland?*. *172*

Calow, Peter, 1976, *Biological Machines: A Cybernetic Approach to Life*, Edward Arnold, London. *25, 25b, 121*

Cannon, Walter, 1932, *The Wisdom of the Body*, Norton, New York. *127, 127b, 128, 128b-129*

Carnap, Rudolph, 1950, 'Testability and meaning', 1936, and 1937, *Philosophy of Science*, Issue 3 (1936) – Issue 4 (1937). *88, 89-90*

Carson, Rachel, 1962, *Silent Spring*, Houghton Mifflin, Boston. *74*

Cattel, Cohen and Travers, eds. 1937, *Human Affairs: Essays on the Application of Science to the Study of Society*, MacMillan, London. *306*

Cavalieri, Liebe F., 1981, *The Double-Edged Helix. Science in the Real World*, Columbia University Press, New York. *316*

Cesaire, Aime, 1972, *Discourse on Colonialism*, Monthly Review Press, New York. *76*

Chaitanya, Krishna, 1972, *The Physics and Chemistry of Freedom*, Somaiya Publications, Bombay. *19, 71*

Chaitanya, Krishna, 1975, *The Biology of Freedom*, Somaiya Publications, Bombay. *13, 104, 227*

Chaitanya, Krishna, 1976, *The Psychology of Freedom*, Somaiya Publications, Bombay. *154, 163*

Chaitanya, Krishna, 1983, 'A Profounder ecology: the Hindu view of man and nature', *The Ecologist*, Vol. 13, No. 4. *345, 346, 347*

Chan, Wing-Tsit, ed. 1963, *A Source Book in Chinese Philosophy*, quoted by Peerenboom, 1991, *Beyond Naturalism*. *344*

Chantepie de la Saussage, Pierre Daniel, 1904, *Manuel d'Histoire des Religions,* Paris. *346*

Chargaff, Erwin, 1976, Letter to Science June 4th, quoted by Culliton, Barbara J., 1978, in 'Science's Restive public', in Holton and Morrison, eds. 1979, *Limits of Scientific Inquiry. 316*

Ch'ien Lung: quoted by Whyte, 1927, quoted by Toynbee, 1934. *175*

Clastres, Pierre, 1976, *Le Societe contre L'Etat,* Les Editions de Minuit, Paris. *336-7, 338*

Clements, Frederick and Shelford, Victor, 1930, *Bio-Ecology,* Wiley, New York. *2*

Cloward, Richard A. and Ohlin, Lloyd E., 1961, *Delinquency and Opportunity,* Free Press of Glencoe, New York. *245*

Codrington, Robert Henry, 1891, *The Melanesians, Studies in their Anthropology and Folklore,* Clarendon, Oxford. *351*

Cody, M. L. and Diamond, J. M., eds. 1975, *Ecology and Evolution of Communities,* Belknap Press, Cambridge, Mass. *59, 204*

Coleman, J. S., 1968, *The Adolescent Society,* The Free Press of Glencoe, New York. *283, 285-6*

Colinvaux, P. A., 1973, *Introduction to Ecology,* Wiley, New York. *18*

Commoner, Barry, 1964, 'DNA and the Chemistry of Inheritance, *American Scientist,* Vol. 52. *226*

Conable, Barber, 1987, *Presidential address to the Board of Governors of the World Bank,* World Bank, Sept. 29th. *373*

Concern, 1981, *The Times,* September 6th. *44*

Connell, J. H., 1980, 'Diversity and the co-evolution of competition, or the ghost of competition past', *Oikos,* 35. *206*

Coomaraswamy, Ananda, 1983, *Symbolism in Indian Architecture,* The Historical Research Documentation Centre, Jaipur. *294*

Cornford, F. M., 1957, *From Religion to Philosophy,* Harper Brothers, New York. *83, 83b, 83c, 194, 299, 309, 343, 345, 347*

Craik, Kenneth, 1952, *The Nature of Explanation,* Cambridge University Press, Cambridge. *3, 49*

Crawford, C. C. and Leitzell, F. M., eds. 1932, *Learning a New Language,* University of Southern California Press, Los Angeles. *159*

Crawford, Michael and Sheilagh, 1972, *What We Eat Today,* Neville Spearman, London. *176-7*

Crawford, O. G. S., 1951, *The Fung Kingdom of Sennar,* John Bellows, Gloucester. *173*

Crick, Francis, 1966, *Of Molecules and Men,* University of Washington Press, Seattle. *17*

Cuenot, Lucien, 1951, *L'Evolution Biologique,* Masson, Paris. *165, 277*

Culliton, Barbara J., 1978, 'Science's Restive public', in Holton and Morrison, eds. 1979, *Limits to Scientific Inquiry. 315-16*

Cumont, Franz, 1956, *Oriental Religions in Roman Paganism,* Dover Publications, New York. *379*

Curtis, J. T., 1959, *The Vegetation of Wisconsin,* University of Wisconsin Press, Madison. *18*


Dalrymple, Theodore, 1991, 'If symptoms persist?', Spectator, September 14th, London. *243*

Dalton, George, 1965, 'Primitive money', *American Anthropologist,* 67. *321*

Dalton, George, ed. 1967, *Tribal and Peasant Economics,* University of Texas Press, Austin. *321*

Dalton, George, ed. 1968, *Primitive, Archaic and Modern Economics, Essays of Karl Polanyi,* Anchor Books. New York. *298, 301-2, 307, 326-7*

Dalton, George, ed. 1971, *Economic Development and Social Change,* The Modernization of Village Communities, The Natural History Press, New York. *302*

Daly, Herman E. and Cobb, John B., 1990, *For the Common Good: Redirecting the Economy Towards Community, the Environment and a Sustainable Future,* Green Print, London. *4*

Dancoff, S. M. and Quastler, H., 'The Information content and error rate of living things', in Quastler, ed. 1953, *Information Theory in Biology. 400-1*

Darwin, Charles, 1952 (original edition 1839), *The Voyage of the Beagle,* quoted by Worster, 1977, *Natures Economy,* J. M. Dent, Guildford. *74*

Darwin, Charles, 1971 (original edition 1859), *On the Origin of Species,* J. M. Dent, Guildford. *71, 166, 195, 203*

Darwin, Charles, 1974 (original edition 1887), *Autobiographical Sketch,* as a section of Darwin, Francis, *The Life and Letters of Charles Darwin,* Oxford University Press, Oxford. *45*

Darwin, Francis, ed. 1887, *The Life and Letters of Charles Darwin,* John Murray, London. *113*

Darwin F. and Seward A. C., eds. 1903, *More Letters of Charles Darwin,* London. *45*

Dawkins, Richard, 1989, *The Selfish Gene,* Oxford University Press, Oxford. *71, 116, 205*

Day, W. R., 1929, 'Environment and disease. A discussion on the parasitism of armillaria mellea', *Forestry,* Vol. 3. *32*

de Beer, Sir Gavin, 1958, *Embryos and Ancestors,* Clarendon Press, Oxford. *108, 142*

de Coulanges, Fustel, 1927, *La Cité Antique,* Hachette, Paris. *336*

de Garine, I., 1979, quoted by Fischer, 1990, 'L'Homnivore, Culture et Nutrition', *Communications,* 31. *310*

de Groot, Jan Jacob Maria, 1910, *The Religion of the Chinese,* Macmillan, New York. *344, 346*

de Haan, J. A. Bierens, 1966, *Animal Psychology,* Hutchinson's University Library, London. *143*

de St Pierre, S. H. B., 1976 (original edition 1784), *Studies of Nature,* Vol: translated by H. Hunter, London, quoted by Egerton. *45*

Dermon, William, 'U.S. Aid in the Sahel, development and poverty', in Barker ed. 1984, *The Politics of Agriculture in Tropical Africa. 373*

Descartes, René, 1946 (original edition 1637), *Discourse on Method,* Everyman, London. *4, 52*

Diamond, Stanley, 1974, *In Search of the Primitive,* Transaction Books, New Brunswick. *338*

Dickey, Lawrence, 'Historicising the Adam Smith Problem', *Journal of Modern History,* No. 58. *244*

Dixon, M. and Webb, E. C., 1964, *Enzymes,* quoted by Thorpe, 1965, *Science Man and Morals,* Longmans, London. *154, 155*

Dobzhansky, Theodosius, 1975, 'Studies in the philosophy of biology', in McConnell and van Dobben eds., *Unifying Concepts in Ecology, 113, 114, 115*

Douglas, Mary, 1963, *The Lele of the Kasai,* Oxford University Press, London. *310*

Douglas, Mary, 1966, *Purity and Danger,* quoted by Nicholas Hildyard, ed.

1978, 'There is more to food than eating', *The Ecologist,* No. 5, Sept/Oct, Routledge and Kegan Paul, London. *351*

Douglas, Mary, 1967, 'Raffia cloth distribution in the Lele economy', in Dalton ed. *Tribal and Peasant Economics. 321-2*

Driesch, Hans, 1908, *The Science and Philosophy of the Organism,* Black, London. *12, 123*

Driver, E., 1961, *Indians of North America,* University of Chicago Press, Chicago. *356*

Dubois, Cora, 1960, *The People of Alor,* Harper, New York. *356*

Dubos, René, 1967, *Man Adapting,* Yale University Press, New Haven, U.S. *31*

Dubos, René, 1970, 'Will man adapt to megalopolis?', *The Ecologist,* Vol. 1, No. 4, October. *289*

Durkheim, Emile, 1964 (original edition 1915), *The Elementary Forms of the Religious Life,* George Allen & Unwin, London. *350*

Durkheim, Emile, 1964 (original edition 1933), *The Division of Labour in Society,* trans. George Simpson, Macmillan, Free Press Paperback edition, London. *241*

Durkheim, Emile, 1966 (original edition in French 1897), *Suicide: A Study in Sociology,* Routledge & Kegan Paul, London. *242, 246*


The Ecologist – 1991 Special Issue: The UN Food and Agricultural Organisation (FAO), 1991, 'Promoting World Hunger', *The Ecologist,* March-April. *336*

Eden, Murray, 1965, 'Mathematical Challenges to the Neo-Darwinian Interpretation of Evolution', Wistar Institute Symposium Monograph, No. 5. *139*

Egerton, Frank, 1973, 'Changing concepts of the balance of nature', *Quarterly Review of Biology,* Vol. 48. *188, 189*

Eibl-Eibesfeldt, Ireneus, 1961, 'The fighting behaviour of animals', *Scientific American,* Dec. *207*

Eiseman, Fred, 1989, *Bali: Sekala and Niskala,* Vol. I, ed. David Pickell, Pickell-Periplus, Berkeley. *294, 346*

Eliade, Mirca, 1959, *The Sacred and the Profane,* Harcourt Brace, Jovanovich, New York. *103, 110, 183, 294*

Eliade, Mirca, 1971 (original edition 1949), *The Myth of the Eternal Return or Cosmos and History,* Princeton University, Princeton. *183*

Engels, Friedrich, 1858, quoted by Worster, 1977, 'The Condition of the Working Class in England', quoted by Worster, 1977, *Nature's Economy. 208*

Evans-Pritchard, E. E., 1937, *Witchcraft, Oracles and Magic Among the Azande,* quoted by Polanyi, 1978, Oxford University Press, Oxford. *93, 94*

Evans-Pritchard, E. E., ed. 1970, Introduction to Hocart, *Kings and Councillors,* University of Chicago Press, Chicago. *190*

Eyre, Edward John, 1945, *Journal of an Expedition of Discovery into Central Australia and Overland from Adelaide to King George's Sound in the years 1840-41. 174*


Fantz, Robert L., 1961, 'The Origin of Form Perception', *Scientific American,* May. *34, 34b*

Farrington, Benjamin, 1973, *Francis Bacon, Philosopher of Industrial Science,* Macmillan, London. *63-64*

Fernea, Robert, A., 1970, *Shayk and Effendi: Changing Patterns of Authority Among The El Shabana of Southern Iraq,* Harvard University Press, Cambridge, Mass. *311*

Fischer, Claude, 1990, *L'Homnivore,* Odile Jacob, Paris. *310*

Fisk, E. K., ed. 1978, *The Adaptation of Traditional Agriculture: Socio-economic Problems of Urbanisation,* Development Studies Centre Monograph, No. 11, Australian National University, Canberra. *304*

Flew, Anthony, 1968, *Evolutionary Ethics,* Macmillan, London. *83*

Food and Agricultural Organisation of the United Nations (FAO), 1984, *Land, Food and People,* Development Series, No. 30, FAO, Rome. *374*

Food and Agricultural Organisation of the United Nations (FAO), 1987, *Agriculture: Towards 2000,* FAO Social and Economic Development Series, No. 27, FAO, Rome. *374*

Forbes, S. A., 1880, 'On some interactions of organisms', *Bulletin of the Illinois State Laboratory of Natural History,* I. *188*

Forrester, Jay W. 1971, 'Alternatives to catastrophe: Understanding the counterintuitive behaviour of social systems', Part 1, *The Ecologist,* Vol. 1, No. 14, August. *248*

Frankl, Viktor E., 1962, *Man's Search for Meaning: An Introduction to Logotherapy,* Washington Square Press, New York. *252*

Frankl, Viktor E., 1972, 'Reductionism and Nihilism', in Koestler and Smythies eds., *Beyond Reductionism. 37*

Frazer, Sir James George, 1935, *Creation and Evolution in Primitive Cosmogonies,* Macmillan & Co., London. *194-5*

Fredericq, Leon, 1889, *Lutte pour l'existence chez les Animaux Marins,* Paris. *127*

Freeman, Peter, 1970, *INEAC, Report on Central African Agronomic Research,* Washington, D.C. *273*

Freud, Sigmund, 1970, *Inhibitions, Symptoms and Anxiety,* Hogarth, London. *76*

Fuller, Robert W. and Putnam, Peter, 1966, 'On the origin of order in behaviour', *General Systems Yearbook,* Vol. II. *23*


Gandhi, M. K., 1949, *An Autobiography,* trans. M. Desai, Phoenix Press, London. *325*

Gaud, William S., Price, Peter W., and Slobodchikoff, C. N., 1984, *The New Ecology, Novel Approaches to Interactive Systems,* John Wiley, New York. *206*

Geist, Valerius, 1974, 'About natural man and environment design', *Proceedings of the Third International Conference on the Unity of the Sciences,* New York. *290-1*

Georgescu-Roegen, Nicholas, 1972, 'Economics and entropy', *The Ecologist,* Vol. 2, No. 7, July. *4*

Georgescu-Roegen, Nicholas, 'Afterword' in Rifkin and Howard eds., 1980, *Entropy. 390*

Gerard, Ralph W., 1949, 'Physiology and psychiatry' *American Journal of Psychiatry,* Vol. 106. *24*

Gerard, Ralph W., 'The biological basis of ethics', *Philosophy of Science,* 9.92. *86*

Gerard, Ralph W., 'Hierarchy, entitation and levels', in Lancelot Law Whyte et alia ed., 1969, *Hierarchical Structures. 301*

Gesell, Arnold, quoted by Sinnott, 1961, in *Cell and Psyche. 104*

Gleason, H. A., 1926, 'The Individualistic concept of the plant association', *Bulletin of the Torrey Botanical Club,* 53. *18, 19, 262*

Goldschmidt, Richard, 1940, *The Material Basis of Evolution,* Yale University Press, New Haven. *410*

Goldsmith, Katherine, Personal communication. *293*

Graham, Frank Jnr., 1980, 'The Witch-hunt of Rachel Carson', *The Ecologist,* Vol. 10, No. 3, March. *75*

Granit, Ragnar, 1974, 'Adaptability of the nervous system and its relation to chance, purposiveness and causality', *Proceedings of the Third International Conference on the Unity of the Sciences,* Vol. 2, International Cultural Foundation, New York. *23, 234*

Granit, Ragnar, 1977, *The Purposive Brain,* M.I.T. Press, Cambridge, Mass. *3, 23, 23b, 25, 145*

Grassé, Pierre-P., 1973, *L'Evolution du vivant,* Albin Michel, Paris. *27, 151, 155, 409*

Grene, Marjorie, 'Hierarchy one word, how many concepts?' in Whyte et alia eds., *Hierarchical Structures. 201*

Grey, Sir George, 1945, quoted by Eyre, Edward John, in *Journal of an Expedition of Discovery into Central Australia and Overland from Adelaide to King George's Sound in the years 1840-41. 174*

Grinewald, Jacques, 1988, 'Sketch for a history of the idea of the biosphere', in Bunyard and Goldsmith eds., *Gaia – the Thesis, the Mechanisms and the Implications. 98, 98b, 99*


Haeckel, Ernest, 1903, *Histoire de la Creation des Etres Organises D'Après les Lois Natureles,* Paris, Librarie C. Reinwald. *108*

Hall, Ross Hume, 1974, *Food for Naught,* Harper and Row, New York. *248*

Hall, A. O. and Fagen, R. G., 1956, *Definition of System,* Systems Year Book, Vol. 1. *198*

Hamberger, V., 1935, 'Regeneration', *Encyclopaedia Britannica,* Vol. XIX, London. *227*

Hammond, Peter Boyd, 1971, *An Introduction to Cultural and Social Anthropology,* Macmillan and Collier Macmillan, London. *116, 288*

Harding, Thomas, G., 1960, 'Adaptation and stability', in Sahlins and Elman eds., *Evolution and Culture. 129-130*

Hardy, Sir Alister, 1965, *The Living Stream. A Restatement of Evolution Theory and its Relation to the Spirit of Man,* Collins, London. *146*

Harlow, H. F., 'The Evolution of learning', in Roe and Simpson eds., 1964, *Behaviour and Evolution. 163*

Harrison, Jane, 1927, *Themis. A Study of the Social Origins of Greek Religion,* Cambridge University Press, Cambridge. *343, 347, 357, 358-9*

Head, H., 1920, *Studies in Neurology,* Oxford University Press, Oxford. *48*

Hearn, Lafcadio, 1904, *Japan: An Attempt at Interpretation,* Macmillan, New York. *109, 355-6, 358*

Heatwold, H. and Levins, R., 1972, 'Trophic structure stability and faunal change during recolonisation', *Ecology,* 53. *131*

Hebb, D. O., 1961, *The Organisation of Behaviour,* John Wiley, New York. *242-3*

Heim, A. W., 1970, *The Appraisal of Intelligence,* National Foundation for Education Research, London. *163*

Herodotus, *The Histories,* quoted by Cornford, 1957, *From Religion to Philosophy. 343*

Herrick C. Judson, 1961, *The Evolution of Human Nature,* Harper & Brothers, New York. *49, 65, 158, 159, 159b, 160, 163, 168*

Hesiod, *Works and Days,* quoted by Cornford, 1957, *From Religion to Philosophy. 83*

Hildyard, Nicholas, 1977, 'Building for collapse', *The Ecologist,* Vol. 8, No. 2, March. *291-2*

Hildyard, Nicholas, 1978, 'There is more to food than eating', *The New Ecologist,* No. 5, Sept-Oct. *351*

Hingston, R. W. G., 1928, *Problems of Instinct and Intelligence among Tropical Insects,* Edward Arnold, London. *163-4*

Hobbes, Thomas, 1968 (original edition 1651), *Leviathan,* Penguin, Harmondsworth. *333*

Hocart, A. M., 1970, *Kings and Councillors,* University of Chicago Press, Chicago. *346*

Holling C. S., 'Resilience and Stability of Ecosystems', in Jantsch and Waddington eds., 1976, *Evolution and Consciousness. 118, 118b*

Holst, Erich von, 1937, 'Vom Wesen der Ordnung in Zentralbervensystem', *Die Naturwissenshafter,* 25, quoted by von Bertalanffy in 'General Systems Theory: A Critical Review'. *145*

Holton, Gerald and Morison, Robert S., 1979, *The Limits of Scientific Inquiry,* Norton, New York. *315, 316*

Horn, F. S., 1975 'Markovian prospects of forest succession', in Cody and

Diamond eds., *Ecology and Evolution of Communities,* quoted by Putman and Wratten, *Principles of Ecology. 59*

Horowitz, Norman H., 1956, 'The Gene', *Scientific American,* October. *47*

Huber, Peter B., 1978, 'Organising production and producing organisation. The sociology of traditional agriculture', in Fisk ed., 1978, *The Adaptation of Traditional Agriculture. 304*

Hughes, J. Donald, 1981, 'Early Greek and Roman environmentalists', *The Ecologist,* Vol. 1, No. 1, Jan-Feb. *348*

Hughes, J. Donald, and Thurgood, J. V., 1982, 'Deforestation in ancient Greece and Rome; a cause of collapse?', *The Ecologist,* Vol. 2, No. 5, Sept-Oct. *356, 357*

Hughes, J. Donald, 1983, 'Gaia: an ancient view of the planet', *The Ecologist,* Vol. 13, No. 2-3. *97, 97b, 97c, 348, 370*

Hull, C. L., 1927, *A Behaviour System,* quoted by Chaitanya, in *The Psychology of Freedom,* Somaiya, Bombay. *154*

Humboldt, Alexander von, 1849, *Cosmos. A Sketch of the Physical Description of the Universe,* 5 Vols, trans. Otte, E. C. and Paul, B. H., Bohns Scientific Library, Henry A. Bohn, London. *39*

Hume, A. O., 1878, *Agricultural Reform in India,* W. H. Allen & Co., London. *41, 42, 312*

Hume, David, 1969 (original edition 1740), *A Treatise on Human Nature,* Penguin, Harmondsworth. *403*

Hutton, James, 1788, 'Theory of the Earth: investigation of the laws observable in the composition, dissolution and restoration of land upon the globe', *Transactions of the Royal Society of Edinburgh,* I, Part 2. *98*

Huxley, T. H. and Huxley, J. S., 1947, *Touchstones for Ethics,* Harper Bros, New York. *84, 85, 86, 137, 364*

Huxley, J. S., 1953, *Evolution in Action,* Harper Bros, New York. *24-25*

Huxley, J. S., 1962, 'Higher and lower organisation in evolution', *Journal of the Royal College of Surgeons,* Edinburgh, quoted by Thorpe, W. H., 1974, in *Science, Man and Morals. 169*


Iamblichus, *Life of Pythagoras,* quoted by Cornford, 1975, *From Religion to Philosophy. 344*

International Cultural Foundation, 1972, *Proceedings of the Third International*

*Conference on the Unity of the Sciences. Science and Absolute Values,* International Cultural Foundation, New York. *23, 234, 290-1*

Isutzu Toshihiko, 1971, *The Conception and Reality of Existence,* The Keio Institute of Culture and Linguistic Studies, Tokyo, quoted by Nandy, 1987, *Traditions, Tyranny and Utopias. Essays in the Politics of Awareness. 64*

Itard, Jean-Marc Gaspard, 1932, *The Wild boy of the Aveyron,* trans. by George and Muriel Humphrey, Appleton Century Crofts, New York. *229*


Jackson, Wes, Personal communication. *223*

Jantsch, Erich, 1980, *The Self-Organizing Universe,* Pergamon Press, Oxford. *362, 363-4*

Janzen, D. H., 1986, 'The natural history of mutualism', in Boucher ed., *The Biology of Mutualism. 214-5*

Jaulin, Robert, 1971, 'Ethnocide. The theory and practice of cultural murder', *The Ecologist,* Vol. 1, No. 18, Dec. *290*

Johnson, C. G., 1963, 'The aerial migration of insects', *Scientific American,* Dec. *153*

Jones, Alwyn, 1983, 'Beyond Industrial Society. Towards Balance and Harmony', *The Ecologist,* Vol. 12, No. 4. *335*

Jones, W. H. S., 1946, 'Philosophy and Medicine in Ancient Greece', *Bulletin of the History of Medicine,* Supplement 8. *188*

Jungk, Robert, 1958, *Brighter than a Thousand Stars,* Penguin, Harmondsworth, quoted by Visvanathan, *Atomic physics: the career of an imagination. 76*

Kaberry, Phyllis Mary, 1939, *Aboriginal Women, Sacred and Profane,* Routledge and Kegan Paul, London. *305*

Kalmus, H. ed., 1967, *Regulation and Control of Living Systems,* John Wiley, New York. *151*

Kardiner, Abraham, 1945, *The Psychological Frontiers of Society,* Columbia University Press, New York. *351*

Katz, S. H. and Young M. V., 1978, 'Biological and social aspects of breast-feeding', *The Ecologist Quarterly,* Spring. *176-7*

Kenyatta, Jomo, 1953, *Facing Mount Kenya,* Secker & Warburg, London. *109, 355*

Keyes, Ralph, 1972, 'We, the lonely people', *Intellectual Digest,* No. 4. *314*

King, F. H., 1904, *Farmers of Forty Centuries,* Rodale Press, Emmaus, Pennsylvania. *300*

Kline, Morris, 1972, *Mathematics in Western Culture,* Penguin, Harmondsworth. *52*

Koestler, Arthur, et al. 1950, *The God that Failed – Six Studies in Communism,* Hamish Hamilton, London. *90*

Koestler, Arthur, 1967, *The Ghost in the Machine,* Hutchinson, London. *37, 109, 159, 383-4*

Koestler, Arthur and Smythies J. R. eds., 1972, *Beyond Reductionism,* Hutchinson, London. *54, 113, 114, 149, 155, 198, 200, 259*

Koestler, Arthur, 1972, 'Beyond Atomism and Holism', in Koestler and Smythies eds., *Beyond Reductionism,* Hutchinson, London. *198*

Koestler, Arthur, 1978, *Janus – A Summing Up,* Hutchinson, London. *139*

Kohler, Wolfgang, 1947, *Gestalt Psychology: An Introduction to New Concepts in Modern Psychology,* Liveright Publications, New York. *19*

Kothari, Manu L., and Mehta, Lopa A., 'Violence in modern medicine in Nandy', ed. 1988, *Science, Hegemony and Violence. 53*

Koyre, Alexander, 1965, *Newtonian Studies,* University of Chicago Press, Chicago. *17*

Krechevsky, I., 'Hypothesis Versus Chance in the Pre-Solution Period in Sensory Discrimination', in Crawford C. C. and Leitzell F. H. eds., 1932, *Learning a New Language. 159*

Krige, Eileen Jensen, 1936, *The Social System of the Zulus,* Longman Green, London. *271*

Kropotkin, Peter, 1914 (original ed. 1902), *Mutual Aid. A Factor in Evolution,* Horizon Books, Boston. *212*

Kuhn, Thomas S., 1970, *The Structure of Scientific Revolutions,* University of Chicago Press, Chicago. *66*

Kuhn, Thomas, 1979, 'Logic of discovery or psychology of research?' in Lakatos and Musgrave eds, 1979, *Criticism and the Growth of Knowledge. 91*

Kuper, Hilda, 1963, *The Swazi. A South African Kingdom,* Holt, Rinehart and Winston, New York. *356-7*

La Barre, Weston, 1954, *The Human Animal,* University of Chicago Press, Chicago. *120*

Lakatos, Imre, and Musgrave Alan eds., 1979, *Criticism and the Growth of Knowledge,* Cambridge University Press, London. *53, 91, 91b, 91c-92*

Lakatos, Imre, 1979, 'Methodology of scientific research programmes', in Lakatos and Musgrave eds., *Criticism and the Growth of Knowledge, 91, 91b, 91c, 92*

Lamarck, J. P., 1964 (original edition, Paris. 1802), *Hydrogeology,* trans. Albert V. Carozzi, University of Chicago Press, Chicago. *98, 98b*

Lamarck, J. P., 1873 (original edition 1809), *Philosophie Zoologique,* 2 Vols, ed. C. Martins, Savy, Paris. *138*

Lashley, Karl, 1960, *The Neuro-Psychology of Lashley,* Selected Papers, New York. *48*

Lee, R. B. and Devore, I. eds., 1968, *Man the Hunter,* Aldine Publishing Co., Chicago. *223*

Leopold, Aldo, 1953, *A Sand County Almanac,* Oxford University Press, Oxford. *86, 97*

Levi-Strauss, Claude, 1955, *Tristes Tropiques,* Plon, Paris. *291*

Lewis, Oscar, 1966, 'The Culture of Poverty', *Scientific American,* October. *243-4*

Liedloff, Jean, Personal communication. *302, 311*

Linnaeus, Carl, 1964 (original edition 1735), *Systema Naturae,* B. de Graaf, Newkoop. *211*

Lods, Adolphe, 1932, *Israel: From its Beginnings to the Middle of the Eighth Century,* trans. S. H. Hooke, Routledge & Kegan Paul, London. *334, 350*

Lorenz, Konrad, 1962, 'Gestalt perception as fundamental to scientific knowledge', in *General Systems Yearbook,* No. 7. *72, 145*

Lorenz, Konrad, 1963, *On Aggression,* Harcourt, Brace, New York. *207*

Lovelock J. E., 1979, *Gaia: A New Look at Life on Earth,* Oxford University Press, Oxford. *125, 178-9*

Lovelock J. E., 'The Gaia Hypothesis', in Bunyard and Goldsmith eds., 1988, *Gaia, The Thesis, the Mechanism and the Implications. 125*

Lovelock, J. E., 1991, *The Practical Science of Planetary Medicine,* Gaia Books, London. *125, 178-9*

Lowie, Robert, 1921, *Primitive Society,* G. Routledge and Sons, London. *337*

Lumsden, Charles J. and Wilson, Edward O., 1981, *Genes, Mind and Culture,* Harvard University Press, Cambridge, Mass. *104*

Lundberg, George A., 1961, quoted by Herrick, *The Evolution of Human Nature. 42*

Lux, Kenneth, 1990, *Adam Smith's Mistake: How a Moral Philosopher Invented Economics and Ended Morality,* Shambhala, Boston. *242, 328*


Mackay, Donald, 1964, 'Communication and Meaning: A Functional Approach', eds. Northrop and Livingstone, *Cross-cultural Understanding. 398*

MacKinnon, Flora ed., 1925, *The Philosophical Writings of Henry More,* Oxford University Press, Oxford. *122*

Macko, D. and Mesarovic M. D., 'Foundations for a scientific theory of hierarchical systems', in Whyte et alia eds., 1969, *Hierarchical Structures. 201*

Maine, Sir Henry Sumner, 1905 (original edition 1861), *Ancient Law: Its Connection with the Early History of Society and its relation to Modern Ideas,* John Murray, London. *333*

Malin, James, 1953, 'Soil, animal and plant relations of the grassland, historically reconsidered', *Scientific Monthly,* 76. *261-2*

Malinowski, Bronislaw, 1937, 'Anthropology as the basis of social science', in Cattel et alia eds., *Human Affairs. 306*

Malinowski, Bronislaw, 1961 (original edition 1922), *Argonauts of the Western Pacific,* E. P. Dutton, New York. *321, 324*

Malinowski, Bronislaw, 1965 (original edition 1945), *The Dynamics of Cultural Change,* Yale University Press, New Haven. *191*

Mann, Robert, Personal communication. *55*

Mann, R. B. 1990, 'Time Running Out. The urgent need for tree-planting in Africa', *The Ecologist,* Vol. 20, March/April. *312*

Margalef, Ramon, 1963, 'On certain unifying principles in ecology', *The American Naturalist,* Nov/Dec, No. 897. *362*

Margalef, Ramon, 'Diversity, Stability and Maturity in Natural Ecosystems', in van Dobben and Lowe McConnel eds., 1975, *Unifying Concepts in Ecology. 54*

Margulis, Lynn, Personal communication. *31*

Marsh, George Perkins, 1965 (original edition 1864), *Man and Nature,* The Belknap Press of Harvard University Press, Cambridge, Mass. *30*

Masterman, Margaret, 'The nature of the paradigm', in Lakatos and Musgrove eds., 1979, *Criticism and the Growth of Knowledge. 53*

Mason, Stephen F., 1956, *Main Currents of Scientific Thought,* Routledge and Kegan Paul, London. *385*

Mathes, J. C. and Gray, Donald H., 1975, 'The Engineer, as social radical', *The Ecologist,* Vol. 5, No. 4. *314*

Mattson W. L. and Addy, N. D., 1972, 'Photophagous insects as regulators of forest primary production', quoted by Owen and Wiegert, 1972, *Mutualism between grasses and grazers. 214*

Mauss, Marcel, 1954, *The Gift. Forms and Functions of Exchange in Archaic Societies,* Cohen and West, London. *320-1*

May, Robert M., 1973, *Stability and Complexity in Model Ecosystems,* Princeton University Press, Princeton. *213, 267*

McCully, Patrick, 1991, 'The Case Against Climate Aid', *The Ecologist,* Vol. 21, No. 6. *314*

McIntosh, Robert P., 1980, 'Some problems of theoretical ecology', in Saarinen ed., *Conceptual Issues in Ecology. 222*

McIntosh Robert P., 1975, 'H. A. Gleason, individualistic ecologist: his contribution to ecological theory', *Bulletin of the Torrey Botanical Club,* Vol. 102. *18, 261*

McIver, Robert, 1964, *The Ramparts We Guard,* Macmillan, New York. *242*

McKinney, H. L., 1966, 'Alfred Russel Wallace and the discovery of natural selection', *Journal of the History of Medicine and Allied Sciences,* 21.33. *188*

McLean, Paul, 'Man and his animal brains', *Modern Medecine,* 1964, quoted by Koestler, 1975, *The Ghost in the Machine. 109*

McNaughton, S. J., 1979, 'Grazing as an optimization process: grass ungulate relationships in Serengeti', *The American Naturalist,* May, Vol. 13, No. 5. *214*

Meadows, Donella and Dennis, 1972, *The Limits to Growth,* Earth Island, London. *75*

Medawar, P. B., 1974, *The Hope of Progress,* Wildwood House, London. *172, 315, 368*

Medawar, P. B. & J. S., 1977, *The Life Science,* Wildwood House, London. *362*

Medawar, P. B., 1982, *Pluto's Republic,* Oxford University Press, Oxford. *45, 91*

Merrell, D. J. and Underhill, J. C., 1956, 'Selection for DDT resistance in inbred laboratory and wild stocks of Drosophila Melanogaster', *Journal of Economic Entymology*, 49. *25, 272*

Merrell, David J., 1985, *Ecological Genetics*, Longman, London. *25, 53, 148, 148b, 149, 149b, 205-6*

Merton, Robert, King, 1951, *Social Theory and Social Structure: Toward the Clarification of Theory and Research*, The Free Press of Glencoe, New York. *245*

Middleton, John, ed., 1970, *From Child to Adult*, The Natural History Press, New York. *285*

Monboddo, Lord, 1784, *Ancient Metaphysics*, Vol. III, James Burnet, London. *14*

Monod, Jacques, 1970, *Le Hasard et La Nécessité*, Les Editions du Seuil, Paris. *85, 85b, 86, 115, 115b, 137, 198, 252*

Mooney, Patrick Roy, 1979, *Seeds of the Earth: A Private and Public Resource*, Inter Pares, Ottawa. *271*

Moore, Barrington, 1917, 'Presidential Address to St. Louis Branch of U.S. Ecological Society'. *2*

More, L. T., 1944, *The Life and Works of the Honourable Robert Boyle*, Oxford University Press, London. *9*

Morenz, Siegfried, 1973, *Egyptian Religion*, trans. by Ann E. Keep, Methuen, London. *344, 345*

Morgan, Thomas, quoted by Worster, 1977, *Nature's Economy*. *97*

Morin, Edgar, 1977 and 1980, *La Methode. Vol. 1. La Nature de la Nature and Vol. 2. La Vie de la Vie*, Seuil, Paris. *10, 186*

Mumford, Lewis, 1967, *The Myth of the Machine*, Secker and Warburg, London. *292*


Nandy, Ashis, Personal communication. *163*

Nandy, Ashis, 1981, *Traditions, Tyranny and Utopia. Essays in the Politics of Awareness*, Oxford University Press, New Delhi. *64*

Nandy, Ashis, 1983, 'The pathology of objectivity', *The Ecologist*, Vol. XIII, No. 6. *64, 76, 76b, 76c*

Nandy, Ashis, 1988, *Science, Hegemony and Violence*, Oxford University Press, New Delhi. *53, 63, 76, 76b*

National Academy of Sciences, 1991, *Policy Implications of Global Warming*, National Academy Press, Washington. D.C., *180*

Ndaw, Alassane, 1983, *La Pensée Africaine*, Les Nouvelles Editions Africaines, Dakar. *351*

Needham, Joseph, 1936, *Order and Life*, M. I. T. Press, Cambridge, Mass. *85, 124*

Needham, Joseph, 1956, *Science and Civilization in China*, Vol. 2, Cambridge University Press, Cambridge. *344*

Nelkin, Dorothy, 1979, 'Threats and promises. Negotiating the control of research', in Holton and Morison eds., *The Limits of Scientific Inquiry*. *315*

Nicholson, A. J., 1933, 'The Balance of animal populations', *Journal of Animal Ecology*, 2. *58*

Noel, Emile ed., 1979, *Le Darwinisme Aujourd'hui*, Le Seuil, Paris. *98*

Northrop F. S. C. and Livingston, Helen H. eds., 1964, *Cross-cultural Understanding*, Harper & Row, New York. *398*


Oatley, Keith, 1978, *Perceptions and Representations*, Methuen, London. *13, 47, 66, 143, 159*

Odum, Eugene and Patten, B. C., 1981, 'The Cybernetic nature of ecosystems', *American Naturalist*, 118. *129*

Odum, Eugene P., 1953, *Fundamentals of Ecology*, W. B. Saunders, Philadelphia. *2*

Odum, Eugene P., 1969, 'The strategy of ecosystems development', *Science*, 164. *265*

Odum, Eugene P., 1983, *Basic Ecology*, Saunders College Publishing, Philadelphia. *13, 21, 117, 130, 130b, 188, 200, 201, 222, 233, 262, 263-4, 280, 324, 367*

Odum, Eugene P., Personal communication. *26*

Odum, Howard, 1971, *Environment, Power and Society*, John Wiley and Sons, New York. *130*

O'Neill, R. V., 1976, 'Paradigms of ecosystems analysis', in Levin 1976 ed., *Ecological Theory and Ecosystems Models*. *54*

Orians, G. H., 1975, 'Diversity, stability and maturity in natural ecosystems', in van Dobben and Lowe McConnell eds., *Unifying Concepts in Ecology*. *117, 135*

Ospovat, Dov, 1981, *The Development of Darwin's Theory*, Cambridge University Press, Cambridge. *211*

Owen, D. F. and Wiegert, R. G., 1981, 'Mutualism between grasses and grazers: an evolutionary hypothesis', *Oikos*, 36. *214*

Pantin, C. P. A., 1968, *The Relations Between the Sciences*, Cambridge University Press, Cambridge. *53*

Pappenheim, F., 1968, quoted by Jones, 1983, in 'Beyond Industrial Society: Towards balance and harmony', *The Alienation of Modern Man*, Modern Reader Paperbacks, London. *335*

Park, Mungo, 1970 (original edition 1799), *Travels in the Interior of Africa*, ed. Ronald Miller, Edito-Service, Geneva. *173, 302*

Parsons, Robert T., 1964, *Religion in an African Society*, E. J. Brill, Leiden. *358*

Passmore, John, 1978, *Science and its Critics*, Duckworth, London. *20, 190*

Patai, Raphael, 1947, *Man and Temple in Ancient Jewish Myth and Ritual*, Thomas Nelson, London. *194, 295*

Pattee, Howard, H., 1973, *Hierarchy Theory: The Challenge of Complex Systems*, George Braziller, New York. *200*

Pattison, James and Kerr, Peter, 1991, 'The Day America told the truth', quoted by Tistall, Simon, *The Guardian*, May 2nd. *244*

Patten, B. C. and Odum, E. P., 1981, 'The cybernetic nature of ecosystems', *American Naturalist*, 118. *129, 130, 232*

Peerenboon, R. D., 1991, 'Beyond naturalism: a reconstruction of Taoist environmental ethics', *Environmental Ethics*, Vol. XIII, Spring. *344*

Piaget, Jean, 1967, *Biologie et Connaissance*, Gallimard, Paris. *165, 259*

Piaget, Jean, 1968, *The Child's Conception of the World*, Adams & Co, Littlefield, New Jersey. *59*

Piaget, Jean, 1971, quoted by Henryk Skolimowski, in Ayala and Dobzhansky eds., 1974, *Studies in the Philosophy of Biology*. *72*

Piaget, Jean, 1976, *Le Comportement, Moteur de l'Evolution*, Gallimard, Paris. *410*

Piaget, Jean and Inhelder, Bärbel, 1972, 'The Gaps in empiricism', in Koestler and Smythies eds., *Beyond Reductionism*. *259-60*

Pirie, N. W., 1969, 'Gardyloo', *The Listener*, 82, 331. *16*

Pittendrigh, Colin, 1958, 'Adaptation, Natural Selection and Behaviour', in Roe and Simpson eds., *Evolution and Behaviour*. *184-5*

Plato, *Menexemus*, quoted by Hughes, 1983, 'Gaia, An ancient view of our planet', *The Ecologist*, Vol. 13, No. 2-3. *97*

Pliny the Elder, *Natural History*, quoted by Hughes and Thurgood, 1982, 'Deforestation in Ancient Greece and Rome; A Cause of Collapse?'. *357*

Polanyi, Karl, 1945, *The Great Transformation*, Victor Gollancz, London. *304, 327*

Polanyi, Karl, 'Societies and Economic Systems', in Dalton ed., 1968, *Primitive Archaic and Modern Economics*. *301-2, 307, 325*

Polanyi, Karl, 'The Self-Regulating Market', in Dalton ed., 1968, *Primitive, Archaic and Modern Economics*. *326-7*

Polanyi, Michael, 1978 (original edition 1958), *Personal Knowledge. Towards a Post-Critical Philosophy*, Routledge and Kegan Paul, London. *37, 37b, 38, 43, 44, 45, 49, 55, 67, 74, 77, 79, 79b, 92, 92b, 93, 93b, 93c, 94, 95, 122, 159, 377*

Pollard, Nigel, 1981, 'The Gezira scheme. A study in failure', *The Ecologist*, Vol. II, No. 1. *173*

Popenoe, David, 1991, 'Family decline in the Swedish welfare state', *The Public Interest*, Winter. *340*

Poncet and Brevedent, quoted by Crawford, *'Fung Kingdom of Sennar'*, quoted by Pollard, 'The Gezira Scheme: A Study in Failure'. *173*

Popper, Karl, 1973 (original edition 1972), *Objective Knowledge*, Clarendon Press, Oxford. *43, 44-45, 67, 90, 90b, 90c*

Popper, Karl, 1983 (original edition 1959), *The Logic of Scientific Discovery*, Hutchinson, London. *80, 91*

Price, Peter W., 'Alternative Paradigms in community ecology', in Gaud, Price and Slobodchikoff eds., 1984, *The New Ecologist*. *206*

Prigogine, Ilya and Stengers, Isabelle, 1979, *La Nouvelle Alliance*, Gallimard, Paris. *9, 9b, 198, 266-7*

Putman, S. D. and Wratten, R. J., 1984, *Principles of Ecology*, Croom Helm, Beckenham, Kent. *54, 58-59, 130, 131, 204, 262-3, 279-280*

Quastler, H. ed., 1953, *Information Theory in Biology*, University of Illinois Press, Urbana. *400-1*

Radcliffe-Brown, A. R., 1965, *Structure and Function in Primitive Society,* Cohen & West, London. *110, 277, 278*

Rappaport, Amos, 1978, 'Culture and environment', *Ecologist Quarterly,* No. 4, Winter. *289*

Rappaport, Roy, A., 1967, *Pigs for the Ancestors,* Yale University Press, New Haven. *129*

Rappaport, Roy, A., 1979, *Ecology, Meaning and Religion,* North Atlantic Books, Richmond/Calif. *60, 63, 335*

Raum, O. F., 1967, *Chaga Childhood,* Oxford University Press, Oxford. *284*

Ravetz, Jerome, R., 1971, *Scientific Knowledge and its Social Problems,* Oxford University Press, Oxford. *89, 315*

Reichel-Dolmatoff, Gerardo, 1977, 'Cosmology as ecological analysis: a view from the rainforest', *The Ecologist,* Vol. 7, No. 1. *294-5, 370*

Reichel-Dolmatoff, Gerardo, 1983, 'The Kogi Indians and the Environment – Impending Disaster', *The Ecologist,* Vol. 13, No. 1, Jan-Feb. *129, 256-7, 309-10*

Ricklefs, R. E., 1973, *Ecology,* Nelson, London. *262*

Ricqlès, Armand de, 1979, 'Darwinisme, paleontologie et anatomie comparée', in Emile Noel ed., *Le Darwinisme Aujourd'hui. 98*

Riedl, Rupert, 1978, *Order in Living Organisms,* John Wiley, New York. *139*

Robertson-Smith, W., 1914, *Essays on the Religion of the Semites,* Adams and Charles Black, London. *355*

Roe, Anne and Simpson, George Gaylord eds., 1958, *Behaviour & Evolution,* Yale University Press, New Haven. *163, 184-5*

Rogers, Everett, M. and Kincaid, D. Lawrence, 1981, *Communications Network: Toward a New Paradigm for Research,* Collier Macmillan, London. *392*

Roszak, Theodore, 1972, *Where the Wasteland Ends,* Faber and Faber, London. *120, 252, 359*

Russell, Peter, 1982, *The Awakening Earth,* Routledge and Kegan Paul, London. *362-3*

Rutherford, Ernest, quoted by John Passmore, 1978, *Science and its Critics. 17*

Ryle, Gilbert, 1949, *The Concept of Mind,* Hutchinson's University Library, London. *41*


Saarinen Esa ed., 1982, *Conceptual Issues in Ecology,* D. Reidel, Dordrecht. *16,*

Sachs, Wolfgang, 1990, 'Six essays on the archeology of development', *Interculture,* 109, 4, Fall. *314*

Sagan, Dorion and Margulis, Lynn, 1983, 'The Gaian perspective of ecology', *The Ecologist,* Vol. 13, No. 5. *100*

Sahlins, Marshall, 'Tribal Economics', in George Dalton ed., 1971, *Economic Development and Social Change. 302, 303*

Salaman, Redcliffe N., 1949, *The History and Social Influences of the Potato,* Cambridge University Press, Cambridge. *328*

Sampson, R. Neil, 1981, *Farmland or Wasteland,* Rodale Press, Emmaus, Pennsylvania. *172*

Santiago, Ramon-y-Cajal, quoted by Sherrington, 1975, *Man on his Nature. 166*

Schebesta, Paul, 1940, *Les Pygmees,* Gallimard, Paris. *351*

Schmalhausen, Ivan, 1949, *Factors of Evolution. The Theory of Stabilising Evolution,* trans. Isadore Dordick, ed. Theodosius Dobzhansky, Blakiston (McGraw-Hill), New York. *410*

Schoepf, Broske Grundfest, 'Man and biosphere in Zaire', in Barker ed., 1984, *The Politics of Agriculture in Tropical Africa. 373*

Scott, James, 1978, 'The Subsistence ethic', *The New Ecologist,* No. 3, May/ June. *273*

Senghor, Leopold, 1983, Preface to Alassane Ndaw: *La Pensee Africaine. 351*

Shannon, Claude E. and Weaver, Warren, 1949, *The Mathematical Theory of Communication,* University of Illinois Press, Urbana. *393-95*

Sharp, R. Lauriston, 'Steel axes for stone age Australians', in Spicer ed., 1952, *Human Problems in Technological Change. 313*

Sheldrake, Rupert, 1988, *The Presence of the Past,* Collins, London. *343*

Sherrington, Sir Charles, 1940, *Man on his Nature,* The Gifford Lectures, 1937-8, Cambridge University Press, Cambridge. *142, 165, 166, 234*

Sherrington, Sir Charles, 1947 (original edition 1906), *The Integration of the Nervous System,* Cambridge University Press, Cambridge. *158*

Simberloff, D. S. 1980, 'A succession of paradigms in ecology', in Saarinen ed., *Conceptual Issues in Ecology. 16*

Simberloff, D. S. and Wilson E. O. L., 1969, 'Experimental zoogeography of islands: the colonization of empty islands', *Ecology,* 50. *131*

Simpson, George Gaylord, 1950, *The Meaning of Evolution. A Study of the History of Life and of its Significance for Man,* Oxford University Press, London. *85, 85b, 86, 113*

Singh, Rev. J. A. L. and Zing, Robert M., 1942, *Wolf Children and Feral Man,* Harper and Bros, New York. *229*

Sinnott, Edmund W., 1961, *Cell and Psyche,* Harper and Rowe, New York. *104, 104b*

Skinner B. F., 1957, *Verbal Behaviour,* quoted by Koestler, 1975, *The Ghost in the Machine. 159*

Skolimowski, Henryk, in Ayala and Dobzzhansky, 1974, *Studies in the Philosophy of Biology. 72*

Skolimowski, Henryk, 1983, *Technology and Human Destiny,* University of Madras, Madras. *211*

Spengler, Oswald, 1939, *The Decline of the West,* Alfred Knopf, New York. *68*

Spicer, E. H. ed., 1952, *Human Problems in Technological Change,* Russell Sage Foundation, New York. *313*

Sprigge, T. L. S., 'The definition of a moral judgement', in Wallace and Walker eds., 1970, *The Definition of Morality. 84*

Stanner, W. E. H., 'The Dreaming', in Hammond ed., 1971, *An Introduction to Cultural and Social Anthropology. 116, 288*

Stent, Gunther, 1978, *Paradoxes of Progress,* W. H. Freeman, San Francisco. *143, 253, 377*

Suess, Edouard, 1875, quoted by Grinewald, 'Sketch for a history of the Biosphere', in Bunyard and Goldsmith eds., 1988, 'Gaia, the Thesis, the Mechanism and the Implications', *Die Entstehung der Alpen,* W. Braumuller, Vienna. *98, 99, 99b*

Sumner, William, Graham, 1963, *Social Darwinism. Selected Essays of William Graham Sumner,* Prentice-Hall, Englewood Cliffs. *333*


Tansley, Arthur, 1920, 'Classification of vegetation, or the concept of development', *Journal of Ecology,* 2. *2, 18, 18b*

Tansley, Arthur, 1935, 'The use and abuse of vegetational concepts and terms', quoted by Worster, 1977, 'Nature's Economy', *Ecology,* 16, July. *261*

Taylor, Bron, 1991, 'The religion and politics of Earth First', *The Ecologist,*

Vol. 21, No. 6, Nov-Dec. *381*

Taylor, John, quoted by *Daily Telegraph,* 1990, '50% Crime Rise Forecast 2000', September 26th *245*

Tempels, Placide, 1948, *La Philosophie Bantoue,* Presence Africaine, Paris. *145, 350, 351*

Thatcher, Margaret, 1989, Speech on the global environment to the United Nations General Assembly, New York, 8th November, typescript only, The Prime Minister's Office, London. *374*

Thoreau, Henry, David, 1906, *The Writings of Henry David Thoreau,* 20 Vols, Houghton Mifflin, Boston. *71*

Thorpe, W. H., 1956, 'Some implications of the study of animal behaviour', *The Advancement of Science,* Vol. 13, No. 50. *21*

Thorpe, W. H., 1965, *Science, Man and Morals,* Methuen & Co, London. *154, 155, 168-9*

Thorpe, W. H., 1969, 'Why the Brain is more than a Mere Computer', *The Times,* London, January 25th. *45*

Thorpe, W. H., Discussion following presentation of Ludwig von Bertalanffy's 'Chance or Law?', in Koestler and Smythies eds., 1972, *Beyond Reductionism,* The Ansback Symposium. *113*

Thurnwald, Richard, 1931, *Die Menschliche Gesellschaft,* quoted by Polanyi, Societies and Economic Systems. *303*

Tillich, Paul, 1952, *Systematic Theology,* Chicago University Press, Chicago. *71*

Tistall, Simon, 1991, *The Guardian,* May 2nd. *244*

Tinbergen, N., 1951, *The Study of Instinct,* The Clarendon Press, Oxford. *34*

Tolman, E. C., 1962, *Purposive Behaviour in Animals and Men,* Century Psychology Series, New York. *41*

Tonnies, Ferdinand, 1955 (original edition 1920), *Community and Association,* Routledge and Kegan Paul, London. *335*

Toynbee, Arnold, J., 1934, *A Study of History,* Royal Institute of International Affairs, London. *175*

Trivers, R. L., Foreword to R. Dawkins, 1976, *The Selfish Gene,* Oxford University Press, Oxford. *71*

Turner, Victor, 'A Ndembu doctor in practice', in Kiev ed., 1967, *Magic, Faith and Healing. 371*

Tyler, Edward, 1903, *Primitive Culture,* John Murray, London. *337*

Uchendu, Victor C., 1966, *The Igbo of Southeast Nigeria,* Holt, Rinehart and Winston, New York. *353*

U.S. Dept. of Education, 1964, *Equality of Education Opportunities,* Washington D.C. *284*

Ungerer, E., 1930, 'Der Aufbau des Naturwissens', Padagogische Hochschule ii, quoted by von Bertalanffy, 1962, *Modern Theories of Development. 277-8*


van der Post, Laurens, 1961, *The Heart of the Hunter,* Hogarth, London. *174-5*

van Dobben, W. H. and Lowe-McConnell, eds., 1975, *Unifying Concepts in Ecology,* Funk, The Hague. *54, 113, 117, 136*

Vastakos, R. K., 1971, 'A Hint from the past', *Alternatives,* Vol. I, No. 1. *288*

Vayda, Andrew, P., 'Maori Warfare', in Bohannan ed., 1967, *Law and Warfare. 207*

Vayda, Andrew P., 1969, *Environment and Cultural Behaviour,* American Museum of Natural History, New York. *173*

Vernadsky Vladmir, quoted by Grinewald, 'Sketch for a history of the Biosphere', in Bunyard and Goldsmith eds., 1988, *Gaia, the Thesis, the Mechanism and the Implications. 98, 99*

Visvanathan, Shiv, 'Atomic physics: the career of an imagination', in Nandy ed., 1988, *Science, Hegemony and Violence. 76*

Voelcker, John Augustus, 1893, *Report on the Improvement of Indian Agriculture,* Eyre and Spottiswoode, London. *311-2*

von Bertalanffy, Ludwig, 1962, *Modern Theories of Development: An Introduction to Theoretical Biology,* trans. J. H. Woodger, 1933, Harper Torchbook, New York. *20, 185, 199, 277*

von Bertalanffy, Ludwig, 1962, 'General systems theory: a critical review', *General Systems Yearbook,* Vol. III. *145*

von Bertalanffy, Ludwig, 'Chance or Law?', in Koestler and Smythies eds., 1972, *Beyond Reductionism. 149*

von Bertalanffy, Ludwig, 1973, *General Systems Theory. Foundations, Development Applications,* Allen Lane, London. *4, 199*

von Feuerbach, Anselm, 1834, *Caspar Hauser,* Simpkin and Marshall, London. *229* von Hilderbrand, Martin, 1981, 'An Amazonian Tribe's View of Cosmology', in Bunyard and Goldsmith eds., *Gaia, The Thesis, the Mechanisms and the Implications*. *300*

Waddington, C. H., 1934, 'Morphogenetic fields', a review of 'The Elements of Experimental Embryology', J. S. Huxley and G. R. de Beer, *Science Progress*, Vol. 29, No. 114, quoted by Chaitanya, 1975, *The Biology of Freedom*. *227*

Waddington, C. H., 1952, *The Listener*, 13th November, quoted by Koestler, 1978, in *Janus: A Summing Up*. *139*

Waddington, C. H., 1969, *Towards a Theoretical Biology*, 2 Vols, Edinburgh University Press, Edinburgh. *228-9, 399, 400, 401, 410*

Waddington, C. H., 1960, *The Ethical Animal*, University of Chicago Press, Chicago. *85, 85b, 86, 115, 364, 405*

Waddington, C. H., 1970, 'Basic ideas of biology', in Waddington ed., 1969, *Towards a Theoretical Biology*, *227, 228, 399, 400, 401, 410*

Waddington, C. H., 'The theory of evolution today', in Koestler and Smythies eds., 1972, *Beyond Reductionism*. *54, 155*

Waddington, C. H., 1975, *The Evolution of an Evolutionist*, Edinburgh University Press, Edinburgh. *72, 134, 274, 284*

Waddington, C. H. and Jantsch eds., 1976, *Evolution and Consciousness – Our Human Systems in Transition*, Addison-Wesley, Reading, Mass. *384*

Wallace A. F. C., 1956, 'Revitalization Movements: Some theoretical considerations for their comparative study', *American Anthropologist*, Vol. 58, April. *379-80*

Wallace A. F. C., 1963, *Culture and Personality*, Random House, New York. *92*

Wallace, Alfred, Russel, quoted by Egerton Frank, 1973, *Changing Concepts of the Balance of Nature*. *189*

Wallace, Alfred Russel, quoted by McKinney, 1966, in 'Alfred Russel Wallace and the discovery of natural selection', quoted by Egerton, in *Changing Concepts of the Balance of Nature*. *189*

Wallace, G. and Walker, A. D. M. eds., 1970, *The Definition of Morality*, Methuen, London. *84*

Ward, Lester, 1893, *The Psychic Factors of Civilization*, quoted by Worster, 'Nature's Economy', Boston. *172*

Warming, Johannes Eugenius, 1909, *The Oecology of Plants: An Introduction to the Study of Plant Communities,* trans. Percy Bloom and Isaac Bailey Balfour, Clarendon Press, Oxford. *211*

Washburn, S., and Lancaster, C., 'The evolution of hunting', in Lee and Devore eds., 1968, *Man the Hunter. 223*

Watkins, John, 'Against Normal Science', in Lakatos and Musgrave, 1979, *Criticism and the Growth of Knowledge. 92*

Watson, John B., 1925, *Behaviourism,* Kegal Paul, Trench, Trubner, London. *41, 41b*

Wiseman, Stephen ed., 1966, 'Intelligence and Ability', *Modern Psychology,* Harmondsworth, London. *163*

Weiss, Paul, 1956, *Proceedings of the National Academy,* 42. *280*

Weiss, Paul, 1971, *Hierarchically Organized Systems in Theory and Practice,* Hafner, New York. *199, 200*

Weiss, Paul, 'The living system, determinism stratified', in Koestler and Smythies eds., 1972, *Beyond Reductionism,* Hutchinson, London. *53*

Weiss, Paul, 1972, Discussion after presentation of his paper 'The living system', Koestler and Smythies eds., *Beyond Reductionism. 114*

Weiss, Paul, 1973, *A Science of Life,* Futura Publishing Co., New York. *12-13, 46, 185, 226, 227, 228, 232-3*

Wheeler, Sir Robert Eric Mortimer, 1959, *Early India and Pakistan,* Thames and Hudson, London, quoted by Vastokas, *A Hint From the Past. 288*

White, Gilbert, 1902 (original edition 1789), *The Natural History of Selborne,* John Lane, London and New York. *211*

Whitehead, A. N., 1958, *Science and the Modern World* (text of the 1925 Lowell Lectures), Mentor, New York. *4, 80, 404*

Whittaker, R. H., 1964, 'Gradient Analysis of Vegetation', *Biological Reviews,* 42. *19, 19b*

Whitten, N. E. Jnr., 1978, 'Ecological imagery and cultural adaptability', *American Anthropologist,* Vol. 80, No. 4, Dec. *60-61*

Whorf, Benjamin Lee, 1956, *Language, Thought and Reality,* M. I. T. Press, Cambridge, Mass. *68, 103*

Whyte, A. F., 1927, *China and Foreign Powers,* Humphrey Milford, London. *175*

Whyte, Lancelot Law, Wilson, Albert G., Wilson, Donna eds., 1969, *Hie-*

*rarchical Structures,* Proceedings of the symposium held Nov. 18-19, 1968 at Douglas Advanced Research Laboratories, Huntington Beach, Calif, American Elsevier, New York. *200*

Wilson, Carrol et alia, 1971, *Man's Impact on the Global Environment. A Study of Critical Environmental Problems,* M. I. T. Press, Cambridge, Mass. *179*

Wilson, Edward O., 1976, 'Sociobiology: A new approach to understanding the basis of human nature', *New Scientist,* 13, May. *190, 405-6*

Woodger, J. H., 1967, *Biological Principles,* Routledge and Kegan Paul, London. *3, 53, 103, 104, 121, 121b, 122, 149-150, 232*

World Bank, 1981, *Accelerated Development in Sub-Saharan Agriculture,* Washington D.C. *313*

Worster, Donald, 1977, *Nature's Economy,* Sierra Club, San Francisco. *64, 74, 86, 97, 122, 123, 172, 208, 260*

Wynne-Edwards, V. C., 1962, *Animal Dispersion in Relation to Socal Behaviour,* Oliver and Boyd, Edinburgh. *86*

Wynne-Edwards, V. C., 1964, 'Population control in animals', *Scientific American,* August. *255-6*


Young, L. Z., 1950, *The Life of Vertebrates,* Oxford University Press, Oxford. *154*

Yu-Lan, Feng, 1984, *A Short History of Chinese Philosophy,* trans. Derek Boddler, Macmillan, New York, quoted by Peerenboom, 1991. *344*


Zuckerman, S., 1932, *The Social Life of Monkeys and Apes,* Kegan Paul Trench Trubner, London. *14, 209*

Zuckerman, S., *Address to U.N. Conference on the Environment,* Stockholm. June, 1972. *75*